MW00803617

Norman Lear

Norman Lear

His Life and Times

Tripp Whetsell

APPLAUSE
THEATRE & CINEMA BOOKS

APPLAUSE
THEATRE & CINEMA BOOKS
Bloomsbury Publishing Group, Inc.
4501 Forbes Blvd., Ste. 200
Lanham, MD 20706
ApplauseBooks.com

Distributed by NATIONAL BOOK NETWORK

Library of Congress Cataloging-in-Publication Data Available

ISBN 9781493068401 (cloth : alk. paper) | ISBN 9781493068418 (ebook)

♾™ The paper used in this publication meets the minimum requirements of American National Standard for Information Sciences—Permanence of Paper for Printed Library Materials, ANSI/NISO Z39.48-1992.

This book is affectionately dedicated to my
all in my family for their love and support.

Contents

PART THREE
THE GLORY YEARS

PART FOUR
THE LATER YEARS

Introduction

No matter who the subject is, writing a biography is always filled with twists and turns at every corner. In early 2021, when I first undertook the challenge of chronicling the still-unfolding life and career of legendary television producer, writer, and activist Norman Lear, who was then ninety-eight and had been one of my biggest heroes for as long as I can remember, I did so fully aware of how much of an uphill climb it would be.

But then after three long years and multiple delays—including a shattered elbow following a bicycling accident that put me out of commission for six weeks—the one thing I never anticipated was Norman's death on December 5, 2023, exactly one week before I was scheduled to turn in the manuscript. Even despite his extremely advanced age of one-hundred-one-and-a-half, it seemed like he would be around forever. I heard the news early that following morning as I was on my way back to Manhattan from my weekend home on Long Island, where I'd been holed up for the past several days writing.

Within minutes of getting an alert of his passing from CNN on my iPhone, I began receiving dozens of phone calls, texts, emails, and Facebook messages from family members and friends. Although many were aware of the biography I was working on, mostly they were condolences from people who knew how much Norman and his sitcoms like *All in the Family*, *Sanford and Son*, *Maude*, and *The Jeffersons* meant to me.

Having grown up watching them as a young child in the 1970s, I carried them in my DNA as much as anything else. In some ways, I feel like Norman helped raise me, and the fact that he was now gone seemed unfathomable. Once I returned to my apartment later that morning, I immediately turned on the television as I sat glued to my computer watching and reading the tributes as they poured in from news outlets around the world and on social media. And sentimentalist that I am, I couldn't help but tear up as the theme songs from his shows, especially "Those Were the Days" from *All in the Family*, played in the background.

I also found it difficult to concentrate when it came to the task at hand of getting back to the book even though most of the heavy lifting had already been done. First, there was the sense of sadness and disbelief I felt now writing about him in the past tense. Far trickier, however, was trying to figure out how to capture the essence of an American icon who had lived for more than a century, who was active until almost the very end, and whose life was far more complicated than most people realize.

It felt like I was starting from scratch.

I was lucky enough to cross paths with Norman (whom I always deferentially addressed as "Mr. Lear") several times over the last decade. The first time was by phone in 2011 for a fortieth-anniversary retrospective I did on *All in the Family* for *TV Guide*. He couldn't have been nicer and even sent me a letter afterward telling me how much he enjoyed the article. I met him a second time in 2015, this time in person, at his New York apartment when I interviewed him for my last book *The Improv: An Oral History of the Comedy Club That Revolutionized Stand-Up*. We had an enjoyable, unhurried chat that concluded with him autographing his recently released memoir *Even This I Get to Experience* and posing for a picture.

Our next encounter was in Boston in 2018 at Emerson College, which he attended briefly, where I'm also an alumnus and an adjunct professor. The occasion was the unveiling of a life-size statue of Norman that stands prominently in the middle of our campus. I didn't know it yet, but two years later, I would be teaching a class there about his sitcoms, which is how this project came about.

Of course, no one knew then either that the world was about to come to a grinding halt during the COVID-19 pandemic during which Norman graciously Zoomed into my class twice. Thus, when this book transpired, my hope was that he would give me his blessing and participate. He even told me he would consider it, and his daughter Kate was also extremely supportive.

So I was surprised, though not entirely shocked, when after reaching out to Norman's publicist and having what appeared to be a promising conversation, she politely declined my request, saying that he was "too busy." But it wasn't a hard "no" either, and while she said he wouldn't be able to commit to an extensive interview, she also told me that he might be willing to answer some questions once the book was close to completion.

Again, this did not surprise me. As an entertainment journalist who has interviewed hundreds of celebrities for my other books and dozens of newspapers and magazines, I've been down this road many times before; plus it fit with Norman's reputation of rarely giving interviews, which was understandable because of who he was and his age. Nevertheless, I thought I might have a shot, especially since he had appeared in my class twice and I'd already interviewed him before. I also tried to emphasize this in my multiple correspondences with his publicist, as did my publisher and literary agent, as we continued our efforts to make my good intentions and desire to ensure accuracy known.

But as time went on, these overtures were simply ignored until I was finally told in the spring of 2023 via email that getting any cooperation from Norman or anyone else from his team at Act III Communications wasn't in the cards, although they wished me well. Happily, however, there were many others connected to him who were willing to talk to me and were treasure troves of information. To supplement the nearly two dozen interviews I conducted, I turned to the publicly available archive of what was already "out there" about Norman, which was enormous. Particularly useful on the electronic front were the Television Academy Foundation's Oral History Collection and the American Comedy Archives at Emerson College, as well as scores of vintage interviews, magazine and newspaper articles, and of course, his vast body of work that far exceeds the trailblazing 1970s sitcoms for which he was best known. There were also numerous books that were extremely helpful, including Norman's own 2014 autobiography *Even This I Get to Experience*, as well as Michael Starr's *Black and Blue: The Redd Foxx Story*, *Warm Up the Snake: A Hollywood Memoir* by director John Rich, Alan Neuwirth's *They'll Never Put That on the Air: An Oral History of Taboo-Breaking TV Comedy*, Shawn Levy's *King of Comedy: The Life and Art of Jerry Lewis*, *This Is CBS . . . A Chronicle of 60 Years* by Robert Slater, *In All His Glory: The Life of William S. Paley, the Legendary Tycoon and His Brilliant Circle*, *Up the Tube: Prime-Time TV in the Silverman Years* by Sally Bedell Smith, among others.

As for a legacy, Norman stands in perpetuity among the most seminal and enduring cultural figures America ever produced. He offered the world a window into the lives and homes of families who looked like the people who were watching them, while also boldly tackling social issues through comedy that no one had ever before dared to take on and gave underrepresented members of society their first-ever prime-time voice.

He was also the first television producer to become as famous as the shows he created. Off-screen, he was an impassioned social activist, a pursuit to which he devoted much of the later part of his life through his progressive advocacy group People for the American Way, dedicated to the preservation of free speech and counteracting the Christian Evangelical right-wing's sway over American politics.

Following his death, headlines around the globe heralded Norman as a visionary and a trailblazer, which, of course, he was. But even more importantly, he was a human being who was not without flaws. At times, this included not giving others enough credit for their role in his success and personifying the negative connotation of the Hollywood limousine liberal who talked the talk without always walking the walk. Pointing this out is not meant to besmirch his legacy, but rather to highlight also that he wasn't always perfect.

What follows, then, is an objective portrait of Norman Lear in full totality for over a century, from the young boy he started out as to the man, comedic auteur, and activist he became, presented and reflected on through the multiple facets of his personal and professional life, his activism, and the people, places, and events that shaped it from the very beginning until the end. While this is the first comprehensive biography about him, no book can ever be completely "definitive" as hard as it may try.

With that being said—and to whatever extent possible—this hopefully comes close.

Part One

The Early Years

CHAPTER 1

Early Childhood and Youth

In December 1971, nearly one year after *All in the Family* premiered, viewers discovered for the first time how Archie and Edith Bunker met. It was revealed in the season-two episode "Cousin Maude's Visit" that became the origin for the eponymous hit spin-off starring Bea Arthur. The premise was that the entire Bunker household got sick with flu, and as Edith's liberal feminist first cousin Maude Findlay, whom Archie despised, came to take care of them, Edith, as only she could, told the meandering story of how Archie, trying to get her attention, stuck his hand into her sundae at an ice cream parlor, and forever captured her heart.

Later recounted again almost verbatim in the final scene of the season-8 flashback episode "Mike and Gloria Meet," it also illustrates just one example of Norman's uncanny knack for mining deeply into the recesses of his past, and with tongue firmly planted in cheek, turning it into comedy gold.

From "stifle," "dingbat," and "meathead" to Archie's beer-stained easy chair, countless aspects from his own life can be found sprinkled throughout his signature sitcom and other shows. In this hilarious bit about how Archie and Edith became a couple, he masterfully played off the circumstances under which his own parents Herman and Jeanette Lear originally got together some fifty years earlier.

But in a very real sense, it was also a prophetic metaphor for how Norman quickly learned to use comedy to survive a childhood that was marred by pain, poverty, and often desperation from a very young age.

The peculiar tale of how his parents crossed paths occurred sometime in the summer of 1921 at a New Haven, Connecticut, ice cream parlor.

Like Archie did with Edith, Herman—in his quest to get Jeanette, who was there on another date, to notice him—thrust his hand into her banana split. Following a brief eight-week courtship, they were married that September. Eleven months later, on July 27, 1922, their first and only son Norman Milton Lear entered this world at New Haven Hospital. Three years after that, on October 25, 1925, Herman and Jeanette became the parents of a daughter, Claire.

An aspiring jazz singer who later performed in nursing homes and was the model for Gloria on *All in the Family*, Claire would spend most of her life in the Connecticut area, where she was a housewife married for sixty years to a metal worker named Richard Brown and the mother of three children, deliberately eschewing the spotlight of her famous older brother. Though they were never estranged, they were never particularly close either. In 1997, Norman told the *Hartford Courant* that he was sometimes "exasperated by her and by her inability to grasp subtleties because she was unaware of the greater events and forces in the world," adding that "in some ways she is as unsophisticated a person as I've ever met."[1]

During the earliest years of his life, the family lived at 45 Mead Street in downtown New Haven, where his mother, Jeanette, allegedly dropped three-month-old Norman on his head while she was bathing him in the kitchen sink, leaving him there alone as she ran next door to a neighbor to get help. "Over the years, this incident seemed increasingly funny to her," he said in his 2014 memoir *Even This I Get to Experience*. "It became a kind of set piece in *her* life story."[2]

According to New Haven historian and author Peter J. Malia, the Lears' long-demolished home on Mead Street was a "late-nineteenth-century tenement with the bottom-floor used for businesses and the top-floors used as apartments, not unlike the Lower East Side of New York in those years."

The years were the "Roaring Twenties," an era that modern history has often romanticized as such because of the optimism and prosperity that came to define it as investors flocked to a rising stock market and companies unveiled cutting-edge new products like the first washing machines and radios. The New Haven of the early 1920s was also a thriving, vibrant city that, as the name suggests, has always prided itself on being a place of hope and opportunity for its citizens. In the meantime, immigration to Connecticut and New Haven particularly continued to flourish in the early twentieth century much as it had during the immediate decades before. It was especially prevalent among Poles, Germans, and Italians, as well as Southern and Eastern European Jews. As New Haven's inner neighborhoods with their overcrowded walk-up apartment buildings continued to evolve through multiple ethnic identities who quickly found work as unskilled factory workers, domestics, tailors, and barbers, generations who came before them found kinship, friendship, and often a place to stay. It isn't surprising, then, that both sides of Norman's family ended up here.

The first to arrive was his paternal grandfather, Solomon Lear, who immigrated to New Haven from Russia just after marrying his half-niece in 1880. On March 19, 1893, Norman's father Herman was born the second of six children. Except for his Uncle Jack, a theatrical publicity agent for MCA whose professional footsteps he initially aspired to follow in, Norman would describe his father and the rest of his siblings (older brother Edward, younger brother Eli, and sisters Jenny and Fanny) as "bent," something he attributed to having grandparents who were uncle and niece, even though details of specific memories were sparse.

On his mother's side, Norman's recollections of his other grandparents were more abundant, albeit occasionally tinged with exaggeration. For years, he claimed that his grandfather used to write letters to the president of the United States every month, something he later incorporated into the second episode of *All in the Family* when Archie got dressed up to write a laudatory letter to Richard Nixon and fantasizes about his reaction. As for the real source of inspiration, however, he later acknowledged that it was his friend's grandfather and not his own who wrote to presidents.

Yet despite such occasional fabrications, his affection for his maternal grandparents, Shia and Elizbeth Sokolovsky (later shortened to Seicol), whom he called my *bubbe* and *zayde*, was genuine and everlasting. In many respects, they were the one and only stable presence throughout much of his early life. Arriving from Russia at New York's Ellis Island in 1904, his grandfather Shia settled in New Haven shortly afterward and sent for his wife and three children.

Their longtime residence was a fourth-floor walk-up apartment at 75 York Street with Shia, who became a dressmaker, eventually opening his own store in downtown New Haven. As a young teenager, Norman worked there on weekends with his cousin Elaine who later married Ed Simmons, his first comedy writing partner.

By stark contrast, Norman's immediate household was almost always in turmoil in one form or another. The family lived, as he often said, quoting his friend the playwright Herb Gardner, "at the ends of their nerves and at the tops of their lungs." Herman Lear (who liked to call himself "H.K.," having added the "K" as an initial he made up that stood for "King"), was a nattily dressed ne'er-do-well. Sporadically working as a traveling salesman, he had an unyielding weakness for getting involved in get-rich-quick schemes that eventually landed him in serious trouble.

Though Norman was too young to realize the seriousness of his father's character flaws at first, the resulting consequences left an indelible imprint that remained with him for the rest of his life. Still, in many of his public recollections over the years, he also downplayed Herman's chicanery, variously describing him as a "salesman/entrepreneur who was going to have a million dollars in ten days to two weeks tops" and of "having a screw in his head, which if turned one way or another might have helped him get right from wrong."

In other moments of nostalgia, Norman described Herman as a "rascal," although in a 2014 interview with the Associated Press's Frazier Moore to promote his memoir when he was ninety-two, he conceded: "I wanted to run as far as I could from anything he stood for. But at the same time, I wished to make him everything I wanted him to be. My favorite way of thinking about him was as a rascal, and not—I have a hard time saying it even now—as a thief."[3]

Jeanette, meanwhile, was cold and indifferent. A hypochondriac who always had difficulty expressing affection or approval, her relationship with Norman would forever be complicated. One underlying reason, he later surmised, may have been a series of illnesses she experienced as a young girl, which contributed to her obsession with doctors and a perpetually bleak outlook on life that was exacerbated by the strains of her tumultuous marriage to Herman that became worse as she got older.

Sometime in 1927 when Norman was five years old—most likely because Herman was down on his luck—the Lears moved to Chelsea, Massachusetts, just across the Mystic River outside Boston. For a Jewish family seeking a fresh start in the United States, Chelsea back then was about as ideal a place as you could get.

Despite a devastating fire that had left 56 percent of the population homeless two decades earlier, by the late 1920s, Chelsea was enjoying something of a renaissance, thanks to a major influx of Russian and Eastern European immigrants, especially Russian Jews. By the early 1930s, the number had doubled to nearly twenty thousand out of a population of almost forty-six thousand, making Chelsea home to the largest number of Jewish residents per square mile of any city outside New York.

Thanks to its prime waterfront location and easy access to Boston's rail hub, Chelsea was home to a slew of flourishing industries from factories that made everything from shoes to elastic goods, adhesives, and stoves—along with shipbuilders, lumberyards, metalworks companies, and machine shops, where employers found an ample supply of eager labor.

The Lears lived at 12 Warren Avenue, and Norman attended the local elementary school, where he was a decent student. It was also here in Chelsea that he discovered America's new favorite pastime, radio, excitedly indulging in a nightly cavalcade of comedians, many of whom had their own shows in those years. Among them was Joe Penner, whose "Wanna buy a duck" was a popular catchphrase in households everywhere, along with Fred Allen, Eddie Cantor, and Edgar Bergan (accompanied by his dummy Charlie McCarthy)—and later—Jack Benny, Burns and Allen, Bob and Ray, *Amos 'n' Andy* and *Fibber McGee and Molly.*

He particularly loved listening to the fights broadcast live from Madison Square Garden in New York on Friday nights while sitting at his father's knee, although sadly, it was a ritual that would not last. One afternoon in the summer of 1931—just out of third grade and two weeks shy of his ninth birthday, as he was preparing to leave for sleepaway camp in Vermont—Norman's world was shattered when Herman was arrested for trying to sell phony bonds to the Boston securities firm E.A. Pierce & Co.

The following day on the Fourth of July, a picture of Herman handcuffed to a policeman and coming down the courthouse steps during his arraignment hearing was plastered across the front pages of the *Boston Globe* and the *Evening Traveler.* Five weeks later, Herman was convicted and served three years at Deer Island Prison, off Boston Harbor.

Norman received another blow on the night of Herman's arrest as well-meaning family and friends congregated at the Lears' home for an impromptu estate sale. Not only were they leaving Chelsea, but Jeanette also planned to send her son to live with relatives while Claire stayed with her. The double whammy devastated the young boy, who in one form or another, immediately felt a pervasive sense of neglect and despair from which he would never fully recover.

Yet what is interesting about this bleak period is that this is also when Norman instinctively began to discover his famous sense of humor that would become his life's calling—something he later called "finding the foolishness of the human condition" amid the pain and sadness of real life. For Norman, this realization actually occurred on the same night of Herman's arrest. As he told the *Times of Israel* in 2015: "There is humor everywhere. Standing with a group of people watching a casket go into the ground and [you see] the chief mourner scratching his [tuchas]. There is humor there. Where there is humanity, there is comedy.

"My mother couldn't live in the house we were living in, she was so ashamed," he recalled. "She was selling the furniture, and somebody was about to buy my father's red leather chair. It was just the worst moment I could live through at nine years of age. And the guy who was buying the chair put his hand on my shoulder and said, 'Well, Norman, you're the man of the house now.' To tell a kid in that situation he's the man—and then two seconds later he was saying, 'There, there, Norman! The man of the house doesn't cry.' I came away from that and the foolishness of the human condition just struck me. And I understood that you can't have a situation where there isn't some humor."[4]

Around this same time also, Norman's lifelong social and political consciousness began to awaken as he became aware of the realities of being Jewish in 1930s America. This epiphany occurred sometime shortly before Herman's arrest when he stumbled upon Father Charles Coughlin, the infamously anti-Semitic, pro-fascist broadcaster considered to be the father of hate radio, while listening to his Crystal radio set one afternoon.

At the height of his popularity in the 1930s, some thirty million faithful listeners tuned in to hear Coughlin's bigoted, rambling rhetoric. As Norman told *Variety* in a 2019 interview: "The Coughlins of the world scared the shit out of me. But it also helped me keep my guard up."[5] Further indicative of Coughlin's lasting impact on his psyche was his decision to call the progressive free-speech advocacy group he founded in 1981 People for the American Way. As the *Variety* article also noted: "Voices like Coughlin's weren't the American way, Lear believed. That's how he came up with the name."[6]

With his father in prison and Jeanette having all but completely washed her hands of her only son, Norman spent the next three years bouncing around between relatives. The first to take him in was Al, Jeanette's brother, who lived in Hartford and managed a ladies' shoe store. Terribly lonely and often feeling invisible—especially after being separated from Jeanette and Claire, whom he rarely saw even though they lived nearby—Norman once again relied on his sense of humor to carry him through, including a newly discovered talent for mimicry.

Around 1932 when he was ten or eleven, Norman returned to New Haven to live with his maternal grandparents, Shia and Elizabeth. But despite their close relationship, he was even more at loose ends about being abandoned yet again by Jeanette who remained behind in Hartford with Claire.

Still, Norman was always a fighter and managed to survive his pre-adolescent days in New Haven relatively unscathed. Other memories from back then—including the weekend double-feature movie matinees he saw at the Roger Sherman Theater and selling souvenirs on The Green, the common area outside the Yale Bowl before Saturday football games—were good ones.

In the summer of 1934, Herman was finally released from prison, and the Lears, reunited for the first time in three years and on the move again, headed for New York. On the day of his parole, Herman boarded a Manhattan-bound train from Boston, while Jeanette, Norman, and Claire anxiously waited at New Haven's Union Station to join him for the rest of the trip.

Of that afternoon and not knowing what to expect, Norman remembered, "I was just a small boy, but I was a crowd of emotions."[7] On the contrary, Herman—who got on the train wearing the same suit he'd worn on the day of his arrest, which was now several sizes too large—was still full of bravado, and as usual, ever the braggart making promises he couldn't possibly keep. He was thinner, yes, but otherwise being behind bars hadn't changed him one iota, as he pledged to take the family on a trip around the world for Norman's upcoming Bar Mitzvah. As for Norman and his sister, it felt as if they were complete strangers.

After arriving at New York's Penn Station, the Lears settled in with another family, sharing a three-bedroom apartment in the Prospect Park neighborhood of Brooklyn on St. Marks Avenue while Herman tried to get back on his feet. At the turn of the twentieth century, Prospect Park had been one of Brooklyn's most affluent areas, as it is again today. However, the Great Depression had forced many of its wealthy residents to scale back their lifestyles and sell their homes, which the landlords who bought them either tore down or turned into tenements. This is likely why the Lears were able to live there, plus Herman and Jeanette already had relatives in New York.

By all accounts, both Lear children acclimated well to their new surroundings as Norman soon enrolled at Samuel Tilden High School and quickly developed a group of friends who lived in his same apartment building. Two of his closest pals were Eddie Pearl and Bernie Fischer with whom he formed a musical trio called the Harmonic Rascals. When they weren't performing together, especially during Halloween, one of their favorite activities was pulling pranks like sticking pins into the doorbells of the apartments on the upper floors, causing them to ring incessantly, and letting the air out of the tires of cars on the block. They also reveled in watching their pal Marty Ellen eat flies for a nickel.

His other Brooklyn friends from around this time were Herbie Lerner and Elliot and Edwin Schwartz, twin brothers who lived in the neighborhood. Together, they belonged to the youth organization Young Israel, where Norman wrote and all three boys performed in the play *Sir Your Cur, or the Villain Gets It in the End*. They also played sports, forming a sandlot football team and naming it ACHVA (the Hebrew name for "brotherhood"), complete with embroidered maroon sweaters with an *A* on the chest and stripes down the sleeves.

In the summer of 1935 shortly after his thirteenth birthday, Norman had his Bar Mitzvah. Though Herman didn't make good on his promise to take the family on a 'round-the-world trip, he nevertheless spared no expense on the milestone event.

The ceremony was held at the Sharri Zedek synagogue on Manhattan's Upper West Side followed by a lavish reception back at the Lears' apartment. As gifts, Norman received a Waterman fountain pen and $32 in cash, which he immediately blew that same afternoon on an impromptu trip with his friends to Coney Island. That following summer when he was fourteen, he got a job at the iconic amusement park as a carnival barker hawking souvenirs.

He returned to work there when he was fifteen, although once again, misfortune befell the family, and as a result, their four years in New York ended abruptly. That following April, Herman was gravely injured on the New Jersey Turnpike, near New Brunswick, when he and five other men later described in a newspaper clipping as "a car full of novelty salesmen" were involved in a two-car collision in which only three of them survived.

Miraculously, Herman was one of them, though his recovery took months and caused him to walk with a permanent limp that sometimes required the use of a cane. Following his long convalescence, the Lears returned to Hartford, where Herman, Jeanette, and Claire remained for the rest of their lives.

Their first home was an apartment on Woodland Street, where Norman enrolled as a sophomore at Weaver High School and Herman eventually found work canvassing door to door for a local building contractor. Within a year, he decided to start his own contracting business, naming the new venture "Norclaire Construction, Inc." and building six Cape Cod–style houses on Woodstock Avenue, one of which they moved into. Of everywhere the family lived while he was growing up, this was the only place Norman ever considered home and where Herman later died.

Norman's teenage years in Hartford were significant for several other reasons as well, including learning to drive, discovering girls, and his first exposure to theater and vaudeville at the State Theater. Originally opened in 1926, it was here where he saw everything from Ritz Brothers films to live performances by Benny Goodman, Ella Fitzgerald, Duke Ellington, Peggy Lee, and a young singing sensation named Frank Sinatra, who would later go on to star as a swinging New York bachelor in his first film *Come Blow Your Horn*.

On the romantic front, Norman's first love was a girl by the name of Adrienne Young. Later, he met Charlotte Rosen, a salesclerk for the local department store G. Fox & Company, who was a year older, on a hayride; she later became his first wife. Meanwhile, at Weaver High School, Norman, by his own description, was "no more than a B student, but with an A profile [even though] it was not the way I saw myself then."[8] After briefly playing football on the junior varsity team, he quickly gained a following writing the senior class play and penning a humor column for the weekly student newspaper, the *Lookout*, called "Notes to You from King Lear."

Though his time as a big-time comedy writer and TV producer was still many years away, it was his first taste of what was to come.

CHAPTER 2

College (Briefly) and Off to War

Norman graduated from high school in the spring of 1940. In his year-book, the *Weaver High School Portal*, there was a paragraph next to each student's photograph summarizing their accomplishments and most unique attributes. This was his:

> This is Lear, the inimitable Lear—clearing house for ancient, medieval, or risqué jokes, past master of the art of reflex-provoking (sneezing, etc.) and if anyone asks him who [gossip columnist Walter] Winchell is—he's New York's Lear. An ultra-sophisticate, the "'King' tells a good story," showers before breakfast, writes poetry, likes debating, acting, orating, and is a famous wit (infamous if you must!). We can't seem to do the old boy justice.[1]

But as foretelling as the approbation was, Norman's goal at this point was not to become a comedy writer, much less for television, which wouldn't become widely available to the public as a mass medium for nearly another decade. Number one on his post–high school to-do list was to be the first person in his family to go to college even though the Lears' precarious financial situation severely diminished the possibilities.

It isn't clear what Herman was doing at this point or if his contracting business had yet gone belly-up as it eventually would. However, his perpetual plight combined with the economic devastation of the Great Depression almost all but guaranteed that Norman wouldn't be able to pursue his dreams of a college education.

He also faced other challenges beyond the family's financial troubles. Most problematic was a national quota system in place at the time restricting the number of Jews, Blacks, and other minorities who were being admitted at many of America's top colleges and universities. During and after World War I, such overt discrimination was rampant, and it remained intact until the late 1960s.

Jews applying to the Big Three Ivy League giants—Harvard, Princeton, and Yale—were among the biggest targets. In fact, the same year Norman was born, Harvard's president A. Lawrence Lowell, in 1922, proposed limiting the number of Jews to a maximum of 15 percent, arguing that the university couldn't survive unless the majority of the students came from old-line American families and that the limits would prevent further anti-Semitism. At the time, Lowell reasoned: "The anti-Semitic feeling among the students is increasing, and it grows in proportion to the number of Jews. If their number should become forty percent of the student body, the race feeling would become intense."[2]

Though he was acutely aware of this reality, Norman was still determined to go to college. Then sometime in the winter of 1940, he providentially learned about a National Oratorical Contest that was being sponsored by the American Legion and decided to enter. As it happened, it was the first year of the competition and the first prize was a full scholarship to Emerson College in Boston, located just across the Charles River from Harvard. The contestants were required to deliver an eight-minute speech about the U.S. Constitution, followed by an extemporaneous four-minute lecture on a related subject, the unknown topic of which wouldn't be given to them by the judges until right before they were to return to the podium for a second time.

Appalled by the notion of quota systems for Jews trying to get into the nation's top colleges and with his childhood memories of hearing the anti-Semitic rhetoric of Father Charles Coughlin still fresh in his mind—on top of the escalating Second World War and rise to power of Nazi dictator Adolf Hitler—the title of the speech Norman prepared was "The Constitution and Me." With an instant command of the audience, he talked candidly about how the constitutional guarantees of equal rights and freedom for all held a special, if not precarious, meaning for him as a member of a minority group. After handily winning the local, regional, and national competitions that spring, he was awarded admission to Emerson's freshman class for the following fall, where he planned to major in either theater or journalism.

Today, Emerson is in the heart of Boston's theater district at the intersection of Tremont and Boylston Streets. With a total enrollment of over four thousand students, it also maintains stand-alone campuses in Los Angeles on

Sunset Boulevard and the Netherlands and is internationally recognized as the only four-year college in America with programs specializing exclusively in communications and the performing arts, including the nation's first comedy major.

With many of its students going on to pursue successful careers in theater, film, television, and radio, a very small list of its most famous alumni includes former *Tonight Show* host Jay Leno; actors Henry Winkler, Spalding Gray, Jennifer Coolidge, and Brandon Lee; TV executives Max Mutchnick, Kevin Bright, Vin Di Bona, and Doug Herzog; makeup artist Bobbi Brown; and comedians Dennis Leary, Mario Cantone, David Cross, Steven Wright, Eddie Brill, and Bill Burr.

Emerson began in 1880 as a school of oratory, founded by its namesake president Charles Wesley Emerson, a Unitarian minister originally from Pittsfield, Vermont, who was a distant cousin of poet Ralph Waldo Emerson. Several years before Norman's arrival in 1940, they dropped the "Oratory" part of the name and were already beginning to gain notoriety for having some of the nation's first programs in radio, television, and theater.

Nevertheless, Emerson hadn't been Norman's first choice. He'd originally set his sights on the much larger Northwestern University outside Chicago, which was also well known as an early pioneer for its programs in theater, radio, and television, along with a more lenient quota system. However, Emerson—which dedicated a life-sized statue of him after Norman established a scholarship in his name in 2018—was his only option, and he immediately took to it like a duck to water.

As it was until the early 2000s, the college in those years was in the Back Bay section of Boston on Beacon Street. During his time there, it had an enrollment of around two hundred students, most of them female. Norman lived with four other male freshmen in a nearby rooming house at 270 Clarendon Street, which they shared with a group of single women in their thirties—and where he was the token Jew—although it never came up. According to the website backbayhouses.org, 270 Clarendon was originally built as a private residence in 1874 and was converted into a rooming house in the same year Norman lived there. It was run dormitory-style by a forty-something Irish couple named Francis and Marion Lawless who also owned another rooming house at 204 Commonwealth Avenue.

Despite everything he had to go through to get there, Norman, for the most part, was a mediocre student at Emerson, although he quickly made a name for himself after performing in several school plays. When he wasn't in class or onstage, one of his favorite haunts was Scollay Square in a now-defunct section of downtown Boston. Today, it is known as Government

Center, a complex of municipal buildings where City Hall, courthouses, and most state and federal offices are located.

The area was originally named for William Scollay, a prominent local developer and militia officer who purchased a landmark four-story merchant building at the intersection of Court and Cambridge Streets in 1795. Officially called Scollay Square in 1838, in the ensuing years it would become one of Boston's major commercial business districts, serving as home base to a diverse assortment of local shop merchants, banks, lawyers, doctors, and dentists. Among them was Dr. William Thomas Green Morton, who was the first dentist to use ether as an anesthetic. What Scollay Square is best remembered for, however, is being the home of the Old Howard Theater, which comedian Fred Allen had once dubbed "Boston's Broadway."

Originally built in 1844, it began as a venue for serious drama, ballet, and opera, playing host to many of the most famous and infamous theatrical stars of the day, including Abraham Lincoln's assassin John Wilkes Booth, who once played Hamlet there. Later, in the 1900s and 1910s, it showcased many of the nation's top vaudeville acts. After falling into steep decline in the 1940s, it became a mecca for burlesque and minstrel shows, gradually changing its image from family-friendly theater as it now primarily catered to sailors on leave and local college students.

Given his well-demonstrated penchant for live theater, it wasn't much of a surprise that Norman was one of the Old Howard's most fervent patrons, attending every performance he could. While he was amused by the boisterous revelry of the comedians and sketches, it was the bump-and-grind burlesque girls who made the biggest impression. Just as important, he also intuitively understood that it was the audience and their shared reaction that gave these performers focus and humanity, bringing them to life even in the absence of all subtlety or any depth.

As Norman began his sophomore year at Emerson in the fall of 1941, all appeared to be chugging along according to plan until an event occurred that not only changed the course of his own life, but also the entire nation. That Sunday, December 7, he was in rehearsals for a school play called *The Two Orphans* when the director and his fellow cast members received word of the surprise Japanese attack on Pearl Harbor, leading to America's formal entry into World War II. With almost-perfect recall, he described the incident to comedian Bill Dana during a 2015 interview for Emerson's American Comedy Archives oral history series:

> We were rehearsing on the Esplanade at the little theater behind 130 Beacon Street. [A woman named] Gertrude Binley Kay was our

director, and [she] wore this huge hat and talked in this high-pitched Brahmin accent. And someone came in at ten o'clock in the morning or something. We had started very early on a Sunday morning, that Sunday morning, and someone came rushing in to say the Japanese had just bombed Pearl Harbor. And Gertrude Binley . . . I don't remember anyone else. We all had these enormous reactions I'm sure, but Ms. Kay went ape and insisted that we go down to Boylston Street where there were some Japanese stores where we could break the windows. It was quite a moment.[3]

At the same time, as Norman struggled with his emotions over the strike, he quickly decided to forgo his relatively happy-go-lucky life as a college student to voluntarily enlist in the US Army Air Force. Like the rest of the country, he was not prepared for this unexpected turn of events. But as he told *People* magazine in 1995, "I just had to get into it. I was Jewish and I wanted to kill Germans."[4] In other interviews over the years, he would offer a similar refrain.

For example, during another wide-ranging five-hour conversation about his life and career with the National Television Academy of Arts and Sciences for its oral history collection in 1997, he said: "I loved the thought of looking down and seeing those bombs dropping and being Jewish had everything in the world to do with it. As a matter of fact, when my tour of duty was over, I volunteered to go into the infantry so I could kill with my hands."[5]

Yet Norman did not enlist immediately, mainly out of deference to his beloved grandfather Sol, who was ninety-two at the time and on his death-bed in New Haven Hospital. When he called to tell him of his plan, the old man who hadn't spoken or reacted to anything in days cried and passed away the following afternoon. In a rare display of emotion, Jeanette cried also, as Herman—who by then had a job recruiting local Connecticut metal workers and tool-and-die makers to manufacture heavy equipment for the military—advised Norman to wait, which he did.

Because he was always extremely guarded about many aspects of his early life, reconstructing certain details is difficult. However, here is what's known. In the immediate months following the attack on Pearl Harbor, Norman remained in Boston, although it's unclear as to whether he was still officially matriculated as a student at Emerson.

What he did do during this period was set up a stand on campus selling school supplies with his friend Nick Stantley, which soon led to another venture selling Defense Stamps and Bonds for the Treasury Department for twenty-five cents apiece. Jack Lear, Norman's press agent uncle, had meanwhile recently gotten a job working for the government as a dollar-a-year man, a term used in World War I and World War II to describe men who offered their expertise and services to the government for one dollar a year. With his background in public relations and natural knack for selling and spinning, Jack was hired to market a new initiative called "Unusual Non-Military War Efforts," which seemed like a perfect fit for his nephew's fledgling enterprise. As soon as he got wind of it, Jack told his boss Milburn McCarthy Jr. who immediately called Norman from Washington to learn more.

McCarthy was so impressed with what Norman told him that he came up with the idea of making Emerson the flagship location of the nation's first Collegiate Stamp Bureau, with plans to expand to other colleges across the country. Although it never got off the ground, the publicity it generated because of Jack's handiwork resulted in an Associated Press story about the venture, which was picked up by the *Boston Globe*.

Several days later, Norman and Nick received an invitation to appear on *The March of Time*, a popular radio program broadcast on CBS, the same network that three decades later would become the television home for many of his classic sitcoms. As a bonus, they received an all-expenses-paid trip to New York, including parlor car seats on the New York, New Haven, and Hartford Railroads and a two-bedroom suite at the Roosevelt, one of Manhattan's poshest hotels.

Unfortunately, Norman's first brush with celebrity was a fleeting one because on the day the show was to air, their segment got bumped to make room for an interview with a young boy wearing braces and stricken with polio who'd just been pictured in a local newspaper kissing President Franklin Delano Roosevelt, who was also a victim of the then-incurable disease. And so, in a telling sign of just how fickle the media business could be even back then, Norman and his friend's fifteen minutes of fame went as fast as it came.

After nine months of back-and-forth, and despite Jeanette's emotional pleas, Norman finally decided to enlist. His military branch (as Archie Bunker's would be) was the US Army Air Forces, also known as the Air Corps. Officially called for duty in early November 1942, he received basic training in Atlantic City, New Jersey. Not long after, he was dispatched to Scott Field in Illinois to receive training as a radio operator, where he learned Morse Code. Next, he went to Laredo, Texas, for ammunitions training before finally being transferred to the University of Buffalo in Buffalo, New York, for flight training in an AT-6 single-engine aircraft where he was also reunited with and got engaged to his former high school sweetheart, Charlotte Rosen, which was a decision he would immediately regret.

The circumstances leading up to the engagement occurred randomly one night as Norman was completing his training. He and another cadet named Jimmy Gorman were on a double date at a revolving cocktail lounge on top of the Statler Hotel in Buffalo called the Circus Bar. Norman's date was a striking young Irish woman named Helen O'Leary, and at some point during the evening—likely attributable to the slight buzz they were both feeling from the Southern Comfort whiskey they'd been drinking—the pair began joking that if Helen were to marry Norman, her name would be Helen O'Leary Lear. And then on an impulse, Norman got up and walked over to the nearby pay phone and placed a person-to-person collect call to Charlotte, who was still living in West Hartford, Connecticut, with her parents.

Though the pair hadn't spoken in over a year, she immediately accepted the charges. After exchanging pleasantries, Norman popped the question, and Charlotte said yes. The ceremony took place two weeks later, on October 21, 1943, in a private room he rented located next to the Circle Bar. The only guests were several of his cadet friends, a couple of whom were in the wedding party, along with Charlotte's parents Rhoda and Al and Herman and Jeanette. A week after the ceremony, Charlotte returned to Connecticut with her parents, and Norman was sent to Nashville, where he had a full physical and underwent a series of mathematical and mechanical tests.

Although he was in excellent health except for a minor sinus condition, he inexplicably failed the physical, which not only made him ineligible to become a pilot, but also to fly as part of the aircrew. Shocked by the disappointing news and fearing he had been grounded, he grew restless until soon enough he received word he was being transferred to Avon Park, Florida, to await assignment to become a radio operator and gunner on either a B-24 or a B-17 fighter plane.

Norman was in Florida for two weeks, where he completed more drill exercises and attended a series of lectures. To help pass the time and get his mind off things, he also responded to a help-wanted notice on one of the bulletin boards at the Army Air Force base and spent a week pushing a wheelbarrow at a nearby fertilizer factory.

Finally, in late October 1943, he received orders to report to the crew of a B-17 fighter plane, also known as a flying fortress, that was bound for either Europe or the South Pacific. Though the crew initially had no knowledge of what their final destination was until receiving word from the captain, Norman was assigned overnight guard duty during their first stopover in Gander, Newfoundland, which was followed by the Azores islands off the coast of Portugal.

Their plane touched down in Foggia, Italy, late on the afternoon of November 1, 1944, where Norman was stationed for the remainder of his tour of duty—and where Archie Bunker, who always referred to World War II as "the big one" on *All in the Family*, was fictitiously said to have been stationed too. Over the next eighteen months, Norman served in the Mediterranean theater (a military term that refers to the area or place where important events are either happening or escalating during warfare).

Here he flew fifty-two combat missions and was later awarded the Air Medal. While he was constantly in harm's way, he fortunately managed to escape any serious injuries during the raids as several members of his squadron got caught in the crossfire.

One of them was his close pal Jimmy Edwards, whose plane was shot down on their first mission and who died almost immediately afterward. The devastation of his friend's death was something Norman would never forget, especially during the immediate aftermath as he tried to remain focused on the future.

In like manner, it was also toward the end of his tour of duty in Foggia during World War II that Norman dipped another toe into the creative waters—this time with a Thanksgiving-themed variety show he wrote, produced, and emceed for the troops called *Holiday Hangovers*, which won rave reviews.

But while the triumph of the show was yet another transformative experience, it still wasn't enough to convince him that he could someday make a living as a comedy writer.

At least not yet.

CHAPTER 3

Return to Civilian Life

A s Americans were breathing a collective sigh of patriotic relief following the official end of World War II in September 1945, Norman, now twenty-four, was trying to figure out what to do with the rest of his life.

Though he'd forfeited his American Legion scholarship at Emerson after dropping out to enlist, he could have undoubtedly still gotten his degree either there or someplace else thanks to the G.I. Bill. But instead, he decided to try his hand at becoming a press agent like his uncle Jack, Herman's brother, who, as he explained repeatedly in interviews throughout the years, always had a brand-new quarter he flipped to Norman every time he saw him—and so Norman assumed that if he could be a press agent, then he could also do the same thing for his own nieces and nephews someday.

Meanwhile, the start of Norman's publicity career, or more precisely his search for a job, began ingeniously at a Foggia printing shop one afternoon shortly after Europe declared the end of the war in the spring of 1945, as he dictated what amounted to a de facto press release extolling his unique qualifications to a barely English-speaking linotype operator.

That same afternoon, he mailed the missive to his uncle Jack, who immediately sent it out to sixteen public relations firms in New York, Chicago, and Los Angeles, eliciting replies from two that were both based in Manhattan. The first was from George Evans, arguably the hottest entertainment PR man in America who repped Frank Sinatra and invited Norman in for a job interview.

The second was from George and Dorothy Ross, a theatrical PR agency that handled both Broadway shows and personalities. They were so impressed with Norman's chutzpah that they hired him on the spot, sight unseen, and he accepted. First, however, there was the matter of his discharge and reuniting with a new bride he barely knew.

Norman was officially and honorably discharged from the army in October 1945. Within hours of landing in Palm Beach that following afternoon, he and the other G.I.s with whom he'd spent the better part of the past year said their goodbyes, and he was bussed off the airfield to a nearby highway, where he hitchhiked to Miami. The plan had been for him to meet up with Charlotte and his new in-laws, Al and Rhoda Rosen, who were now living there, although the fact that they hadn't made the trip to Palm Beach to meet Norman would prove to be the first of many red flags.

In lieu of a welcome-home dinner that evening at their apartment, Al ordered takeout from a local deli. Meanwhile, Norman and Charlotte's first night back together by his own description was "perfunctory, half-hearted and forced." Nonetheless, he made the first of what turned out to be many attempts to try and stick it out. Several weeks later, they were back in New York, where he soon reported for work as a junior press agent for George and Dorothy Ross earning thirty dollars a week.

Again, because Norman was always reluctant to share many intimate details about his early personal life, where they were living at the time is unclear as is almost everything else about Charlotte. Virtually no comprehensive information exists about her in his memoir, in any of the hundreds of newspaper and magazine profiles that have been written about him, or online either.

What is clear, however, is that Norman appeared to enjoy his time as a fledgling press agent for George and Dorothy Ross, and it's not difficult to understand why. The immediate postwar years that followed would be heady ones in the American theater. Without question, the influx of classic musicals on the Great White Way throughout the 1940s and 1950s like *Oklahoma!*, *Carousel*, *Annie Get Your Gun*, *Kiss Me Kate*, and *South Pacific* is why most historians resoundingly consider this era to be the Golden Age of Broadway. American newspapers were also thriving, especially in major cities like New York, which had eight dailies—among them the *Times*, the *Daily News*, the *Post*, the *Daily Mirror*, the *Sun*, and the *Herald Tribune*—along with an army of columnists on both coasts and in between covering the latest Broadway shows and hottest entertainers.

In Hollywood, there was Louella Parsons and Hedda Hopper, whose long-standing rivalry was as legendary as Hopper's flamboyant hats. In Chicago, there was Irv Kupcinet whose venerable "Kup's Column" first launched in 1943 and was a daily fixture in the *Sun-Times* for over six decades. And in New York, there were the likes of Earl Wilson, Ed Sullivan, Leonard Lyons, Dorothy Kilgallen, and Walter Winchell, the kingpin of them all, whose syndicated column "On Broadway" was filled with rumors about celebrities.

As it still is for publicists today, Norman's main job was to get ink for his clients, and it was a skill he very quickly proved to be adept at as evidenced by the hyperbolic self-proclamation he'd sent George and Dorothy Ross that got him hired in the first place. In fact, many of the items he placed in the various gossip columns were bon mots he wrote himself and were so good they often ran verbatim.

One such tidbit involved actress Kitty Carlisle and her husband Moss Hart, the famed playwright and screenwriter behind such Broadway and big-screen masterpieces as *You Can't Take It with You*, *The Man Who Came to Dinner*, *Gentleman's Agreement*, *Hans Christian Andersen*, and *A Star Is Born*. Both Carlisle and Hart were clients of George and Dorothy Ross at the time, and Norman, in his fertile imagination, came up with a premise in which Carlisle had given Hart a pocket flask as a gift that was custom-measured to his hip while he napped.

Though the piece was completely fabricated, it all seemed perfectly innocent to the young spinmeister and accomplished its mission. Not only was it picked up by the *New York Journal-American*'s first-string gossip columnist Dorothy Kilgallen who ran it word for word, it was a twofer—meaning that two of the firm's biggest clients were mentioned in the same column. It also momentarily made Norman the man of the hour, although the wind suddenly shifted when Kilgallen called his bosses and admonished them to have him tone his creative writing down—which they did, along with cutting his salary to thirty-five dollars a week—even though Kilgallen later admitted the item was clever.

However, a second incident occurred several months later when he was publicizing a hit musical revue called *Are You with It?*, starring Johnny Downs, Lew Parker, and Dolores Gray, who were among Broadway's biggest stars at the time. Also in the cast was a popular vaudeville act called Buster Shaver and His Midgets, whose midgets were named George and Olive. Once more, Norman's clever repartee hit double pay dirt with Kilgallen who again ran the item word for word. But then, she was called out for it and complained to Norman's bosses, insisting they fire him this time.

Fearing Kilgallen would permanently blacklist their other clients from her column, George and Dorothy Ross unfortunately relented. Though it must have been a tough decision for them to make—and despite his pleas for forgiveness and offering to take another salary cut—Norman was summarily shown the door without severance pay, ending his career as a press agent after less than a year.

Several days after losing his job in the early winter of 1946, Norman and Charlotte learned she was pregnant. Strapped for cash and with a new baby now on the way, they were forced to move back to Hartford and live with Jeanette and Herman, who by then was in a new line of work. Having made several contacts recruiting local manufacturers around Connecticut to donate parts for military equipment during the war, he was now in the manufacturing business.

As usual, Herman fantasized big-time, naming his latest endeavor Lear, Incorporated and predicting it would become the next General Electric. For a while—with the postwar economy booming and demand for everything from washing machines and stoves to refrigerators, freezers, and coffeemakers revving up—it seemed as if Herman might really make a go of it this time.

So much so that Norman, against his better judgment, decided to go in with him, first making electric hot plates and then teakettles. But then predicably—and despite the backing of a local company in Hartford that was the regional Connecticut distributor for GE—their partnership didn't last.

Still, for all its setbacks, the year 1946 did mark two major milestones for Norman. That summer, he and Charlotte purchased their first home in the Hartford suburb of Windsor, assisted by Herman who hocked his pinkie ring to help cover the $1,500 down payment. Then, on September 15, Norman became a first-time father, welcoming his oldest daughter, Ellen, into the world at Hartford Hospital.

Not long afterward in 1947, Norman also came up with the idea for what he thought was a surefire moneymaking product at a time when practically everyone smoked. Then a two pack-a-day smoker himself, it was for a detachable silver-plated ashtray that clipped directly onto the rim of a coffee saucer, so dinner-party guests could flick their cigarette ashes directly into the dish when coffee and dessert were served.

Norman teamed up with a tool-and-die manufacturer named Lester Gowen whom he had met and befriended when he was working with Herman. Calling their new gizmo the Demi-Tray, they made a prototype and began searching for a distributor, which—unexpectedly and seemingly miraculously—they found in New York on their first try.

The too-good-to-refuse offer to bring the Demi-Tray to market came from Carole Stupell, Ltd., then one of the most exclusive high-end gift shops on Madison Avenue that is still widely credited for creating the bridal registry. What's more, the offer came directly from the owner Carole Stupell herself, who greeted Norman at the door and enthusiastically agreed to become the supplier. During their auspicious first meeting, she immediately put in a large order for that year's Christmas season. With plans to retail the Demi-Trays for $12.95 under the tagline: "A practical measure for smoking pleasure," they were even advertised in the *New Yorker* magazine.

Stupell also ordered a separate line of Demi-Trays in sterling silver, which she sold for $35.95. At her urging, Norman and Gowen soon began making plans to unveil a series of other products for that following year, including candle snuffers and a silent butler, which fit into a larger ashtray that contained a lid so that maids and dinner hostesses could empty the smaller containers into it throughout the evening.

But with virtually no knowledge about the ins and outs of retailing—mainly that you couldn't make money by marking up knockoffs, which the candle snuffers and silent butlers were, even though they'd slightly altered the design—Stupell pulled out of the deal, and the boys lost every cent they'd made. Yet for whatever Norman did or didn't learn from the experience, one thing is for certain: his ability to come up with the idea and take it as far as he did spoke to his determination and talent for knowing what the public wanted, which proved to serve him well as he later evolved into a successful writer and television producer.

Though the birth of Ellen didn't improve their marriage any, by 1949 the Lears were comfortably settled in Windsor. There, Norman spent much of his spare time as a member of the Hartford Players Guild, a local theater troupe that staged four plays a year, many of which he acted in. Meanwhile, Lear, Incorporated, where he still sporadically worked, was on the verge of collapse.

The straw that broke the camel's back occurred during the spring of 1949 when the state of Connecticut ordered the company to cease operations because Herman hadn't filed an annual report in over two years. Feeling increasingly at loose ends on top of the Demi-Tray debacle and about to turn twenty-seven, it was at this precarious moment that Norman decided to take another shot at being a press agent.

This time, however, his sights were set on moving to California and becoming a studio film publicist. At least that was his goal initially, although aside from loading his young family into a car and pointing it west, he didn't have any sort of an immediate game plan—much less the slightest inkling about the drastic turn his life would soon take.

CHAPTER 4

California Dreaming

As he put the house in Windsor up for sale and planned for their move to the West Coast, this time around Norman didn't enlist the help of his Uncle Jack to try and help him find a job in Los Angeles as he had in New York after the war. Curiously also, he opted not to reach out to his first cousin David Susskind, the future TV talk show host and producer, who by then was already heading up the newly minted television-programming division for Music Corporation of America (MCA). Norman was determined to do it all on his own. And somehow, he did, no doubt buoyed by the prospect of starting life anew and being able to finally break free of Herman and Jeanette, whose reaction upon hearing the news was typically negative. Though Charlotte had also initially been reluctant about going, they set out for Los Angeles with their now-two-and-a-half-year-old daughter, Ellen, in tow in late May, making the cross-country drive in a used Oldsmobile convertible he purchased at Herman's urging. News of their departure even made the newspaper, with the *Hartford Courant* running an item in its "City Briefs" column.

They arrived in Los Angeles a little over a week later, late on a Saturday afternoon in June of 1949. After checking into a motel on Sunset Boulevard near Western Avenue, Norman left Charlotte and Ellen behind as he went out to buy an early edition of the Sunday *L.A. Times*, hoping to find an affordable place to live in the classified ads and soaking in the sights like a kid in a candy store as he puffed on a cigarette, driving past landmarks like the Cafe Trocadero and Schwab's Pharmacy.

A couple of hours later, his dreams stretched even further as he headed back to the motel and stumbled upon the ninety-seat theater-in-the-round Circle Theatre, where they were about to begin opening night performances of his favorite play by his favorite playwright: *Major Barbara* by George Bernard Shaw. Pulling up in front of the building, he encountered a man with a broom sweeping the sidewalk named George Boroff, who ran the theater. Immediately, they struck up a conversation, and after learning why he had just moved to California, Boroff offered him an unpaid apprenticeship with the theater's publicist along with a free seat in the second row for that night's show, which was starting in half an hour.

Norman, suffice it to say, was on cloud nine. Adding to his excitement, even more than his new gig or the magnificent performance, was that the actor playing the lead, Andrew Undershaft, was Charlie Chaplin's son Sydney. The pièce de résistance was Charlie Chaplin himself, who arose from his seat following the curtain call afterward—and in appreciation—flawlessly began a pantomime of a slightly inebriated man trying to reach a mailbox in high wind, letter in hand.

On his very first night in Hollywood, not only had Norman crossed paths with the greatest silent-film star of all time, but he also saw him perform live. However, there would be hell to pay, because when Norman arrived back at their motel later that evening—in yet another sign of just how ill-matched they were—his ebullient mood was quickly dashed by Charlotte's wrath as she refused to talk to him for being gone so long.

The following day, Norman found them a place to live in a small one-bedroom cottage behind a larger house on Kenmore Street, located one block off Beverly Boulevard. He spotted it just as the female owner, still dressed in her bathrobe and nightgown, was about to hammer a For Rent sign into the lawn, and the deal was done. However, his early efforts trying to find work as a film publicist didn't yield the same results. After weeks of pounding the pavement in vain, he was nearly broke as he began to wonder if moving to California had been a huge mistake. His near breaking point came one afternoon not long after his arrival while driving around L.A. trying to find the cheapest deal on used tires for his car.

Soon enough, however, Norman befriended Ed Simmons, who was married to his first cousin Elaine. Originally from Boston and three years older than Norman, Simmons had recently moved to California to become a comedy writer. Like Norman, he went on to have a phenomenal career in show business. His apex also occurred three decades later in the 1970s when Simmons won five Emmys as head writer and producer for Carol Burnett's long-running CBS variety show—which, in an interesting twist of fate, aired Saturday nights opposite *All in the Family* alongside *The Mary Tyler Moore Show*, *M*A*S*H* and *The Bob Newhart Show*—on what is still considered the greatest prime-time lineup ever in television history.

But as pivotal as their friendship turned out to be, it didn't involve writing comedy, at least not together at first. In the interim, Simmons threw Norman a lifeline when he got him a job selling door to door for Gans Brothers, a home-furnishings company he was working for while they continued to pursue their respective career goals.

Together, the two men also embarked on several side ventures to earn extra cash, including peddling baby pictures and selling maps containing the home addresses of movie stars through the newspaper classifieds—six for a dollar—so fans who couldn't visit Hollywood could write to them instead. Another enterprise involved a professional wrestler who sang baritone. In quick succession, however, each of these efforts failed, although better times were on the horizon.

The watershed moment occurred one night in early 1950 when they were at Norman's house babysitting their young daughters while their wives were at the movies. At some point during the evening, Simmons asked Norman to help him with a parody he was working on of "The Sheik of Araby," the popular jazz song by Harry B. Smith and Francis Wheeler written on the heels of the 1921 Rudolph Valentino film, *The Sheik*. An immediate smash for New York's storied sheet music behemoth Tin Pan Alley, it had also been a hit among early jazz bands, especially in New Orleans, including a verse that appears in the F. Scott Fitzgerald classic *The Great Gatsby* that had made it both a jazz standard and a well-recognized part of popular culture.

With time on their hands before their wives got home, they began polishing the routine as each one drew inspiration from the other. Of particular importance—though Simmons still didn't know what he wanted to do with it—were the big laughs they got after performing it for their wives when they returned. Vibrating with excitement, Norman immediately suggested they form a comedy writing team. With fresh material in hand and motivated by their spouses' positive responses, he also told Simmons they should begin making the rounds of L.A.'s fertile nightclub scene that night to try and find a comedian to sell it to.

Up until then, the idea of becoming writing partners had never occurred to either of them. However, as Norman easily convinced Simmons, this proved to be their launching pad. An hour or so later, on their first try at a supper club called Bar of Music on Beverly Boulevard, they met a comedienne named Carole Abbot, who was seated at the piano and immediately bought the parody for thirty-five dollars, which they split between them.

After that, they never looked back.

CHAPTER 5

Major Break #1

Norman and Simmons continued writing together at night and peddling baby pictures by day, eventually earning enough money to rent a small office above a delicatessen on Beverly Boulevard for six dollars a month.

It wasn't long into their collaboration, sometime in the early summer of 1950, when they had an idea for comedian Danny Thomas, who was the hottest nightclub entertainer in America at the time. Their idea was a routine about Yiddish words that don't have counterparts in any other languages. "And he talked about three Yiddish words, *Tsimsht, Fardrayt* and *Farblonjet*," Norman later recalled during a 1986 seminar at the Museum of Broadcasting (now the Paley Center for Media) in New York.[1]

Though neither of them had ever met Thomas before, both were familiar with his act, and they wasted no time making their next move once the creative wheels were in motion. Procuring the name of Thomas's agent from *Daily Variety*, Norman called pretending to be a *New York Times* reporter on deadline. When the agent's secretary answered, he told her that he needed to ask Thomas a follow-up question for a profile he was writing about him. He then proceeded to request Thomas's home phone number, which the secretary gave to him with no questions asked.

During the 1986 Museum of Broadcasting seminar, Norman described the encounter like this: "I had a friend when I was a little boy by the name of Merle Robinson. I would use his name anytime I was in trouble. If I was in trouble in the army, if an MP stopped me or I didn't want to be talked to, I was Merle Robinson. So, I called the William Morris office who was Danny Thomas's agent and said, 'My name is Merle Robinson. I'm with the *New*

York Times. I've been doing a story on Danny Thomas. I'm at the airport now, I'm on my way back to New York. I want to write the story and title it when I get there. I only have two minutes left. I have a question for Mr. Thomas.' And I scared his agent's secretary to death, so they gave me his number. I called Thomas and he said, 'How the hell'd you get this number?'"[2]

By sheer fluke, Thomas happened to be in rehearsals with his pianist Wally Popp at the exact moment that same afternoon Norman called. It happened also that they were scrambling to come up with fresh material for an upcoming Friars Frolic the following evening at Ciro's, the iconic Sunset Boulevard nightclub that in the 1940s and 1950s was the epitome of old-school Hollywood glamour frequented by a galaxy of A-list stars of the day, where the famed Comedy Store comedy club is located now.

Amused by how he had finagled his number, Thomas immediately invited Norman to pitch their idea, which he described as "short" and elicited the positive response he'd been hoping for. But when Thomas gave him his address in Beverly Hills and instructed him to get over there with Simmons as soon as possible, there was still one slight problem. The pair hadn't written a single word, and so in yet one more clever trick, Norman feigned another excuse. He told Thomas that they would be tied up for the next several hours but promised to be there by six o'clock. Almost certainly still in shock after realizing what he had just done and how he'd managed to pull it off, as soon as Norman hung up, he and Simmons sat down to write the bit. Once completed, they finally arrived at Thomas's house at the appointed hour.

In what would prove to be their first of many career-defining moments, Thomas's reaction was so enthusiastic after hearing it that he immediately bought the routine, paying them five hundred dollars with the promise of an additional thousand if it went over well when he performed it the following night at Ciro's, which it did. Not only would Thomas continue using the monologue in his act for years afterward, even more consequential was what happened next for Norman and Simmons.

Though they never received the extra thousand dollars, serendipitously sitting in the audience at Ciro's that evening was Norman's cousin David Susskind, who was in Los Angeles on a talent-scouting trip for MCA. Susskind was so knocked out by the material that he went up to Thomas afterward to find out who the writers were. Astonished to learn that one of them was Norman, Susskind called him the next morning with an offer he and Simmons couldn't refuse and urging them to get to New York as quickly as possible.

Susskind, as it turned out, was MCA's representative for a new musical-comedy variety show that was about to go into production for NBC called

Ford Star Revue. Sponsored by Ford Motor Company and hosted by Jack Haley, the actor best known for his role as the Tin Man in *The Wizard of Oz,* Susskind wanted to hire Norman and Simmons as writers and asked them to develop a few sketches for Haley.

As author Stephen Battaglio described the exchange in his 2010 biography *David Susskind: A Televised Life*:

> "Listen," Susskind told Lear. "I'm going to New York tonight. Send a couple of samples of your work over to the hotel so I can show them to Haley."
>
> "What samples?" asked Lear, who revealed that he and Simmons had no material other than the one Thomas routine.
>
> "Listen," Susskind said. "You guys write."
>
> "Yeah."
>
> "You think you write funny."
>
> "Yeah."
>
> "You write a couple of funny things, send it over to the hotel and I'll give someone thirty dollars to make it look like a television script."[3]

Providentially once again, meanwhile, the live-in boyfriend of Norman's landlady was a young actor named Ted Stanhope who had appeared in several television shows and lent them some scripts to look at. With these as their template, they penned two sketches called "Blind Date" and "School of Comics," which Susskind took back to New York and presented to Haley who was as awed with their talent as Thomas had been.

Soon afterward, Norman received word from Susskind that Haley was prepared to roll out the proverbial red carpet with an offer for them to become junior staff writers for $700 an episode. To entice them even further, he also wanted to use one of their sketches on his very first show.

And then just like that, two days later they were flying first-class on an American Airlines flight bound for New York—with NBC picking up the tab no less.

Part Two

On the Ascent

CHAPTER 6

Live from New York

Unexpected as it was, Norman and Simmons's initial foray as TV comedy writers could not have come at a more opportune moment for variety shows. By the early 1950s, the genre was white-hot, most notably with Milton Berle's *Texaco Star Theater*, airing live on Tuesday nights at 9 p.m. from Studio 6B inside NBC's Rockefeller Center headquarters in New York. Debuting on June 8, 1948, just as the networks were beginning to broadcast seven nights a week, it was television's first breakout hit, largely credited for taking TV from a "futuristic toy" to a common household item as sales of new sets went through the roof so that viewers could tune in each week to catch the latest rapid-fire antics and one-liners of Uncle Miltie.

At the time of *The Texaco Star Theater*'s first show, Berle—then forty and an ex-vaudevillian who started in show business when he was five years old but later flopped in radio—was the current king of nightclub comics, earning $10,000 a week. Even though he had only been hired to guest-host *Texaco's* first four installments, his summertime debut was such a smash that he was named permanent host by that fall. Just days after its premiere, *Variety* had already hailed Berle as "one of those naturals," calling the show's frenetic, vaudeville-influenced format "vaudeo" and declaring it "television's hottest development."

Another case in point was the blockbuster ratings. By the end of 1948, *The Texaco Star Theater* was seen by 80 percent of all viewers each week and would remain the number-one program in the country until 1951, quickly earning Berle the sobriquet "Mr. Television," with *Time* and *Newsweek* both putting him on their covers within the same week in May 1949.

Equally as important and by happy coincidence, CBS's *The Toast of the Town* premiered just two weeks after Berle on June 20, 1948, hosted by nationally syndicated *New York Daily News* gossip columnist and former sportswriter Ed Sullivan. Though it would be the first television program to give national exposure to scores of twentieth-century musical and comedy icons from Elvis to the Beatles and the Rolling Stones and from Rodney Dangerfield to George Carlin and Joan Rivers, in the beginning Sullivan seemed like the dark horse of the two. Despite having successfully hosted a similar program on radio, he was frequently mocked for his stiff and awkward stage presence.

Significantly, one of his biggest detractors in the beginning was CBS founder and chairman William Paley, who acknowledged in his 1979 memoir *As It Happened* that "Ed Sullivan was hired as a temporary master of ceremonies for a variety program I wanted in 1948 because the CBS programming department could not find anyone like Milton Berle."[1]

A decade later, Paley's biographer Sally Bedell Smith also offered this similar account in her 1990 book *In All His Glory: The Life of William S. Paley, the Legendary Tycoon and His Brilliant Circle*: "Sullivan was an artless performer, with his high-pitched nasal voice, awkward gestures, bungled introductions, and peculiar grimaces. Paley objected immediately to Sullivan's gauche mannerisms and wanted to remove the show after the first week in 1948."[2] Just two weeks after its premiere, the *New York Times*'s television critic Jack Gould also opined that "the choice of Ed Sullivan as master of ceremonies seems ill-advised."[3]

Sullivan would, of course, quickly prove his naysayers wrong. With a knack for spotting talent—and even more importantly presenting it—*Toast of the Town* (later renamed *The Ed Sullivan Show* in 1955) went on to become a Sunday night institution on CBS for twenty-three years until 1971, while Berle relinquished his hosting duties on *Texaco* in 1956 after only eight seasons.

As a result of the success of both shows, scores of other variety shows soon followed, making up nearly one-third of all prime-time series by 1951 and remaining one of television's most popular programming staples for nearly three decades. Within a few short years of Berle and Sullivan's arrivals, dozens of relatively unknown performers, among them Red Skelton, Danny Kaye, Jackie Gleason, Dinah Shore, and Perry Como, were becoming major stars with variety series of their own. Along with a host, an opening monologue and a live audience, almost all of them included a curtain, sketches, and guests ranging from film, Broadway, and recording stars to classical musicians and comedians—and plenty of pratfalls and pie throwing.

In addition—and in a class by itself—was NBC's *Your Show of Shows*, the ingenious, ninety-minute comedy-variety sketch show created by Broadway impresario Max Liebman, starring Sid Caesar, Imogene Coca, Carl Reiner, and Howard Morris. Several members of the iconic ensemble would later go on to appear in its successor, *Caesar's Hour*, which in both incarnations counted among its writers arguably the greatest group ever assembled on one television program up until this day. Led by Caesar and future *All in the Family* scribe Mel Tolkin, they included, among others, Mel Brooks, Woody Allen, Carl Reiner, Neil and Danny Simon, and *M*A*S*H* creator Larry Gelbart.

Hence, not only had Norman and Simmons's entrance into variety television been perfectly timed, but their new employer NBC also offered a particularly welcoming environment for creative funny people thanks to the arrival of Pat Weaver, who became vice president of television in 1949. Born in Los Angeles, Weaver was already a twenty-year media-industry veteran, first as an advertising executive with the American Tobacco Company and Young and Rubicam, before cutting his broadcasting teeth as a joke writer and producer for comedian Fred Allen's eponymous radio show in the 1940s.

Following his move to television, Weaver would leave an indelible imprint as one of its most influential early innovators, championing not only *Your Show of Shows* and the venerable public affairs program *Meet the Press*, but also helping to create *The Today Show* in 1952 and *The Tonight Show* in 1954 (first called *Tonight Starring Steve Allen*). Additionally, he was a major champion for live dramas like *Hallmark Hall of Fame* and *Philco TV Playhouse*, along with launching NBC's *Producer's Showcase*, which broadcast a series of live theatrical productions, including *Peter Pan*, with legendary Broadway actor Mary Martin; a musical version of Thornton Wilder's *Our Town*, starring Frank Sinatra; and *The Petrified Forest*, with Lauren Bacall, Humphrey Bogart, and Henry Fonda.

A profile in the *New Yorker* magazine from around this time described Weaver as "not only the leading showman in television," but also its "most unrelenting thinker and most vocal theorist."[4] With a particular predilection for comedy-variety shows, another example of his Midas touch was *All Star Revue*. Airing from 1950 until 1953 and originally billed as *Four Star Revue* for its rotating roster of guest hosts, they included Ed Wynn, Jimmy Durante, film actor Jack Carson, and (significantly for his connection to Norman) Danny Thomas. In *King of the Half Hour*, David Everitt's 2001 biography of *All Star Revue* head writer Nat Hiken, the author offered the following assessment of Weaver's programming prowess:

> True to his gag-writing roots, Weaver was especially keen on humorous programming. In fact, he regarded it as the lynchpin of his prime-time

schedule, in which the eight o'clock slot every night would be set aside for comedy. The thinking was that funny shows such as *Texaco Star Theater* would attract the entire family until nine o'clock, at which time parents would put their small children to bed and stay tuned for the dramas that would follow. Weaver also made sure there would be something amusing on the air to wrap up the evening's viewing. At first, this late-night slot was filled by *Broadway Open House*, alternately hosted by comedians Jerry Lester and Morey Amsterdam. Replacing this program in 1954 was another Weaver-instigated institution, *The Tonight Show*.[5]

Premiering in the summer of 1950, meanwhile, was *Ford Star Revue*, which had been launched as a replacement series for bandleader *Kay Kyser's Kollege of Musical Knowledge* before briefly being given its own regular time slot in early 1951. Though the show struggled to find its footing from day one—and host Jack Haley, despite his notoriety from *The Wizard of Oz*, failed to catch on as the front man—it made Norman and Simmons two of the most sought-after comedy writers in television almost immediately.

Without spouses and children, the two men arrived in New York on a warm summer evening in late June, having toasted their success with their wives over a pint of Fleischman's gin during a celebratory dinner at the Simmonses' Los Angeles apartment the night before. Upon landing at La Guardia Airport, Norman elatedly called his parents in Connecticut to let them know that he was back on the East Coast to write for a new variety show on NBC. But instead of getting his old man's approval, Herman was nonplussed.

Awaiting them at the airport was a car NBC had sent for them, complete with a uniformed driver standing at the baggage claim and holding up a sign that read: SIMMONS AND LEAR. After retrieving their suitcases, they were shuttled off to the Hotel Wellington in Midtown Manhattan, located at Seventh Avenue and West 55th Street around the corner from NBC, where a small suite with twin beds had been reserved.

Haley's first episode of *Ford Star Revue* was scheduled to air live on national television on Wednesday, July 6, 1950, at 9 p.m. With little more than four days to prepare an entire show, including the opening monologue, two major sketches, and incidental material, Norman and Simmons were immediately put to the test. While they often wrote alone, they both thrived on collaboration. They also had a terrific sense of comic timing, an essential skill that would continue to serve them well in the years to come.

Not only were Norman and Simmons now bona-fide TV comedy writers, but they also had a small budget to hire someone else. It was at this point, in yet one more incredible stroke of good luck, that they crossed paths with another up-and-coming young writer named Danny Simon. Accompanying him for their first meeting was Danny's kid brother Neil—then known as Doc—whom Danny was mentoring at the time and had nicknamed "Doc" after he saw him playing with a toy stethoscope when they were growing up.

"Doc" would, of course, become the most celebrated and prolific Broadway playwright of the mid-twentieth century, capturing the American psyche in more than thirty plays, including such seminal classics as *Barefoot in the Park*, *The Odd Couple*, *Plaza Suite*, *The Sunshine Boys*, *The Goodbye Girl*, *California Suite*, and later *Brighton Beach Memoirs*, *Biloxi Blues*, *Lost in Yonkers*, and *Laughter on the 23rd Floor*, most of which became successful films, earning him more Tony and Oscar nominations than any other writer. Notably, *Come Blow Your Horn*—Simon's first hit play about a young man leaving the nest to join his bachelor big brother in Manhattan—was later brought to the big screen by Norman and his then–future partner Bud Yorkin, with Norman also writing the screenplay and Frank Sinatra starring in the film.

Eight years Neil's senior, Danny Simon would also rack up an impressive list of credits in his own right, becoming the head writer on *The Danny Thomas Show/Make Room for Daddy* and a contributor to *The Carol Burnett Show*, as well as such Norman-produced sitcoms as *Diff'rent Strokes* and *The Facts of Life*. He also later wrote jokes for Alan King, Joan Rivers, and country music singer Mac Davis, along with lecturing about comedy writing at Duke University and the University of Southern California.

But for most of his life, Danny was unfortunately overshadowed by Neil's breakout success, as his sporadic triumphs were often trumped by his own bitterness for his less-than-flattering portrayal as the muse for many of the characters in the younger Simon's most beloved plays—among them the finicky divorcee Felix Unger in *The Odd Couple*, the older brother in *Brighton Beach Memoirs* and *Come Blow Your Horn*, and the Hollywood producer in *Plaza Suite*. Yet as a comedy writing duo—and especially early on—the Simon brothers quickly proved to be a winning formula as Neil readily acknowledged in his 1996 memoir *Rewrites*. "The fact is, I probably never would have been a writer if it were not for Danny," he wrote. "Once, when I was fifteen years old, he said to me, 'You're going to be the funniest comedy writer in America.' Why? Based on what? How funny I could be at fifteen?"[6]

At the time of their auspicious first meeting with Norman and Simmons—who immediately hired them after discovering that their budget for one writer covered their asking price as a team—it was Danny whose star was on the ascent. The oldest son of Mamie and Irving Simon, born and raised in the Bronx, he inadvertently began writing comedy in 1947 at the age of nineteen while working as an assistant buyer for the Brooklyn department store Abraham & Strauss.

After flubbing his lines so badly during rehearsals for an annual employee holiday show, the frustrated producer told him to write his own skit, which Danny did that same evening at home with Neil's help. As the incident was related by the *Washington Post*'s Adam Bernstein in Danny's 2005 obituary: "Neil would sit there doing his homework. And I'd say, 'Be my sounding board. Just sit there and talk to me.' And he would come up with these funny lines, just like he always had. I didn't teach him to be funny. God came up with that."[7]

The Simons officially became a comedy writing team in the late 1940s. Like Norman, Danny also began his fledgling show business career as a press agent—in Danny's case, in the publicity department of Warner Brothers in New York—with Neil joining him there as a clerk following his discharge from the air force.

As one thing led to the next, the brothers soon began writing television and radio scripts, first for *The Ford Star Revue* and then for the likes of Phil Silvers, Milton Berle, Jackie Gleason, Jerry Lester, and most memorably Sid Caesar on both *Your Show of Shows* and later *Caesar's Hour*, eventually earning $1,600 a week before Neil decided to strike out on his own to write plays.

As it happened, however, Norman and Simmons's time as junior writers for Jack Haley's *Ford Star Revue* lasted only a couple of weeks, although their brief tenure wasn't a result of the show's lackluster ratings. It was because of the other audition sketch they'd written called "Blind Date," which scored big when it aired during the second episode. And then, in another major coup, comedian Jerry Lewis was watching that night and immediately recruited them just as he was about to become a rotating host with singer Dean Martin on *The Colgate Comedy Hour*, which was set to premiere on NBC that September. Gobsmacked by the surprise of their latest stroke of good luck, Norman told *Variety* in 2015: "Ed Simmons and I had written a routine for Danny Thomas's nightclub act, which led to New York and Jack Haley's *Ford Star Revue*. Jerry Lewis saw a sketch that he knew he could do better, so he wanted us. MCA handled both shows, so it was easy to move over to Martin and Lewis. Within three weeks, we were writing for *The Colgate Comedy Hour*. Suddenly Simmons and Lear were major comedy writers. All these other writers came out of radio, but we were *the* TV writers. But the joke of jokes was that we didn't have any experience."[8]

Never afraid to take risks, wunderkind programming chief Pat Weaver was hedging practically all of NBC's bets on the success of *Colgate*. Launched two years before *The Today Show* and four years before *The Tonight Show*, it had been his most ambitious undertaking yet, designed to take direct aim at CBS's powerhouse *Ed Sullivan Show*, still called *Toast of the Town*, and airing opposite it on Sunday nights at 8 p.m.

In 1950, Dean Martin and Jerry Lewis were also the hottest comedy team in America, so it was little wonder they had been Weaver's first choice to become the hosts. Martin and Lewis had initially crossed paths five years earlier in 1945 at New York's Glass Hat Club before officially debuting as a comedy team at the 500 Club in Atlantic City on July 25, 1946.

Quickly rising to prominence as bigger gigs along the East Coast and in Chicago soon followed, by the summer of 1948 they were headlining at the Copacabana, the crown jewel of nightclubs on Manhattan's Upper East Side, while also performing nightly at the six-thousand-seat Roxy Theater in Midtown. With audiences doubled over by Lewis heckling Martin while he tried to sing, their boyish good looks and pitch-perfect chemistry coupled by ad-libbed improvisational segments added a unique quality to their act unlike anything show business had ever seen before.

The public couldn't seem to get enough of them either. After first becoming an overnight sensation as a nightclub duo, they starred on their own radio program, *The Martin and Lewis Show*, on NBC. Soon they were signed by Hal Wallis, the legendary Paramount producer behind both Elvis Presley's slipshod film career along with such classics as *Casablanca*, *The Adventures of Robin Hood*, and *True Grit*, to star in a series of their own films, beginning with the 1949 screwball comedy *My Friend Irma* and its sequel *My Friend Irma Goes West* in 1950. On television, they made their debut on the inaugural episode of Ed Sullivan's *Toast of the Town* in June 1948 followed by appearances on NBC's *Welcome Aboard* in October 1949 and *The Texaco Star Theater* in 1950.

However, when it came to doing a variety show of their own, Pat Weaver's pitch to Lewis proved to be a much tougher sell at first. During a 2000 interview for the National Television Academy of Arts and Sciences' Oral History Collection, he offered this recollection:

> Pat Weaver had a great idea. He talked to us about doing a weekly show and I said, "No, we're going to get burned out doing a weekly show and I won't do that." Well, the interesting thing is he got the same response from Abbott and Costello and Eddie Cantor, so his idea was, "I'll tell you what we'll do. We'll put you on every six weeks. You'll do eight shows a season and you'll do it with Abbott and Costello, Eddie Cantor, Donald O'Connor and Ed Wynn." That's how *The Colgate Comedy Hour* started.

I accepted that and I told Dean, and Dean said, "You know, they're talking about thirty-nine weeks." And I said, "Yeah, they're talking about disaster. You don't want to do that." And he respected my opinion relative to burning out. So, we did *The Colgate Comedy Hour.* We were on against Sullivan on Sunday nights at eight o'clock and we beat Sullivan forty-eight times in a row for the eight years we did it.

Nobody beat Sullivan. Nobody. Any of the specials that NBC threw at Sullivan, they didn't beat him, [but] Dean and I beat him by twelve, thirteen, fourteen points.[9]

With that, so began this big-budget comedy extravaganza featuring the first major television appearances of most of the top names in show business for which its sponsor, the consumer products giant Colgate-Palmolive, would reportedly shell out over $3 million during the first season alone. Keeping true to Weaver's word, the original goal was to have three rotating elements that—as explained by television historians Tim Brooks and Earl Marsh in their book *The Complete Directory to Prime-Time Network and Cable TV Shows 1946–Present*—was "each a complete series of its own, starring Eddie Cantor, Martin and Lewis, and Fred Allen respectively."[10]

In what was to be another defining moment in Norman and Simmons's early comedic climb, Martin and Lewis quickly became and would remain *Colgate*'s biggest draws. Officially premiering on September 10, 1950, at 8 p.m., *Colgate* was broadcast live on the East Coast from the newly refurbished Park Theater near Columbus Circle in New York, with episodes fed by kinescope to audiences on the West Coast airing on a one-week delay. Martin and Lewis in the meantime were ready for television and vice versa. In his 1996 biography, *King of Comedy: The Life and Art of Jerry Lewis*, author Shawn Levy concludes this resoundingly, also offering this behind-the-scenes glimpse of how the show came together once the deal was signed:

> Television was their last frontier. Even though it had movie men like Hal Wallis worrying holes through their stomachs, television was becoming a miraculous cash cow of show business. And along with the realization that Dean and Jerry were becoming the biggest thing in movies came the suspicion that they would also be a natural for TV.
>
> Norman Blackburn and the MCA crew spent the summer of 1950 assembling a creative team for the Martin and Lewis leg of *The Colgate Comedy Hour* and then brought the principals together for a skull session in August. Making the trip out west for the meeting would be the producer Blackburn had hired, Ernest Glucksman, a lumpy, well-dressed

man born in Vienna in 1902—an unlikely regent, at first blush, to the Prince of Mirth. But Glucksman's background was unique: He had roots in both the Borsch Belt, where he'd run summer stock theaters and done stints as a social director, and in early television, where he'd worked on *Your Show of Shows* with Sid Caesar and *The Phil Silvers Arrow Show*. The combination made him a serendipitous find.[11]

So, too, was another young man from Pennsylvania named Alan "Bud" Yorkin, who had originally been hired as an NBC cameraman before quickly being promoted, first as *The Colgate Comedy Hour*'s stage manager, and then at Norman and Pat Weaver's behest, to director. Far more consequential, however, is that *Colgate* was where Norman and Yorkin first met, by default setting the stage for one of the most prolific creative partnerships in the history of Hollywood. But that wouldn't happen until much later.

At that juncture, Norman and Simmons were simply trying to adjust to their new surroundings. Adding to their jitters was their boss, a veteran radio writer named Harry Crane, who intimidated them both at first. To combat their nerves and lack of sleep wrought by the grueling hours and unwieldy production demands of live television, they often survived on a steady diet of Seconal and Dexedrine, which they procured over the counter from the nearby Alwyn Pharmacy.

Martin and Lewis's inaugural show aired on September 17, one week after *Colgate*'s premiere. Along with banter for the opening monologue, Norman and Simmons wrote three sketches: a bit depicting life behind the scenes of a live television show, a song parody of the ballad "Frankie and Johnny," and a satire about the film industry's anxieties about television called "Movies Are Better Than Ever."

The latter featured Martin portraying the manager of an empty movie theater and starlet Marilyn Maxwell, a moderately successful radio and film actress of the time, as the buxom box office clerk who does a striptease to attract customers, one of whom was Lewis playing a guy named Melvin. Though, of course, significant problems would later emerge, leading to their eventual breakup as a comedy team in 1956 and a twenty-year estrangement, Martin and Lewis immediately brought out the best of each other on the small screen just as they had in nightclubs, radio, and films.

Yet even fifty years after the show's premiere, Lewis remained circumspect about the audience's positive reception, telling the Television Foundation in 2000 that "We were not the ones to get any kind of a gauge from because we were so hot that anything we did we had the viewer. With the first

Colgate Comedy Hour, we had the largest audience that any *Colgate Comedy Hour* ever had or ever would have."[12]

Further proof of Martin and Lewis's star power was reflected in the reviews, almost all of which were resoundingly positive. The most ostensibly laudatory was from the man widely considered to be television's most influential critic during the medium's early years, the *New York Times*'s Jack Gould. Heralding Dean and Jerry as "a pair of mad zanies of the first rank," he went on to sum up the first show as "sixty minutes of slapstick and horseplay that for the most part were swell nonsense."[13]

But for all the review's glowing platitudes in the lead paragraph, what followed was far less flattering, with Gould also declaring: "It is the Lewis half of the partnership who is the works. . . . He was a one-man Hellzapoppin' who clowned his way through everything and everybody."[14]

Gould was even more derisive in his appraisal of Martin's talent, describing him as "a competent straight man" with "a baritone voice that should not offend either [Bing] Cosby or [Perry] Como fans." He concluded the review by asserting that Lewis "should have more support on future programs."[15]

Also problematic was the negative reaction among film producers and theater owners over how the "Movies Are Better Than Ever" sketch had ridiculed the motion picture industry's resentment of television. Consider biographer Shawn Levy's account of the fallout in his book, *King of Comedy*:

> The very day the skit aired, the *Motion Picture Herald* had declared Dean and Jerry the "Stars of Tomorrow" in its annual exhibitor's poll, the first team and the first comics ever so honored. Unable to reach Dean and Jerry, who'd left New York for a string of club dates, enraged exhibitors began assailing [film producer] Hal Wallis's office with telegrams and letters of protest. Wallis already hated their being on television: Not only did it overexpose them, he felt, but they would be subject to what he considered inferior writing and direction, thus jeopardizing their pull at the box office. . . . Dean and Jerry took out ads in *Variety* and *The Hollywood Reporter* to apologize for the flap, and even gave a free performance in Pittsburgh for a convention of Allied theater owners by way of apology. Jerry typed out a personal note to Wallis from Pittsburgh ("Dean joins me in sending fondest regards," he assured his boss) and signed it "MOVIES ARE BETTER THAN EVER."[16]

When viewed through the lens of history today, the flack over "Movies Are Better Than Ever" might have been a foretelling sign of what was to come for Norman, who never shied away from controversy. Nevertheless, it was a momentous battle to have been confronted with so early in his career, and the criticism stung. At the same time, he also questioned his abilities as a writer, later acknowledging in his memoir that "as that first broadcast ended, I was dissatisfied."[17]

But as the outcry over "Movies Are Better" subsided, *Colgate* quickly rallied. As the ingredients came together and it became clearer and clearer *Colgate* had lightning in a bottle, Norman and Simmons were increasingly beginning to feel within their element, plus they were having a lot of fun too. Also, because of the show's rotating roster of hosts who each had separate writers, Norman and Simmons were therefore only responsible for one show a month. Describing those years as an "accident of fate" during a 2005 interview with comedian Bill Dana for Emerson College's American Comedy Archives, Norman recalled:

> It could have been film. It happened to be television. But having made film and television, they're delights in different ways. The joy of making television in those years is that there were only three networks, so we had huge audiences. And to have an idea on a given Tuesday and know that four Tuesdays or six Tuesdays from then, you might be making sixty million people laugh because that was the size of the audiences. One specific delight: "Oo, I can get this to that big an audience that quickly." But you couldn't make love to the product. You had to let it go. And, you know, the great joy of film among other joys, the great creative joy is you finish it and then you've got the great post-production period when editing is every bit as creative as writing. And I always thought about it as being able to make love to the product for months and months.[18]

The early through mid-1950s would continue to be a golden era for Martin and Lewis. Not only were they the hottest comedy team in America, but they were also the highest-paid act in show business. Releasing one film after another on top of their appearances on *Colgate*, sold-out nightclub performances, and a new radio program for Chesterfield cigarettes, which Norman and Simmons would also write for, nearly everything they touched turned to gold. In *King of Comedy*, Lewis's biographer Shawn Levy vividly illustrates both the financial rewards that the duo reaped during this period, along with the pandemonium they ignited:

> In July 1951 Dean and Jerry were booked into the Paramount Theater in support of *Dear Brat*. . . . The Paramount was the nation's premiere

presentation house, a picture palace that had survived the demise of vaudeville with its prestige intact. . . . They would play six shows a day (seven on Saturday) for a guaranteed paycheck of $50,000 a week, plus fifty percent of all weekly receipts above $100,000.

They created virtual gridlock around Broadway and Forty-fourth Street. In order to empty the auditorium and sell more tickets . . . management promised the audience that Jerry and Dean would perform impromptu shows for them from the window of their dressing room. . . . After the Paramount, they hit Chicago and Detroit, to similarly incendiary receptions. *Life* [magazine] put them on its cover that August.[19]

For Norman and Simmons, meanwhile, an even more unforgettable incident happened in Chicago. In March 1950, they flew out to the Windy City to hand-deliver their second radio script to Martin and Lewis, who were booked for a two-week engagement at the ritzy Chez Paree supper club. They were all staying at the posh Ambassador East Hotel in the Gold Coast area. One night during a break from their performances on the eve of Lewis's twenty-fourth birthday, Norman and Simmons knocked on his door and were shocked to find the comedian lying alone with a candle affixed to his penis, as he then proceeded to light the wick and started singing the "Happy Birthday" song to his erect genitalia.

Back in New York, they continued churning out Martin and Lewis's TV and radio scripts for the remainder of *Colgate*'s first season. With Charlotte and Ellen eventually making the move east also, the Lears rented a tenth-floor apartment on Manhattan's Upper West Side.

However, as the season drew to a close and the first nationwide transcontinental coaxial cable was installed, now making it possible to air programming live from coast to coast, Pat Weaver decided to move the shows featuring Martin and Lewis and Abbott and Costello to Los Angeles. As *Colgate* became NBC's first regularly scheduled west-to-east broadcast, Norman and Simmons followed suit.

CHAPTER 7

Up and Down the Martin and Lewis Merry-Go-Round

With technical operations set up in New York, Chicago, and Los Angeles, the first West Coast episode of *The Colgate Comedy Hour* featuring Martin and Lewis aired on November 10, 1951. The guests were Dorothy Dandridge, who went on to become the first African American film star to be nominated for an Oscar for Best Actress in the 1954 movie *Carmen Jones*; the Mayo Brothers comedy team, making their first national television appearance; character actor Marion Marshall; radio announcer Jimmy Wallington; and bandleader Dick Stable.

In the opening sketch, Martin played Lewis's life-sized dummy as they passed themselves off as a ventriloquism act for a talent agent, followed by Martin singing "Solitaire" and Lewis's lip-syncing "Be My Love." Other pieces that night included Lewis going undercover as a prisoner, Dandridge singing "Blow Out the Candle," and the finale in which Martin attempted to sing with Lewis conducting and disrupting the orchestra.

NBC, correctly anticipating that *Colgate* would continue its winning streak, spared no expense. That following April, the network signed a fifteen-year lease at a cost of $30,000 a year at the lavish El Capitan Theatre in West Hollywood—now the home for *Jimmy Kimmel Live!* and the place from which Richard Nixon delivered his famous "Checkers Speech" on national television in 1952—where the Martin and Lewis and Abbott and Costello installments originated.

On the domestic front, Norman, Charlotte, and Ellen took up residence on the lower floor of a Hollywood duplex on North Orange Drive owned by the 1932 gold medal Olympic swimmer-turned-actor Buster Crabbe. Soon afterward, Charlotte's parents also made the move to Los Angeles and took an apartment around the corner. It was around this time as well that the normally nonchalant Jeanette began begging Norman to come home for a visit to Hartford the next time he was in New York so she could show him off to friends and family.

As Norman and Simmons's star continued to rise on the set of *Colgate*, both Hollywood and the media took notice. "Their wild imaginings have raised M&L to the peerage of their particular type of comedy," gushed *Variety* in one review that was typical of the buzz they were receiving.[1] Lavish in their prasie as well—at least in public—were Martin and Lewis, who also took out a full-page ad in the venerable entertainment trade in the spring of 1951 expressing their gratitude:

> Writers have always been the unsung heroes of our business. This is to tell you publicly how grateful we are for all the wonderful sketches you've written for us, and to sing songs of praise for two great guys, as well as two great talents.[2]

Privately, however, the notoriously egomaniacal Lewis had no interest in sharing the spotlight. As a matter of fact, he resented Norman and Simmons. According to Lewis's biographer Shawn Levy, much of Lewis's animosity stemmed from his own lack of writing credits, even though he was the one who had recruited Norman and Simmons.

> Late in life, Jerry spoke of himself as a writer first and foremost—"I began as a writer and that's been the secret of much of my success: what I've been able to get down on paper."
> But during the 1950s, though he took (and undoubtedly deserved) credit in interviews for much of the material he and Dean performed, he had never received a credit for a film or TV show.[3]

In an interview for Levy's biography several years before his death in 1998, Simmons offered his own take. Describing Lewis as an "unwilling collaborator," he recalled: "Jerry couldn't sit down and write like a writing-type person," also adding, "Jerry never met with us. We'd have to go chase after him and pin him down. We pretty much had free reign."[4]

This was the crux of it: Lewis didn't have the self-discipline or time to write, and his abilities to write his own material were severely limited. Not surprising either is that in countless interviews and several books throughout the remainder of his life, he seldom admitted he had ever used writers. He also never again publicly acknowledged Norman and Simmons's contributions.

At *Colgate*, Norman, Simmons, and director Bud Yorkin used the fact that Martin and Lewis were often too busy to supervise scripts to their advantage, waiting instead until rehearsals to show them the material after the sets and costumes had been designed and it was too late to make any changes. Off-set, meanwhile, at least for a time, they enjoyed a cordial, if not affable, relationship—until they didn't.

Norman and Simmons remained with *Colgate* for three seasons, also turning out scripts for Martin and Lewis's radio program and punching up their films in between gin rummy games in a rented apartment complex on North Flores Drive they used as their office along with several writers who rented space.

But the good times and conviviality were short-lived. As Martin and Lewis's fame grew, so did Lewis's refusal to take advice from Norman and Simmons. As Norman surmised to biographer Shawn Levy: "He never understood the essences of Jerry Lewis. He never understood what was best about him. So he accentuated some of the things that were the most irritating. He hasn't welcomed collaboration in his life. He stopped doing that early in our career together. He just didn't require it."[5]

The beginning of the end came in November 1953 after NBC awarded Norman and Simmons an unprecedented seven-year contract at $10,400 an episode, making them the highest-paid writers in television. With *Billboard*, *TV Guide*, and *Variety* all reporting it, Lewis was naturally livid. Then, one month later, they were summarily fired without warning. Though they immediately threatened to sue (and they won) without going to court and NBC honored their contract, the die had already been cast. For the first half of the 1953–1954 season, Lewis threw everything they wrote into the trash.

Adding insult to injury, he also brought in a new team of writers—among them Harry Crane, who went on to help create *The Honeymooners*, and Danny Arnold, who later produced the sitcoms *Barney Miller*, *That Girl*, and *Bewitched*—until Norman and Simmons had finally had enough and quit that spring.

Norman was now thirty-two, and despite being out of work, the world was his oyster. Just how big his pearl would be someday was still anybody's guess.

CHAPTER 8

Putting Words into the Big Mouth and Other Adventures

Extricating themselves from the toxic grip of Lewis's out-of-control ego undoubtedly reinvigorated Norman and Simmons, who were effectively now free agents and not unemployed for long.

Still riding high from their fabulous success on *Colgate*—and perhaps because of the circumstances leading to their departure—Norman was immediately brought on board as a writer to help salvage the low-rated CBS sitcom *Honestly, Celeste!*, starring actor Celeste Holm, which was canceled after only eight episodes. Soon afterward, in late 1953, Norman and Simmons were hired again together as the replacement for writer-producer Nat Hiken on NBC's highly popular *The Martha Raye Show* as Hiken went on to major success as the creator of the classic sitcoms *Car 54, Where Are You?*, and *The Phil Silvers Show*.

Martha Raye, too, was a force of nature to be reckoned with. Aptly known as "The Big Mouth," she was also a volatile, often self-destructive enigma who is today largely a footnote in the annals of early television history. For those who grew up in the 1970s and 1980s, she is likely best remembered as the pitchwoman for Polident denture cleaner and her appearances in the Sid and Marty Kroft films *Pufnstuf* and *The Bugaloos*. Television audiences from back then might also remember her occasional guest turns on *The Love Boat* and *McMillan & Wife*, and her recurring role as Carrie Sharpels, the eccentric mother of short-order diner cook Mel Sharples on the CBS sitcom *Alice*.

But in the 1950s, Raye was the Tina Fey of her day and the precursor to Carol Burnett. In a career lasting nearly six decades, she sang, danced, acted on Broadway, appeared on radio and in films, and was also known for her work entertaining the troops overseas during three wars, earning her the nickname "Colonel Maggie." Born in the charity ward of a Butte, Montana, hospital on August 27, 1916, her real name was Maggie Yvonne Reed. Her Irish immigrant parents were a vaudeville song-and-dance team. By age three, Raye was already honing her act. When she was fifteen, she chose her stage name out of the phone book, racking up the credits and never looking back.

Eventually finding her way to Hollywood, her big break came one night in the mid-1930s while performing at the famed Trocadero nightclub and catching the eye of producer Norman Taurog after convincing fellow comics Joe E. Lewis and Jimmy Durante to play her straight men onstage. The following day she was cast in the 1936 film *Rhythm on the Range*, starring crooner Bing Crosby, and became a star overnight after performing a slapstick drunk scene.

Besides being funny, what made Raye such a novelty was her brash, take-no-prisoners persona during Hollywood's golden age when such open displays of bravado were rare among female performers. But it was also her Achilles' heel in a life that was marred by depression, drug and alcohol abuse, seven marriages—including her final one to Mark Harris, a man thirty-two years her junior with whom she tied the knot in 1991 just two weeks after they met—and her rocky relationship with her only child Melodye. As Milton Berle, who gave Raye her start in television, observed, "She was one of the world's four best comediennes, but she lived a life of personal disaster."[1]

By the time she made her small-screen debut on Uncle Miltie's *Texaco Star Theater* in April 1949 (coincidentally performing alongside Berle in a parody sketch of the film *The Shaik of Araby*, whose theme song had been the catalyst for Norman and Simmons becoming writing partners), Raye's own movie career was virtually nonexistent after having burned practically every bridge in Hollywood. Berle had first met Raye eight years earlier in Detroit during out-of-town tryouts for the 1941 Broadway musical *Hold on to Your Hats*, costarring and produced by her old friend Al Jolson. The musical was short-lived, and Raye began performing in nightclubs around the country, which is how she crossed paths with Berle again.

Already in the throes of a messy divorce from her second husband, the British composer David Rose, Raye suffered multiple injuries in a near-fatal car crash near her home in Los Angeles the month before the show was scheduled to open at Detroit's Cass Theatre for a two-week engagement on June 30. Still, she managed to somehow rally. Following the show's successful opening night in Detroit, Raye, Jolson, and most of the other cast members attended a party afterward at the Bowery nightclub, where Berle was headlining.

In the summer of 1941, she was working at a club in Miami called the Royal Palm where Berle was the headliner on the same bill. Performing also was a men's singing group who were regulars unrelated to Berle's act. While they were up onstage, he decided to join them—stumbling, blundering, ad-libbing, and doing all the things for which he was famous—as the audience delighted in the intrusion. Berle's shenanigans went over so well, in fact, that the singers decided to work him into their act for the remainder of his engagement.

In the meantime, Raye had also been scheduled to perform. But when she arrived at the club the night she was supposed to go on, instead of doing her own act, she decided to join in on the riotous fun, ad-libbing and clowning right along with Berle without missing a beat. This kismet chemistry also fit seamlessly into television, as Raye went on to appear eleven more times between 1949 and 1955 on *The Texaco Star Theater*, later renamed *The Milton Berle Show*.

Beginning in 1951, she also got a new professional lease on life as a regular on NBC's *All Star Revue*—the retitled and recast version of *Four Star Revue* that was also the launching pad for the short-lived *Jack Haley's Ford Star Revue*, where Norman and Simmons had gotten their television start. Raye became so popular she soon started appearing in a series of eponymous specials. After beginning as an occasional replacement for *The Milton Berle Show* and *Your Show of Shows*, Raye eventually got her own hour-long program called *The Martha Raye Show*, which aired every other Tuesday night on NBC at 8 p.m. from January 1954 until May 1956.

The original specials were helmed by Nat Hiken, who also doubled as the head writer for *All Star Revue* and its predecessor, along with briefly penning scripts for *The Colgate Comedy Hour*, which is where he first met Norman and Ed Simmons in 1952.

According to biographer David Everitt: "Hiken set Raye on the right course in the show's first installment. The character he created for Raye was manic, aggressive, and man-hungry but also sweet-natured and vulnerable. In stark contrast to glossy variety shows of later years, the program revolved around Raye's rat-trap apartment in Flatbush, where her neighbor was a frowzy Jewish hausfrau named Mrs. Storecheese. Hiken defined Ray's love life in the first scene, when a friend calls to fix her up on a blind date. The audience hears only Raye's side of the conversation: "About his eyes. . . . Never mind the color. How many?"[2]

Among the press, her biggest cheerleader was *Variety*, who in its critique of one early episode called that show an "excellent fusion of Miss Raye's talents with good writing and good production," also applauding the commercials.[3] With Hiken's steady hand at the wheel, Raye's recurring specials continued under the *All Star Revue* umbrella until its cancellation at the end of the 1952–1953 season. After expanding from sixty to ninety minutes in what would be the beginning of *The Martha Raye Show*'s third season, it was moved to the coveted 9 p.m. timeslot on Saturday nights as a once-a-month replacement for *Your Show of Shows*. Predictably, the media immediately took notice, with the *New York Times* magazine, *Look*, *Life*, and *Time* all running major feature articles.

But while Raye and Hiken should have been over the moon about this latest feat, backstage things were beginning to fall apart amid creative differences that were eerily like what Norman and Simmons had encountered with Jerry Lewis. According to what codirector Grey Lockwood told Hiken's biographer, mainly at issue was "what may have been a simmering resentment on Raye's part."

"The word was out that it's this guy behind those words and those ideas—she's a great performer but where would she be without Nat?" Lockwood said. "She apparently couldn't handle it too well. It bugged her."[4]

At that point, Raye's personal life was also again in tatters as she began showing up late to rehearsals not knowing her lines. Complicating things even further was a dustup between Hiken and Lockwood over top billing in the opening credits. Though eventually resolved, it would ultimately be the straw that broke the camel's back as Hiken inked a lucrative five-year deal with NBC's archrival CBS, paying him an annual six-figure salary as a producer-director.

And that was that: Hiken was out, and Norman and Simmons were in, inheriting many of Hiken's same problems with Raye, plus several new ones along the way, although at first, Norman was ecstatic. "Simmons and I loved Martha, were crazy about the book-musical format and felt challenged about the idea of replacing Nat Hiken," he said.[5]

Unfortunately, there was still one major hurdle. *The Martha Raye Show* was based in New York. That meant moving back to the East Coast, which Charlotte adamantly refused to do. Their loveless marriage was on its last legs by then, and Ellen, now six, was in the first grade. While Norman's overriding concern was for his daughter's well-being in his absence, the main reason Charlotte didn't want to move was because she would have to give up her therapist, whom she saw five times a week.

So after meeting with the shrink himself, an agreement was reached. It was decided that Norman would accept the job in New York and all three of them would live there if *The Martha Raye Show* got renewed the following year. At the urging of Charlotte's shrink, she and Ellen stayed behind in Los

Angeles, with Norman calling Ellen daily and commuting to the West Coast every other weekend.

For a moment, the arrangement went accordingly, even amicably. But then, out of the blue, the other shoe dropped after Charlotte informed Norman she'd made another appointment for them to see her therapist during one of his visits to California. While the session was predictably a disaster, it didn't really matter. By this point, Norman had long had enough. Citing irreconcilable differences, they soon began divorce proceedings.

In the meantime, the New York dream home Norman had hoped they would someday share—and now never would—was a palatial three-story penthouse, complete with a winding spiral staircase and rooftop garden overlooking the East River at 25 Tudor City Place in Murray Hill. During their first year on *The Martha Raye Show*, Ed Simmons also lived there, and they frequently hosted parties in between shows. At one time or another, Gordon MacRae, Red Buttons, Imogene Coca, Henny Youngman, Jack E. Leonard, as well as Raye herself entertaining from the staircase, were among the guests at these soirees.

As a stand-alone series airing every other week, the first episode of *The Martha Raye Show* debuted on January 23, 1954. Sponsored by the cosmetics manufacturing giant Revlon, it featured Raye, Rocky Graziano, Edward G. Robinson, and Cesar Romero, with Norman and Simmons officially taking over from Hiken as head writers that following fall on September 28. Appearing alongside Raye and Graziano on their first show was comedian Wally Cox, then costarring with actor Tony Randall on the hit NBC sitcom *Mister Peepers*, and Paul Lynde, the campy character actor best known for his frequent guest stints in the 1960s and 1970s on *Bewitched* and *The Hollywood Squares*.

With Norman now pulling double duty as codirector of *The Martha Raye Show* with Grey Lockwood, Hiken's act proved to be a tough one to follow; a fact not lost on reviewers even as ratings for the 1954–1955 season rose steadily from number seventeen to number nine. Opining in the *New York Times* that "Raye's exasperating excesses were creeping back once again, and she was badly in need of bright material and discipline," television critic Jack Gould also noted that "Miss Raye can be an immensely funny woman, and surely will be again. But she should learn to keep her guard up against the false friends who sometimes may lack the fortitude to tell her 'no.'"[6]

Though such caustic critiques and inevitable comparisons to Hiken continued throughout Norman and Simmons's tenure, they still managed to rise to the occasion even as it turned out to be one of the toughest endurance tests of their career. In the spring of 1955, Norman's romantic life took a positive turn when he met Frances Loeb, a sportswear buyer for the department store giant Lord & Taylor.

A year younger and an avowed feminist, Frances was the one who gave him his trademark white hat so he wouldn't pick at his scalp when he wrote. Most significant of all, she became his second wife for thirty years, the mother of his two middle daughters, Kate and Maggie, and the inspiration for his second-most-famous sitcom character: Maude Findlay.

"I was very much a part of his thinking," Frances declared following their divorce in 1986, culminating in a $110 million divorce settlement that was one of the largest in Hollywood history, which she used to launch *Lear's* magazine in 1988. "Norman could not have done his shows without me, and I didn't get that without earning it. Believe me, I earned it."[7]

No doubt also, is that Frances, whose roller-coaster personal life was shaped by multiple demons, including alcoholism, three suicide attempts, sexual affairs with men and women, and bipolar disorder, entered this world with the odds stacked almost insurmountably against her as she readily admitted. The only child of an unwed mother and unknown father, she was born in Hudson, New York, on July 14, 1923, at the Vanderheyden Home for Wayward Girls.

Her birth name was Evelyn, and she was renamed Frances by her adoptive parents, Aline and Herbert Loeb, when she was fourteen months old. Raised in the New York City suburb of Larchmont, Aline was a mercurial, emotionally distant figure whose second husband sexually abused Frances when she was twelve years old following Herbert's suicide during the Depression.

In high school, Frances attended the now-defunct Mary A. Burnham School for Girls in Northampton, Massachusetts, before moving to New York and working primarily in retail and advertising in the late 1940s and early 1950s. For a brief time also, she worked as a camera girl at the famed Copacabana nightclub in Manhattan, a position that ended abruptly when she allegedly asked the publicity-shy gangster Frank Costello if he wanted to have his picture taken and her boss picked her up by the armpits, carried her out to the street, and after kissing her goodbye, fired her.

By the time she met Norman, Frances had already been married twice. Her first marriage to a Charleston, South Carolina, Navy Yard traffic manager named Harold Weiss lasted less than two years. Her second union to Morton Kaufman was even shorter, ending within its first year, leading to her first suicide attempt and a three-week stay at New York's Bellevue Hospital in the psychiatric ward.

Norman first crossed paths with Frances midway through his first year on *The Martha Raye Show*. It happened after he received a random phone call from his old friend Leonard Sosna, a World War II Bomb Squadron buddy he hadn't seen in nearly a decade, who was in town from Chicago and had gotten his private number from NBC. Sosna and another male friend had come to New York to visit a girl, who, as it turned out, was Frances.

Though he would never see Sosna again, Norman's second encounter with Frances happened several weeks later after they exchanged phone numbers when she called to ask him to be her escort at a dinner the following Saturday night. As smitten as he was, however, Norman was still ensnarled in a messy divorce and custody battle over Ellen with Charlotte, and it would be another year before he and Frances were free to tie the knot.

That spring and summer of 1955, meanwhile, were marked by more joy and sadness. In the positive column was the news that *The Martha Raye Show* had been renewed for a third season. But just as Norman was savoring his success, his father Herman—in debt deeper than ever before—was nearly killed when his pickup truck was struck by an oncoming eight-car New Haven Railroad passenger train.

Near death in a coma for over a week and with no witnesses, Herman claimed that it had been an accident after his truck stalled, although both Jeanette and Norman believed otherwise. Though there was no mention of his famous son, the collision made front-page news the next day with the headline: "Train Shatters Truck, Injures One in Windsor" in the *Hartford Courant*'s April 27 edition. Identifying Herman as "head of the Concord Modernizing Co. of Windsor" and describing the truck as "a three-quarter ton stake body model carrying business equipment," the newspaper also published a grisly black-and-white photograph of the mangled truck that was practically severed in two, accompanied by the following caption:

> SIDETRACKED: Although the driver of this truck, Herman K. Lear, sixty-two, of 68 Woodstock St., Hartford, escaped death when it was struck by a train Tuesday at the Pierson Lane tracks grade crossing in Windsor, the vehicle was demolished and dumped into a gully beside the tracks. Lear was taken to Hartford Hospital with head, leg and other injuries and in critical condition.[8]

That summer, Norman rented a cottage in Ocean Beach, the secluded seaside hamlet and unofficial capital of Fire Island. Stretching for thirty-two miles off the coast of Long Island just two hours away from Manhattan, it was the perfect place for him to rejuvenate and unwind, with Frances coming out from the city on weekends as their romance blossomed and Ellen joined them for a month.

Living two doors away were Carl Reiner; his wife, Estelle; their nine-year-old son and future *All in the Family* star, Rob; and six-year-old daughter, Annie. Then in his early thirties like Norman, Carl's star was also on the ascent as a writer-performer on *Caesar's Hour*, which had premiered on NBC just one day before *The Martha Raye Show* in September 1954, and was the follow-up series to Sid Caesar's trailblazing variety program *Your Show of Shows*, for which Carl had also written and performed. The Reiners first began vacationing on Fire Island in 1951 at the suggestion of fellow *Your Show of Shows* writer Mel Tolkin, who went on to be the story editor on *All in the Family* and its spinoff, *Archie Bunker's Place*. It was here where Carl wrote what became the first thirteen episodes of *The Dick Van Dyke Show*, as well as his semiautobiographical first novel, *Enter Laughing*, which novelist Herman Wouk was among the first to read.

Additionally, two other pivotal events transpired during that summer when Norman and the Reiners were neighbors. One of them, monumentally, was Norman's discovery that Rob Reiner had inherited his father's comedic chops. It was an unexpected revelation that occurred randomly one afternoon while Rob was teaching Ellen how to play jacks and he noticed the funny expressions on his face and the inflections in his voice as the young Reiner demonstrated how to toss the ball and pick up the jacks. And then—either shortly before or after—it was also at a dinner party at Carl Reiner's house, where Reiner stood up at some point during the evening and pretended to be the host of a TV talk show as he proceeded to interview several of the guests on a portable reel-to-reel tape recorder. When he got around to interviewing Mel Brooks—who also began improvising and pretended to be a man who seemed to know everything—Reiner then asked how he could have known about something that had taken place centuries before. To which without any prompting, Brooks responded that he was two thousand years old in what became the impetus for their iconic comedy routine "The 2,000-Year-Old Man," which they would soon perform that fall on national television on *Your Show of Shows*.

That fall also, plans got underway for the fifth season of *The Martha Raye Show*, which as it turned out, was the last. Hosting the September 20 season opener was Tallulah Bankhead, the hard-drinking, foghorn-voiced stage actress best known for her performances on Broadway in *The Little Foxes* and *The Skin of Our Teeth*, and her appearance in the 1944 Alfred Hitchcock film *Lifeboat*.

Several weeks before *The Martha Raye Show*'s fifth-season premiere, a twelve-year-old spelling prodigy from Baltimore named Gloria Lockerman won the grand prize on *The $64,000 Question*, the hit CBS quiz show, also sponsored by Revlon, after she correctly spelled the word "antidisestablish-mentarianism." Adding to the excitement was that Lockerman was African American, making her a national celebrity practically overnight as the media wasted no time writing about it. Most vociferous was *Jet* magazine, which proclaimed that Lockerman had "emerged as the brightest Negro juvenile entertainer since the heyday of boogie-woogie pianist Sugar Chile Robinson."[9]

Taking notice also were Norman and Simmons who immediately booked Lockerman on the show. It's also important to note that the main sketch they wrote—centering around a little girl fantasizing about her Good Fairy, played by Raye, and her Bad Fairy, played to perfection by the fiery, foulmouthed Bankhead—was still nearly a decade ahead of the civil rights moment. However, the studio audience still loved it and instantly fell in love with Lockerman.

So, too, did Raye and Bankhead. Caught up in the excitement of the moment as they were taking their bows at the end of the show, both women began hugging and kissing the young girl on national television, never considering what the rest of America watching at home might think, as consequently NBC and Revlon were flooded with scores of angry letters of protest.

Though *The Martha Raye Show* wasn't immediately canceled, they were put on notice, and it was the first nail in the coffin. One reason it was initially given a reprieve was that Revlon founder Charles Revson, despite not being a fan of Raye's personally, still enjoyed reaping the benefits of the show's strong ratings.

While Revson never openly criticized Raye and Bankhead for their on-air displays of affection toward Lockerman, his private rebuke to the staff was a different story. At first, Revson insisted that he and his team didn't mind what they did personally. But then he backpedaled, telling them also that Revlon had a product to protect, and that as a result, they were still obligated to take what he called "corporate exception" to the incident. Furthermore, Revson admonished Raye to find a way to perform without being physical or unwomanly.

Then more problems arose the following week when actor Douglas Fairbanks Jr.—then starring in his own namesake syndicated anthology series distributed by NBC—hosted the second show on October 11. The issue this time was over a sketch based on comedian Red Skelton's classic vaudeville routine "Guzzler's Gin," in which Raye was preparing a tropical drink for Fairbanks's character, not realizing that its contents were from a whisky bottle and got increasingly smashed.

In the way Norman and Simmons originally conceived it, Raye's character was only supposed to get slightly inebriated, not drunk. Raye, however, had other ideas. And so with the coercion of her ex-husband and still-manager, Nick Condos—who was there in the studio when the show went live—instead of getting tipsy, Raye got plastered. With the cameras rolling, she lifted the bottle, pouring its contents into her cleavage, flinging it up into her armpits, and then, after taking a long swig, dousing it into Fairbanks's face with her ample mouth.

While the studio audience and the est of America watching at home howled, Revson was not amused, and T e Martha Raye Show was axed. But then to underscore how innocuous the sketch really was, it wasn't yanked immediately, and they were allowed to finish out the season.

After eight more shows, Raye ended its run on May 29, 1956. The twenty-eighth and final show featured Cesar Romero and veteran character actor Fritz Field. After that, it disappeared onto the scrapheap of other long-forgotten variety shows, although it can still be found on YouTube.

As for Norman and Simmons, they were once again out of work.

CHAPTER 9

Marriage #2 and Other Ups and Downs

As Norman was trying to figure out his next move professionally, negotiations over his divorce settlement with Charlotte lingered for nearly six months. Her attorney, also the father of nine children, had suggested an implausibly one-sided arrangement in which Charlotte would receive full alimony and child support, which she would automatically forfeit if she ever remarried. If she divorced again within two years, however, those payments would be automatically reinstated.

Not surprisingly, Norman's initial reaction was to reject the idea outright. But after more wrangling and hoping to get things over with as quickly as possible, he eventually agreed to it against the advice of his lawyer. Finally, in late October, a settlement was reached for an undisclosed amount.

Norman could not have been more relieved. Immediately afterward, he temporarily relocated to Las Vegas, where, then as now, divorces were granted within six weeks as long as one of the spouses could show proof of residency. As it turned out, Norman's proof was a local hotel he paid top rates for, in exchange for which he managed to convince one of the desk clerks to vouch for his whereabouts even though he was rarely there. Instead, he spent most of his time in L.A. writing new material and looking for work.

When the divorce was finalized on December 7, 1956, Norman arranged to marry Frances that same afternoon at the home of a local rabbi, with Simmons serving as his best man. Following the nuptials, Simmons flew back to L.A., while the newlyweds headed to Caesar's Palace for dinner and saw Milton Berle perform.

Several days later, they returned to Los Angeles with plans to live there permanently in a rented bungalow on Mulholland Drive. By March, Frances learned she was pregnant. Unfortunately, Norman and Simmons were unable to find work that was financially commensurate with what they had been earning on *The Colgate Comedy Hour* and *The Martha Raye Show*, so they opted to hold out for something better even as their bank accounts dwindled.

One job they were up for during this period was to become head writers for crooner Perry Como's eponymous musical-variety show on NBC. Along with Bing Crosby and Frank Sinatra at that time, Como was one of the era's hottest singers and nightclub headliners. A former barber famous for his cardigan sweaters and silky baritone vocals, he had already recorded such chart-topping hits as "Till the End of Time," "Prisoner of Love," and "Papa Loves Mambo" when *The Chesterfield Supper Club*—his first TV series and the first ever to be simulcast on both radio and television—began airing on NBC in December 1948.

In 1950, he moved over to CBS, where the first incarnation of the then-titled *Perry Como Chesterfield Show* aired as a fifteen-minute thrice-weekly program that ran for five years before returning to NBC in September 1955. Now simply called *The Perry Como Show* and lasting another eight years, it became a prime-time, hourlong variety series, first airing on Saturday nights opposite CBS's powerhouse *The Jackie Gleason Show* from 8 until 9 p.m., then on Wednesdays from 9 until 10 p.m. from 1959 until 1963.

At first, it seemed as if Norman and Simmons were shoo-ins, their stellar track record with NBC having almost assuredly given them the inside track, even though it would have also meant moving back to New York. Norman—who, by this point was increasingly growing restless and facing mounting financial pressures with a new wife, alimony, child support, and another baby on the way—was especially gung-ho. It's also not a stretch to say that even with all his success, he likely feared losing everything, his mind-set at the time no doubt inextricably affected by the scars of his childhood, having grown up in the Great Depression and endured his family's perennially hardscrabble existence because of Herman.

But to his great disappointment, he soon learned that the job had gone to another pair of writers represented by MCA, also the packager for *The Perry Como Show*. Making matters worse was his discovery that they had never been candidates at all, something he realized during an impromptu visit to the agent's office a couple of days after receiving the bad news and getting the runaround.

The tip-off occurred halfway into the meeting when Norman asked to see a copy of a pitch letter the agent claimed he'd written to *Como*'s producers. Attempting to placate him, the agent asked his secretary to retrieve the correspondence from the file room. Then, after the agent politely asked him to wait in the adjacent empty office, Norman discovered he'd been conned as he walked back into the hallway and spotted the secretary stationed in a cubicle outside the agent's office.

With the telephone affixed to one ear, she was seated at the typewriter typing the letter she was supposed to retrieve while the agent was dictating it to her from behind his closed door. Needless to say, Norman was livid, and after confronting the agent, he severed all ties.

But then fortunately—and just in the nick of time—another opportunity came his way. It happened courtesy of his future producing partner Bud Yorkin, who had recently moved to Los Angeles, where he was now the director of country-and-western singer Tennessee Ernie Ford's new weekly half-hour variety program on NBC.

The offer was for Norman and Simmons to become writers, though not head writers, working under Roland Kibbee, the three-time Emmy-winning writer best known for his work on such shows as *The Alfred Hitchcock Hour*, *It Takes a Thief*, *The Virginian*, and *Columbo*, and a longtime film collaborator with actor Burt Lancaster, whom Norman would credit as one of his mentors. Also on the writing staff was Danny Arnold who had replaced Norman and Simmons on *The Colgate Comedy Hour*.

Of the writers' instrumental role in the success of *Tennessee Ernie Ford*, Yorkin recalled: "We probably had the best writing staff ever put together for a comedy show [with] Danny Arnold, Norman Lear and Roland Kibbee. You couldn't miss with these three guys. We'd sit on a Monday night, the three writers and myself, and we'd have the entire show written by five o'clock the next morning. I never had an experience like that, and I then learned after all those years that you can forget everything if you don't have the writers."[1]

Absent from Yorkin's glowing sentiments, however, was Simmons, who had turned the offer down. His reason was that the $1,500-a-week salary, which came out to $750 apiece split between him and Norman, had been their starting pay on *The Jack Haley Show*, and he refused to consider it. With this came the unofficial end of the comedy-writing team of Norman Lear and Ed Simmons. Though the parting was amicable, they never worked together again. By this time also, Simmons had split from Norman's cousin Elaine, so the familiar part of their lives was over too, and they seldom had much interaction after that except for occasionally running into each other in the hallways at CBS Television City in 1970s.

The main draw for *The Tennessee Ernie Ford Show*—also known as *The Ford Show* and *The Ford Show, Starring Tennessee Ernie Ford*—was its bass-baritone country-singing host. Born in Bristol, Tennessee, Ford caught the show-business bug early, performing in the choir of his Methodist Church and singing at family get-togethers before getting his first professional job as a ten-dollar-a-week disc jockey on the local radio station WOPI in 1937.

Using that to help fund his education at the Cincinnati Conservatory of Music, he returned to WOPI's announcer's booth in 1939, where he remained for two more years before moving on to other radio stations in Knoxville and Atlanta. After serving in the US Army Air Corps. during World War II (the same military branch as Norman), Ford resumed his career as a disc jockey at radio stations in Pasadena and San Bernadino, California. It was during his time as an early-morning DJ for the country music program *Bar Nothin' Ranch Time* on San Bernadino's KXFM that his hillbilly alter ego "Tennessee Ernie" first emerged.

The character became so popular that he was hired by KXLA in San Bernadino. This quickly led to a series of musical tours and an offer to become a disc jockey on the ABC radio network in 1952, followed by guest spots on NBC-TV's *Kay Kyser's Kollege of Musical Knowledge* in 1953.

Then in 1955, Ford recorded the smash hit "Sixteen Tons" for Capitol Records, which became one of the biggest country singles of all time, selling more than twenty million copies worldwide. But although he would go on to record nearly fifty more songs throughout the remainder of the decade, it was largely because of Ford's three appearances during seasons 3 and 4 of *I Love Lucy* as Lucy Ricardo's hayseed "Cousin Ernie" that he became a household name.

The variety program NBC had in mind was essentially another extension of Ford's exaggerated folksy persona, which, as Norman observed, "was perfect for the television show he did and the audience who cared to see him."[2] Fittingly sponsored by the Ford Motor Company and debuting on October 4, 1956, it was broadcast live from NBC's West Almeda Avenue studios in Burbank. Backed during the first season by "The Voices of Walter Schulman" choral group, it became a huge hit overnight as Ford's folksy catchphrases like "Nervous as a long-tailed cat in a roomful of rockin' chairs" and "Bless your pea-pickin' hearts" won the hearts of the nation—especially in middle America.

Critics surprisingly liked it as well as this review from the *New York Times*'s often-acerbic Jack Gould—also evaluating the inaugural episodes of CBS's classic anthology series *Playhouse 90* and the ABC variety show *Circus Times* in the same article—illustrates:

Tennessee Ernie Ford sauntered onto after-dark television last night on Channel 4. His personable drawl, ingratiating smile and unhurried manner provided a jovial and pleasant restful half-hour. [Actors] Greer Garson and Reginald Gardner contributed to the first show of the new series.

Their British accents clashed admirably with Mr. Ford's back-home speech. A regular feature of the show will be the Voices of Walter Schumann chorus, a group that is remarkably well-triggered to handle anything from a grunt to a tone poem. This talent was employed both amusingly and artistically by Mr. Ford.

All in all, the new show gives promise of being a relaxing stopover during the television evening.[3]

Appearing as guests was a Who's Who list of such notables as Ronald Reagan and his ex-wife Jane Wyman, singers Rosemary Clooney and Nelson Eddy, crime novelist Mickey Spillane, actors Zsa Zsa Gabor, Carol Channing, and Douglas Fairbanks Jr., and gossip columnist Hedda Hopper—many of whom appeared during the show's first season, where it was ranked among the top-ten programs. *Ford* is also significant for the fact that it was one of the first shows on television to introduce the animated version of cartoonist Charles M. Schulz's Peanuts characters and ventriloquist Shari Lewis's sock puppet Lamb Chop.

Norman's main responsibility was writing the monologues—a role that while at times harrowing—he nonetheless grew to relish as he witnessed firsthand the fruits of his labor on full display every week on national television. With his creative and financial fortunes once again on the rise, in October 1957, he and Frances moved to a larger home nearby on Mulholland Drive that was equipped with a full nursery. On December 13, she gave birth to their oldest daughter, Kate.

But then, exactly seven days after the blessed event, on December 23, Norman received the sad news from his sister Claire back East that their father had died of a heart attack. The official cause was coronary thrombosis resulting from the erosion of plaque in the arteries forming clots in the heart. He was sixty-four years old.

As much as he resented his father's deception and misdeeds, losing Herman was a devastating blow for Norman, also spilling over into his complicated relationship with Jeanette. Pouring more salt into the wound amid his grief, he was further anguished to learn from Claire that their mother was planning a funeral despite Herman's explicit wishes to be cremated without a service.

A couple of days later, Norman flew to Connecticut from California alone. When he arrived at the funeral home in Hartford just as they were about to transport Herman's body to the synagogue, he was horrified when the undertaker told him that per Jeannette's instructions, it was to be an open-casket funeral. This was too much for him to bear. In spite of everything Herman had put them all through, Norman still thought he deserved the respect of having his final wishes carried out. Expressing his outrage in his memoir more than five decades later, he recalled: "I could have slapped my mother. This wasn't just adding insult to injury. I thought this was the crown jewel of her narcissism. And of course, it played out just that way."[4]

Following a perfunctory service led by a rabbi who had never met Herman, he was laid to rest at John Hay Memorial Park in Hartford. Etched in capital letters at the bottom of his tombstone was the word *FATHER*. Owing the bank and other creditors over $100,000 at the time of his death, his obituary in the *Hartford Courant* described him as a "retired salesman and veteran of World War I who lived in Hartford for nineteen years."[5]

Less than a year later, Jeanette remarried. Her new husband was Charles Gladstein, a Bridgeport hardware store owner, who passed away in 1968. Jeanette, meanwhile, lived another twenty-two years. Her relationship with Norman would always remain strained.

~

Although *The Tennessee Ernie Ford Show* stayed on the air for another four years—the last three of which were in color—Norman left after only one season, when he received a too-good-to-refuse offer to become the producer and head writer of *The George Gobel Show*, another monster hit variety program on NBC that was being expanded to a full hour. Though he is mostly now another long-forgotten footnote in the annals of early television history, in the 1950s, the crewcut-capped Gobel was one of the medium's biggest comedy stars.

Soft-spoken and mild-mannered, the Chicago native was best known to his legions of fans by his self-appropriated nickname "Lonesome George," as well as for the quirky catchphrases "We don't hardly get those no more" and "Well, I'll be a dirty bird." *The George Gobel Show* first premiered on October 2, 1954, airing as a half-hour vehicle on NBC on Saturday nights from ten o'clock until ten thirty, with Gobel winning an Emmy that year for Outstanding New Personality.

The centerpieces were his deadpan monologue and sketches, often consisting of bits about his home life and wife, Alice, who was nicknamed

"Spooky Old Alice" and played for comedic effect by actor Jean Marie "Jeff" Donnell. The show also featured a high-wattage galaxy of guest stars such as Kirk Douglas, Jimmy Stewart, Henry Fonda, Shirley MacLaine, and Fred MacMurray.

Following its expansion, NBC plucked Norman to replace Hal Kanter—the Emmy-winning writer, director, and producer who was still nearly ten years away from creating the groundbreaking sitcom *Julia*, TV's first show about the professional life of an African American woman played by Diahann Carroll—as *Gobel*'s director and head writer. Fondly remembering the experience, Norman said, "*The George Gobel Show* was as strong and joyful a building block as I could have wished for at this transition in my career."[6]

His tenure there lasted two years before he teamed up with Roland Kibbee to create *The Deputy*, a half-hour Western starring Henry Fonda for NBC. Set during the early 1880s in the Arizona Territory, it is notable both for being the first episodic television show Norman created, as well as the first program Fonda appeared on as a series regular. After that, they would continue to work together over the years, first on a special Norman cowrote for CBS in 1962, and then in 1974 when Fonda hosted an hourlong retrospective celebrating *All in the Family*'s one-hundredth episode. They also worked together again two years later in 1976, with Fonda appearing as himself in the season-4 *Maude* two-parter "Maude's Mood," in which Maude launches a relentless campaign to get him elected president of the United States and it is revealed she suffers from manic depression.

On top of this, Fonda was one of the original owners of a home in the upscale L.A. neighborhood of Brentwood that Norman and Frances eventually purchased in the late 1960s. But in the meantime, another even more significant event occurred after Norman and Bud Yorkin's paths crossed again in 1958.

CHAPTER 10

In Tandem

When Norman and Bud Yorkin first met on *The Colgate Comedy Hour* in the fall of 1950, neither of them could have ever possibly predicted the major role they would someday play in each other's lives. But fate can be a strange thing. Six years later, when Norman desperately needed a job, it was Yorkin after all who hired him to be on the writing staff of *The Tennessee Ernie Ford Show*. And then not long afterward, it quickly became apparent that Yorkin was destined for much bigger things, although there was still no inkling about what the future had in store for them together.

Yorkin was four years younger than Norman, born on February 22, 1926, in Washington, Pennsylvania, a suburb of Pittsburgh. Though his real name was Alan David Yorkin, the circumstances under which he acquired the nickname "Bud" occurred randomly when he was just a small boy. "My family and I were crossing a bridge one time," he recalled during a 1997 interview for the Television Academy Foundation. "My father gave me a quarter to give to the toll booth keeper, and he gave me ten cents change and said, 'Thanks Bud.' That's been my name ever since."[1]

The only boy and youngest child of three, Yorkin's father, Maurice, owned a local women's wear/jewelry store. Jesse, his mother, was a home-maker whose nephew was *Gone with the Wind* producer David O. Selznick. By Yorkin's own description, he grew up in a household that was middle class where as a young teenager he became an avid radio listener, particularly of comedy shows like *Fibber McGee and Molly* and the early programs of Jack Benny, Bob Hope, and Red Skelton, never imagining that he would one day work with some of them. Like most kids his age, he often spent Saturday afternoons at the movies watching the latest Westerns.

A gifted high school athlete with a bent toward math and science, he won a scholarship to the prestigious Carnegie Institute of Technology (now Carnegie Mellon University) in Pittsburgh with plans to become an engineer. However, his college education was temporarily interrupted midway through his sophomore year when he voluntarily enlisted in the navy. He was stationed in Gulfport, Mississippi, and—as Norman had during his time in Foggia, Italy, in World War II—Yorkin first discovered his passion for writing while penning sketches for the base's comedy shows.

Back in Pittsburgh, he again toyed with the idea of pursuing a career in show business. While he continued to study electronics, he dabbled in acting classes in Carnegie Tech's theater department, also then as now renowned for its nationally ranked drama program. It was here that he first met and eventually teamed up with Ken Welch, the five-time Emmy-winning composer who went on to become the musical director of Carol Burnett's long-running CBS variety show.

Together during their junior year in 1947, they wrote the annual play for Carnegie's student theatrical troupe Scotch 'n Soda. But because switching majors at that point would have meant losing a year's worth of credits, Yorkin opted to stick with his original plan.

After finally earning his degree in electrical engineering in 1948, much to his dad's chagrin, he decided to move to New York to try his hand at becoming a comedy writer. With money still left on his G.I. Bill, Yorkin enrolled in Columbia University's master's program in literature shortly after arriving in New York. But then, his interest in the still-nascent medium of television began to take shape when he got a job as a repairman for the United States Television Company, one of the nation's first manufacturers of projection TVs.

The offices were located on Long Island, which is where he and another colleague were one night after everyone else had left and the phone rang. The call was from a desperate bar owner in Manhattan whose television was on the fritz. After convincing them to drive all the way into the city to fix the broken set for which they were paid two-hundred dollars, Yorkin and his friend decided to start their own side business repairing televisions at night.

He did this for two years in between juggling his day job and classes at Columbia even though he never graduated. Instead, after learning through a newspaper ad that NBC was hiring for a series of executive engineering jobs, the then-twenty-five-year-old applied in person and was immediately hired the same day. While he didn't become a writer (at least not at first), Yorkin fast became a much-in-demand cameraman working on practically every live NBC variety program that originated from New York in those years, including Milton Berle's *Texaco Star Theater* and Sid Caesar's *Your Show of Shows*.

From the very beginning, however, he had his eye set on an even bigger prize: producing and directing. So much so that Yorkin soon began sending critiques of NBC's shows to the network's brass. Though he never received a response, in 1950 he was elected to help negotiate a new contract on behalf of his union with NBC. Having skillfully proven his mettle and that he knew what it took to get ahead in the TV business, Yorkin quickly began rising through the NBC production ranks—first as a stage manager on *Philco TV Playhouse* and *The Colgate Comedy Hour* (which he also directed) and later as a producer-director on *The Dinah Shore Show*, *The Tony Martin Show*, *The George Gobel Show*, and *The Tennessee Ernie Ford Show*.

In October 1954, Yorkin teamed up with his first cousin, the celebrated film producer David O. Selznick, on the epic television spectacular *Light's Diamond Jubilee* commemorating the seventy-fifth anniversary of Thomas Edison's invention of the electric light bulb. Budgeted at the then-astounding sum of $350,000, the special was a remarkable feat for several reasons: first, for the fact that it was simulcast on all four US networks of the time (CBS, NBC, ABC, and DuMont) and carried across over 350 television stations; second, for its deft blending of music, drama, and comedy; and third, for its astounding all-star cast, which, among others, included Humphrey Bogart and Lauren Bacall in their first live television appearance, Eddie Fisher and Debbie Reynolds, Helen Hayes, David Niven, Dorothy Dandridge, Kim Novak, and a fireside chat by President Dwight D. Eisenhower during the close. In addition to Selznick, the writers included the likes of Irwin Shaw, John Steinbeck, and Max Shulman, with an Emmy win that year for Victor Young for Best Music for a Prime-Time or Variety Series.

Yorkin's star steadily continued to rise for the remainder of the 1950s as more offers poured in. But by 1957, he had increasingly begun to grow tired of the frenetic pace of live weekly variety television. Ready to stop and smell the roses and in the enviable position of being able to write his own ticket, he decided to focus his efforts instead on specials and trying to find his first movie to direct.

When it came to his next project, the small screen came calling first. At that time, Bing Crosby, Gene Kelly, and Fred Astaire—three of Hollywood's biggest stars of all time—were preparing to host their first TV specials. Yorkin was offered all three and decided to go with Astaire.

The hour-long *An Evening with Fred Astaire* was broadcast live on NBC on October 17, 1958. Originating from the network's Burbank studios and sponsored by the Chrysler Corporation, it was billed as something of a comeback for the iconic hoofer, who was then fifty-nine, and introduced Astaire's new dance partner, Barrie Chase. It was also a coming-out party of sorts for Yorkin, showcasing his magnificent instincts as a writer-producer-director.

"We rehearsed for about eight weeks, and it was so big that we took every stage in Burbank," he recalled. "Every number would be full stage and during commercial breaks we'd have Astaire changing costumes walking across the hall. I used four control rooms with four different crews. I had sixteen cameras, and we piped the music."[2]

During the afterparty at the Beverly Hills Hotel later that evening, Astaire received congratulatory phone calls from President Eisenhower and Ed Sullivan. *An Evening* was also nominated for and won nine Emmy Awards for most outstanding single television program of the year, best single performance by an actor, best choreography for television, best musical contribution to a television program, best art direction in a live television program, best live camera work, best writing of a single musical or variety program, best direction of a single musical or variety program, and best special musical or variety program—one hour or longer. Additionally, it was the first major television show to be recorded in color on videotape and was later rebroadcast twice, spawning three more specials.

With Yorkin himself taking home three statues for best writing, producing, and directing, his next offer was to direct Helen Hayes in the musical *Mrs. Harris Goes to Paris* on Broadway, which he turned down—and as it turned out—never made it to the Great White Way. Soon afterward, however, another gig came his way to direct Jack Benny in an hour-long TV special that aired on CBS in 1959, costarring Bob Hope, Mitzi Gaynor, and ventriloquist Señor Wences.

Amid all Yorkin's massive success, Norman was at something of a creative crossroads. It was also around this same time when he and Frances became close friends with Yorkin and his wife, Peg. Born in New York in 1927, Peg, like Frances, was an early women's rights activist and cofounder and longtime chair of the nonprofit Feminist Majority Foundation, to which she personally donated $10 million in 1991, then the largest gift ever made for women's rights.

Besides the two couples' mutual creative, political, and philanthropic interests, the Yorkins' two children Nicole and David, were the same ages as the Lears' daughters, Kate and Maggie, and the two families often spent time together. Soon joining them also was Norman's oldest daughter, Ellen, who came to live with Norman, Frances, Kate, and Maggie permanently the year she turned fourteen in 1962.

In the late fall of 1958, meanwhile, several weeks after Yorkin's mammoth triumph with the Fred Astaire special, while Norman was pondering his next career move, the two couples were out to dinner one evening in Beverly Hills. Making small talk afterward as they walked back to their cars, Peg—in what must certainly have seemed like it came completely from out of left field—suggested to Norman that he and Yorkin should become producing partners, telling him that by combining their respective strengths, together they would be unstoppable.

Though they hadn't considered the prospect before, both men were intrigued. That same evening, the two couples went out for a nightcap to discuss the idea. A few short weeks later, Tandem Productions—the inspiration for their new company's name derived from the image of two men pedaling a bicycle for two uphill—was born.

"Our thinking was primarily that we really wanted to own our own company and create our own particular shows," Yorkin told the Television Academy Foundation, adding also that "there was a lot of love and respect between the two of us" and "we [believed] that it certainly would be an [attractive] package for motion pictures, which it turned out to be [because] we could write, produce and direct the whole ball of wax."[3]

Formalizing the arrangement was Yorkin's powerhouse Hollywood attorney Greg Bautzer, whose client roster included Howard Hughes, Ginger Rogers, Joan Crawford, Ingrid Bergman, Rock Hudson, Darryl Zanuck, and *The Hollywood Reporter* founder William R. Wilkerson. Soon afterward, Bautzer landed Tandem a cushy three-year development deal with Paramount Pictures that included feature films, specials, and six television pilots. To celebrate the milestone, Peg and Frances surprised their husbands with a tandem bicycle, which they had delivered to the Paramount lot.

Their inaugural project was the first broadcast of the *TV Guide Awards*, an annual awards show sponsored as a reader's poll by the editors of the venerable television listings magazine that ran for four years on NBC from 1960 until 1964. With winners chosen from 289,000 mail-in ballots, the first broadcast aired in color on March 25, 1960. It was hosted by *Father Knows Best* and future *Marcus Welby, M.D.* star Robert Young, with skits by actors Nanette Fabray and Fred MacMurray.

Between 1961 and 1962, Tandem also made a series of other specials for NBC. Their first was with singer Bobby Darin, who in the late 1950s had become a major recording star with such classics as "Splish Splash" and "Mack the Knife." Their next one was with Danny Kaye, the impish, lithe-limbed comedian and actor who'd risen to fame on Broadway in the 1941 Ira Gershwin–Moss Hart musical *Lady in the Dark* and became an even bigger star on radio and in such films as *The Kid from Brooklyn*, *The Secret Life of Walter Mitty*, *The Inspector General*, *Hans Christian Anderson*, *White Christmas*, and *The Court Jester*.

Directed by Yorkin and cowritten by Norman and Hal Kanter, the special was to be a litmus test for grooming and gauging Kaye's appeal for television, where he went on to star in his own weekly variety series costarring Harvey Korman and Joyce Van Patten. It ran for four years on CBS and won both Emmy and Peabody Awards. Yorkin also won a Director's Guild Award for the special. But as far as the experience itself was concerned, it was one of the worst of his career—something he blamed Kaye's wife Sylvia Fine for.

"I never got along with Danny, I think, because of his wife," Yorkin recalled. "I insisted she couldn't write the special. She wrote all his material, and I told her that if she wanted me to do the show, she couldn't write it. But she was [still] in the background criticizing all the time and that made him come to me. And I feel badly about that, because I told him that I didn't enjoy working on the show and we had kind of a falling-out after it was over."[4]

More gratifying and far more ambitious was an hour-long comedy special examining the contemporary American family that Norman and Yorkin did for CBS in February 1962 called *Henry Fonda and the Family*. Costarring Dick Van Dyke, Paul Lynde, Verna Felton, Dan Blocker, and Michael J. Pollard, it was directed by Yorkin and cowritten by Norman and humorist Tom Koch. While in many ways it was a run-of-the-mill variety special of that era—shot in black and white with flimsy sets, schmaltzy up-tempo background music, and stock characters—in other respects, *Fonda* had the look and feel of the classic Thornton Wilder play *Our Town*. At the same time, it tackled a host of easily identifiable family themes about the complexities of domestic life in ways that were funny, simplistic, and profound, with Fonda either narrating or becoming a secondary character in every scene.

But even though the special was highly touted by CBS largely on the strength of Fonda, critical reception was decidedly mixed. Its harshest review came from Jack Gould of the *New York Times*, who wrote that "except for an amusing line or two on the apprehensions and eccentric appetite of the young mother-to-be, the material painted the American family as composed of lamebrains given to untidy smooching or fulltime idiocy. Norman Lear and Tom Koch who prepared the script, obviously have been watching too much television."[5]

Nevertheless, *Fonda and the Family* still stands out as a perfect early example of Norman and Yorkin's astute sophistication and splendid range at the time, if not an indication of Tandem's future. Such was also the case that same year in the first of a series of specials they did with singer Andy

Williams directed by Yorkin and cowritten with Norman that aired May 4, 1962, on NBC. Also costarring Dick Van Dyke, Andy Griffith, and Ann-Margret with music by Henry Mancini, it was an instant hit.

So too was Williams's weekly variety show, which ran on NBC for nine years, with Yorkin directing many of its early episodes, along with a 1967 Christmas special and then—also under the Tandem canopy—*An Evening with Carol Channing*, which won an Emmy for outstanding achievement in variety in 1966.

Among Norman and Yorkin's early television pilot endeavors was a series about the international adventures of two airline pilots and one stewardess called *Three to Get Ready*. Another project in the offing was *Band of Gold*, an ensemble comedy featuring the same set of actors playing different characters in different locations in a series of unrelated storylines about couples who were either married or unmarried. Considering the taboo-busting sitcoms Norman did later, the farcical premise seems inconceivable in retrospect.

Yet, as they became famous for doing in all their endeavors, Norman and Yorkin assembled a stellar cast with *Band*. The two leads were James Franciscus—the character actor best known for his tough-guy roles in scores of films and six television series, including *Doc Elliot*, *Hunter*, *Mr. Novak*, *Longstreet*, *The Investigators*, and *Naked City*—and the raspy-voiced Suzanne Pleshette, who went on to play Emily Hartley, Bob Newhart's wife, on the . comedian's eponymous 1970s sitcom.

With *Band*'s pilot seemingly a slam dunk, Norman and Yorkin were both convinced they had struck gold. But then it wound up in the wrong hands when it was sent to James Aubrey, CBS's pugnacious head of programming, who was widely known within broadcasting circles as "The Smiling Cobra" and a man of stark contrasts. Under Aubrey's leadership in the early to mid-1960s, for example, CBS's profits rose from $25 million in 1959 to $49 million in 1964. To accomplish this, however, he would also make a mockery out of the vaunted Tiffany Network, becoming its chief purveyor of such shows as *Mister Ed*, *The Munsters*, *Green Acres*, and *The Beverly Hillbillies* (the kind of lowbrow fare that CBS's urbane founder and chairman William Paley loathed), and in an interesting twist, a major reason why *All in the Family* eventually got on the air in a direct effort to replace them.

Of course, *AITF* was not even a gleam in Norman's eye when they were trying to sell *Band of Gold*. At that time also, the events leading to Aubrey's dismissal in February 1965 for alleged financial mismanagement and plotting to have Bill Paley ousted from his own company—"circumstances," that, as the *New York Times* declared in a front-page article the following day, "rivaled the best of CBS mystery or adventure shows"—had not come to light yet.[6]

However, Aubrey, then at the height of his power in 1961, took an immediate liking to Norman and Yorkin's high-concept premise. To their great delight and surprise, he called the very same day he read the script, not only raving about it, but requesting a meeting in his office to discuss plans to add *Band* to the fall schedule. He was so enthusiastic about its prospects, in fact, that he already had a time slot picked out on Tuesday nights at eight thirty.

Norman and Yorkin were over the moon even though they had heard rumors about Aubrey's difficult reputation. However, they hadn't experienced it firsthand and at the time had no reason to suspect anything might be awry. In fact, after hearing the good news and telling Aubrey they were planning to celebrate by taking their wives to Acapulco for a long weekend, he told the two men to have a good time. He even ended the meeting unexpectedly by giving them a hug and sending them on their way.

But then, as things turned out, it was all a smoke screen. Following a blissful few days in Mexico with Frances and Peg, Norman and Yorkin returned to L.A. to discover that *Band* wouldn't be airing at all. Aubrey had instead awarded the coveted time slot to his best friend Keefe Brasselle—a modestly successful actor best known for his title role in the 1953 biopic *The Eddie Cantor Story*—for another series that hadn't been developed yet.

However, despite their obvious disappointment, the debacle was kismet. Norman and Yorkin already had plenty of other irons in the fire. One of the most promising embers ignited during the first year of their development deal with Paramount. The proverbial spark came from Norman's old friend Neil Simon, who had sent him a copy of his first play *Come Blow Your Horn*, which was soon heading to Broadway. The premise centered around Buddy Baker, an impressionable, still-wet-behind-the-ears twenty-one-year-old, who decides to leave his suburban home to move to New York and live with older brother Alan, a ladies' man who lives in a swinging bachelor pad in the East Sixties on Manhattan's Upper East Side.

After Normal had rewritten the script more than two dozen times, *Horn* made its hit Broadway premiere at the Brooks Atkinson Theatre (now the Lena Horne Theatre) on February 22, 1961, forever cementing Simon's reputation as one of America's most prolific playwrights. In the cast were Hal March—the actor and quiz show host best known for his years as the front man on the 1950s game show *The $64,000 Question* and his multiple sitcom appearances on *I Love Lucy* and the original radio version of *The George Burns and Gracie Allen Show*—along with actors Arlene Golonka, Warren Berlinger, Lou Jacobi, and Pert Kelton, who originated the role of Alice Kramden on *The Honeymooners*.

But as gung-ho as Norman and Yorkin were about *Horn*'s big-screen prospects, they also felt that March wasn't a big enough name to play the lead. As a matter of fact, the only person they could envision was Frank Sinatra. If everything went accordingly and he agreed to make the film, Paramount would finance and distribute it. However, at the time they made the deal, there was still one problem: Sinatra wasn't even aware of the project.

And thus they commenced what turned out to be a nearly-yearlong crusade, sparing almost no expense and pulling out all the stops, trying to get the Chairman of the Board on board. How their persistence finally paid off is truly the stuff of Hollywood legend.

It began with a phone call from Norman pitching the project to Sinatra's then-producer, Howard Koch, who went on to run Paramount Pictures. Koch loved the script and thought Sinatra would be perfect for the lead. But when all of Koch's initial attempts to get him to read the screenplay proved futile, Norman and Yorkin shifted into high gear. Because of the premise—about a sophisticated New York bachelor trying to teach his shy younger brother about the ways of the world, particularly women—they changed the title to *Cock-a-Doodle-Doo* to emphasize the film's coming-of-age theme.

With a copy of the script always in hand, Norman then spent the next several months trying to track Sinatra down in restaurants, hotel bars, recording studios, and all his other usual L.A. haunts to no avail. Sinatra was so stealthy that he managed to throw him off the scent everywhere he went. Finally, in early 1962, Norman caught a break when he learned the crooner was appearing on an upcoming television special with Judy Garland. He even got past security at NBC in Burbank and onto the soundstage where the special was being filmed. As soon as he saw him, Sinatra—who was by now familiar enough with what Norman looked like that he'd even nicknamed his balding pate "The Helmet"—boisterously addressed him as such accompanied by a few expletives shouted into a microphone from across the room as a guard escorted Norman out.

Norman was still unfazed. Sensing by the impishly sarcastic tone in his voice that Sinatra was actually getting a kick out of the cat-and-mouse game—and as if on a dare—Norman proceeded to mount a full-court press. After getting his home address from Howard Koch, Norman sent Sinatra a cage of roosters to his home along with another copy of the script. Then after changing the name of the film back to *Come Blow Your Horn*, he sent over a box of toy trumpets.

Sinatra, meanwhile, continued giving him the slip until Norman industriously devised what he was sure was a can't-miss last ploy. With the help of the Paramount prop department, he decided to build Sinatra a reading kit—complete with a full-size floor lamp, an easy chair, a rug, a pipe, a smoking jacket, and an ashtray—having it sent over to his house with another copy of the script. To add to the ambiance, he even threw in a record player and a copy of Jackie Gleason's *Music to Read By* album.

Taking his cues from Howard Koch, who informed Norman that Sinatra was in New York, it was decided the kit would be delivered to the house the night he was supposed to return to L.A. when there weren't any servants around. In the meantime, Norman left instructions with the deliveryman to set things up on Sinatra's front lawn and to turn on the lamp and the record player before he drove away.

Flush with excitement over what he was certain Sinatra's positive response would be, Norman spent the next forty-eight hours anxiously awaiting a phone call from him that never came. As it turned out, the reason why he didn't hear from him was because Koch had been wrong: Sinatra's housekeeper was there that night after all and had dismantled the reading kit before he got home. The only thing left over was the smoking jacket, which she hung up in his closet.

In the meantime, the more time that passed, the more Norman was convinced Sinatra had completely written him off. Compounding his angst was knowing that without Sinatra, their deal with Paramount was off. With dashed hopes, Norman glumly put in a call to Sinatra's manager Hank Sanicola, telling him he'd finally gotten the message that Sinatra wasn't interested and promising not to bother him again.

But then as their conversation wound down, Norman told Sanicola about his latest stunt, and he laughed. Reassuring him that the reason why he hadn't heard anything about the reading kit from Sinatra was because he didn't know anything about it, Sanicola called the singer and told him the story. Then that following day, Norman also got another call. This time, it was from Sinatra, telling him how much he loved the ingenuity of the reading kit. He also told Norman that he'd read the script and agreed to do the film. And then, with tongue firmly planted in cheek, he reprimanded Norman for taking so long to get it to him.

With both men coproducing, Yorkin directing, and Norman writing the screenplay, the world premiere of *Come Blow Your Horn* was in May 1963 in Palm Springs. Hosting it was Barbara Marx, the wife of Marx Brother Zeppo, at their home. Several weeks later, on June 5, 1963, *Horn* officially opened in New York at Radio City Music Hall. Yet despite Sinatra's star power, many critics were not overly enthused. Consider this jagged opener from the zinger fired off by *New York Times* film critic Bosley Crowther the day after *Horn*'s debut at Radio City: "Have you ever had to sit and listen patiently while a clumsy raconteur butchered a funny story you'd already heard a couple of times? That's how it is to be exposed to the movie Bud Yorkin and Norman Lear have made from Neil Simon's unspectacular but lively stage play *Come Blow Your Horn*. For the dismal fact is that the producers and Frank Sinatra have really butchered the play in their garish screen version, which came to the Music Hall yesterday."[7]

Nevertheless, *Horn* was the first big-budget motion picture with "Screenplay by Norman Lear," "Produced by Norman Lear and Bud Yorkin," and "Directed by Bud Yorkin" emblazoned across the screen. What's more, it went on to become the fifteenth-highest-grossing film of 1963, with an Oscar nomination for Best Art Direction. Riding the momentum, Tandem was increasingly becoming a major player in Hollywood, and so—ever more by default—were Norman and Yorkin even with the occasional missteps along the way.

One of their biggest blunders was not stepping up to the plate fast enough after being offered the chance to produce the movie versions of Neil Simon's next two plays, which became among his most famous: *Barefoot in the Park* and *The Odd Couple*, which Paramount also owned the film rights to. It was a decision Norman later described as "foolish" and "unintentional."

In retrospect, though, it isn't difficult to understand the reasons for the oversight. Despite all its success at the time, Tandem was still in growth mode and eagerly trying to spread its wings. Also, according to Yorkin, they didn't want to become pigeonholed as a company that only produced films adapted from Broadway shows. Toward this end, Norman took another giant leap off the creative cliff during this period when he attempted to option the film rights to a book called *Fear on Trial* by Henry Faulk.

Faulk had been a popular radio and television personality in New York during the height of the McCarthyism "Red Scare" era of the 1950s. He was blacklisted and subsequently won a $3,500,000 judgment in what was then the largest-ever settlement in a libel case. *Fear* was his gripping firsthand account of the ordeal. As soon as Norman read it, he became enamored with turning it into a film, because nearly everything in and around the story that would later become a lynchpin of his political activism resonated with him.

No doubt adding to the intrigue was the fact that it also involved numerous famous people, including Ed Sullivan and Norman's own cousin David Susskind along with journalists Edward R. Murrow and Charles Collingwood; actors Lee Grant, Myrna Loy, and Tony Randall; game show producer Mark Goodson; and attorneys Roy Cohn and Louis Nizer. And so, Norman began working on the screenplay, although unfortunately Tandem never made the movie when an arrangement with National General Corporation to finance the film as part of a two-picture deal fell through. However, the project did resurface a decade later in 1975 as a CBS Movie of the Week starring William Devane, George C. Scott, and Dorothy Tristan. Using the same title as the original book, this time it was helmed by Alan Landsburg, the Emmy-winning producer behind such telefilms as *Bill* starring Mickey Rooney, the early TV reality series *In Search of . . .* and *That's Incredible*, and the 1983 *Jaws* sequel *Jaws 3-D*.

In the meantime, with Paramount having now rescinded their offer to Tandem to produce *Barefoot in the Park* and *The Odd Couple*, their second film was *Never Too Late*, with Norman producing and Yorkin directing. Released by Warner Brothers in November 1965, it was based on the hit Broadway play by Sumner Arthur Long, who also wrote the screenplay, and costarred Maureen O'Sullivan and Paul Ford reprising their roles in the film.

It told the story of Edith Lambert (O'Sullivan), a fifty-something middle-aged housewife married to Henry (Ford), a lumber company executive who recently lost his bid to become mayor of their small New England town. After twenty-five years of marriage, their lives are upended when Edith discovers she's pregnant for the second time. Complicating matters for them are their self-centered adult daughter Kate and scatterbrained son-in-law Jim who are living with them.

Suitably cast as Kate was Connie Stevens, the blond bombshell singer and actor who first rose to fame in the 1950s for her starring role as Cricket on the ABC detective series *Hawaiian Eye* and with such hit recordings as "Sixteen Reasons" and "Kookie, Kookie (Lend Me Your Comb)." The part of Stevens's onscreen husband—originally auditioned for by Bob Crane, who was then starring in the CBS military sitcom *Hogan's Heroes*—went to Jim Hutton, the actor best known for his role as mystery writer Ellery Queen in the 1970s NBC adventure series reboot of the same name, who later played Julie Cooper's much-older love interest in a season-3 four-parter of Norman's original *One Day at a Time*.

Shot on location in Concord, Massachusetts, *Never Too Late* translated well to the small screen and was generally well-received. Though several critics invariably panned the film, it was far more for the style rather than its treatment of the subject matter. Sharpening his pen in particular again (and not surprisingly given his scathing critique of *Come Blow Your Horn* two years earlier) was Bosley Crowther, writing condescendingly in the *New York Times* that "they don't make pictures like *Never Too Late* in Hollywood anymore—at least not very often. For that we can thank our lucky stars, because no matter how much this screen version of Sumner Arthur Long's pellucid play, which ran for more than two years on Broadway, may hash and rehash the same jokes that clobbered the Broadway suckers while offering the same horse-faced Paul Ford in the role of the thunder-struck husband he gulped and gargled on the stage, it is still pretty small potatoes up there on the Panavision screen."[8]

Nonetheless, for the most part the reviews were positive, even glowing in their praise of *Never*'s deft portrayal of what was largely still considered to be a taboo theme. Seeming to sum up the general consensus at the time were the following sentiments expressed by the now-defunct *Los Angeles Evening Citizen News*'s Nadine Edwards:

> The ambitious producer-director team of Norman Lear and Bud Yorkin have decided it's never too late for a winner and forthwith have given theatergoers one of the year's funnier themes; one which should tickle the funny bone of Mom and Dad, to say nothing of their young, married offspring.
>
> Delightfully homespun with shades of sophistication, *Never Too Late* takes gentle exception to the fact that there is nothing new under the sun—it's just the way you present it. In other words, the picture is laced with the usual cliches, innuendos and tried-and-true situation comedy, but injected with so much more warmth and humor and charm, that it seems almost new in concept.[9]

In 1967, Norman and Yorkin turned their attention to yet another delicate topic in *Divorce American Style*, costarring Dick Van Dyke and Debbie Reynolds alongside Jason Robards, Van Johnson, and British actress Jean Simmons. Distributed by Columbia Pictures and billed as a comedy satire with Norman penning the screenplay and Yorkin directing, the film concerned Richard Harmon (Van Dyke) and his wife Barbara (Reynolds), an affluent married couple from suburban Los Angeles who seem to have it all. After seventeen years of marriage, however, they find themselves constantly at odds with one another as it becomes increasingly apparent they can no longer live together. In a last-dich effort to save their faltering marriage, they seek counseling, emptying out their joint bank account in the process and ultimately decide to divorce.

In the meantime, Richard is forced to move into a modest apartment as he struggles to survive on $87.30 a week after high alimony payments wreak havoc on his wallet. Living in the same building is Nelson Downs (Robards), also a recent divorcee, who introduces Richard to his ex-wife Nancy (Simmons) in the hopes of marrying her off so that he can marry his ex-fiancée.

Nancy is also eager to marry Richard because she's lonely. But before they can, they first have to figure out a way to solve Richard's alimony troubles. Ultimately, they concoct a scheme to introduce Barbara to Big Al Yearling, a millionaire auto dealer played by Johnson, and the two soon begin a relationship.

The story then takes a sudden and dramatic twist the night before Harmon's divorce is set to become final. As all three couples meet at an L.A. nightclub to celebrate their respective plans, a hypnotist puts Barbara in a trance after pulling her from the audience. This leads to Barbara performing a mock striptease at the prompting of the hypnotist, who then tells her to kiss her true love, whereupon she kisses Richard, and they decide to give their marriage another try, while Nelson plays matchmaker with Nancy and Big Al.

In many ways, *Divorce* was yet another predictive sign of the sophisticated subject matter that was to become an integral part of Norman's sitcom canon in the 1970s. No doubt in other ways (even if he didn't realize it at the time), it was also a fictionalized version of a real-life fantasy he may well have had following his own divorce from Charlotte.

And it struck an immediate chord with moviegoers and critics alike. In one of his earliest reviews for the *Chicago Sun-Times*, Roger Ebert hailed the film as "a member of that rare species, the Hollywood comedy with teeth in it," also adding that "Bud Yorkin has directed it with wit and style, and the cast, which seems unlikely on paper, comes across splendidly onscreen . . . the charm of the film [being] in its lowkey approach. The plot isn't milked for humor or pathos. Both emerge naturally from familiar situations."[10]

Singing its praises as well was *Variety*, writing: "Comedy and satire, not feverish melodrama, are the best weapons with which to harpoon social mores. An outstanding example is *Divorce American Style* . . . which pokes incisive, sometimes chilling, fun at the U.S. marriage-divorce problems."[11]

Eviscerating Norman and Yorkin once again, however, was the *New York Times*'s Bosley Crowther, who said of *Divorce*, "It is rather depressing, saddening and annoying, largely because it does labor to turn a solemn subject into a great big American-boob joke." He also took potshots at Van Dyke's performance, describing him as "too much of a giggler, too much of a dyed-in-the-wool television comedian for this serio-comic husband role."[12]

Nevertheless, *Divorce* cleaned up at the box office as nearly every Columbia film in the late 1960s did. Norman, meanwhile, was nominated for both an Academy Award for Best Original Screenplay and for Best Comedy by the Writer's Guild.

With Tandem now having hit its stride, they would strike box office gold again in 1968 with two more films. Yorkin directed Alan Arkin in *Inspector Clouseau*, which was the third installment of the Pink Panther film franchise filmed in London. Closer to home, meanwhile, Norman wrote and produced the musical comedy *The Night They Raided Minsky's* not knowing how difficult the project was going to be, or that it would be the impetus for his eventual return to television.

Part Three

The Glory Years

CHAPTER 11

Family Ties

The inspiration for what became Norman's crowning achievement all started because of the Cowardly Lion. More specifically, the genesis of *All in the Family* began because Bert Lahr, the actor and comedian who played him in *The Wizard of Oz*, died suddenly during the production of Norman's latest film *The Night They Raided Minsky's* in 1967.

Based on author Rowland Barber's 1960 novel of the same name, the film tells the story of Rachel Schpitendavel, an ambitious but naïve Amish girl (played by Swedish actress, model, and singer Britt Ekland) who flees her strict rural Pennsylvania roots in search of fame and fortune as a dancer in the big city. Hoping to set New York's theater world on its ear through dances she's invented based on Bible stories, Rachel winds up on Manhattan's Lower East Side circa 1925 and accidentally invents the striptease after auditioning at a burlesque house called Minsky's.

By the time Tandem acquired the film rights in mid-1965, the property had been up for grabs for nearly four years. Among its earliest contenders was Broadway producer Leonard Key, who outbid several others for the stage rights, including actress Debbie Reynolds, who'd also been vying to bring *Minsky's* to the big screen.

Then reportedly the highest price ever paid for stage or screen rights, Key had even enlisted screenwriter Julius J. Epstein for the project along with Henry Mancini and Sammy Cahn to write the music. But after he was unable to find adequate financial backing before the two-year limit on the stage rights ended in 1963, Key's involvement ultimately fell by the wayside.

No doubt feeling a sense of nostalgia about the many wistful hours he'd spent taking in the latest burlesque shows at the Old Howard Theater in

Boston during his years as a student at Emerson College, Norman relished the opportunity to do a film like *Minsky's*. Once aboard after officially acquiring the rights in September 1965, he assumed full control of the project, becoming sole producer and co-writing the script, for which he shared onscreen credits behind Arnold Schulman and Sidney Michaels.

Filming on location in New York was originally set to begin in the fall of 1966, although casting and production logistics quickly proved to be a massive challenge, delaying its start for another year. Most difficult initially was the cast, or more accurately, the unavailability of the actors Norman wanted to use because of other commitments. The first person considered for the lead as theater owner Billy Minsky was comedian Dick Shawn, but it later went to Elliott Gould, then married to Barbra Streisand, making his feature film debut.

First up for the part of Raymond (and initially slated to become one of *Minsky's* producers also), was Norman's friend Tony Curtis, who quit after just one month after winning the coveted title role of Albert DeSalvo in the 1968 true crime film *The Boston Strangler*. Next was Alan Alda, who had to turn it down because he was already starring in *The Apple Tree* on Broadway, as did Walter Matthau due to another scheduling conflict, and so Jason Robards stepped in one month before filming got underway.

Briefly in the running to become Chick Williams, Raymond's sidekick, was Mickey Rooney (also Norman's first choice to play Archie Bunker), although the part went to Joel Grey, then headlining on Broadway in *Cabaret*, who also had to turn it down because he was slated to begin rehearsals for a new musical about composer George M. Cohan. Fortuitously available and cast, however, was British comedian Norman Wisdom hot off the heels of a recent Tony Award nomination for his appearance in the musical comedy *Walking Happy*.

To direct *Minsky's*, Norman hired William Friedkin. Having recently made his directorial debut in the 1967 film *Good Times* starring Sonny and Cher, Friedkin would go on to a spectacular career as the Oscar-winning director of such classics as *The French Connection*, *The Boys in the Band*, and *The Exorcist*, as well as become one of the key figures closely associated with the New Hollywood movement of the 1970s.

But at the time Norman hired him, he was still a greenhorn, at one point feeling so out of his league that he even asked Norman to fire him, according to his 2013 memoir *The Friedkin Connection*. Recalling the experience with bloggers Alex Simon and Terry Keefe for *The Hollywood Interview* in 2008, Friedkin also said:

Minsky's was way over my head. I didn't have a clue what to do. Norman produced it and he was a very difficult, tough guy to work with, but I learned a great deal from him, and I was struggling every day on the set. It wasn't a great script . . . it was a lot of schtick. But it would've been a lot better if I'd been more familiar with that world of burlesque in the twenties, which I wasn't. So because of that I think the film suffers to a great degree from that.[1]

Among others rounding out the cast were Rudy Vallée as the film's narrator, Forrest Tucker as theater patron Trim Houlihan, Joseph Weisman as Billy Minsky's father, comedian Jack Burns as the candy butcher, and Bert Lahr in what would be his last role as long-in-the-tooth vaudeville performer Professor Spats. Penning the film's musical score was the Broadway lyricist and composer team of Charles Strouse and Lee Adams.

Production on *Minsky's* finally got under way in October 1967 and was the first film musical ever shot on location in New York City, with a budget of over $3 million, also making it the most expensive movie ever made there at the time. For the exteriors, an entire block of East 26th Street between First and Second Avenues was transformed to resemble the Lower East Side of the mid-1920s.

To preserve the area's authenticity, Norman managed to persuade Mayor John Lindsay to postpone an urban renewal project and delay plans to demolish a group of abandoned tenements while they filmed there for two weeks as barrels and garbage cans were set up to camouflage parking meters. A partial replica of an elevated train station was also built on the site, while a subway scene inside a vintage train car was filmed in Brooklyn and some of the other interiors were shot at Chelsea Studios. For scenes taking place at the fictionalized Minsky's Burlesque, the real-life Gayety Theater (now the Village East Cinema) on the Lower East Side was used.

Despite the initial casing and logistical hurdles, once filming began it proceeded mostly without incident. But then in late November, Bert Lahr was suddenly hospitalized with what was thought to be a back ailment. Though he'd been expected to fully recover, he died two weeks later at Columbia Presbyterian Hospital at the age of seventy-two. In his 1969 book, *Notes on a Cowardly Lion: The Biography of Bert Lahr*, the account offered by John Lahr, the actor's son and former theater critic for the *New Yorker*, was this:

Bert Lahr died in the early morning of December 4, 1967, for what was reported as a back ailment. Two weeks before, he had returned home at two a.m., chilled and feverish, from the damp studio where *The Night They Raided Minsky's* was being filmed. Ordinarily, a man of his age and reputation would not have had to perform that late into the night, but he had waived that proviso in his contract because of his trust in the producer and his need to work. The newspapers reported the cause of death as pneumonia; but he succumbed to cancer, a disease he feared but never knew he had.[2]

Naturally, everyone was upset by Lahr's sudden death, especially Norman. Though Lahr wasn't a principal character and most of his scenes had already been shot, editing the film turned out to be a nightmare that would take nearly a year even as Norman attempted to put the best spin on it, telling the *New York Times* that "through judicious editing, we will be able to shoot the rest of the film so that his wonderful performance will remain intact."[3]

Meanwhile, legendary film editor Ralph Rosenblum offered a completely different take, describing the first screening of *Minsky's* with William Friedkin and Norman as "disastrous" in his 1979 book *When the Shooting Stops . . . the Cutting Begins*. "I had taken *Minsky's* on not because I believed it would be a great editorial challenge but because I saw it as a lark," he recalled. According to Rosenblum, United Artists executive vice president David Picker called it "the worst first cut I've ever seen," also telling Rosenblum and Norman, "Whatever you want to do, go ahead, take your time, and do it."[4] In the end, Lahr's test footage along with burlesque comic Joey Faye pinch-hitting as a body double and an uncredited voice were used to complete the role.

Minsky's premiered in Los Angeles on December 18, 1968, before opening nationwide on December 22, exactly one year after filming was completed and garnering mostly positive critical nods for its homage to old-time burlesque. One of the most favorable was Roger Ebert's review in the *Chicago Sun-Times*, saying:

> *The Night They Raided Minsky's* is being promoted as some sort of laff-a-minit, slapstick extravaganza, but it isn't. It has the courage to try for more than that and just about succeeds. It avoids the phony glamour and romanticism that the movies usually use to smother burlesque (as in *Gypsy*) and it really seems to understand this most-American art form.[5]

Sharing Ebert's sentiments was Judith Crist, calling it "really just what we were wishing for at Christmas" in *New York* magazine and writing, "What a delight to have a chance to laugh out loud at sex!"

Like the burlesque it glorifies—and with tender loving care—this boisterous, colorful, wiggling eulogy to the Lower East Side bump-and-grind culture of the 1920s is plotless, frenetic, funny and just as good as the real thing. It's nostalgic as all get out to see the lumpy dumpy chorus, the snores and the leerers and the lechers around the runway, the Crazy House bit and the spielers and, beyond the theater, the East Side in its glory from the barrels of half-sours to the knishes to the Murphy-bedded hotel rooms. Director William Friedkin (this was his pre-*The Birthday Party* film) proves his sense of cinema again by remarkable interslicing of newsreels and striking use of black-and-white fade-ins to color.[6]

Time magazine also hailed the film as "a valedictory valentine to old-time burlesque," with some of the most lavish praise going to Bert Lahr:

In legend, the girls were glamorous, and every baggy-pants buffoon was a second W.C. Fields. In truth, the institution was as coarse as its audiences. *Minsky's* mixes both fact and fancy in a surprisingly success-ful musical. . . . *Minsky's* was fifty-eight days in the shooting and ten months in the editing—and shows it. Marred by grainy film and fleshed out with documentary and pseudo-newsreel footage of the 1920s, the film spends too much time on pickles, pushcarts and passersby. But it compensates with a fond, nostalgic score, a bumping, grinding chorus line and a series of closeups of the late Bert Lahr, who plays a retired burlesque comedian. Like Lahr, the film offers an engaging blend of mockery and melancholy.[7]

Minsky's also did far better at the box office than anyone expected, gross-ing $197,152 in its first twenty-three days playing at two theaters in New York alone. Nonetheless, it's little wonder that as much as Norman enjoyed making the film initially, having it behind him was an enormous relief.

Compounding the difficulties caused by Lahr's death was the toll that Norman's decision to bring Frances, Kate, and Maggie with him to New York took on his personal life. While Ellen, who was now twenty and in col-lege, didn't join them, being uprooted from their friends in Los Angeles was especially difficult for Norman and Frances's two young daughters, who were enrolled at P.S. 6 on East 82nd and Madison Avenue. Frances, on the other hand, was initially excited about the move.

The Lears rented a three-bedroom apartment near the girls' school in a prewar doorman building on Fifth Avenue. In the beginning, Frances enjoyed redecorating it to her taste and reconnecting with old New York friends. Yet, as Norman became more and more preoccupied with *Minsky's*, she felt increasingly lonely and overshadowed by his career. As the years progressed, it was a rift that only grew and would ultimately doom their marriage.

During *Minsky's* filming and postproduction, Norman continued to develop and search for new projects as Yorkin remained in England shooting *Inspector Clouseau* with Alan Arkin. On the film front was an idea called *Two Times Two* about two sets of male twins who get mixed at birth after being born in the middle of the night.

Another intriguing idea was a film about quitting smoking, which became *Cold Turkey*, released in February 1971. Third was a spoof of soap operas to air late at night five nights a week and was the concept that later became *Mary Hartman, Mary Hartman* starring Louise Lasser and premiering in 1976.

Meanwhile, in 1968, as he was scrambling to salvage Lahr's truncated *Minsky's* appearance in the editing suite, Norman learned about a TV show making waves over in England called *Till Death Us Do Part*. Its premise about the dysfunctional family dynamics of a working-class bigot from London's East End constantly at odds with his socialist liberal son-in-law resonated with him. He also began to think something like it might work in the United States and set out to buy the American rights—sight unseen.

CHAPTER 12

On a Mission

How *Till Death Us Do Part* first landed on Norman's radar screen is said to have happened in several ways. By most accounts, including the one in his memoir, it originally came to his attention after he read an item about it in *TV Guide* during the editing debacle of *The Night They Raided Minsky's*, although in some instances over the years he said he read about it in *Variety*.

Bud Yorkin had also seen an episode when he was living in England working on the film *Inspector Clouseau* with Alan Arkin and sent a tape of *Till Death* back to Norman, something that would prompt finger pointing five decades later from Yorkin's first wife Peg and their daughter Nicole. According to multiple sources—including the *Los Angeles Times* following the publication of Norman's autobiography *Even This I Get to Experience* in 2014, as well as Yorkin's obituary in the *Hollywood Reporter* a year later, and then again in the *L.A. Times* in 2019 after Norman was nominated for an Emmy for the first installment of his *Live in Front of a Studio Audience* specials with Jimmy Kimmel—the Yorkins were angered all over again by what had apparently been a long-simmering resentment that he had never received enough credit for *All in the Family* and the other shows it spawned.

The *Hollywood Reporter* obit ("Bud Yorkin, Overlooked *All in the Family* Legend, Dies at 89")[1] and the 2019 *L.A. Times* piece ("Norman Lear's Latest Emmy Win Writes His Partner Out of History—Again")[2] even made these assertions directly in the headlines. For his part, Yorkin had always maintained that he mailed Norman the videotape on something of a lark, telling the Television Academy Foundation in 1997: "I said this will blow your mind, [but] never did it dawn on me . . . that was Norman's idea totally of trying to do it here. I just said, 'Want to have some fun? Watch this show.'"[3]

At the time of Yorkin's death, meanwhile, Norman said in a statement to the press: "His was the horse we rode in on and I couldn't love or appreciate him more."[4] What he never did do, however, was publicly acknowledge Yorkin for giving him the tape, always proclaiming that even though he never saw an episode before deciding to bid on it, he and Yorkin discussed it first. Moreover, when it came to his motivation for doing so, Norman's goal, according to what he told author Ronald Brownstein, was not to change television.

"I never, ever remembered thinking, 'Oh, we're doing something outlandish, riotously different,'" he said in Brownstein's 2021 book, *Rock Me on the Water: 1974—The Year Los Angeles Transformed Movies, Music, Television, and Politics*. "I wasn't on any mission. And I don't think I knew I was breaking such ground. I didn't watch *Petticoat Junction*, for Chrissake. I didn't watch *Beverly Hillbillies*. I didn't know what I was doing."[5]

It was a similar refrain to the explanation he offered in countless other interviews, also telling *Rolling Stone* in 2016: "Well, I had realized that the shows that were on television for years like *The Beverly Hillbillies* and *Petticoat Junction*, which are perfectly good shows, had episodes where the biggest problem a family might face would have been that the roast was ruined when the boss was coming over to dinner. That was fine, but it made a giant statement, too. There were no women or their problems in American life on television. There were no economic problems. The worst thing that could happen was the roast would be ruined. I realized that was a giant statement—that we *weren't* making any statements."[6]

And to the *Harvard Business Review* in 2014: "I never thought of these shows as groundbreaking, because every American understood so easily what they were about. The issues were around their dinner tables. The language was in their school yards. It was nothing new. Before *All in the Family*, there were a lot of families on television, but the biggest problem they faced was mom dented the fender or the boss is coming to dinner and the roast is ruined. America had no racial problems, no economic problems. Women didn't get breast cancer, men didn't get hypertension."[7]

Whatever the route or Norman's motives (aside from being able to relate to *Till Death*'s two principals, he had also long aspired to have his own sitcom someday in order to reap the financial rewards in syndication if it was successful), that summer of 1968, he immersed himself on a mission to buy the American rights to *Till Death Us Do Part*.

At the heart of the British show was the story of two political polar opposites living under the same roof in the blue-collar Wapping section of London's East End. Alf Garnett, the family patriarch (played by actor Warren Mitchell), was a bigoted British dockworker who constantly locked horns with his liberal socialist son-in-law Mike Rawlins (Anthony Boothe). Elise (played by Dandy Nichols) was Alf's long-suffering wife, and they had one daughter: Rita (Una Stubbs) who was married to Mike.

Like Archie Bunker, Alf was the archetypal uneducated white reactionary whose limited worldview and political knowledge was expressed through a thick cockney accent in colorful language deemed unacceptable for 1960s British television. And as Archie did also, Alf referred to virtually every minority group in existence in derisive terms while constantly putting down his son-in-law, calling him a "Shirley Temple" or a "Randy Scouse Git," a phrase meaning "horny, Liverpudlian jerk" in American English that caught the ear of Mickey Dolenz, the drummer-vocalist for the American pop rock band the Monkees, who, after seeing an episode of the show while on tour in the U.K., wound up turning it into the title of one of their biggest hit songs.

❧

Till Death was the brainchild of writer-producer Johnny Speight who was two years older than Norman. Both shared left-leaning political views and similar career paths as comedy writers. A lifelong socialist, Speight was born in the Canning Town district of East London on June 2, 1920. After dropping out of school at the age of fourteen, he held a series of factory jobs before becoming inspired by the playwright George Bernard Shaw and deciding to pursue a career in show business as a writer.

Just as Norman had cut his TV comedy writing teeth on some of America's most popular 1950s variety shows, Speight's first job was as a writer for the popular BBC sketch comedy series *Great Scott—It's Maynard!* in 1955. His next big gig was a stint on the black-and-white BBC sitcom *Sykes and a . . .* writing alongside comedian Spike Milligan before hitting the big time with *Till Death Do Us Part* in July 1965.

The show originally started out as a single episode on the BBC's long-running one-off sitcom anthology series *Comedy Playhouse* before beginning its run as a regular program that following year and becoming an instant hit in multiple incarnations. First airing as a stand-alone series on the BBC from 1966 until 1968, and again from 1972 until 1975, this was followed by a six-episode spinoff called *Till Death* that aired on BBC rival ITV in 1981 and then a sequel called *In Sickness and in Health*, which ran on the BBC from 1985 until 1992.

Comparably to *All in the Family* in the United States throughout the 1970s, a key part of the show's appeal was that it tapped in to the general public perception of Great Britain's widening generation gap in the 1960s, exploring the new sexual and social mores of the era. At the same time, it realistically addressed racial and political issues that had become increasingly prevalent in British society, with Alf Garnett representing the England old guard and referring to wife Elise as a "silly old moo" (a substitute for the word "cow"), which became a popular catchphrase on the show, just as Archie's "stifle," "dingbat," and "meathead" did on *All in the Family*.

As Speight told an interviewer in 1995: "I didn't invent Alf. He was created by society. I just guessed on him. I observed him, and unfortunately the world is full of Alf Garnetts. You can't encourage racists to be any worse than they are. And the fact that you raise these points of view and make fun of them makes people inclined to think about them. If you never mention them, they just go on."[8]

To a certain extent, of course, this was also true of *All in the Family*, although unlike Archie who genuinely loved Edith, Alf and Elise's marriage was far more dysfunctional. For instance, while Edith rarely reacted when Archie called her "dingbat" or shared his prejudices, Elise often called Alf a "pig" whenever he insulted her and held many of the same racist views.

∼

During the summer of 1968, Norman began outlining the storyline and characters for the show's pilot, at first calling it *Justice for All*. He next enlisted Sam Cohn to represent the project, the powerful and eccentric New York talent agent known as much for his hard-nosed negotiating skills as he was for his slovenly grooming habits and nervous tic of absent-mindedly chewing on paper napkins. Between early August and late September, Cohn, who would go on to become one of the founding partners of International Creative Management in 1974, acquired the American rights from Beryl Vertue, the British agent for *Till Death Us Do Part*.

Acting on his indefatigable instincts and figuring he had nothing to lose, Cohn's first inclination was to pitch the project to ABC—then the perennially third-ranked network as it would remain until the mid-1970s—which already had its eye on *Till Death* and immediately commissioned a pilot. As Leonard Goldberg, ABC's head of programming at the time, recalled: "I had always felt that at ABC you had to do something *different* to attract audiences. . . . So when the idea was presented, and then I read the script and committed to the pilot, I thought, 'This is a very daring show.' But if you're ABC, you can't just play it safe. You play it safe, you lose. So, we had to try it—it excited me."[9]

"ABC was the third network. CBS and NBC were the twin Rocks of Gibraltar—and for Len and I, the challenge was fun," added Goldberg's second in command Martin Starger.

> We were able to take chances 'cause we had nothing to lose, much like Fox Broadcasting later. In this era, just to give you the context of time, I had two assistants, one after another. Barry Diller was my executive assistant. He was Len's—and when Len left, he became *my* assistant. Some time later, when I put him in charge of movies for television, Michael Eisner became my assistant. We had some pretty good people in a very small department. It was electric. We were all young, we could try anything.
>
> We needed comedies. *Bewitched* was one. We had a couple, but a weakness at ABC was half-hour comedies.
>
> Norman Lear—who was not the Norman Lear we think of today—had this show he wanted to do. And it was exciting. It was different. I said to myself, "Great idea. Terrific talent. An urban half-hour comedy." We would've given anything to have Jackie Gleason in *The Honeymooners*, but CBS had that. So, we did the first pilot.[10]

Unfortunately, getting the show on the air wasn't the slam dunk Norman had hoped for. Neither was casting for the lead role of Archie Bunker, whose last name was still Justice after Mickey Rooney, the only actor Norman had in mind, flatly turned him down. The role, of course, went to Carroll O'Connor, who went on to earn eight Emmy Awards and still consistently ranks among the greatest television characters of all time in countless polls.

During this period when Norman was casting for the ABC pilot, the burly Bronx-born O'Connor, then in his mid-forties, was already a semi-well-known character actor who had appeared on scores of television shows throughout the 1950s and 1960s, including *The United States Steel Hour*, *Armstrong Circle Theatre*, *Bonanza*, *The Fugitive*, *The Man from U.N.C.L.E.*, *The Defenders*, *Dr. Kildare*, *The Outer Limits*, *Mission Impossible*, *Gunsmoke*, and *That Girl*. He had also been an early contender for the roles of Dr. Smith on *Lost in Space* and the Skipper on *Gilligan's Island*, along with appearances in such films as *Lonely Are the Brave*, *Cleopatra*, *In Harm's Way*, and *What Did You Do in the War, Daddy?*, which is where Norman had first seen him.

And like Norman did after high school, O'Connor briefly attended college before voluntarily dropping out when the United States entered World War II. However, when it came to how he first read for the role that would make him a star, O'Connor's account is starkly different from Norman's. According to what Norman said in his memoir, it was through casting agent Marion Dougherty and another woman who worked at Tandem Productions named Marian Rees:

> The actors Marion Dougherty brought in for me to read had all seen the script and had a chance to think about the role. When Carroll came to audition, he entered as the cultured, New York– and Dublin-trained actor he was. In that mode, we discussed the script and the role of Archie quite thoroughly, and I couldn't be sure what he really thought of it. When he turned to the script to read, however, his voice, his eyes, and the attitude of his body shifted, he opened his mouth, and out poured Archie Bunker.

Of their first meeting, O'Connor would describe Norman as "very nice" and "very cordial,"[11] although the lesser-known story is how O'Connor's initial involvement in the show came about. According to what he told the Television Academy Foundation in 1998 and wrote in his autobiography *I Think I'm Outta Here: A Memoir of All My Families*, which was published that same year by Simon & Schuster, it began with Howard Adelman, an independent producer who had been involved early on in the deal to bring *Till Death Us Do Part* to the United States. "He was talking to ABC and someone from ABC told him to sign me to play that part," O'Connor said in the Television Academy Foundation interview. "And he did to make a long story short. He and I made a deal, and then one day he called me up and said ABC wanted him to join forces with the Yorkin and Lear production team and did I mind. I said, 'I don't mind, Howard, as long as my deal with you goes onto these guys.' Nobody knew the kind of hit it was going to become and so I didn't care if I did it or not. That's what happened and Norman Lear became associated with the show shortly thereafter."[12]

In his memoir, O'Connor also recalled reading about *Till Death* in *The Saturday Review* shortly before he was asked to audition. "Not two weeks after reading an item about the British show, I got a call from my agent Jack Gilardi, who said that someone wanted to talk to me about doing the same show here, an American version."

I could hardly believe it: the ABC network was interested in doing this mad thing and had agreed to work with a smart young fellow who had secured the American rights to it. ABC had told him to sign me to play the lead. I said, "Jack, I'll talk to him. The thing is sure a disaster, but the explosion will get us a lot of attention." A pleasant young man with an eastern college look to him, Howard Edelman, came out to Malibu Beach where [wife] Nancy and I and [son] Hugh were staying in the summer of 1968, and I made a deal with him, script unseen. We began talking about where the principal character came from, and agreed on New York, though someone had suggested Texas to Howard: we talked about casting, and Howard began seeing pairs of kids for the parts of the daughter and son-in-law, and some actresses' names to consider for the part of the wife but didn't suggest that I meet anybody.[13]

In the end, Norman would ultimately and irrefutably be the one to acquire the American rights and create the character of Archie Bunker. Yet even so—and even though neither he nor Yorkin ever publicly admitted or denied it—Adelman's early involvement is also indisputable, a fact further underscored both by the Internet Movie Database, which lists him as a producer for the original *Justice for All* pilot, as well as what O'Connor said in his memoir along similar lines of his remarks in the Television Academy Foundation interview.

"Howard told me one day that ABC wanted him to associate himself with Bud Yorkin and Norman Lear, a team experienced in producing TV comedy specials," O'Connor wrote. "He asked me how I felt about this, and I said I felt alright provided my deal with him went unchanged in any way, and that he remained prominent as the producer in control of the material. His tenure was important to me; he had agreed with me from the start that the leading character in this play, this TV series, was the archetypical American wage-earning guy. Howard, being Jewish and educated, had observed the character only at a distance. He saw that I possessed a singular insight into the motives and behavior of the character, and he was happy to share control of the material with me. He assured me that none of our agreements would change."[14]

But there was also apparently already trouble on the horizon, because at some point Adelman parted company with Norman and Yorkin for reasons neither of them ever revealed publicly. Not known either is just how Adelman's association with Norman and the project first came about. However, almost two years to the exact date of *All in the Family*'s eventual premiere on CBS, Adelman filed a lawsuit in Manhattan Federal Court against Tandem

Productions for $6.5 million on January 11, 1973. It claimed, among other things, that Adelman had been the one who first told Norman about *Till Death Us Do Part*, that bringing the show to the United States and its concept and characters were his idea, and that he would be a joint owner if the show was picked up as a regular series.

Norman vehemently denied all of Adelman's charges except for one: in September 1967, the two had indeed collaborated on another prospective daytime series called *The Bickersons*, which never sold. Nonetheless, the case was later settled out of court for an undisclosed sum. Producers run the risk of being sued all the time even though ideas, facts, and concepts aren't protected by copyright law, and while no one else ever questioned that Norman had legitimately acquired the rights and conceived what *All in the Family* became, he likely decided to settle anyway to avoid any negative publicity.

Carroll O'Connor would, of course, still play Archie—and in an early sign of his many creative battles with Norman that were to come—he immediately took issue with the pilot script, which he called "terrible"[15] and rewrote in pencil.

Recalled Norman: "He had rewritten the entire first act! That was the first of endless confrontations. That was something that went on for all the years."[16] But then luckily, hiring leading lady Jean Stapleton to play Edith (whom Norman had originally called Agnes and cast first) would prove far easier.

Though Stapleton also wasn't a household name, like O'Connor she already had a substantial résumé at the time of her audition. Born in Manhattan in 1923, she began her career in summer stock before making her New York debut in the off-Broadway play *American Gothic* followed by roles on Broadway in such hit musicals as *Funny Girl*, *Juno*, *Damn Yankees*, and *Bells Are Ringing*, reprising her parts in the film versions of the latter two.

She also worked steadily on television throughout the 1950s and 1960s with minor roles on such dramas and comedies as *Robert Montgomery Presents*, *Route 66*, *The Philco-Goodyear Television Playhouse*, *Dr. Kildare*, *Car 54 Where Are You?*, *The Patty Duke Show*, *Dennis the Menace*, and *My Three Sons* in addition to appearing alongside O'Connor in a 1962 episode of the E. G. Marshall courtroom drama *The Defenders*, and as a pitchwoman for Ivory soap and Gleem toothpaste. "My agent called me to come up and see Norman Lear about this part in a series. . . . Norman said that he had seen me in *Damn Yankees*, and that's how I came to his attention. And so I read," Stapleton recalled.

And I was just amazed by its quality. Really good script. A comedy based in character and situation and so forth. And I thought to myself, "Wow, this on TV, how wonderful." Even then I thought that. And I read for him, and then I went back to Pennsylvania. Then I think I was called up again. . . . Now I don't know their names, but I know that he saw every character actress in town for this part. He read everybody. And that's how I got the part.

[Edith] just had a zinger, about one line a page, that just broke his hot air. Every time it was a laugh. And so I think I said it in quite a wry and wise manner, knowingly, you know, a zinger. Bursts his bubble. And that's the way I played the first—the pilots and the first—which became the first show, because I had nothing else to base it on. You don't know what comes later. You don't know much about these parts.[17]

For Mike (who was originally called Richard) and Gloria, Norman initially cast the much younger, lesser-known actors Tim McIntire and Kelly Jean Peters, who, respectively, went on to appear in such films and TV series as *Stand by Your Man*, *The Gumball Rally*, *Brubaker*, *Quincy*, *Newhart*, *Cagney & Lacey*, *Growing Pains*, and *L.A. Law*. To write the theme song "Those Were the Days," he turned to his old pals Charles Strouse and Lee Adams, the Broadway lyricist and composer team already renowned for such hit musicals as *Bye Bye Birdie* and *Golden Boy* who had written the film score for *The Night They Raided Minsky's* and would later go on to even greater acclaim for the musicals *Applause* and *Annie*.

ABC taped the first pilot in front of a live audience in New York in late September 1968 using what would become *All in the Family*'s premiere episode, "Meet the Bunkers." Available today on YouTube, both the script and the original opening sequence are nearly identical, minus Archie and Edith seated at the piano. First, we see an aerial view of the Manhattan skyline, then Queens, and then the cluster of two-family rowhouses before the camera pans back into their home with a shot of a welcome mat with "Justice" across it at the front door.

Though the set used in the initial pilot was entirely different from the actual show, the theme song was mostly the same, except for a few lyric changes and Edith's voice, which is even more shrill. As for the debut performances of O'Connor and Stapleton as Archie and Edith, they were spot-on and revealed instant chemistry, although ABC got nervous and put the kibosh on it immediately.

Disappointed but undeterred, Norman would have been all too happy to take the project elsewhere. However, the property was still under contract with ABC for another year, which meant that the network had the right to exercise its option to order a second pilot, as it did that following February with directives to tone Archie down.

While he wasn't willing to do so, Norman did agree that the chemistry hadn't been right between O'Connor, Stapleton, and the two actors who played Gloria and Richard (soon changed to Dickie), so they were recast. For Gloria, he chose Brooklyn-born actor Candice Azzara whom he'd first seen in the 1968 Broadway play *Lovers and Other Strangers* and with whom he'd struck up a conversation afterward at the cast party.

The director was actor Charles Grodin who made the introduction. "It was at my friend's apartment on West Eleventh Street where I used to live, and I made the lasagna," Azzara recalled. "Chuck Grodin came up to me and said, 'This is Norman Lear, and he likes your acting.'"

> And then suddenly, I got a call to fly out to California to do this pilot. I remember how much I loved the seriousness of the comedy, and I remember Jean and I just sitting down quietly and going over our lines. The only trouble . . . I remember having trouble kissing the guy. I get very embarrassed kissing and Norman Lear said, "You just kiss him like *this*," and he kissed me.[18]

The new person Norman hired to play Dickie was Chip Oliver, a former linebacker for the Oakland Raiders who'd left the team after only one season to join the One World Family Commune in San Francisco before trying his hand at acting.

Codirecting with Yorkin—and using the same script and set, with Archie and Edith now seated at the upright piano singing "Those Were the Days, which became the show's new title—the second pilot was again filmed in front of a live audience, this time at ABC's Prospect Avenue Studios in Los Angeles. As they had before (and in an ominous sign of what was to come), the network added the warning line: "For Mature Audiences Only" underneath the title during the opening sequence.

And then they pulled the plug again.

The problem this time was the timing, which couldn't have been worse. During the same month Norman filmed the second pilot, the network suddenly found itself in hot water after the disastrous single episode of an overly hyped new sketch comedy series called *Turn-On* that had already been turned down by CBS and NBC.

Created by *Laugh-In* producers Ed Friendly and George Schlatter and sponsored by the pharmaceutical manufacturing giant Bristol-Meyers, the

On a Mission

show had been picked up by ABC for a projected thirteen-week run, premiering at 8:30 p.m. on Wednesday, February 5, 1969, and preempting the hit prime-time soap opera *Peyton Place*. With the same producers at the helm and Albert Brooks among its writing staff, it had been highly touted as the second coming of *Laugh-In* and featured comedian Tim Conway as guest host of the inaugural show.

A central part of *Turn-On*'s premise—and what ABC was banking on—was that the star was a mock-up computer in what Digby Wolfe, one of the program's other producers, described as a "visual, comedic, sensory assault involving . . . animation, videotape, stop-action film, electronic distortion, computer graphics—even people."[19]

What it wound up being, however, was a strained and sophomoric attempt at cheap laughs, which was so laced with sexual inuendo and double entendres that ABC canceled it before the first episode ended, never airing it on the West Coast and deciding not to move forward with Norman's second pilot.

Though *Those Were the Days* was effectively dead, helping to cushion the blow shortly before the second pilot was shot was also the news that Norman and Yorkin had been offered a three-picture deal by United Artists on the heels of UA honcho Arthur Krim having seen a rough cut of Norman's most recent film *Cold Turkey*—a satire about quitting smoking written and directed by Norman, starring Dick Van Dyke and a Who's Who of comedic actors, including Bob Newhart, Tom Poston, Bob and Ray, Pippa Scott, Jean Stapleton, Everett Horton, and Vincent Gardenia. Once again in due time, was the possibility of doing a movie version of *Those Were the Days*.

Only, instead, the project wound up at CBS—and this time Norman was in the catbird's seat.

CHAPTER 13

Rube Tube Awakening

On Wednesday, January 8, 1964, television scored what would become the most-watched half-hour broadcast in the entire history of the medium. That night, at 9 p.m. Eastern Time, sixty-five million viewers were tuned into "The Giant Jackrabbit" episode of the long-running CBS sitcom *The Beverly Hillbillies*.

The inane plot was also one for the record books: in need of food because of the poor hunting conditions in Beverly Hills, the Clampetts call a local catering service, which refuses to take the order. Meanwhile, their banker Mr. Drysdale, has been given a kangaroo as a joke, which gets loose and wanders into the Clampetts's backyard, whereupon Granny sees it and thinks it's a giant jackrabbit.

This episode is notable for more than just the silly storyline and enormous ratings it scored. It followed what turned out to be President Lyndon B. Johnson's first State of the Union address to the nation after John F. Kennedy's assassination the previous November.

However, the fact that it aired when it did wasn't surprising, especially given the wave of escapist programs that permeated American television at the time. Throughout the 1960s (and with the rare exception of the evening news), the three networks all but turned a blind eye to the simultaneous realities of the decade: the nightly carnage in Vietnam, the antiwar and civil rights movements, the assassinations of three of the nation's most prominent political leaders, the growing drug culture, and the emerging feminist and sexual revolutions.

At the time "The Giant Jackrabbit" episode first aired, *The Beverly Hillbillies* was already in its second season and had been a hit right out of the box.

It would also make history again the following week when the next episode, "The Girl from Home," became number four on the most-watched list of television programs of the decade.

Meanwhile, less than a year before the *Hillbillies* premiere, newly installed Federal Communications chairman Newton Minnow made his famous speech before members of the National Association of Broadcasters in Washington in which he declared television a "vast wasteland" and urged executives to clean up their act by providing programs that were "in the public interest."

While the timing of the speech was certainly propitious, Minnow's message nevertheless fell mostly on deaf ears as the "wasteland" he was referring to grew even vaster in the immediate years afterward. And CBS became the unabashed leader of the pack, with James T. Aubrey—the network's colorful and controversial chief of programming who would kill Norman's very first sitcom attempt *Band of Gold* in its cradle—as the chief purveyor. As one former colleague summed up Aubrey's style in a memo that was accidentally leaked to a congressional committee in the mid-1960s, "His formula for success was simple—and simpleminded: broads, bosoms and fun."[1]

Early on in Aubrey's tenure, one of CBS's biggest hits was *The Andy Griffith Show*, which premiered in October 1960 and would remain a top-ten hit throughout its entire eight-season run. Seeking to capitalize on *Griffith*'s enormously successful premise about a small-town sheriff and its citizens in the fictitious sleepy southern hamlet of Mayberry, North Carolina, Aubrey quickly greenlit a string of less sophisticated, more outlandish rural comedies, including *The Beverly Hillbillies* (1962–1971), *Petticoat Junction* (1963–1971), and *Green Acres* (1965–1971), which were all created and produced by the same person, writer-producer Paul Henning, who began his career as one of the first staff writers for George Burns, penning scripts for both his radio and television programs. Also premiering in 1964 was *Gomer Pyle U.S.M.C.*, which put *The Andy Griffith Show*'s former gas station attendant front and center, wreaking havoc on the Marine Corps and never once acknowledging the Vietnam War that was in full expansion, even though it was a military comedy.

To be sure (and with the exception of *Andy Griffith*), most critics and CBS executives, including founder and chairman William Paley, hated these shows. However, they also couldn't ignore the enormous profits and blockbuster ratings as Aubrey became the first network president to control all aspects of programming. As Paley's biographer Sally Bedell Smith noted in her 1990 book *In All His Glory*: "He [Aubrey] jettisoned all live drama and moved entirely to filmed weekly series in two categories: inane comedy and fast-action adventure."

With hits like *The Beverly Hillbillies*, *Petticoat Junction*, *Green Acres* and *My Favorite Martian*, CBS surged ahead of NBC in popularity. In the 1962-63 television season, CBS had eight of the top ten television programs, seven of them comedies. It was CBS's most shameless excursion down the low road.

Except as a rubber stamp, Paley had little part in deciding what programs appeared on CBS's airwaves. He professed dismay at some of Aubrey's choices (although he did nothing to stand in the way) and was apparently incredulous in 1962 when Aubrey and his executives outlined a show about a suddenly oil-rich family from the Ozarks that moves into a mansion in Beverly Hills. "What the hell *is* this?" Paley whispered to [network president Frank] Stanton, who reassured him that it was probably just a "one-joke-show." Paley "genuinely disliked *The Beverly Hillbillies*," Aubrey recalled. "But he put it on the schedule anyway."[2]

CBS was hardly alone. Throughout the decade on all three networks, sprinkled around and among the *Hillbillies* was a seemingly endless spectacle of peculiar and outlandishly unbelievable characters on such half-hour comedies as *Bewitched*, *I Dream of Jeannie*, *My Mother the Car*, *Mister Ed*, *The Flying Nun*, *Gilligan's Island*, *The Addams Family*, *Hogan's Heroes*, and many others.

Sandwiched between were scores of other moralistic family sitcoms, variety shows, and Westerns, many of which were leftovers from the 1950s. Yet nearly all of them (some deservedly so) achieved "classic" status and remain among the most beloved programs of all time, also spawning generations of new fans well into the twenty-first century thanks to cable, video, DVDs, and more recently, streaming services, though virtually none of them tackled any groundbreaking themes.

ABC, then the weakest of the three networks, was the first to make any efforts to lure younger and more urban audiences with programs like the private detective drama *77 Sunset Strip* and *That Girl* starring Marlo Thomas, although neither show made any direct attempts to tackle any of the social changes unfolding in real life. The first formidable effort to do so occurred in 1968 with *The Mod Squad*, producer Aaron Spelling's mixed-race drama—"One black, one white, one blonde," as the show's advertising campaign described it—about three disenfranchised young hippies working as undercover vice cops in Los Angeles.

NBC tentatively followed suit that same year with *Julia*, starring Diahann Carroll in TV's first prime-time sitcom that cast an African American woman in a leading role who was also a professional, with Carroll portraying a nurse who works for a white doctor, although the subject of race never came up. NBC also scored another major coup in 1968 with *Rowan & Martin's Laugh-In*, the irreverently fast-paced sketch-comedy series that helped elect Richard Nixon president and set the stage for *Saturday Night Live* even though *Laugh-In*'s humor was essentially toothless.

Again in 1969 also, ABC would take another baby step with *Room 222*, a dramedy by producer James L. Brooks, who went on to create *The Mary Tyler Moore Show*, *Taxi*, and *The Simpsons*, about the struggles of young students and teachers at an integrated Los Angeles high school. CBS's first attempt toward relevance, meanwhile, was with *The Smothers Brothers Comedy Hour*, premiering in February 1967 and starring sibling comedy duo Tom and Dick Smothers. The Brothers had first gained a following in the early 1960s with their popular nightclub act and a series of albums that combined stand-up and folk music parodies. In 1965, this led to their first association with CBS in a short-lived sitcom called *The Smothers Brothers Show*, which lasted for one season. Their new CBS show was the pet project of Mike Dann, the longtime vice president of programming who stepped into the president's chair after James Aubrey was fired in 1965.

However, Dann's quest to bring the Smothers Brothers to television wasn't because of any desire to break down social barriers. For Dann—whom the *New York Times* described as "one of the most powerful programmers in network television in the 1950s and 1960s [who] proved an astute judge of audience appeal, a master of scheduling and a shrewd marketer"[3]—it was to take direct aim at *Bonanza*, NBC's powerhouse Western series that had dominated the 9 p.m. Sunday-night time slot for over a decade.

Dann's instincts proved correct as *The Smothers Brothers Comedy Hour* became an instant hit, edging out *Bonanza* in the ratings, winning multiple Emmys, and attracting a younger audience electrified by its anti-establishment tone, political humor, and musical guests like Pete Seeger, Simon & Garfunkel, the Who, Buffalo Springfield, and Joan Baez. The show also had a stable of irreverent young writers, including Steve Martin, Rob Reiner, Bob Einstein, and Carl Gottlieb, best known for cowriting the screenplay for *Jaws* and its two sequels.

But as its audience grew and Tom Smothers in particular became emboldened to use the show as a liberal bully pulpit on contemporary themes—namely the Vietnam War, the drug culture, and civil rights—it constantly ran afoul of CBS censors. Though *Comedy Hour* also had allies within the network, particularly Mike Dann, some became increasingly nervous about alienating affiliates in the South on top of mounting frustrations over the constant confrontations with Smothers. To remedy the situation as the 1968–1969 season got underway, CBS ordered that they deliver their shows ten days ahead of their scheduled airdates so they could be reviewed by censors.

Predictably, this only fueled the fire as the network cut two lines from a satire of the show's chief competitor *Bonanza*, as well as a full segment set against the backdrop of the mayhem at the 1968 Democratic Convention in Chicago featuring Harry Belafonte singing, "Lord, Don't Stop the Carnival," during the season premiere.

Things then grew even more contentious as the season wore on, most notably concerning a sermon comedian David Steinberg delivered about Moses and the Burning Bush, resulting in a slew of complaints, and prompting CBS to offer affiliates the chance to preview each future episode ahead of time so they could decide whether to air it. Steinberg, however, wasn't banned. Instead, the Smothers Brothers were informed that he could return to the show on the condition that he didn't doing any more sermons, which, of course, Smothers gleefully asked him to do—this time delivering a biblical parody of "Jonah and the Whale" that never aired.

The final straw came in April 1969. After the Smothers turned in one of the episodes past the due date stipulated in their contract, CBS abruptly canceled the show three months after Richard Nixon became president, with many suspecting that the move was politically motivated, although a dip in the ratings didn't help matters. Wielding the proverbial ax was newly installed CBS president Robert D. Wood, who had assumed the network presidency less than two months before and who, ironically, along with Mike Dann who would eventually resign, was among *All in the Family*'s earliest allies.

However, the Smothers Brothers not only won two Emmys for Outstanding Variety Series and Outstanding Writing Achievement, but they also garnered significant support from the press, including a cover story in *Look* magazine and an editorial in the *New York Times*, later winning a breach-of-contract lawsuit against CBS. In the meantime, the network wasted no time, almost immediately replacing the Smothers Brothers with another rural comedy: *Hee Haw*, which premiered in *Comedy Hour*'s old time slot on June 15, 1969.

But the handwriting was on the wall. With CBS increasingly becoming branded the "Hillbilly Network" and the "Country Broadcasting System," the first cracks in its façade began to unfurl at the end of the 1969 season when NBC beat CBS out by a third of a point in the ratings for the first time and both NBC and ABC started to successfully lure larger advertisers with the promise of younger, more affluent demographics. As Cecil Smith, the celebrated television critic of the *Los Angeles Times*, noted, "How many farmers CBS had didn't matter unless you sold tractors."[4]

Something else was also indisputable. For the first time in its history, CBS was on the ropes, and while newly minted president Robert D. Wood hadn't been elevated to the top post with an agenda to transform the network, he immediately jumped into the fray. Originally from Boise, Idaho, Wood had started his broadcasting career in ad sales during the late 1940s, first for CBS's radio affiliate, KNX, and then its television affiliate, KNXT. Rapidly rising through ranks, where he and KNXT endorsed Ronald Reagan in his successful bid for California governor against Democrat incumbent Pat Brown in 1966, shortly afterward CBS plucked Wood to become executive vice president of CBS's Television Stations division, promoting him to president in 1967 and then again to president of the CBS Television Network on February 14, 1969, Valentine's Day.

All too aware that CBS's aging prime-time schedule was on the wane in major cities like New York, L.A., and Chicago, his first order of business, as he put it, was "how to get the wrinkles out of our network without eroding our popularity."[5] But though this was his goal, Wood also knew that many of these shows remained highly popular, and so he instituted a plan, later known as the "rural purge," in which CBS would gradually begin phasing out *The Beverly Hillbillies*, *Petticoat Junction*, *Green Acres*, *Gomer Pyle U.S.M.C.*, and *The Andy Griffith Show* spinoff *Mayberry R.F.D.* over the next two years.

Also on the chopping block and eventually canceled were such long-running variety programs as *The Ed Sullivan Show*, *The Jackie Gleason Show*, and *The Red Skelton Hour*, as well as *Lassie*, as NBC and ABC quickly followed suit. In the fall of 1970, as all three networks replaced them with a slew of new shows aimed at younger audiences on their schedules. Debuting on CBS alone was *Storefront Lawyers* about a high-power Los Angeles attorney giving up his job to start an inner-city community legal services firm; *The Interns*, starring Broderick Crawford; and Andy Griffith returning to television as the principal of an exclusive California private school in *The Headmaster*. Though each of these programs were spectacular flops, a fourth one—*The Mary Tyler Moore Show* about a single working woman from Minneapolis premiering that September—wasn't.

It was also the first major win for Fred Silverman, the newly installed vice president of programming whose talent for picking hits earned him the nickname "The Man with the Golden Gut" as the only television executive to head programming for all three networks.

Another series that Silverman and Wood were contemplating around this time was *All in the Family*—still under the moniker *Those Were the Days*—which first landed on the CBS antenna in late 1968, when another CBS executive named Marc Golden who was a former CIA agent and Mike Dann's right-hand man saw an episode of *Till Death Us Do Part*. According to author Sally Bedell Smith's 1981 book, *Up the Tube: Prime-Time TV in the Silverman Years*, "Golden carried home an episode about a contentious Christmas dinner at the Garnetts and showed it to his colleagues in New York. They termed it brilliant. Programming vice president Irwin Segelstein suggested that an American version with CBS star Jackie Gleason might work well. Dann was intrigued enough to authorize CBS to buy the rights to the British show, [but] the CBS executives lost out to a balding, slightly built comedy writer and film director named Norman Lear."[6]

In early 1970, meanwhile, Sam Cohn, who was still Norman's agent, pitched the second ABC pilot to Dann and Segelstein, whose reaction was even more favorable than before, although they were still unwilling to commit. Several months later, however, that all changed when Bud Yorkin who was at CBS meeting with Wood about another Tandem project mentioned the second pilot.

That following day, as Dann—who would soon depart CBS for a job with PBS's Children's Television Workshop—watched a videotape of the show in his office and was laughing so hard that Silverman could hear him all the way down the hall. After poking his head in to see what all the uproar was about, they replayed the tape, and, as Yorkin later recalled, "Fred Silverman sits down, watches it, and says, 'I've got to have this. This thing is going on CBS.'"[7]

Watching it next was Robert Wood who also laughed uproariously. Immediately, he ordered thirteen first-run episodes with a guarantee for thirteen repeats.

CHAPTER 14

On the Air

Bob Wood's and Fred Silverman's support and a thirteen-week commitment notwithstanding, the yet-to-be-titled *All in the Family* still had significant hurdles to overcome. One of them was CBS founder chairman Bill Paley, who had a particularly strong contempt for Archie and called the show "vulgar," even though he supported the decision to air it.

In the meantime, many of those closest to Norman, including Frances, thought it was too big a gamble for him to take. Norman also had some misgivings the more he thought about it. When he received the news from CBS that the show had been picked up in the spring of 1970, he was just about to sign the three-picture deal with United Artists, realizing that as much as he wanted to do *AITF*, the film deal was a much surer thing. "He [CBS president Robert Wood] wanted to take a chance, but he fought me tooth and nail," recalled Norman, noting also that most of the network's uncertainty was a fear of the unknown. "That's all they worried about. It's as simple as 'We don't know if this works. We know the *Hillbillies* and *Petticoat Junction*, we know that works. We don't know if *this* works."[1]

That summer, as he weighed the pros and cons of both, Norman traveled to Des Moines, Iowa, to begin production for his anti-smoking satire film *Cold Turkey*, for which he received an Oscar nod for Best Screenplay that following year. In Iowa making the film with Norman that summer also was Jean Stapleton, who played Mrs. Wappler, one of the residents in the fictional town of Eagle Rock, where the movie took place. "We were in Iowa shooting the film and [one day] Norm came along and said, 'It looks like we've been picked up,'" she recalled. "And then he said, 'Don't celebrate until you're in the studio making it.'"[2]

Sometime afterward, Norman called Carroll O'Connor, then living in Italy, to let him know also. However, he was even more tepid in his enthusiasm than Norman had been with Stapleton. In fact, he was so dubious about its prospects that before returning to the United States, O'Connor made Norman agree to pay for first-class round-trip airline tickets for him and his family to Rome and held on to his apartment there just in case the show got canceled.

When production on *Cold Turkey* wrapped at the end of the summer, Norman returned to Los Angeles to begin recasting for the Bunkers' daughter and son-in-law. For the male lead (whose name was now Mike), he chose Rob Reiner, who had known Norman since childhood and regarded him as a second father. Reiner's real father, of course, was the comedy legend Carl Reiner, who was also Norman's longtime close friend.

Born in the Bronx in 1947, the younger Reiner grew up surrounded by fellow comedy icons like Mel Brooks, Imogene Coca, and Sid Caesar while his dad penned sketches for Caesar's iconic NBC variety show. As a young boy, Reiner was painfully shy and introverted, although he eventually grew out of it after the Reiners moved to Beverly Hills in 1958, where Carl went on to create *The Dick Van Dyke Show*.

After attending Beverly Hills High School and dropping out of UCLA, Reiner, along with fellow classmates Richard Dreyfuss and Albert Brooks, formed a comedy troupe called The Session before being plucked to perform in the famed improv troupe The Committee. In the late 1960s, Reiner was also featured in a number of bit sitcom parts, often playing cartoonish hippies on such shows as *The Beverly Hillbillies*, *The Andy Griffith Show*, *Gomer Pyle U.S.M.C.*, *That Girl*, and *The Partridge Family* before getting his big break at age twenty-two when he and his friend and writing partner Steve Martin were hired as junior writers on *The Smothers Brothers Comedy Hour* during its final season.

With left-leaning political views and shoulder-length hair, Reiner had wanted to play Archie's liberal son-in-law in the original pilot, although Norman thought he was too young at the time. But then in early 1970—after seeing his portrayal of a high school teacher who had an affair with one of his students in the short-lived CBS series *The Headmaster*—Norman changed his mind.

Briefly considered for the part of Gloria was Reiner's then-fiancée Penny Marshall, though Norman didn't think their on-screen chemistry was right. In the meantime, he remembered having recently seen a young actor named Sally Struthers dancing on *The Return of Smothers Brothers Comedy Hour*,

ABC's short-lived attempt to revive the sibling comedians' controversial CBS variety show in early 1970—and invited her to read for *All in the Family*.

Despite having laryngitis during the audition, Struthers—who earlier that year had also appeared on comedian Tim Conway's CBS variety show and in the film *Five Easy Pieces* playing Jack Nicholson's lover Betty—won Norman over and soon got the role. To direct, Norman hired sitcom veteran John Rich. Norman had first met Rich on *The Colgate Comedy Hour*, where he was one of the stage managers, and he would go on to become one of Hollywood's most-sought-after directors whose many other TV comedy credits at the time included *Gomer Pyle U.S.M.C.*, *Gilligan's Island*, *The Brady Bunch*, *Our Miss Brooks*, and *I Married Joan*, as well as such dramatic series as *Bonanza*, *The Twilight Zone*, and *Gunsmoke*, and the feature films *Easy Come, Easy Go* and *Roustabout* starring Elvis Presley, *Boeing Boeing*, *The New Interns*, and *Wives and Lovers*.

Rich had also directed nearly fifty episodes of *The Dick Van Dyke Show* (where he won his first Emmy in 1963 and worked closely with Mary Tyler Moore), who actually called him on the exact same day Norman did in 1970, asking him to direct the premiere episode of her eponymous sitcom. But though he declined in favor of the more daring *All in the Family*, Rich still had reservations. "I had my doubts about the network's ability to live up to this commitment, but the attempt intrigued me," he remembered.[3]

However, even before the show premiered, Rich and Norman disagreed over who should play the part of Lionel Jefferson, the Bunker's eventual African American next-door neighbor, who from the very beginning stole many of the scenes for his deft razzing of Archie who never realizes he's being one-upped. Norman had wanted Tony and Drama Desk Award–winning stage actor Cleavon Little, then appearing in the Broadway musical *Purlie*, who would go on to star in Mel Brooks's classic 1974 comedy film *Blazing Saddles* in what became his best-known role as Sheriff Bart. But Rich thought Little was too threatening. Instead, he wanted and managed to persuade Norman to go with Mike Evans, an acting student at Los Angeles City College who had no professional experience but had blown Rich away when he read for the part during an open audition at CBS.

To pen the additional twelve scripts CBS had ordered, meanwhile, Norman enlisted the team of Don Nicholl, Michael "Micky" Ross, and Bernie West. From 1971 until 1974, the three would serve together as the show's head writers, script consultants and story editors before going on to write and produce *The Jeffersons*, *Three's Company*, and its two spin-offs, *The Roper's* and *Three's a Crowd*.

After nearly three years of starts and stops, *All in the Family* was finally added to CBS's prime-time lineup in the fall of 1970. Set to premiere as a mid-season replacement that January, the show took up residence in Studio Thirty-One inside CBS's mammoth Television City production facility located in L.A.'s Fairfax District. However, even with the show now a done deal with an official time slot on the schedule, Norman still faced considerable resistance from the network about *AITF*'s coarse language. They also wanted to air the more innocuous second episode first, although he held firm after having already shot the pilot three times. Additionally, from day one, Norman had always believed that the key to making the show work—and the only way that it could—was to dive in headfirst, with all of Archie's animosity and bigotry (and the other cast members reacting to it) on full display. "It was deliberately based on the slightest of stories, which gave me the opportunity to present 360 degrees of everyone, but especially Archie—his attitudes on race, religion, politics, sex and family, holding nothing back," said Norman. "Metaphorically, you can't get any wetter than wet, I told Mr. Wood, so we all needed to jump in the pool and get soaking wet together the first time out."[4]

And yet while he prevailed, the fact that the show ever got on the air at all was nothing short of miraculous. Even watching it today more than half a century later is still shocking. In the now-familiar storyline, Mike and Gloria are planning a surprise Sunday brunch to celebrate Archie and Edith's twenty-second wedding anniversary while they're at church. In the opening scene, they arrive home early to find an amorous Mike kissing Gloria, lifting her in his arms and preparing to carry her upstairs to their bedroom as an incensed Archie walks in on them and says, "Eleven ten on a Sunday morning."

With this, they were off to the races as Archie went ballistic—first railing at Mike about the promiscuity of today's youth and then almost in the same breath—raging about "your spics and your spades," "black beauties" and "Hebes," also telling Edith to "stifle" and calling her a "dingbat." He then proceeded to put Mike down as a "dumb pollack," also calling him "Meathead" and proclaiming him to be the "laziest white man I have ever seen," both of which were also insults Herman used to hurl at Norman.

Meanwhile, Mike—who, as the series begins, is a college student majoring in sociology depicted as representing the ideals of the 1960s counterculture minus drug use and "free love"—is no less worked up into a frenzy than Archie, telling him that he and Gloria see no evidence of God and blaming America's crime problem on poverty, which, of course, enrages Archie even more. Rounding things out is Lionel who gets the reactionary Archie's guff by needling him with broad African American stereotypes.

In general, the version of "Meet the Bunkers" that aired as the first episode was essentially the same as the two original pilots. One concession Norman did agree to make was eliminating a scene at the beginning that showed Mike zipping up his fly as he and Gloria walked downstairs after making love.

CBS, meanwhile, found itself in the unenviable position of not being able to sell any advertising as the premiere date grew closer. Even after offering it at cut rates, they still only sold one spot before it went on the air. According to author Sally Bedell Smith: "At first the network had thought of promoting the show in the *I Love Lucy* vein by showing Archie grabbing a coffee pot by the spout instead of a handle. But they decided on a forthright if muted approach instead. The CBS advertisement said, 'You are about to see something entirely new in comedy. Real people.'"[5]

To cover the network's back with the affiliates in the weeks before the show's premiere, Robert Wood also sent a telegram featuring excerpts from a speech he'd delivered the previous spring. It read: "We have to broaden our base. We have to attract new viewers. We're going to operate on the theory that it is better to try something new than not to try it and wonder what would have happened if we had."[6]

All in the Family debuted at 9:30 p.m. Eastern on Tuesday, January 12, 1971, taking over the time slot of another sitcom called *To Rome with Love* about a widowed college professor from Iowa who moves to Italy with his three daughters. The three shows that immediately preceded it that night were *The Beverly Hillbillies*, *Green Acres*, and *Hee Haw*, while a blurb appearing in *TV Guide* that same week alerted viewers of what was to come: "This series will explore American prejudices by looking at those of one middle-class family—if viewers can take the heat. There's plenty of abrasive language and subject matter to keep the cards and letters pouring in."[7]

Out in Hollywood on the night of the premiere, meanwhile, the cast was already dress-rehearsing on the set for the sixth episode, "Gloria Has a Belly Full," still facing the possibility that CBS might chicken out at the eleventh hour and not air the pilot first. With both Norman and John Rich threatening to walk if they reneged, the network still wanted them to eliminate Archie's "Sunday morning" line at the beginning of the episode when he sees Mike and Gloria coming downstairs, fearing that it might offend viewers in middle America.

Not that Norman or Rich would have even considered taking it out. "It's easy to understand their nervousness, but it didn't make us pull any punches in the pilot episode," Rich recalled.[8] Following the five-thirty dress-rehearsal taping in front of a live studio audience, the entire cast and many of the crew gathered in the small control room above the soundstage, keeping an eye on the clock as Norman and Rich continued to fret.

With the three-hour time difference between the two coasts, at the appointed time—9:30 in New York and 6:30 in L.A.—everyone nervously turned their attention to the TV monitors, holding their collective breaths, still not knowing which episode was going to air as the soon-to-be immortal images of Archie and Edith seated at the piano singing the theme song flickered onto the screen for the first time.

But then exactly fifty seconds later, the camera panned into the Bunkers' living room, with Gloria dressed in a miniskirt as Mike opened the door and said the first line. Presaged by an announcer reading an advisory warning, CBS had opted to air the pilot after all. As an added precaution, the network had also hired extra operators to man the switchboards in New York and Los Angeles to handle the anticipated flood of phone calls from irate viewers.

Yet, to everyone's surprise, the tidal wave they were expecting was barely a trickle. That evening, CBS only received a thousand telephone calls in five of the largest markets, with over 60 percent of them applauding the show. And yet still, with only a 28 percent share in the ratings, *All in the Family* had entered America's living rooms with not a bang but a whimper.

CHAPTER 15

The Makings of a Hit

Despite anemic ratings at first, Norman's insistence that from the very beginning *All in the Family* had to get, as he often put it, "all wet at once" would indeed serve both him and the show well throughout the first season and beyond. In this regard—and thus consequently—by marking his territory and shooting the flames higher and higher each week, he not only demonstrated a resolute commitment to producing high-quality shows that continuously pushed the envelope, but also his already considerable clout at CBS.

Although the second episode "Writing the President," in which Archie dresses up in a suit and tie to write a fawning letter of praise to Richard Nixon with the salutation "Dear Mr. President, Your Honor, Sir," isn't as edgy as the first, it is still notable. As the plot unfolds, it is discovered that Archie did so after he found out Mike had written a critical letter to the commander in chief condemning him for his policies. Given who the characters were and when this episode originally aired, there was nothing overly surprising about its theme. Still, what made it significant was the sheer novelty of being the first entertainment program ever to devote an entire half hour to tackling both America's ever-widening generation gap, as well as the country's divisive attitudes toward the president from both sides of the political spectrum as Nixon became one of *AITF*'s biggest adversaries.

Two weeks later, with "Judging Books by Covers" in week four, *All in the Family* took on what was arguably at the very top of the list of its most daring subjects of the entire series, and a first-ever for television: homosexuality. Originally airing on February 5, 1971—less than two years after police raided the Stonewall Inn, a popular gay bar in New York's Greenwich Village, setting off a three-day riot that became the catalyst for the modern-day gay rights movement—the episode was not only the first to acknowledge that homosexuality existed, but it also paved the way for all other gay characters on television, from Jodie Dallas (Billy Crystal) as the first openly gay character as a series regular on the late1970s sitcom *Soap* to Ellen DeGeneres on *Ellen* and *Will & Grace* two decades later.

In what would become typical Norman fashion, the episode demonstrated the absurdity of inherent prejudice against homosexuals through Archie's ignorance as Mike and Gloria's intellectual friend Roger (portrayed by actor Anthony Geary, who would go on to major stardom as one of the most famous soap opera characters in history as Luke Spencer on *General Hospital*) stops by for a visit after a trip to Europe and Archie takes one look at him and automatically assumes he's gay.

Although it turns out Roger is straight, it is later revealed that Steve, Archie's macho former football player drinking buddy from Kelsey's Bar—played by Phil Carey, the actor who is best-known for his role as Texas billionaire Asa Buchanan on the long-running ABC soap *One Life to Live*—is. "I wouldn't let them do what they did unless I punched him in the arm," Carey recalled.

> Of course, I had lines like, "Did you ever see me with a woman?" And the funny part is the guy on *General Hospital* Tony Geary was the guy they all thought was gay. The scene was that the bartender calls Archie's son-in-law Mike over and says, "We don't mind Steve coming in here, but that . . . that's got to stop." Mike says, "What . . . you mean?" [And the bartender says], "Oh yeah, but we accept him." And that's how it all started. Anyway, when it finished, I said, "I'm gonna punch him in the arm," and I give him a shot, walk out and he says, "Nah, it could never be."[1]

In like manner during episode four, *AITF* deftly tackled another topic that was fast becoming a national crisis in 1971: America's blood shortage. At the beginning of the story, Archie is unwilling to donate blood and is ridiculed, all the while raising awareness through satire that there were millions of others out there just like him who refused to donate. Then as Mike and Gloria finally convince him to go to the local neighborhood blood bank with them, the show sparked even further discussion, first on the importance of blood donation as an essential part of modern health care—and then race—as Archie worries that the beneficiary of his vital fluids might be a minority.

Yet even as *AITF* fearlessly kept challenging traditional America week in and week out, ratings did not improve. Unable to crack the top forty TV shows within its first month on the air, by late February, cancellation, despite CBS's thirteen-episode-thirteen-repeats commitment—seemed imminent as many critics denounced the show for promoting bigotry.

Harshest of all was the assessment of *Life* magazine's John Leonard, who in a scathing review accompanied by the headline "Bigotry as a Dirty Joke" called it a "wretched program," asking also, "Why review a wretched program? Well, why vacuum the living room or fix the septic tank? Every once in a while, the reviewer must assume the role of a bottle of Johnson's No-Roach with the spray applicator: let's clean up this culture."[2]

Also bemoaning the show were African American journalist Whitney M. Young Jr. of the *Los Angeles Sentinel* who said "it has to be a new low in taste"[3] and an irate Lucille Ball, outraged about the fact that *All in the Family* was on CBS, where she was still one of its biggest stars. "How awful," she complained to the *Los Angeles Times*'s Cecil Smith after watching the first episode. "How could they put anything like this on the air, particularly at CBS, my station?"[4]

Bill Cosby, who in the early 1970s was one of the nation's most prominent African American entertainers—a revered stand-up comic who had been the first person of color to star in the lead role of a prime-time network TV show in the NBC espionage series *I Spy* for which he won an Emmy, a pitchman for Coke and Jell-O pudding, and a respected family man three decades before being outed and convicted as a sexual predator—also angrily sounded off on the show, saying that, "Some watch the show and love Archie because they think he's right. . . . Names have a tendency to stay. Names like *kike*, *nigger*, and the rest of them never seem to die. Archie says them in his home where in his mind it's safe. I guess what I dislike most about him is he never says what he does is wrong."[5]

On the other hand, there were plenty of fans as well. Among *AITF*'s biggest was *L.A. Times* TV critic Cecil Smith who disagreed with Ball and wrote: "Another thing you have to give *All in the Family*—it's funny. Not gently funny, not sophisticated funny, not intellectually funny, not relevantly funny—but raw, rough, roaring, falling down in the aisles funny."[6]

Variety also hailed it as the "best TV comedy since the original *The Honeymooners*" with the "best casting since Sgt. Bilko's squad" and predicted that it should be the "biggest hit since *Laugh-In*, or the Neilson sample is in need of severe revision."[7] Also abundant in his praise was Cleveland Amory who wrote in *TV Guide* that "*All in the Family* is not just the best-written, best-directed and best-acted show on television, it is the best show on television."[8]

In what was literally a love letter from beginning to end, he added: "It is also a landmark show—a complete breakthrough—one which opens up a whole new world for television and has already made the old world seem so dated that we very much doubt that any new program, from here on in, will ever be quite the same again."[9]

For the normally acerbic Jack Gould of the *New York Times*, it was also a welcome breath of fresh air. Accompanied by the headline: "Can Bigotry Be Laughed Away? It's Worth a Try," he wrote that "Except for *All in the Family* it is difficult to recall another TV attempt to bring the disease of bigotry and prejudicial epithets out in the open with the aim one hopes of applying the test of corrosive recollection and humor."[10]

It was in this manner that the show began eventually picking up steam, even as CBS continued to have doubts and even rebuked Merv Griffin for inviting the cast to appear on his talk show that March. According to his 2003 autobiography *Merv*, the network asked him point-blank: "Why are you putting them on? The show probably won't last the season."[11]

But that all soon changed as whatever remaining reservations CBS may have had were permanently erased. The turning point occurred at that year's Emmy Awards in May when *All in the Family* won for Outstanding New Comedy Series and Jean Stapleton took home the statuette for Outstanding Continued Performance by an Actor in a Leading Role in a Comedy Series, beating out both Marlo Thomas and Mary Tyler Moore.

Emceeing the Emmys that year was *Tonight Show* host Johnny Carson, who, in acknowledgment of the show's central theme, kiddingly said to Norman as he went up to accept the award: "I would like to congratulate Norman Lear. He's a great guy—for a Hebe."[12]

Several days later, the show would get another unexpected boost from the unlikeliest of sources when an incensed Richard Nixon (who eventually put Norman on his infamous "Enemies" list) watched the episode "Judging Books by Covers" in reruns from the White House with chief of staff H. R. Haldeman (and in comments secretly recorded on audiotape that were later released to the public) proclaimed: "Archie is sitting here with his hippie son-in-law, married to the screwball daughter. . . . The son-in-law apparently goes both ways" (and calling Mike's friend Roger, whom Archie thinks is gay) "obviously queer" [because] "he wears an ascot, and so forth." Not surprisingly, however, Nixon was generous in his praise of Archie, calling him a "hard hat," with Haldeman also noting that the show "seeks to downgrade him and make the square hard hat out to be bad."[13]

In a way, Nixon's comments, even though they weren't made public until nearly six months later, may have also indirectly been a catalyst for the turning point as much as the Emmys because immediately after that, *All in the Family*'s fortunes changed on every front. That following week, it catapulted from near obscurity in Nielson's to the top as much of America tuned in for the first time.

Meanwhile, as the show quickly became the most-talked-about program in the country, that summer network president Robert Wood and vice president of programming Fred Silverman began cleaning house as *The Beverly Hillbillies*, *Mayberry R.F.D.*, *Green Acres*, *Hee Haw*, and *The Jim Neighbors Hour* were all canceled in one fell swoop. Also getting the axe were *The Red Skelton Show*, *The Jackie Gleason Show*, and *The Ed Sullivan Show*, which had been CBS mainstays for more than two decades.

If timing is everything in comedy, then *All in the Family*'s time had finally come.

CHAPTER 16

Lightning in a Bottle

With the show gaining more and more momentum in summer reruns, Norman and the network brass suddenly found themselves facing the dilemma of when *All in the Family* should air once the new fall season got underway. Though everyone agreed it needed to be moved from 9:30 p.m. on Tuesdays to a better slot, the man who had ultimate final say—Bill Paley, CBS's stately founder and chairman—remained skittish.

Despite all the post-Emmy buzz, he adamantly insisted that *AITF* not go on before 9:00 any night. At first, the plan was to put it on at 10:30 on Mondays after the long-running sitcom *My Three Sons* starring Fred McMurray, which was in its eleventh and final season. But then another predicament arose when they realized that it would still be competing with ABC's powerhouse *Monday Night Football* and the *Monday Night Movie* on NBC. And so that August, Fred Silverman, the ever-industrious vice president of programming, came up with an alternative to make *All in the Family* the lead-in on Saturday night at eight o'clock followed by *The Mary Tyler Moore Show* at eight thirty.

"A couple of things struck me," he recalled.

They were taping *All in the Family* and these shows were terrific. The second thing is that we [already] had *Mary Tyler Moore* scheduled on Tuesday nights at eight o'clock between *The Beverly Hillbillies* and *Hee Haw*, so that was the schedule and I looked at *Mary Tyler Moore* and said, "This is such a terrific show and we've got it sitting here in the middle of all these shit-kicker shows."

I called [Bob] Wood a couple of weeks before the season was to begin and said, "We've got some resources and we've got to deploy them in a better way. I think *All in the Family* can be a major hit for us, let's get it out of that time period. Put it at the beginning of Saturday. Let's do a simple flip. We'll take *All in the Family* and put it on at eight, and we'll take *My Three Sons* and put it on at ten-thirty Monday. It's the last year anyway." I said, "The second thing you should consider doing is *Mary Tyler Moore* is such a smart show. Let's put it on Saturday night and let Tuesday night be the receptacle for all that crap we weren't able to cancel yet."[1]

Wisely, Wood and eventually Paley listened, putting complete faith in Silverman's programming intuition. As for Silverman himself—aside from being one of the first to green-light both *All in the Family* and *The Mary Tyler Moore Show*—it would be one of his biggest victories at CBS. Not only did *AITF* become the number-one show in the Nielsens for the five years it aired there from 1971 until 1975, along with *MTM* and eventually *M*A*S*H*, *The Bob Newhart Show*, and *The Carol Burnett Show*; it became the anchor for what is still regarded as the greatest lineup in TV history.

Returning to the airwaves on September 25, the season-2 opener was "Gloria Poses in the Nude" in which Mike's famous artist friend Zabo offers to paint Gloria in her birthday suit, much to Archie's and eventually Mike's chagrin, followed by "The Saga of Cousin Oscar," where Archie's ne'er-do-well cousin dies while staying at the Bunkers and Archie is forced to pay for the funeral when none of the other relatives are willing to chip in.

Both episodes were written by Norman with pitch-perfect appearances by Mike Evans—who would later share the cover of *TV Guide* with O'Connor in 1973—again reprising his role as Lionel Jefferson and now living next door with his mother Louise (Isabel Sanford) and Uncle Henry (Mel Stewart)—verbally castigating a completely oblivious Archie. Meanwhile, with most of the country now tuning in each week to catch the latest goings-on of the Bunkers at 704 Hauser Street (usually from Archie's greasy, beer-stained easy chair), CBS censors began giving the show considerably more leeway.

"When you hear about the other shows not being able to say this or that, it's nice to be with a show where we can be as free as we are," observed head writer and story editor Bernie West in 1974. "I'm not just talking about profanity either. It's the topics, the treatments, and the latitude we have to make things as funny and true-to-life as possible."[2]

It was also around this same time that critics almost universally began praising the show. At that same time, schoolteachers started writing to CBS asking for *All in the Family* study guides as a whole new lingo called "Archie Bunkerisms" emerged and the show went further and further out on a limb.

Added during season 2 to its usual bill of fare of race, politics, and bigotry were menopause and impotence. Almost without fail, audiences roared with laughter week in and week out, not only because the way that the Bunkers and Stivics dealt with such highly personal issues was hysterically funny, but because they could all identify with the characters' reactions.

Yet, as commercially popular as it was, the show still wasn't immune from criticism, much of it directed at Norman, and none harsher than a scathing three-page essay published in the Sunday Arts section of the *New York Times* two weeks before the second-season premiere on September 12, 1971, called "As I Listened to Archie Say Hebe . . ." Penning it was Laura Z. Hobson, the liberal feminist author best known for her novels *Gentleman's Agreement* exploring anti-Semitism and *Consenting Adults* about homosexuality. The *Times* piece began with: "I have a most peculiar complaint about the bigotry in the hit TV comedy *All in the Family*. There's not enough of it."[3]

That the shellacking appeared in the *New York Times*, of course, gave it even more gravitas. "Hebe, spic, coon, Polack—these are words that it's central character Archie Bunker is forever using," she continued, "plus endless variations like jungle bunnies, black beauties, the chosen people, yenta, gook, chink, spook and so on. Quite a splashing display of bigotry, but I repeat, nowhere near enough of it."[4]

She then went on to accuse both Norman and CBS of being dishonest for softening the threat of prejudice by not using harsher derogatory terms like "kike" and the N-word, also questioning whether, intentionally or not, they were trying to make bigotry more acceptable, and in doing so, if less-educated viewers would feel superior to Archie's flaws because they didn't know any better.

Hobson—who was said to have initially been inspired to write the essay after Johnny Carson called Norman a "Hebe" as he accepted his Emmy Award that May—apparently decided to publish it in America's newspaper of record when Norman refused to take her phone calls over the summer to express her views—and at which point he also graciously invited her to California to meet with him in person instead, but she declined.

Three weeks after Hobson's manifesto was published, Norman put pen to paper and wrote a rebuttal. Also appearing in the *Times* but on the op-ed pages with the headline ". . . As I Read How Laura Saw Archie," he said: "In answering Laura Z. Hobson's novella attacking *All in the Family*, I'd like to first welcome her back to the fight against prejudice. The world needs every voice that speaks out of this area, and we are proud that we had something to do with the return of Mrs. Hobson's thunder after a twenty-four-year silence." He added: "I am twenty-two years your junior, madam, and meaning you no disrespect, if you have not known lovable bigots in different stripes and attitudes and varying degrees, we are obviously aging in different wine cellars."[5]

After both pieces came out, the *Times* received numerous letters to the editor from readers with a consensus that, in a revealing indication of how passionately most viewers were about the show, was evenly split. With some siding with Hobson and some with Norman, others criticized him for responding to her at all. In the meantime, as *All in the Family*'s ratings continued to climb, rising also was the strain between Norman and O'Connor over the direction of the scripts. "Carroll sat down to every reading worried and unhappy," Norman remembered. "It seemed to make little difference whether his problems with the script turned out to be few or many, small or large. Most of the time we'd hear, 'It just doesn't work.'"[6]

One of the most contentious incidents occurred midway through the second season in an episode called "The Elevator Story," which originally aired on New Year's Day 1972. It involved Archie getting trapped in a stalled elevator with a pregnant Puerto Rican woman who delivers right there; it is regarded as one of O'Connor's finest performances of the entire series. However, after looking at the script during the first table read in mid-December, he almost didn't do the show, insisting that five people in an elevator for an entire half hour would be impossible to shoot.

As usual, he also refused to listen to reason as Norman and John Rich both tried to reassure him that it could be done. Making matters even more complicated was that because of the upcoming holidays, it was the only completed script they had available to shoot. And then, instead of trying to work things out and reach some sort of compromise, O'Connor stormed out of the rehearsal hall, and the rest of the cast was sent home.

Later that same afternoon, at O'Connor's request, an emergency meeting was held in CBS president Bob Wood's office. Along with O'Connor, his agent, and his attorney, in attendance were Norman and his lawyer and Wood, with O'Connor still grumbling and protesting about the script. "Carroll said flat-out that he thought this week's script was repulsive and unplayable and that in no way was he going to do it," Norman recalled.[7]

Then, at some point during the meeting, according to Norman, O'Connor had a complete meltdown and started to cry. At the same time Norman became increasingly aware of the precarious position the entire show was now in and feared that it would collapse if O'Connor was allowed to prevail. Meanwhile, the network had already warned Tandem Productions,

O'Connor and his team, and Norman personally that *All in the Family* would be canceled with further legal action if "The Elevator Story" wasn't ready to air on the scheduled date.

By six o'clock that evening, with CBS's position clear, Norman assured Wood that everything would be fine—and O'Connor got up and left. And as a result, the well-oiled machine that was normally *All in the Family*'s production week was suddenly now in free fall.

The following morning on Tuesday, Stapleton, Reiner, Struthers, and the rest of the supporting cast showed up for rehearsal at Television City without O'Connor. On Wednesday, he was still a no-show as Norman continued to worry, not only about whether CBS would make good on its threat to cancel the show if they didn't complete the episode, but also how they would be able to do it without O'Connor.

And so on it went, until early that evening when, by whatever miraculous means, Norman received word from his attorney that O'Connor would be returning to work the next day. After scheduling a series of makeup rehearsals over the weekend, that Tuesday "The Elevator Story" was taped, and the studio audience's reaction was unbelievable. In the crescendo scene in the elevator when the pregnant woman is about to give birth, the camera pulled in tight to reveal the face of the expectant mother assisted by her husband talking to her in Spanish as she grunts, pushes, and yells until finally the baby comes out, and Archie, as he hears the first cry, turns around and melts at the wonderment of having witnessed the miracle of birth, his facial expression priceless. O'Connor's performance was pure magic, though his friction with Norman only grew worse.

Six weeks after "The Elevator Story," *All in the Family* aired what arguably became the show's singularly most famous episode, if not the most celebrated guest appearance in sitcom history, when singer Sammy Davis Jr. showed up on the Bunkers' doorstep. Davis and Norman had been friends ever since his days writing for Dean Martin and Jerry Lewis on *The Colgate Comedy Hour*, and by the early 1970s, Davis had been one of the most popular figures in American entertainment for decades who had already played himself on countless TV shows.

He was also a fervent fan of *All in the Family*. So much so that whenever he was scheduled to perform on Saturday nights, he would move the start time back thirty minutes so he could catch the latest episode in his dressing room before the concert. Itching to confront Archie himself ever since the series began, Davis actively pursued Norman for an invitation to appear for nearly a year, even remarking to Johnny Carson on *The Tonight Show*, "Imagine a one-eyed colored Jew going head-to-head with Bunker."[8]

But to Davis's great surprise and disappointment, neither Norman nor John Rich were interested even though both Davis and his agent Si Marsh persisted. According to Rich,

> We were pleased to get such wonderful publicity as we struggled to find our audience. But we did not expect to hear from Sammy's agent at the William Morris Office as we did. One day, Lear told me Si Marsh had called [again], wanting to know when we were going to book Sammy on the show. Norman asked me what I thought of the idea. "Not much," I said. We both agreed that it wouldn't work. To have a star of Davis's magnitude show up at the Bunkers' home would be too unbelievable. Marsh was persistent, saying Sammy could play any part we wanted. But Davis was such a distinctive personality, we insisted it was clear he could only appear as himself. Besides, we really wanted to avoid the business of guest-star visits, no matter who they might be, and we informed the agent of our decision.[9]

Still refusing to take no for an answer, Davis and Marsh continued their crusade—with Davis continuing to talk the show up on interviews every chance he got and even announcing he was going to appear—until finally, after months of back-and-forth, Norman and Rich relented. No less determined to be involved, meanwhile, was Norman's old pal Bill Dana, the comedian and comedy writer best known for his alter ego José Jiménez, the bumbling English-mangling bellboy first made famous in a sketch on *The Steve Allen Show*.

Dana, who had also attended Emerson College in Boston and first met Norman at NBC in the 1950s, had been clamoring to write for *All in the Family* ever since the show went on the air. Thus far, however, his efforts had been for naught. "I had heard about the success of *All in the Family*, [which at the time] was the biggest hit in the world and I called Norman Lear who was my oldest and dearest friend in the business and asked if I could pitch an episode," remembered Dana. "He said, 'It's impossible, please come by and say hello, but have zero expectations because we're already over committed and blah, blah, blah.' So I went up there and by luck he said, 'There's one possibility. If you can come up with a way that the real Sammy Davis ends up in the mythical Bunker household, then you can write that script. So, we just spit-balled around and we came up with the idea."[10]

What Dana and Norman came up with was "Sammy's Visit," which aired on February 19, 1972. To summarize the plot: Davis accidentally leaves his briefcase in Archie's cab, and the family and several of the neighbors go berserk when they learn the entertainer is dropping by to pick it up. Having begun laying the groundwork in several earlier episodes so that Davis could be Archie's passenger, Norman and Rich decided Archie would moonlight as a taxi driver for his friend Burt Munson.

As "Sammy's Visit" opened, a normally gruff Archie arrives home with the news that his otherwise-humdrum night driving the cab had one bright spot: picking up a VIP passenger whose identity he makes everyone guess before finally revealing it is Sammy Davis Jr., with Archie telling them also that he had given the singer their address so he could mail them an autographed picture. A few minutes later, Davis calls to say he has left his briefcase in the cab, and Archie tells the family that the megastar is going to stop by on his way to Kennedy Airport to pick it up.

It was under these rather simplistic circumstances that the show then brilliantly zeroed in like a laser beam on the fundamental ignorance of Archie's narrow-mindedness. From the moment Davis rings the Bunkers' doorbell, Archie spews off a series of offensive remarks about the fact that Davis is both African American and Jewish (including the word "colored" and asking him how he "turned Jew"). Archie then blithely complains to him about how Mike and Gloria are always calling him prejudiced. At first Davis is incredulous. But then he looks at Archie, and with a completely straight face, replies: "You prejudiced? Look, if you were prejudiced, Archie, when I came to your house, you would have called me coon or a nigger. But you didn't say that . . . you said colored."

And then: "If you were prejudiced, you'd walk around thinking you were better than anybody else in the world. But I can honestly say, having spent these marvelous moments with you, you ain't better than nobody."[11]

Of course, Archie was so clueless that he took this as the supreme compliment. He also didn't have the slightest idea that his comments and behavior—including telling Davis that he was a "tribute to his race" or offering him a Twinkie because he thought that's what African Americans ate—was the least bit offensive. In Archie's misguided mind, he thought he was making intelligent, normal conversation.

A little bit later in the setup for the scene for which the episode will always be remembered, Archie and Davis veer into the topic of Caucasians and African Americans kissing and hugging on television. Once again, Davis played masterfully right into Archie's hands, telling him that he was required to do it because of a clause in his contract, as Archie, staying ever true to the gullibility of his character, expresses his surprise.

And then came the kiss.

When Munson arrives at the house to deliver the briefcase and asks Davis to pose for a picture, this was the moment the singer had been waiting for: one that no one else but Norman and Rich knew about and the audience could never have anticipated. As the camera clicked on the count of three, Davis proceeded to plant a big wet one on Archie's cheek and wordlessly exited through the Bunkers' front door. Archie goes into a state of shock. Standing motionless, his eyes twitching, mouth wide open, blood draining from his face, the studio audience's reaction off the charts. For a moment it seems like Archie is going to keel over until finally he gathers his composure and says, "What the hell. He said it was in his contract."[12]

Fade out.

Recalled Rich: "On the night we shot the show, the moment when Sammy Davis, Jr. kisses Archie Bunker earned us the biggest, longest laugh I have ever experienced. The audience howled and applauded and kept it up so long we had to shorten the moment for the home audience. Carroll O'Connor's shock take was awesome, as was Sammy's entire performance. Our adventure into a 'one in a million' story had worked superbly. But we vowed never to do it again."[13]

And they never did, even as this episode forever cemented *All in the Family*'s place in the pantheon of popular culture while also flawlessly illustrating the key ingredients that were the very essence of the show.

CHAPTER 17

The Tandem Sitcom Machine
Swings into High Gear

With *All in the Family* already television's singular biggest sensation of the decade by the time of its second-season premiere in the fall of 1971, Norman and Bud Yorkin wasted no time in search of Tandem's next big hit.

Once again, it was Great Britian that brought good tidings.

Their source this time was *Steptoe and Son*, an English sitcom about a feuding father and son who ran a junk business in London's Shepard's Bush section that had been another gigantic smash on the BBC. It was the creation of Ray Galton and Alan Simpson, the prolific British comedy-writing duo, who, after meeting under the unfunniest of circumstances while recovering from tuberculosis in a Surrey, England, sanitorium in 1948, formed a comedy writing partnership that lasted over fifty years.

While *Happy Go Lucky*—the BBC radio program starring British comedian Derek Roy where they had gotten their big break—was a colossal flop, as a writing team they quickly became the equivalent of what Norman and Ed Simmons had been on American television's earliest variety shows throughout the 1950s. It was during this same period, in fact, beginning in 1954 that they wrote for *Hancock's Half Hour*, the sitcom still regarded as one of the best in British history. Also simulcast on radio where it started throughout much of its seven-season run, it starred British comedian Tony Hancock and South African actor and comedian Sid James as his second banana.

But then, they endured a highly public split from Hancock in 1961, as did Norman and Simmons quitting *The Colgate Comedy Hour* in 1953 because of Jerry Lewis's megalomaniacal personality, although in Galton and Simpson's case the separation was the result of Hancock's alcohol-infused paranoia of becoming a one-trick-pony sitcom star, from which his career never recovered, and he committed suicide seven years later.

Soon after the rift, however, they were hired on the long-running BBC anthology series *Comedy Playhouse* where they wrote ten one-off half-hour plays, including *The Offer*, from which *Steptoe and Son* emerged in two incarnations: first in black and white from 1962 until 1965, and again in color from 1970 until 1974.

It costarred Wilfred Brambell, the British actor best known to American audiences for his turn in the 1964 Beatles film *A Hard Day's Night*, and Harry H. Corbett. Together, they played Albert and Harold Steptoe, a widowed, semi-illiterate junk dealer (known as the "rag-and-bone" trade in England) who runs roughshod over his son, who works with him and often calls him a "dirty old man," which became the series catchphrase. While Harold aspires to a better life, he can never bring himself to leave his father even though they constantly bicker.

Set in mid-twentieth-century England, much of the humor arose from the intergenerational conflict of the two main characters' lives, with many episodes revolving around Albert and Harold's dysfunctional relationship even though they loved one another, or Albert's get-rich-quick schemes and Harold's mostly futile attempts to get laid. Rounding out the cast, meanwhile, was a large collection of family and friends who usually dropped in unannounced.

Bud Yorkin first saw an episode of *Steptoe* in 1970 while he was in England directing the film *Start the Revolution without Me* costarring Gene Wilder and Donald Sutherland. Though it isn't clear how or when Norman initially learned about the show, he quickly expressed interest when Yorkin floated the possibility of bringing it to the United States and asked him to take charge of the project because he was still consumed with getting *All in the Family* off the ground. Accordingly, by mid-1971—and working again with Beryl Virtue, the British agent who represented Galton and Simpson and brokered the deal for *Till Death Us Do Part*—Tandem also now had the American rights to *Steptoe*. To develop the series, Yorkin (at Norman's behest) hired Aaron Ruben, the veteran sitcom showrunner whose credits included *The Phil Silvers Show*, *The Andy Griffith Show*, and *Gomer Pyle U.S.M.C.*, which he created.

Ruben could not have been happier. He had known Norman and Yorkin ever since his days at NBC directing *Caesar's Hour* in the 1950s and accepted immediately without hesitation. "I'd never worked with them before, but I knew Norman from way back in New York," remembered Ruben. "He called me one day to tell me that he and Bud had just bought this property called

Steptoe and Son and it's about a father and son who own a junkyard and they were Cockney. It was one of the funniest shows I'd ever looked at. It was wonderful and the writing was incredible."[1]

Yet as enamored as he was with the concept, casting what would of course become *Sanford and Son*, starring comedian Redd Foxx as the cantankerous, chest-clutching Los Angeles junk man Fred Sanford, would at first prove to be a seemingly impossible task. In his 2011 book *Black and Blue*, Foxx's biographer Michael Starr chronicled the challenges that Norman, Yorkin, and Ruben faced, and why, in addition to doing the show with an all-Black cast, they chose Foxx as the lead:

> The problem was, they just couldn't find the right combination of actors to play the bickering yet loving father and son—and they couldn't decide on the character's ethnicity. Initially the show was going to be set in New York. "Mainly, we had in mind Jewish and Italian actors, since most of the junk peddlers in New York are of that origin," Ruben said. "But we couldn't find the right characters—those wonderful old-timers are all gone, and you're not going to bring Jimmy [Cagney] out of retirement either."[2]

Still, the choice of the then-forty-nine-year-old Foxx as the show's lead seemed to be—and was, as it turned out—a huge gamble on multiple fronts. To age himself for the part of the sixty-five-year-old Fred Sanford, the notoriously temperamental funnyman grew a scruffy beard, wore heavy stage makeup, and dyed his hair gray in addition to incorporating a bowlegged shuffle to the character's gait. Additionally, the comedian suggested using his real-life surname Sanford for the last name of his character, hence the title of the show becoming *Sanford and Son*, with Foxx also requesting that his onscreen son be named Lamont after his childhood friend Lamont Ousley. On the set, meanwhile, Foxx made no secret of his love for cocaine, openly doing drugs in rehearsals and wearing a gold coke spoon around his neck. He also briefly left the series over a salary dispute along with demanding to have windows installed in his dressing room and his own customized golf cart, requests that were all ultimately met as his frequent complaints about racism eventually led both Yorkin and Ruben to quit.

According to Illunga Adell, who served as the show's first Black staff writer, Foxx's contempt toward Yorkin was especially vitriolic: "Redd Foxx did not like Bud Yorkin . . . I repeat, Redd Foxx did not like Bud Yorkin. I remember sitting at the writer's table in between table reads one time when Redd told Aaron Ruben—and this is almost verbatim—'You tell Bud I don't want to see him around here anymore.' Well, Aaron kind of chuckled looking a little uncomfortable and said, 'Redd, I can't, he's the executive producer of the show.' And Foxx repeats, 'You tell Bud Yorkin that I don't want to see him around here anymore.' After that, Bud stopped coming around. He didn't come to the table reads anymore and he didn't come to the tapings again until Redd dropped out over more money during season three."[3]

It was a true testament to Foxx's star power at the time. And at the time of his casting—years before Richard Pryor and the legions of other Black comedians who followed like Eddie Murphy, Chris Rock, Tracy Morgan, Kevin Hart, Bernie Mac, Martin Lawrence, and Dave Chappelle dominated the stand-up scene with their raunchy acts—Foxx had long reigned supreme. Known as the dean of X-rated comedians both before and during the civil rights movement, he perfected not only the art of the dirty joke, but also risqué storytelling, becoming the first Black comedian to play white audiences on the Las Vegas strip.

One of his biggest fans was Norman: "I'd seen him often in nightclubs with an act that was as scatological as could be . . . scatological as could be," he recalled. "But . . . Redd Foxx . . . God makes a clown every one-hundred-fifty years or so [and] Redd Foxx was a real clown. He could walk into a room and tell you that your mother had died and make you laugh. . . . Redd Foxx was just funny."[4]

Born John Elroy Sanford in St. Louis and raised in Chicago, Foxx dropped out of school when he was thirteen, eventually making his way to New York aboard a freight train in 1939 with a group of friends to try and break into show business. There he and his pals played in a washtub band called The Five Hip Cats on the street corners of Harlem, sometimes earning as much as fifty dollars a night and performing on *The Major Bows Amateur Hour* radio show that same year. It was in Harlem also that he got the nickname "Red" because of his ruddy hair color and skin complexion, and later he added an extra "d."

But after World War II began and having successfully dodged the draft by eating a half bar of soap before his physical to cause heart palpitations, lean times followed. After a series of odd jobs—including washing dishes, working at Jimmy's Chicken Shack in Harlem, where he befriended future civil rights activist Malcom X, as well as briefly doing time on Rikers Island for stealing a bottle of milk—Foxx eventually found work telling off-color jokes on the Chitlin' Circuit, the trade name for Black clubs and music halls around the country.

His big break came in the winter of 1951 after blues singer Dinah Washington, who'd seen him perform on the East Coast, coaxed him into moving to Los Angeles to become her opening act. Though the new gig ended after just four weeks, Foxx eventually caught the eye of record producer Dootsie Williams while performing at a nightclub called the Brass Rail in downtown L.A. in 1955. Then in 1956, he recorded the first of his popular "party albums" (spoken comedy without music often sold in the back of record stores in a brown paper wrapping with a warning sticker, and a genre he took credit for originating), first for Williams's Dootone Records and later for Frank Sinatra's Reprise label—gradually building a loyal fan base among Black and white audiences alike, and eventually recording fifty albums, which sold over ten million copies.

However, as Foxx conceded to an interviewer in 1982: "No one expected me to be on television because I had a reputation from the party records as X-rated, but that's the type of humor I liked. That's the humor they had in the ghettos. They didn't pull no punches and they didn't want to hear about Little Boy Blue and Cinderella. So I gave them what they wanted. I busted loose."[5]

A decade earlier, meanwhile, Norman and Yorkin's decision to create *Sanford and Son* as a predominantly Black show when the nation was still racked with racial tension was a gutsy move to be sure. From *Amos and Andy* to *Beulah* and *Julia*, there had, of course, been sitcoms featuring Black main characters before. But *S&S* was something altogether different, becoming, as screenwriter and TV historian Kendall Rivers observed, "not only the first mega hit sitcom starring an all-African American cast that appealed to every one of every color, but also the first African American sitcom to make it to the coveted one-hundredth episode, not to mention go past it."[6]

Explaining Norman and Yorkin's rationale in his 2001 book *Primetime Blues: African Americans on Network Television*, author and media studies professor Donald Bogle also noted:

> Both men had noticed the altered perspectives already then taking root in popular culture. Not only had *The Flip Wilson Show* proved that a black TV star could appeal to a mainstream audience but so too had such crossover movie stars of the 1960s and early 1970s as Motown's Supremes and the Temptations as well as Atlantic [Records'] queen of soul Aretha Franklin. Younger audiences were conferring superstar status on African American entertainers who in the past would have been denied such a broad audience. The success of black movies like *Shaft* and *Cotton Comes to Harlem* were also a sign of a new African American audience.[7]

Once Foxx had been signed on, the next part to cast was his thirty-two-year-old son, Lamont. It, of course, went to Demond Wilson, a Vietnam veteran originally from Valdosta, Georgia, who had been acting since the age of four. By the time of his *Sanford and Son* audition twenty years later, he had already done several plays on and off Broadway, including *The Boys in the Band* and *Ceremonies in Dark Old*, as well as such films as *The Organization* starring Sidney Poitier and *Daring*, along with the CBS action-adventure series *Mission Impossible* in 1971.

That same year Wilson landed on Norman and Yorkin's radar screen when he and actor Cleavon Little played a pair of burglars who broke into Archie's house in the *All in the Family* episode "Edith Writes a Song." Yet Wilson had reservations about doing *Sanford and Son* when Aaron Ruben first approached him. Nevertheless, he still agreed to fly to Las Vegas along with Ruben and his wife to meet Foxx. In the end, what changed Wilson's mind was seeing Foxx perform at the Hilton and then staying up all night to discuss the project with him and Ruben afterward.

With the two principals now aboard and convinced that, with the mammoth success of *All in the Family*, CBS would immediately snap it up, Norman, Yorkin, and Ruben next set out to film the pilot. To their great surprise, however, nobody from the network wanted it because they thought it was little more than a carbon copy of *All in the Family*.

According to the account given by Foxx's biographer Michael Starr: "Redd and Demond Wilson began rehearsing a scene for the pilot at CBS's Fairfax studio. But there was a problem: Yorkin and Lear couldn't get any network officials, particularly Fred Silverman, to come over and watch rehearsals."

> "We were rehearsing *All in the Family* at CBS and any date I made for the CBS brass to see Redd Foxx in rehearsal, for some reason they couldn't make or they broke the date or whatever," Lear said. Said Yorkin: "We had a problem with Fred Silverman."
>
> Silverman remembers the story a bit differently—and still rues the day he passed on the Yorkin and Lear pilot.
>
> "It was one of the stupidest things I did at CBS," Silverman said thirty years later: "We had *All in the Family* on the air and Bud and Norman came in with the idea, and it was called *Steptoe and Son*. They failed to mention that Redd Foxx was on it, or that it was going to be a black show. They never said that. And they just described it and I said, 'Well, I don't understand, you are selling us a show we already have. I mean, we have *All in the Family* and we have Archie and Meathead. What's the

difference?' And there was silence. I said, 'We're not interested.' There was never any run-through, or never any talk of a run-through. It's one of the decisions I regretted for the next three or four years."[8]

Undiscouraged, Norman and Yorkin plowed ahead, nevertheless. Their next step was NBC, where fortuitously Yorkin's old pal Herb Schlosser—who had already forever left his mark on the network after having negotiated Johnny Carson's first deal to host *The Tonight Show* in 1962, along with getting *Rowan & Martin's Laugh-In* on the air in 1968, and later becoming a central figure in the development of *Saturday Night Live* in 1975—was the network's West Coast operations president. As it turned out also, Schlosser had previously made a deal for NBC to acquire the rights to *Steptoe*, which had fallen through, clearing the way for Tandem. And in the meantime, Schlosser had been searching for a potential vehicle for Foxx to star in ever since his appearance playing a reporter interviewing the first Black vice president of the United States (played by Foxx's old friend Slappy White) on the 1967 prime-time George Schlatter special, *Soul*, which made Yorkin's pitch even more irresistible.

However, there was still another hurdle to overcome: how to get Schlosser over to CBS to watch the pilot, which at first he resisted, until Norman and Yorkin came up with a plan. Tracking him down through his secretary at NBC while he was having lunch with the network's East Coast head of programming at the famed Brown Derby restaurant in the fall of 1971, they invited them over to CBS to watch the taping, where the cast of *All in the Family* was also rehearsing across the hall.

Remembered Schlosser: "Yorkin had arranged with me that he was going to call me at lunch. He called me during the middle of my cobb salad and said, 'We would like to show you a run-through of the pilot script.' It was at the CBS studios on Fairmont [and] so I told Mort they wanted to show us a run-through. So, we went down there and on one of the rehearsal stages they did a run-through of that pilot with Redd Foxx playing the father and a fellow we'd never heard of named Demond Wilson playing the son.

"The audience for the show was the cast of *All in the Family*, and of course, everybody laughed and when we walked out [Norman and Yorkin] said, 'Do we have a commitment?' Mort and I agreed all the time, and so I said, 'As far as I'm concerned, we're going to push this thing through, and Mort said, 'yep.' We walked out and Mort said to me, 'You wait and see, Demond Wilson is going to be the star of the show.' He wouldn't give me 100 percent. He gave me 99.9, but I can say we were both aboard, and we went to New York and we scheduled it."[9]

Wasting no time revving up the NBC publicity machine as it heavily promoted the show with the slogan, "America, you're in for a yock; Archie, you're in for a shock!"[10] beginning in late November, both the *New York Times* and the *L.A. Times* ran features that same month. In December, meanwhile, NBC booked Foxx on *The Flip Wilson Show* as Wilson (who had actually gotten his big break on *The Tonight Show* because of Foxx singing his praises to Carson during a 1965 guest appearance) was now all-too-happy to return the favor, extolling *Sanford and Son* to one local Los Angeles interviewer at the time as "television's first really black show" with "black people acting and talking like black people really do."[11]

The first *Sanford and Son* taping in front of a live studio audience at NBC's Burbank Studios was on December 30, with the show premiering nearly a month later on Friday, January 17, 1972, at 8 p.m., remaining there for all six seasons and originally airing opposite *The Brady Bunch* on ABC and *The Sonny and Cher Comedy Hour* on CBS.

Set in Los Angeles's predominantly Black working-class section of Watts, which had been the scene of one of the country's worst race riots in 1968 (and with most of the action taking place in the Sanfords' ramshackle, clutter-strewn two-story home in the middle of their junkyard), unlike *All in the Family* it was an instant hit and was renewed for a second season almost immediately as NBC, seeking to capitalize on the show's popularity, booked Wilson and Foxx in a series of live stage shows around the country. Almost instantly also, Fred Sanford was anointed a classic television character in the same league as Ralph Kramden, Lucy Ricardo, Barney Fife, and Archie Bunker.

With its funky opening theme "The Street Beater," scored by legendary composer Quincy Jones, the first episode, "Crossed Swords" (written by Aaron Ruben and adapted from an episode of *Steptoe* as several other early episodes were to save time), established the dynamics of Fred and Lamont's complicated relationship right from the get-go.

The storyline centers around Lamont buying a valuable porcelain figurine from an aging white former silent-film actress for fifteen dollars while out on his daily junk rounds in Hollywood. Although the woman's asking price is ten dollars, Lamont offers her an extra five, which infuriates Fred who then remarks that "there's nothing uglier than an old white woman."[12] After taking the statue to a local antiques dealer in Beverly Hills who tells them it's very valuable and offers them $800, Lamont, thinking they can get more, wants to auction it off instead, and they attend the auction pretending to be buyers where Lamont manages to artificially inflate the price to $1,500. But to Lamont's dismay, Fred bids $2,000, wins the statue, and then accidentally drops it, smashing it to pieces. Fred threatens to kill himself, and Lamont's dreams of breaking free are put on hold indefinitely.

Still hysterical more than five decades later, the first episode also introduced many of the show's most famous catchphrases and running gags: Fred's first fake heart attack (complete with him clutching his chest, staring heavenward, and proclaiming to his long-dead wife, "You hear that, Elizabeth? I'm comin' to join you, honey!"), the first "You big dummy," and "How would you like one 'cross your lips?" Fred also sifted through a tangled pile of old reading glasses to find the ones he needed and had his first attack of *arthur-itis*, which is how he wound up breaking the statue.

On hand as the series progressed, meanwhile, were a baker's dozen of other memorable recurring characters serving both as Fred and Lamont's cronies and comedic foils. Introduced during seasons 1 and 2 were Melvin (played by Slappy White, whose real name was Melvin); Bubba (Don Bexley) and Skillet and Leroy (as Fred's pals who were also Foxx's real-life friends from the Chitlin' Circuit); police officer "Smitty" Smith (Hal Williams) and his partner Officer "Hoppie" Swanhauser (Noam Pitnik); the Sanfords' Puerto Rican next-door neighbor, Julio Fuentes (Gregory Sierra); Lamont's smooth-talking best friend Rollo Larson (Nathaniel Taylor); and nurse Donna Harris (Lynn Hamilton) as Fred's on-again, off-again girlfriend.

Added into the mix later was Fred's slow-moving, easily confused friend Grady Wilson (Whitman Mayo), who was later spun off into his own series after briefly moving into the Sanfords' house for six episodes during season three when Foxx was off the show because of a contract dispute, and whose catchphrase was "Good Goobily Goop!" And, of course, there was Aunt Esther as Fred's Bible-toting sister-in-law who couldn't stand him and vice versa. Played to perfection by Foxx's childhood friend LaWanda Page, many of the show's most unforgettable scenes involved Fred and Esther going at it, with him insulting her, and her unleashing what would become two of the show's other most famous catchphrases: "You a heathen!" and "Watch it, Sucka!" usually uttered as she was hitting him with her purse. On hand also were Woody (Raymond Allen) as Aunt Esther's hard-drinking henpecked husband, who owns a hardware store, and Pat Morita, the future *Karate Kid* star who played Lamont's Asian friend Ah Chew (and whose intentional mispronunciation by Fred was another one of the show's running gags with the middle initial *G* in his name for which he would make up various funny names for what it stood for as they fit the moment).

What made *Sanford and Son* so popular in sharp contrast to *All in the Family* was that it was pure comedy, never deliberately setting out to tackle any serious social issues or make a statement which, if it did, was entirely unplanned. It also came along at a time when political incorrectness was acceptable on prime-time television as Fred used the N-word freely while saving his sharpest barbs for the show's two Asian and Puerto Rican characters A Choo and Julio.

Nevertheless, *S&S*, like *All in the Family*, predictably had its critics even as Norman, just three days before the show's premiere, insisted to the *Washington Post* that "*Sanford* is not sensational like *All in the Family*" and "deserves to be considered on its own merits," with producer Aaron Ruben adding in the same article that: "The only similarity may be some kind of breakthrough away from the safe antiseptic series where you're convinced the houses don't even have bathrooms."[13]

In fact, in another article reminiscent of Laura Hobson's scathing *New York Times* essay on *All in the Family* in the fall of 1972, author and Black literature professor Eugenia Collier wrote a similarly blistering op-ed also appearing in the *Times* in June 1972, calling *Sanford and Son* "white to the core" in its headline, decrying the show as "insidious and dangerous" and saying that "the Sanfords themselves are great examples of sick American humor."

Also describing the show as "funny as a one-legged man with a broken crutch" and Fred Sanford as "a racist who is not even consistent in his obnoxious ways" and Lamont as "nobody's dream man" who is "not even his own man," Collier went on to say:

> There's nothing new here that has traditionally motivated black humor—no redemptive suffering, no strength, no tragedy behind the humor. Fred Sanford and his little boy Lamont, conceived by white minds and based upon a white value system, are not strong black men capable of achieving or even understanding—liberation. They are merely two more American child-men. We—all of us—need to be surrounded by positive—and *true* images of blackness based upon black realities, not upon white aberrations.[14]

However, much of Collier's argument fell short—especially her "white to the core" allegations—never once mentioning the fact that the show did indeed have Black writers, including comedian Richard Pryor and Paul Mooney and later staff writer Ilunga Adell Stevenson who wrote scripts on such topics as racial profiling, interracial marriage, and Pan-Africanism.

Still, in a broader context, *Sanford and Son*'s legacy more than fifty years later remains something of a double-edged sword, the complexities of which author Donald Bogle summarized in his book *Primetime Blues*:

What can account for the fact that the series was so "beloved" by viewers, black and white? Some might argue that the white audiences felt comfortable because none of its perceptions (or rather misconceptions) about African Americans was challenged by the series; the images alleviated white fears of black anger. Watching *Sanford and Son*, all that political dissent and turmoil of the 1960s seemed like no more than a bad dream. Those old-style genial Negros had *some* gripes but posed no threat. . . .

But for the African American audience, something else transpired on the show. No white critic may ever understand the pleasure the African American audience experienced (at this time in history) at again seeing African American performers relate to one another, establishing a semblance of a black community and an approximation of black life and culture. . . .There was the pleasure of seeing Sanford speak his mind, especially about race.[15]

After six seasons and 136 episodes, *Sanford and Son* finished its original run on March 25, 1977. Though the show never had an official finale and its two spin-offs *Sanford Arms* and *Sanford* quickly faltered, the extraordinary popularity of the series has remained in the ensuing decades. What's more, it was an indisputable trailblazer for scores of other Black-led sitcoms in the years that followed—a feat that, in the end, remains its biggest legacy.

CHAPTER 18

. . . And Then There's *Maude*

I n December 1971, almost one month to the day before *Sanford and Son*'s premiere, Norman was already laying the groundwork for what was to become his next big hit and the first direct spin-off of *All in the Family*, only he didn't know it yet.

With *AITF*'s second season half underway and its four main principals by now well-established, his only objective initially was to try and spice things up by bringing in somebody from the outside onto the show for one appearance, who could, as he put it, "kill Archie verbally . . . destroy him."[1] Recalling his rationale at the time, he told interviewer Morrie Gelman in 1998: "Mike fought with him all the time and Mike was as poor a liberal in terms of being well founded in his views as Archie was a conservative, so I thought given my family life it had to be somebody out of his deep past that could hammer him over a twenty-year period."[2]

That somebody, of course, was Maude Findlay, Edith's outspoken liberal feminist cousin, who despised Archie and vehemently opposed their marriage. Brash, brassy, four-times-married, and loosely based on Norman's second wife, Frances, the character first entered the fray in "Cousin Maude's Visit," which was the twenty-fifth overall episode of *All in the Family* and the twelfth of the season, cowritten by Rob Reiner's longtime writing partner Phil Mishkin, along with Michael Ross and Bernie West.

In it, Archie, Mike, and Gloria have all come down with the flu, and Edith is running herself ragged until, much to Archie's chagrin, Maude arrives unannounced and uninvited to nurse them back to health as the battle lines are drawn and more arguing and commotion ensues. Drawing inspiration from *Till Death Us Do Part*, where the Garnetts had a cousin named Maud, when it came to casting what was only planned as a single guest appearance, Norman could only think of one person: his old friend veteran stage actor Bea Arthur, who had won a Tony Award in 1966 for her performance as Vera Charles in the original Broadway production of *Mame*. Two months older and often cited by Norman as his most favorite performer he ever worked with, the husky-voiced Arthur (born Bernice Frankel) had served as a Women's Reservist in the Marine Corps during World War II and briefly studied to become a medical technician before moving to New York to pursue acting and getting her first big break when she landed a role off-Broadway appearing as Lucy Brown opposite Lotte Lenya in *The Threepenny Opera* in 1954.

That following year, she was hired to perform as a torch singer in the off-Broadway musical *Ben Bagley's Shoestring Revue*, which is where she and Norman first met one night when he was in the audience. Instantly enamored of her talent, he told *TV Guide* in 1972: "I'll never forget her singing a torch song called 'Garbage.' She sang it while leaning up against a streetlamp with a single spotlight on her. The idea was, 'Garbage, he treated me like garbage,' and every time Bea sang the word *garbage* the house rocked with laughter and I was afraid they'd have to send out for coffee and doughnuts for the survivors."[3]

Five years later—and five weeks before it was canceled—Norman hired Arthur for a guest spot on *The George Gobel Show*. In the twelve years since, the two had remained close, so naturally when he called to offer her a coveted guest role on *All in the Family*, he assumed she would accept. But to his great surprise, Arthur, who was married to film director Gene Saks at the time and living in New York raising two young sons, said no.

"Norman and I had become very, very friendly, and as a matter of fact, he came to [New York] to see me in a show that had closed out of town trying to help me in a thing called *Mother's Kisses*, which bombed," she recalled. "Anyway, Norman was always available and when the show [*All in the Family*] started, he asked me to come out and play a part. And I thought, 'Oh, God, first of all, I don't enjoy flying and what if you write something for me and I don't like it or I don't think it's important enough. I'd feel terrible."[4]

Norman, however, was undeterred. Aware that she was already planning a trip to the West Coast because her husband was directing the film *The Last of the Red-Hot Lovers*, he made her a no-strings-attached proposition she couldn't refuse: to write something for her anyway and find another actress if she didn't like it. Fortunately, Arthur came around. Figuring she had nothing to lose after flying to L.A. and reading the script, she agreed to do the show even though she couldn't figure out what the character was about at first.

But by the time of the taping in mid-November, Arthur had the part down cold. And then on December 11, 1971—the night "Cousin Maude's Visit" originally aired—Norman received an enthusiastic phone call from CBS's programming chief Fred Silverman as the closing credits were rolling, requesting that she immediately be given a series of her own. Intrigued by the prospect, Norman didn't need any cajoling nor did Arthur this time around. "What happened was a few weeks after we finished, I was back in New York and Norman called me. He said, 'The president of CBS said, 'Who is that girl. Let's give her her own show.' That's how it all started. I call it a middle-aged Cinderella story. There we were, my husband, my two kids and me. We got some summer clothes and toys for the kids and came out. We had thirteen weeks and we rented a house and the thing just took off."[5]

With a backdoor pilot scheduled to air as *All in the Family*'s second-season finale in mid-March, Norman's first order of business was to develop the concept for the series, which he did with the aid of Rod Parker, who became the executive producer of what would be *Maude*, revolving around its title character and her husband. Setting the show in the New York City suburb of Tuckahoe in Westchester County, the pilot (also called "Maude") involves Archie and Edith traveling upstate to attend the second wedding of Maude's daughter Carol (originally played by actor Marcia Rodd) in which Archie immediately insults the groom, David, upon learning he's Jewish. Archie isn't the only one to hurl insults, however. After an alcohol-fueled argument with Carol in which David informs her that he expects her to be a stay-at-home mom and has purchased a house without her permission, the wedding is called off.

Having now established *Maude*'s premise and the storyline for the back-door pilot, the next task was finding someone to play Walter, Maude's long-suffering fourth husband, who owns an appliance store in Tuckahoe. As was his predilection when it came to casting, Norman again turned to the theater, where he recruited actor Bill Macy, who had recently appeared as a policeman on the *All in the Family* episode "Archie Sees a Mugging."

Then fifty and mostly a struggling New York actor who'd spent more than a decade driving a cab before becoming Walter Matthau's Broadway understudy in *Once More, with Feeling* in 1958, Macy had previously appeared on the soap opera *The Edge of Night* in 1966 and in the 1968 film version of Mel Brooks's *The Producers*, where he played a jury foreman. His first big break onstage came in 1969 in *Oh! Calcutta!*, the avant-garde off-Broadway musical revue about sex and sexual mores, where he met future wife Samantha Harper and his character Monte—a role he later reprised in the 1972 film version—appeared onstage nude.

Norman had first seen Macy in 1966 in the off-Broadway play *American Hurrah*, a satirical trilogy of one-act dramas featuring one particularly memorable scene in which his character was choking to death on a chicken bone that forever left an impression. "It was a tour de force performance and if I live to be a thousand, I'll never forget it," he remembered.[6]

Though Arthur and Macy had never met or worked together, their on-screen chemistry was instant, and they quickly became friends, often carpooling to the studio together. His widow Samantha Harper Macy recalled fondly how he acclimated to his best-known role and the affinity he had for Arthur: "Bill took every part of himself into every job he ever had and fitted it into the circumstances of his character. And he absolutely loved Bea . . . he was just madly in love with her. One of his favorite stories happened early in the series when they were on a slow elevator one afternoon at CBS and she said, 'Walter/Bill, you're a rock. Despite your lack of humor, you are a rock.'

"Then they got off the elevator and she got a good laugh out of it. He was just himself in that role, in love with that woman, in dealing with the problems they had, he just loved her. Every morning on taping day, he would go to a deli and bring her a hot corned beef sandwich."[7]

Replacing Marcia Rodd in the series and supporting Arthur and Macy as Carol Traynor, Maude's twenty-seven-year-old daughter from a previous marriage, would be Adrienne Barbeau, the buxom young actor who had recently been nominated for a Tony Award for her portrayal of tough-girl Rizzo in the original Broadway production of *Grease*. But despite having already amassed an impressive list of stage credits (including also playing Bette Midler's sister Hodel on Broadway in *Fiddler on the Roof*), Barbeau had no previous television experience and was totally taken aback after being asked to audition for the role of Carol, a single mother who lived with her young son, Phillip (first played by Brian Morrison and later Kraig Metzinger), under the same roof with the Findlays. She also continued to have doubts even after winning the part. "I didn't know anything about television or Norman," Barbeau said. "All my professional career, I'd been on Broadway working at night, so I never watched TV. The first thing I remember is sitting around the writer's table, looking at Norman and thinking to myself, 'Oh my God, he's a genius,' because he knew what to do to a script to make it funnier. He didn't necessarily write the best scripts, but he could take any script and make it the best script. Another clear memory I have of Norman from then is being in his office and him saying to me, 'Look, if you don't trust yourself, trust me. I know you can do this.'"[8]

With the three principals now in place, there were still several other roles to fill. At first on tap to play Maude's ditzy best friend Vivian Cavender was

Doris Roberts, the veteran character actor who would become best known for playing Ray Romano's acerbic meddlesome mother Marie Barone on *Everybody Loves Raymond*. But after wooing her for weeks and finally hearing her read for the part, producer Rod Parker thought Roberts's onscreen persona was too much like Arthur's and so she was let go. Replacing her instead was Rue McClanahan, who had first come to Norman's attention in 1969 in the off-Broadway play *Tonight in Living Color*. As she recounted in her 2007 autobiography *My First Five Husbands . . . And the Ones Who Got Away: A Memoir*, he came up to her afterward and said, "Your performance is amazing. I hope I'll be able to hire you someday."[9]

And then, lo and behold, three years later in the fall of 1972, he cast her on *All in the Family* opposite Vincent Gardenia as a wife-swapping couple who try to have their way with Archie and Edith in the episode "The Bunkers and the Swingers," whose teleplay by Lee Kalcheim won an Emmy for Best Writing. Recalled Bob LaHendro who directed it: "The beauty of it is that these characters by that time were so well defined that all the audience had to know was who the swingers were, and they could already anticipate the reaction of Archie and Edith as they slowly discover what they're involved with."[10]

As for McClanahan's own performance, Norman was so impressed during *AITF*'s rehearsals that he immediately asked her to audition for *Maude* at the same time. McClanahan really wanted to do it, but there was a slight problem: she had just recently won the coveted lead in the Broadway play *Sticks and Bones*, and the director, legendary theater impresario Joseph Papp, refused to let her out of the show.

McLanahan was still determined, however, and so she came up with a plan. In exchange for being able to audition for *Maude*, she offered to relinquish her role in *Sticks and Bones* and become the understudy, a proposal to which Papp eventually reluctantly agreed—and whereupon Norman hired her on the spot—although she didn't appear until the ninth episode and wasn't made a series regular until the fourth season.

Playing McClanahan's eventual onscreen husband and on the show from the very start was Canadian actor and comedian Conrad Bain, whom Norman had seen in the off-Broadway plays *Scuba Duba* and *Steambath* and who would go on to star in his own Tandem-produced series *Diff'rent Strokes*. On *Maude*, he portrayed Dr. Arthur Harmon, the Findlays' conservative, cornball next-door neighbor, who had served in the army with Walter and was his best friend, as well as a constant thorn in Maude's side. Rounding things out—and serving as another comedic foil—was Esther Rolle as Florida Evans, Maude's caustic, no-nonsense maid, who would eventually be given her own series.

On *Maude's* writing staff, meanwhile, were the veteran sitcom scribes Bob Schiller and Bob Weiskopf—also known as "the Bobs," most notably for their work on *I Love Lucy*—alongside Budd Grossman and newcomers Charlie Hauk and Elliot Schoenman. "I had just turned twenty-seven and it was Schiller, Weiskopf, Budd Grossman, Rod Parker and me in these small offices," said Schoenman, who officially joined the show at the beginning of the third season.

The next youngest guy from me was maybe fifty-two. I didn't know from anything and across the hall were the *All in the Family* guys like Don Nicholl, Mickey Ross, Bernie West, Lou Derman, and Bill Davenport, who were these veteran comedy writers going all the way back to radio. We were all on top of each other in these tiny offices and we kind of interacted with each other, which was amazing, because I had to learn really fast how to do it all. It was like going to graduate school for twenty minutes and it was absolutely all consuming.

You'd turn the scripts in to Rod, who would eventually show them to Norman after we'd gotten them in some kind of shape. Then Norman would give his notes, which were kind of all-powerful, because what he wanted was what we ended up doing. The first time I met him was during the hiatus between when I first got there and the third season I was on staff. They'd given me a first-class ticket after I'd gone to New York to get my stuff to move to L.A. and I ended up on the same flight as Norman and Jerry Perenchio from Tandem Productions. I went up and introduced myself to Norman, and he was great. Those were days when they had the lounge upstairs on planes and they invited me to join them for drinks after we ate.

That's where we bonded, and I had a very unique relationship with both him and Bea. Once I started on the show, I suddenly became very hot in the business and I got a call one day from an agent at William Morris who said, "There's this guy who's a film director who wants to write a story and needs a young writer to do it with." At first, I said I couldn't do it because of how swamped I was with *Maude*, but then when he told me that the director was Bea's husband, Gene Saks, I agreed to meet with him at the Warner Brothers commissary.

I still didn't want to do it, but I figured it would be good to meet him and so I went. The interesting aside to this was that one of my favorite things that got me into writing was the film *A Thousand Clowns* where Gene played Chuckles the Chipmunk, Jason Robards's crazy boss. As soon as I saw Gene, I did a doubletake. I said, "Holy shit, it's Chuckles the Chipmunk!" And then from there, it turned out we had a thousand things in common and there was just no way I wasn't going to do this.

What he wanted was to do a story about an eccentric uncle of Bea's, and he would occasionally come over to CBS at lunchtime and we would write. I would also go over to their house a lot on weekends, and after they moved to Sullivan Canyon, I was there every weekend, and I spent a lot of time with both of them. My own father died when I was very young, and so Norman, Bea and Gene kind of became like parent figures to me.

Whenever I'd be over there on the weekends, Bea would always ask how next week's script was, and I'd say, "Norman likes it." And then I would come in on Monday and either Norman, Rod Parker, or whoever else was there would ask how Bea was over the weekend. So even though I was the youngest guy there, I sort of became the conduit in between everything. It was all quite heady stuff.[11]

Maude premiered on September 12, 1972, at 8 p.m. and became an immediate hit. Though its connection to the Bunkers was never directly acknowledged on the show, the link still occasionally surfaced in various media coverage of Arthur such as one profile in the *New York Times* two months after its debut, accompanied by the headline: "She Gave Archie His First Comeuppance."[12] Reviews were also mostly positive. While *TV Guide* had already branded the Maude character as a "caricature of the knee-jerk liberal"[13] before the show even went on the air, among the most lavish early praise came that of *New York Times* television critic John J. O'Connor, who enthusiastically declared, "Fact No. 1 about the new series: The executive producer is Norman Lear, whose TV credits encompass *All in the Family* and *Sanford and Son*, two of the most successful audience grabbers in recent seasons" and "Fact No, 2: The title role is played by Beatrice Arthur. That fact alone may keep Mr. Lear's winning record intact."[14]

O'Connor's prediction proved correct on both counts as the show, even despite its flaws, represented a radical departure from the way white suburban middle-class families had been depicted on television in the past. This was instantly apparent in the catchy but not happy-go-lucky opening theme "And Then There's Maude"—written by Alan and Marilyn Bergman and Dave Grusin and performed by singer Donny Hathaway—comparing the titular character, whose trademark catchphrases were "God'll get you for that!" and "I'll rip your heart out," to such strong-willed female historical figures as Joan of Arc, Lady Godiva, Isadora Duncan, and Betsy Ross.

Immediately evident was the absence of traditional family and gender roles, which had long been sitcom staples along with white picket fences, cardigan-sweater- and pearl-necklace-wearing parents, perfectly mannered kids, and virtually nonexistent problems. Instead, like the Bunkers had before them—except in more affluent surroundings—the Findlays argued about everything, as the imposing, opinionated, feminist liberal progressive Maude spoke out sometimes even more boisterously on certain issues than Archie, with politics, gender, class, and race almost always the linchpin of the debates.

Meanwhile, in the middle of the Findlays' spacious living room—unlike the orderly suburban family sitcom homes of the past and a frequent centerpiece for much of the action during the first season—was an L-shaped mahogany bar with half-empty bottles of vodka. Also different was the wardrobe, with Maude seldom seen in a dress or a skirt and often favoring red, brown, or burgundy floor-length vests and gowns; Walter usually in dark polyester suits or pants, wide-collared shirts and neckties; and Carol almost always in form-fitting blouses and dresses revealing her ample breasts.

True to form as he'd been with *All in the Family*, Norman was once again determined to mark *Maude*'s territory and establish its characters from day one. In doing so, the debut episode "Maude's Problem" dove headfirst into what was still uncharted waters at the time: mental health and the stigma of seeking professional help. With an early draft by Susan Silver—a former casting director for *Rowan & Martin's Laugh-In*, who had previously penned scripts for *That Girl*, *Love, American Style*, *Room 222*, *The Partridge Family*, and *The Mary Tyler Moore Show*—the episode opens with Carol walking through the Findlays' front door as Maude immediately suspects she is having an affair. However, when she discovers Carol's been seeing a therapist and that the sunglasses are to conceal her tears, she becomes hysterical, believing that she is to blame. She then takes it upon herself to pay a visit to Carol's shrink only to find herself in analysis venting about her own life.

Recalling how she first got the assignment and her experience on the show, Silver noted: "I knew Norman because I had done a pilot for Bud Yorkin, and I was asked to do the pilot for *Maude* because it was a spin-off of *All in the Family* and they didn't have one. Norman was out of town, so I met with Rod Parker and since Maude was essentially my own mother, I pitched the story of how I went to therapy.

"That was basically it. I wrote the script, and he liked it very much. But then Norman came back, and because Maude was essentially his wife Frances, and he knew the character so well, he wanted to do some rewriting. I thought the show was excellent because it was like my mother, and he was kind enough to give me a writing credit, although I didn't go to the taping because I was afraid of Bea Arthur. I didn't want to meet her, and I didn't go back to the show after that because I understood that Norman knew what he wanted and that he was going to rewrite everybody, but he was always a gentleman and a lovely guy."[15]

Confronting and normalizing the fears most people had and still have about psychotherapy in its inaugural show would indeed prove to be the first of *Maude*'s many feats as it became a de facto bully pulpit for bringing a kaleidoscope of contemporary, often uncomfortable issues such as marijuana legalization, mental illness, alcoholism, domestic violence, malpractice, cosmetic surgery, gay rights, suicide, sexual harassment, et cetera to the forefront through the comedic lens of television. And, of course, on top of all that, Norman decided to tackle the topic for which, above all others, the show is forever remembered—abortion—in the two-part "Maude's Dilemma," which were the ninth and tenth episodes of the first season.

His inspiration was a 1972 contest sponsored by the birth-control advocacy group Zero Population Growth that was awarding a ten-thousand-dollar prize for comedies with the most innovative stories about population control. As Norman and Rod Parker, who were both intrigued by the creative challenge, began tossing around ideas, several scenarios came to mind. Initially in the offing was a storyline involving the pregnancy of Maude's neighbor Vivian in what would be Rue McClanahan's first appearance, with the two women also talking about contraception and the possibility of Walter getting a vasectomy, which was quickly nixed.

Briefly under consideration as well were either a false pregnancy, which Norman ultimately felt would be a copout, or a miscarriage, though he decided against the latter as well because Gloria had already had one on *All in the Family*. So instead, and because of Austin and Irma Kalish—the veteran husband-and-wife comedy-writing duo who had written for dozens of television shows (including two pivotal episodes of *All in the Family* on which Gloria was sexually assaulted and Edith suspected she had breast cancer) and pitched the idea—it was ultimately decided that Maude, after becoming pregnant at the age of forty-seven, would have an abortion.

"The more interesting story seemed to be, what would this forty-seven-year-old woman really do in her life," Norman later told the *Chicago Tribune*. "And the conclusion we reached was that her family would be thoroughly involved in the deepest concern about all this. We knew where the daughter [Carol] would be on all this and that Maude would be absolutely torn, but that she'd come down on the side, given her age, of not having a child."[16]

Yet, despite the Kalishes' extensive list of credits, Norman had someone else in mind to write the script. The person he chose was a talented young woman named Susan Harris—who would go on to create two of TV's most successful sitcoms of all time, *Soap* and *The Golden Girls*—and had already written two episodes of *All in the Family*, along with scripts for *The Courtship of Eddie's Father*, *The Partridge Family*, and *Love, American Style*. Remembered Harris:

> Norman wanted an abortion episode for Maude's neighbor Vivian. I thought it was a wonderful idea. I thought it was something that absolutely should be addressed, and I liked tackling issues as well as entertaining. I gave it to him, and he said, "This is too good for Vivian. We have to give it to Maude." I wasn't surprised he asked me [to write it] because he had seen my work on *All in the Family* and he had confidence in me. I knew it would be an intense reaction [from viewers]. I knew people felt very strongly about it one way or the other—but something like that would never deter me.[17]

To be sure, the prospect of taking on a highly charged issue like abortion on national television was still a dicey if not dangerous proposition in 1972 even if *Maude*'s wasn't TV's first. The first had occurred a decade earlier in 1962—on the legal drama *The Defenders* on which father and son attorneys Lawrence and Kenneth Preston (played by E. G. Marshall and Robert Reed) defended a doctor arrested for performing illegal abortions—followed by another woman having the procedure on the NBC soap opera *Another World* in 1964.

But *Maude*'s was the first by a lead character on a prime-time sitcom—occurring nearly a year before *Roe v. Wade* made it legal in all fifty states—so CBS was understandably worried. "They were very nervous to say the least," recalled Rod Parker. "The thing we had going for us was that *Maude* was a hit, so the network said okay. But they requested we give another side, so we (wrote) in a neighbor who had a lot of children and was very happy.[18]

Added Norman: "You know, I don't think of it as winning and losing. By the time I did that episode, we had a good relationship with the guy who ran program practices at CBS—William Tankersley—and we would talk about these things. On the abortion episode, he said [at first]: 'God, no. No way we're going to do that.' And we talked and talked. As a result of the conversation, we made it a two-parter and in one, we introduced a friend of Maude's who was pregnant. She had four children that she could ill-afford and was pregnant with a fifth and she in no way would think of an abortion. That was the result of the conversation, to give people who agreed with that point of view an opportunity to be represented also, so it was much more even-handed in terms of the debate."[19]

For actor Adrienne Barbeau, doing the abortion show hit home on a much deeper level.

> It was a very important episode to me and on the hiatus that followed the first season, I went to work at a women's healthcare clinic assisting in providing birth control information and abortion counseling. It was all volunteer work, but I did it because [in addition to what we had done on *Maude*], years earlier I had a girlfriend who needed an abortion, and I was working in a nightclub out in New Jersey that was run by people who had "contacts."
>
> And so, I arranged with my boss for this friend to come out to the club and someone met her there, took her to a hotel room and performed the procedure. [Afterward they] brought her back to the club and told her that she couldn't take any aspirin, or any painkillers, or drink any booze and that she would miscarry in twenty-four hours. Well, she started miscarrying about an hour later and I got her back to my apartment in Manhattan, where she lost the baby in my bathroom. It had an enormous impact on me.[20]

At CBS, the one person who was apparently (and surprisingly) never skittish about Maude having an abortion was founder and chairman William S. Paley who, despite having once described *All in the Family* as "vulgar," was now one of *Maude*'s biggest fans and a fervent supporter of Norman's. According to Hal Cooper, who directed the second installment: "The sales department of CBS were afraid they were going to lose clients and William Paley finally got into it and said in effect from what I heard, 'Norman Lear has never embarrassed this network and I think if he says it's not the wrong thing to do and it'll be done with taste, you have to leave him alone and let him do it.' He [Paley] was the big boss, and of course we did do it, and it was tasteful."[21]

"Maude's Dilemma" originally aired on November 14 and 21, 1972. The first installment began with a visibly stunned Maude returning home from a routine checkup, where despite being well past the age of forty and on birth control, she's just learned she's pregnant. After breaking the news to Vivian—in what Norman described as "a lay down brilliant comic moment that was minutes of laughter and a great situation for these two women"[22]—Maude instructs her to tell Carol, who is shocked, as is the Findlays' maid, Florida, who tries to offer Maude moral support as Carol immediately suggests she get an abortion.

Entering seconds later in the same scene is their goofball other neighbor, Dr. Arthur Harmon, who is there because he and Vivian were supposed to play bridge with the Findlays that night. Having already learned that Maude was pregnant from another colleague at the hospital, instead of trying to help, he only makes matters worse by laughing at her predicament. Meanwhile, as Maude tries to figure out how she is going to tell Walter, who has been away at an appliance convention, she also grapples with the pros and cons of having another child. And then—whereupon returning home and learning she's expecting while he's in the middle of having dinner—Walter (in a bit borrowed from the off-Broadway play *American Hurrah* where Norman had first discovered Bill Macy) begins choking on a chicken bone.

Once Walter regains his composure, he calmly tells her that the decision is hers. This convinces Maude to keep the child because Walter has never had one and she thinks he secretly wants to become a father. At the same time, Walter, also believing that Maude wants the baby, informs Arthur that he does too for her sake. But then in the second episode (after volunteering to get a vasectomy and getting cold feet at the last minute), Maude and Walter both agree that neither of them wants a child at this stage of their lives, so they mutually decide to go through with the abortion.

Despite their delicate and balanced treatment of the subject—and even with the support of both CBS chairman and founder Wiliam Paley and chief censor Bill Tankersly—the network nevertheless remained jittery as the date of the scheduled taping approached. Then they asked for a delay that same day and even threatened not to pay for the taping unless Norman agreed to postpone it, although he vehemently stood his ground, vowing not to put anything in their place if the two episodes weren't filmed and aired as planned.

And then something else that was equally significant happened after the network finally acquiesced. When the first part of "Maude's Dilemma" aired on time for the first time on November 14, only two of CBS's nearly two hundred affiliates, both in Illinois—WCIA-TV in Champaign and WMBD-TV in Peoria—refused to broadcast it.

While some additional public outcry was inevitable, the initial fallout was relatively minimal with nearly equal support. Indeed, after the first installment aired, CBS received some seven thousand letters of protest—something that Norman regarded as an approbation—remarking at the time: "I enjoy stirring feelings, even negative feelings, because I think that is what theater is about. It's marvelous to know that you have engaged the feelings of millions of people."[23] However, of the four hundred phone calls the network received after setting up extra phone lines in New York the night the first episode ran, only ten were in protest.

In the meantime, between October and December 1972 after both episodes had aired, ratings soared, catapulting *Maude* from number twelve to number seven in the Nielsens practically overnight. But then that following summer in August 1973, the other shoe dropped when the episodes reran eight months after the Supreme Court passage of *Roe v. Wade*, making abortion legal in all fifty states.

This time, CBS aired the two episodes with a disclaimer, warning viewers that: "Tonight's episode of *Maude* was originally broadcast in November of 1972. Since it deals with 'Maude's Dilemma' as she contemplates the possibility of abortion, you may wish to refrain from watching it, if you believe the broadcast may disturb you or others in your family."[24]

Yet such precautions did little to dissuade the angry protests from anti-abortion groups and the religious right who picketed with signs in front of CBS—with several demonstrators lying down in front of Bill Paley's car outside Black Rock, the network's Rockefeller Center headquarters in New York, and others doing the same in front of Norman's car in L.A. at CBS Television City, with some of them even plastering pictures of dead fetuses on Paley and Norman's windshields—in turn, prompting nearly forty affiliates not to air the episodes in reruns, and eliciting more than seventeen thousand letters of complaint.

But even so in the end, neither the protestors nor the squeamish affiliates could circumvent the fact that an estimated sixty-five million viewers had seen at least one of the two episodes, either that summer or the previous fall. By any barometer, Norman had won.

He knew it too. Emboldened even more as the stakes got higher and higher, he also knew that victory had not been merely coincidental.

CHAPTER 19

Tandemonium

Nineteen seventy-three was another momentous year for Norman and Yorkin. With three hit shows now on the air on two networks and an endless stream of mostly positive press—including lengthy cover stories in both *Newsweek* and *Time*, along with two in the *New York Times Magazine* and five in *TV Guide*—Tandem had without question become a bona-fide industry powerhouse. On any given day, it seemed, publicists from CBS and NBC were shepherding journalists from at least one, and usually more major magazine or newspaper outlets in between the various studios and Norman and Yorkin's offices.

Moreover, the explosive successes of *All in the Family*, *Sanford and Son*, and *Maude* certainly made it network television's most important purveyor of sitcoms even as it faced some formidable competition from MTM Enterprises, whose juggernauts *The Mary Tyler Moore Show* and *The Bob Newhart Show* were now airing opposite *AITF* Saturday nights on CBS alongside *M*A*S*H* and *The Carol Burnett Show*. Over at ABC, meanwhile, producer Garry Marshall was making a splash with the TV adaptation of *The Odd Couple*, where he would, of course, go on to become a major 1970s sitcom player in his own right as the creator of such beloved classics as *Happy Days*, *Laverne and Shirley*, and *Mork and Mindy*.

Nevertheless, for anyone who wrote for sitcoms back then—and especially newcomers—Norman's shows were still the grand prize. Jay Moriarity, who penned episodes for *All in the Family*, *Maude*, and *Good Times* along with *That's My Mama* and *Chico and the Man* before becoming a staff writer and later executive producer on *The Jeffersons*, recalled the thrill of simply showing up for work "because you never knew what was going to happen or who you were going to see."[1]

Moriarity also recalled the excitement he felt after seeing Norman warm up the studio audience for *All in the Family* in 1972, inspiring him to write the episode "The Draft Dodger," which launched his career even though it was rejected at first and didn't air for another six years. "I was at the taping at CBS with my parents and when Norman came out, the way he talked and everything he said, I could just identify with this guy," Moriarity recalled. "I thought it was the best thing. There was just something about Norman that made me want to jump over the rail and tell him I wanted to work for him. It was like hearing Mark Twain or Will Rogers talk. He was charismatic like that, and he had this [terrific] mustache. I was like, 'yeah,' and then I thought, 'you can do topical stuff.' I went home that night and wrote a treatment for 'The Draft Dodger.'"[2]

As the new fall season got underway in September 1973, *All in the Family* instantly reclaimed its spot as the number-one show in America with an astounding twenty-two million viewers a week. Every taping at CBS Television City now had the aura of a big-time rock concert with Norman, often accompanied by his daughter Kate assisting him, warming up the audience in his trademark white hat as fans wrote away months in advance for free tickets. On taping days, those who couldn't procure them by mail, routinely congregated at dawn at CBS hoping to get standby tickets for either the 5:30 dress rehearsal or the 8 p.m. taping, which were rare since almost everyone who had a ticket showed up, including celebrities.

As for the actors on the show who were now celebrities themselves, it got to the point where they couldn't go anywhere without being hounded. "Rob was the only member of the cast who could go to lunch with me at the food stalls at the Farmers Market [across the street from CBS], where I loved to eat," recalled actor Betty Garrett, who, along with Vincent Gardenia, joined *All in the Family* in the show's fourth season as the Bunkers' next-door neighbors Frank and Irene Lorenzo.

Carroll, Jean and Sally could not go because they would be mobbed. People would just gather around and literally prevent them from eating. But all Rob had to do was leave his toupee back at the studio and nobody knew who he was. I was always glad I never had that kind of celebrity, although one day one lady behind a coffee counter did recognize me. "I admire you so much," she said. "I know everything you've ever done." She started talking about *All in the Family* and then she went on to name every movie I had made, every Broadway show I had been in, and on and on.[3]

Maintaining the momentum were also the accolades the show continued to rack up as Jean Stapleton alone won seven Emmy Awards for Best Actress five years in a row between 1971 and 1975, followed by two more in 1977 and 1978.

After Stapleton's first triumph in 1971, her son—actor-director John Putch, who also made one *All in the Family* appearance playing a boy scout during the season-3 episode "Archie Is Branded" before winning the recurring role of Bob Morton on the original *One Day at a Time*—remembered: "There was an immediate change in anything that happened to us whenever we went out in public for dinner, shopping, or whatever it was. People would just . . . not swarm her . . . but they would stop her and want to talk to her or shake her hand and take a photo, or get an autograph, or something. There was a great deal of that and a lot of personal space interruption. We'd be at a restaurant and people would come up as we were trying to eat, so my sister and I were really, really on the defensive because we didn't want our parents to be disturbed at the dinner table because that was bad manners, which we were taught. But mom was always very kind to the person, and sometimes she would have to reprimand them for trying to take a photo without asking. She did it in such a polite and teaching way that we were just stunned, because all we wanted to do was get up and punch these people."[4]

After again sweeping the 1972 Emmy Awards with eleven nominations and seven statues as Carroll O'Connor and Stapleton opened the telecast and host Johnny Carson called it an "An Evening with Norman Lear," *All in the Family* went on to receive seven more nominations and two awards that following year for Outstanding Comedy Series and Outstanding Writing Achievement. Adding to their achievements in 1973 were two Golden Globes for Best TV Show and Best Actress (Stapleton), with O'Connor, Rob Reiner, and Sally Struthers also getting nods, as did *Sanford and Son* and *Maude*, both of which received multiple Emmy and Golden Globe nominations as Redd Foxx took home his first and only Golden Globe for Outstanding Lead Actor in a Comedy Series.

While the ratings for *Sanford and Son* and *Maude* dipped slightly that fall from the previous spring—with *S&S* going from number two to number three and *Maude* from number four to number six as *The Waltons* and *Hawaii Five-O* nipped at their respective heels—America's affection for the Bunkers, the Sanfords, and the Findlays did not falter. *Time*, in a revealing 1972 profile, offered the following account of not only the fervor the shows were creating, but also the atmosphere at Tandem and the contrasting personalities of Norman and Bud Yorkin:

> Yorkin and Lear's profits from their three shows this year could reach $5,000,000 not counting their take from books, records and other merchandising. With offers of other projects pouring in, their Tandem Productions is the hottest TV production office in Hollywood. . . .
>
> Lear, who spends most of his time at CBS as executive producer of *Family* and *Maude*, is a dapper, droopy-moustached man of fifty with a comedy writer's congenial air of melai choly like a sensitive spaniel: he tends to be the spokesman for the team. Yorkin, forty-six, who concentrates on being the producer of *Sanford* at NBC, is a beefy, genial soul with a flushed face and a habit of punctuating his speech with a stabbing thumb one senses could easily become a fist.[5]

Tandem's first merchandising bonanza was an *All in the Family* LP album released by Atlantic Records in the fall of 1971. With a cast photograph set against a pink backdrop for the cover, it featured the theme song and twelve short recordings of dialogue from the first season. The recording did so well, in fact, that it quickly made the top-100 in the music industry trade magazine *Cashbox* followed by two others: *All in the Family: 2nd Album* released in 1972—this time with the four principals against a white backdrop next to the Bunkers' coatrack, and Edith, Mike, and Gloria standing behind Archie chomping on a cigar in his easy chair with five dialogue cuts from season 2, including "Cousin Maude's Visit," "Sammy's Visit," and "The Elevator Story"—and 1973's *Archie & Edith Side by Side: An Evening of Songs and Fun with the Bunkers* with Archie and Edith seated at the piano.

Not long after the first album release, there was also a fan magazine called *All You'd Like to Know about "All in the Family"* along with a series of Gloria Bunker paper dolls. During the 1972 presidential election between Richard Nixon and George McGovern, meanwhile, *All in the Family* also experienced what can only be described as a merchandising tsunami as an "Archie Bunker for President" movement unexpectedly took on a life of its own with "Archie Bunker Campaign" headquarters cropping up across the country in such major national retail outlets as Montgomery Ward, and Archie even receiving a vote for the vice presidency at that summer's Democratic National Convention in Miami.

While neither Norman nor O'Connor had deliberately sought such notoriety for TV's most famous sitcom character on the national political stage, they certainly didn't reject it either. Suddenly—and again to a lesser extent during the 1976 presidential race between Gerald Ford and Jimmy Carter—Archie's picture was everywhere: on beer mugs, on coffee cups, on T-shirts, on posters, on bumper stickers, on wristwatches, and on political buttons wielding such slogans as "America's Foist Family, the Bunkers," "Back Bunker," and "Another Meathead for Bunker."

And the *All in the Family* merchandising machine wasn't limited to only record albums and presidential elections. Over the course of the series' run, there was also a groundswell of other *All in the Family* swag, including a board game from Milton Bradley in 1972, a fourteen-inch "Archie Bunker's Grandson" doll manufactured by Ideal Toys in 1976 billed as "the first anatomically correct male doll," as well as student study guides from Scholastic Reader and a series of books, including *The Wit and Wisdom of Archie Bunker* and *Edith Bunker's "All in the Family" Cookbook*. Even ministers began devoting entire sermons to the show. One of them notably was Spencer Marsh, a Presbyterian pastor from Portland, Oregon, who in 1975 and again in 1977, penned the books *God, Man, and Archie Bunker* and *Edith the Good: The Transformation of Edith Bunker from Whole Woman to Total Person*, both published by Harper & Row with forewords by O'Connor and Stapleton.

No doubt inspired by *All in the Family*'s success was Johnny Speight, who remounted its antecedent *Till Death Us Do Part* for a second run on the BBC beginning in September 1972. Here in the United States that same month, Marvel Productions also began airing the animated sitcom *The Barkleys* on NBC. Seemingly taking a page straight from the playbook of the hugely popular 1960s animated Stone Age series *The Flintstones*, which had drawn inspiration from *The Honeymooners*, *The Barkleys* was similarly inspired by *All in the Family*. The story centered around an anthropomorphic family of dogs led by Arnie, a loudmouthed, potbellied bus driver who sounded like a cross between Fred Flintstone and Ralph Kramden; his long-suffering wife, Agnes; and their three kids Terry, Roger, and Chester. Ironically, it was also written by Woody Kling and Larry Rhine, who would go on to become the lead story editors for *AITF* during its later seasons where they were responsible for some of its most memorable shows, including "Birth of the Baby," "Joey's Baptism," "Archie's Brief Encounter," and "Edith's Crisis of Faith." Even so, the writing on *The Barkleys* often fell flat, the characters felt contrived, and it was canceled after only thirteen episodes. With *All in the Family* continuing to attract millions of viewers by the week, CBS was increasingly giving Norman freer and freer rein. Meanwhile, as Norman's own notoriety continued to rise, he became even more of a household name, often overshadowing Yorkin, as the following profile in June 1973 from the *New York Times Magazine* illustrates:

"In the beginning," Yorkin says a shade wryly, "I was the one being written about." In 1959, Yorkin, the beefy-armed son of a Washington, PA dress shop owner, was the foremost director of prestige TV specials, showcasing stars like Fred Astaire and Jack Benny. Such specials were Tandem's initial stock and trade, although the team had so little clout at first that Marilyn Monroe made them wait for hours to see her about an idea for a TV musical and never showed up. Later their dreams of movie glory and Lear's protean television creations changed the nature of the relationship. These days Yorkin dismisses all the inevitable talk of disunity with bland comments like, "Whatever is good for me is good for Norman and vice versa." He is content to leave television pre-eminence to Lear and live a more even life than his intense partner.[6]

Although this was the story he presented to the public at the time, it's still hard to know for sure the extent to which Yorkin's sentiments were genuine or simply spin, especially since he and Norman had always kept a tight lid around the intricacies of their then-fourteen-year professional partnership, which subsequently came to an end just a little over a year later. Nevertheless, when it came to the frenetic atmosphere behind the scenes at all three shows, there was no denying the fact that tensions increasingly ran high.

Topping the list at *All in the Family* early on was that even as Tandem raked in millions from merchandising revenue, none of the cast profited. The reason why is because it wasn't in their original five-year contracts, nor at this time, in fairness to Norman and Yorkin, were there yet any formal rules in place from SAG and AFTRA, then two separately run actors' unions, requiring producers to make any concessions, so they often didn't, though not necessarily intentionally or out of greed. Today, of course, things are different. But back then, it was a typical case of out of sight, out of mind.

Such was also mostly the case for residuals at that time, which can explain why Bill Macy echoed a similar complaint in 2018, more than four decades after *Maude* premiered. As the cast of *All in the Family* had, he also signed a standard contract when *Maude* first went on the air in 1972. Unlike now, there were only three networks, there was no cable, and no one had the slightest inkling there would someday be on-demand streaming services and DVDs where people could watch any episode of their favorite show anytime, almost anywhere they wanted. Another major difference was that TV shows then weren't usually even considered viable for syndication until their fifth season, even though both SAG and AFTRA had been successfully negotiating residuals for weekly episodic series in reruns as far back as the mid-1950s. Yet they were still dependent on an actor's original contract and structured to slowly decrease over time, which is why so many popular TV actors from the 1950s to the 1970s received little if any residuals at all.

And so understandably, as *Maude* underwent something of a resurgence thanks to cable reruns on outlets like TV Land and Antenna TV beginning in the mid-1990s, followed by the release of its first season on DVD in 2007, Macy began to feel a sense of resentment that he'd been taken advantage of. As he told an interviewer in 2018: "We did the show from 1972 until 1978. We did 144 episodes, and I did 143. When I first signed a contract with Norman, my agent wasn't present and he [Norman] said, 'In case we go to syndication, there'll be a thing called residuals. You'll have the first year and I'll have everything after that. At that point, I was innocent and inexperienced and I said, 'Okay.' So now for all these years, he's been getting residuals, my residuals. He's a billionaire and I need the money. I think that's very naughty of him."[7]

Of all the actors he ever worked with, Rob Reiner was, of course, among the closest to Norman. However, that still didn't prevent him from occasionally speaking out. In November 1971, two months into *All in the Family*'s second season, for example, he uncharacteristically sounded off about the social relevance (or what he apparently deemed as a lack thereof at the time) on the show that had already made him a star, telling *Newsweek*, "Look, we got an entertainment vehicle, that's all."[8]

In the same article, Mike Evans, who played Lionel Jefferson, groused about being underpaid and his character in general. Complaining that it wasn't rounded or human enough, he said: "There's an unbelievability about it when a character can put up with all the stuff Lionel takes."[9] Sally Struthers, meanwhile, made noise about being typecast and Norman's apparent refusal to let Gloria wear more stylish clothes. Anxious that it would prevent her from landing future film roles, she lamented, "If I don't get to look my best, producers will think I'm a plain, average American girl."[10]

Although Jean Stapleton too would occasionally take issue with the direction of her character, the worst strife by far was the ongoing hostility between O'Connor and Norman, which was exacerbated the more successful Norman and the show became. "With Norman, it was like going to see the king," recalled Elliot Schoenman, a staff writer for *Maude*, which shared offices and studio space with *All in the Family* at CBS Television City during the early seasons of both shows. "And it was always very, very intense because he loved Bea Arthur, so if Norman gave notes about a particular script she would just say, 'OK.' But he was always at war with Carroll O'Connor, and their relationship was terrible. Everyone talked about it in the halls, and it sort of dominated the whole atmosphere."[11]

ROGER SHERMAN THEATRE
The new Roger Sherman Theatre, at 70 College Street, opened on March 12 with a showing of John Barrymore in "The Sea Beast". The theatre is one of the most modern in the East and is equipped to give dramatic as well as motion picture performances.

Early photo of the Roger Sherman Theater, Downtown New Haven (Yale Daily News, *March 20, 1926).* Courtesy Yale University

Southeast corner Chapel Street, New Haven, Connecticut. Courtesy New Haven Museum, New Haven, Connecticut

Southwest corner of Church and Chapel Street, Dudley Clothing, New Haven, Connecticut. Courtesy New Haven Museum, New Haven, Connecticut

New Haven Hospital—Nurses Dormitory, c. 1890. Courtesy New Haven Museum, New Haven, Connecticut

Norman and Jean Stapleton. CBS Photo Archives/Courtesy Estate of Jean Stapleton

Norman Lear and All in the Family *story editors Don Nicholls, Michael Ross, and Bernie West (1974).* Photo by Brian Hammill/Getty Images

The cast of All in the Family *and Norman at the Smithsonian.* Stapleton/Putch Archives/Courtesy Estate of Jean Stapleton

All in the Family *backstage.* Courtesy Estate of Jean Stapleton

All in the Family *backstage.* Courtesy Estate of Jean Stapleton

Norman Lear with Good Times *cast.* UPI Photo/Jim Ruymen/ Alamy Stock Photo

Norman Lear, with actress Louise Lasser, announces the cancellation of Mary Hartman, Mary Hartman *before the show could lose popularity (1977).* Photofest

Norman and Frances Lear,
Los Angeles, 1980. Photofest

Hollywood, California: Milton
Berle, Lucille Ball, former CBS
chairman William Paley, and
producer Norman Lear smile
for photographers as they are
inducted into the Academy of
Television Arts and Sciences
Hall of Fame. Photo by
Bettmann/Getty Images,
January 21, 1984

All in the Family (CBS) TV Series, 1971–1979. Shown on the set, from left: Jean
Stapleton, Carroll O'Connor, producer Norman Lear, Rob Reiner, Sally Struthers, and
Mike Evans. CBS/Photofest © CBS

All in the Family *(CBS) 20th Anniversary Reunion, 1991. Shown from left: Jean Stapleton, Carroll O'Connor, producer Norman Lear, Sally Struthers, and Rob Reiner.* CBS/Photofest © CBS

All in the Family. *Carroll O'Connor, Norman Lear, and Mike Salisbury (April 9, 2001).* © Globe Photos/ZUMAPRESS.com/Alamy Stock Photo

Bea Arthur, Norman Lear, and Jean Stapleton, December 30, 2005, New York City. © Judie Burstein/Globe Photos/ZUMAPRESS.com/Alamy Stock Photo

Norman and wife Lyn attending Cagney the Musical *in Los Angeles, 2017.* Courtesy Riki Kane Larimer and Kate Edleman, producers, and actor Robert Creigton

Norman pictured with actor Robert Creighton and producer Kate Edleman at Cagney the Musical *in Los Angeles, 2017.* Photo courtesy of Riki Kane Larimer and Kate Edelman, producers, and actor Robert Creigton

Norman Lear with his wife Lyn and their family arriving at the Ocean's 13 *premiere at the Chinese Theatre in Los Angeles, June 4, 2007.* Tsuni USA/Alamy Stock Photos

First Collegiate Defense Stamp Bureau

Norman M. Lear, son of Mr. and Mrs. H. K. Lear, 68 Woodstock St., oversees operation of the Defense Stamp Bureau he conceived at Emerson College. Federal authorities are said to be contemplating a campaign to establish other such bureaus as a result.

Norman opens the first National Collegiate Stamp Bureau at Emerson College (c. 1940s). Emerson College Alumni Records/Courtesy Emerson College

Norman standing next to his statue during the dedication at Emerson College, 2018. Emerson College Photograph Collection/ Courtesy Emerson College

The 2017 Kennedy Center Honor Award recipients: First row left to right: Carmen de Lavallade, Norman Lear, and Gloria Estefan. Second row: LL Cool J and Lionel Ritchie (December 2, 2017, Washington, DC). US State Department/Alamy Stock Photo

Attempting to untangle the undercurrent of their acrimony through O'Connor's own words in her book, *Archie & Edith, Mike & Gloria: The Tumultuous History of "All in the Family,"* author Donna McCrohan noted the difference between O'Connor and a star like Jackie Gleason:

> The difficulty, to some degree, lay in the fact that Gleason produced and created, as well as starred in Gleason's programs. In the case of *All in the Family*, O'Connor had to share these honors with Norman Lear. Elsewhere O'Connor had said, "His [Lear's] idea of comedy, I think, is at variance with mine, and we've disagreed over material from the very beginning of the show over what made naturalistic comedy. I had one idea; he had another. But my ideas prevailed. . . . If there is a battle and I keep winning, one of us keeps winning, there are hard feelings. And that's the best way I can put it."[12]

O'Connor also had this to say in his 1998 memoir, *I Think I'm Outta Here*:

> Our Archie joke writers were the cleverest jokes draftsmen in television and what they delivered every week was the very special product they were hired to write. But I refused to play the naked joke, to do the setup-punchline routine, and asked them to recast the jokes as characteristic thrusts and rejoinders, and rework sketch material to the emotional dimensions of a short play. They often balked and more than once threatened to quit, but I too more than once threatened to quit. Lear didn't write for the show, but he gave the writers orders, watched dress rehearsals and gave notes. He hated to tamper with a joke, and he and I had frequent arguments about jokes. He was glad to have other TV projects to turn his attention to—spinoffs from our series like *Maude* and *The Jeffersons* and several other sitcom plunges—glad to see less of me, as I was to see less of him.[13]

In a similar vein, during a 1999 interview with the Television Academy Foundation, O'Connor talked about Norman's supposed reluctance to share writing credits with him even though, according to O'Connor, he rewrote many of the scripts—including the first episode "Meet the Bunkers"—as well as his lingering resentment toward Norman for allegedly not giving him a share of the profits from the shows he spun off from *All in the Family*. Said O'Connor:

We wrote at night at rehearsal, and I would rewrite at home at night, and I would bring in my script of the rewrites in the next day. And then Norman, I think, soon perceived we didn't like each other very much. I was nasty to him on occasion. I should have kept my cool, but you make these mistakes. I'd say outrageous things to him, and he got pretty sore. I got sore at him, too, and then he spun these shows off my show [and] he never offered me a piece of any show. And, of course, I'm very materialistic. That's a euphemism for greedy. I thought that since it's my show and he's doing this thing from my show, it's customary in this business to give a piece. But on any of his shows that spun off from my show, no way. He wouldn't give me any money or any credit or anything even until this day.[14]

On the other hand, while Norman never denied their relationship had been at times strained, he also insisted to Larry King that he never felt any ill will toward O'Connor during an appearance on *Larry King Now* to promote his memoir *Even This I Get to Experience* in 2014. When King—who quoted Norman's "murderously difficult" description of O'Connor from the book—asked about the root cause of their perennial friction and how they each made peace with one another in their own way, Norman explained that "He was basically afraid of being Archie Bunker."

I struggle with it because it's so human and complex. He was very unhappy with certain aspects of our relationship, but when he passed and I went to the house to visit his wife Nancy with a lot of other people, she asked me to wait until the others had left. When we were alone, she took me into a hallway into a room and opened the doors. It was locked and it was his study. The desk was empty except for a piece of paper, a letter I had written him four years before telling him how much I loved him and how much I hated some of the time we spent together fighting, but basically how grateful I was. That was the only piece of paper on his desk.

In the same interview, Norman added: "He didn't like most of what he read. Now, I was wise enough at my age to understand that he was carrying a load—that boom, this show made him a star and a bigot at that—and he was an extremely intellectual guy, a Dublin theater kind of intellectual, with one of the best hearts and wisest minds, so playing this bigot was not easy, although I didn't have to talk him into it. He ached to do it. I put words on paper, and he inhabited them."[15]

However, when it came to O'Connor's seemingly ever-present ire, Norman wasn't the only person with whom he had an axe to grind. Practically from day one, he was also at frequent odds with director John Rich. In addition to one particularly contentious incident that occurred during the week leading up to the season-2 taping of "The Elevator Story," another major blow-up occurred several weeks earlier during the episode "Christmas Day at the Bunkers." At issue then was O'Connor's objection to a scene that had Louise Jefferson, the Bunkers' African American next-door neighbor, standing under some mistletoe with Lionel goading Archie to kiss her.

Though he prevailed again this time, things quickly went from bad to worse—with O'Connor soon demanding his own private dressing room at CBS complete with a color television and couches (another request he was granted)—as Norman refused to allow him to accept a lucrative offer to appear in beer commercials that would have netted him hundreds of thousands of dollars on top of the twenty-five-thousand per episode that he was already earning playing Archie Bunker.

Meanwhile, in an April 1974 article entitled "The Uprising in Lear's Kingdom," *TV Guide* reported one occasion during which O'Connor allegedly lashed out at John Rich for asking him to repeat a line. According to the account offered in the story, O'Connor said, "If I make a change, I'll make it for a reason. If anybody up there in the booth wants to come down and play my part, OK. Meantime, I'm exercising my right of approval on the script."[16]

Three months later, the manure really hit the sewer (as Archie might have said) when O'Connor walked off the set as production for *AITF*'s fifth season got underway in the summer of 1974. Among other things, he filed a lawsuit against Tandem seeking $65,000 in back salary, his name above the title in the show's opening sequence, and clarification of his contract. In turn, Norman immediately got an injunction barring O'Connor from performing until the lawsuit—which O'Connor later conceded "was only kind of a make-up thing to cover myself from walking off" and from out of which he received a $5,000 per episode raise—was settled. "I said they hadn't lived up to the contract," O'Connor recalled. "My original contract called for me to be in an executive capacity, whatever the billing, but that I would have script control and that I would be a script writer on the show. Not just in fact as I was, but de jure. And I also wanted five thousand dollars more an episode, but nobody thought I was going to get any of that. I got the money, but I didn't get the other stuff and the show went on."[17]

To cover their bases while the dispute was still being settled, Norman and Rich forwent plans to open the fourth season with a four-parter about inflation. In its place instead, the writers cleverly came up with another three-part storyline during which Edith, Gloria, and Mike are frantic with worry when Archie goes missing at a veteran's convention in Buffalo, with the still-unknown outcome in the third installment hinged on whether O'Connor would return. These episodes also introduced a new character to the show: Stretch Cunningham, Archie's goofball, joke-cracking coworker from the loading dock, who up until then had been talked about but never seen. He was played by James Cromwell, the actor and activist who would become best known for his Academy Award–nominated turn as the farmer who dances with the pig in the 1995 film *Babe*, and more recently for his Emmy-winning portrayal of Ewan Roy in the hit HBO drama *Succession*. A classically trained actor born into Hollywood royalty as the son of actress Kay Johnson and film director John Cromwell, he was thirty-four years old when he landed the role of Stretch Cunningham on *All in the Family*, where the writers had also briefly considered making his character the much-younger love interest of Irene Lorenzo following the departure of Vincent Gardenia at the end of season 4. At the time, Cromwell, who'd recently moved to Los Angeles and briefly worked as a probation officer after hitchhiking around the world for eighteen months, had just gotten his first television role playing a tennis instructor on the NBC detective series *The Rockford Files* starring James Garner. It was sometime shortly thereafter (thanks to Michael Sevareid, also an actor and the son of legendary CBS newsman Eric Sevareid, with whom Cromwell had attended Middlebury College in Vermont) that he first landed on the radar of Tandem casting director Jane Murray. "The only person I knew in L.A. was Michael, and as a favor to me he sent me down to be interviewed by [casting director] Jane [Murray]," he recalled.

> I'd done ten years of theater by this point, and she picked out the one thing that I actually was not completely forthright with, which was that I understudied the role of King Claudius from *Hamlet* at the Connecticut Shakespeare Festival. I did go on, but I wasn't cast in the role originally, so I thought that was the end of that.
>
> And then about three months later, the phone rang on a Friday afternoon around five o'clock and it was my agent telling me to get down to CBS right away and audition for Norman Lear. [Back then], I didn't watch television at all. I didn't know who Norman was, I didn't know Carroll O'Connor, I didn't know there was a show called *All in the*

Family. So I just went down there, she handed me the pages, I went out into the waiting room to work on it for about five minutes and she said, "Okay, come in and do it for me."

After I did, she told me to go back to the waiting room and then the director came down and I read for him. I don't think it was John Rich. It was one of the other directors who said, "Okay, that's great. Let's go up and talk to Norman." And I went up and talked to Norman, who said, "I'll see you on Monday." I had just channeled Stretch Cunningham, and then later when I heard it, I realized that I had sort of channeled Art Carney from *The Honeymooners*, but I didn't do it on purpose.

It just seemed to fit the character. I loved that he was the unfunniest funnyman and that I didn't know what the circumstances were, which was that Carroll wasn't there and that there was a possibility that they might kill him off.[18]

Luckily for the show, O'Connor would, of course, return, although his conflicts with Norman persisted throughout the remainder of the series. Yet another major source of contention between the two men was allowing the show to continue as *Archie Bunker's Place*, as it did until 1983 against Norman's wishes even as O'Connor began showing remorse about some of his conduct toward the end of *All in the Family*'s original run, telling *TV Guide* in 1979, "I regret nothing about my years on *All in the Family* except my own anger."[19]

Amid all the rancor with O'Connor, Norman also encountered his fair share of difficulties with Sally Struthers, who felt increasingly overshadowed by her costars. Frustrated that Gloria had become little more than window dressing, she also wanted to do movies. Then in 1975, just as the writers had begun developing a new storyline in which Gloria becomes pregnant with Archie's grandson, Joey, she sued Tandem to try and get out of her contract. Consequently, as it had with O'Connor, Tandem retaliated. It successfully obtained an injunction that, according to *Variety*, "not only ordered her to refrain from working in TV or radio until after all the first-run segments of *All in the Family* are completed, but also in the event Tandem should continue her contract for the part's remaining two years," decreeing also that "she is to further refrain from working on other entertainment media while *All in the Family* is in production."[20]

While Struthers would remain with the show for another three seasons, she apparently still held a grudge against Norman about the incident over forty years later. In 2021, during an appearance on *Gilbert Gottfried's Amazing Colossal Podcast!*, here's what she told Gottfried and cohost Frank Santopadre word for word:

> Norman wouldn't let me out to do a movie, a big motion picture, *The Day of the Locust*. The award-winning British director John Schlessinger was directing it, and I was going to be the lead in the film. My agent and I went to Norman and said, "Can I get out of the last four tapings of the season to shoot this film?" He said, "Absolutely not." . . . The next year, he let Rob Reiner out of several shows to shoot a film with Alan Arkin called *Fire Sale*, and I found a lawyer and said, "Get me off this effing show, the nepotism and the misogynistic attitude around here, I want out."[21]

Adding further fuel to the fire was Struthers's rocky relationship with director John Rich, whom she claimed bullied her. In the same interview for *Gilbert Gottfried's Amazing Colossal Podcast!*, she detailed one incident when things got out of hand:

> One day in rehearsal hall, Betty Garrett and I were coloring in our coloring books and they were starting act one, which was a scene between Mike and Edith in the kitchen. [John] says, "Yes, we're starting from act one and I want you to get over there in place outside the Bunker's doorway and wait for your entrance. . . . I don't want to hear your platform shoes clomping across the floor while they're doing their scene. Get over here now." And I did the worst thing a human being can do and I've never forgiven myself for it because he was of the Jewish faith. I clicked my heels together, raised my hand in a Nazi salute and said, "Yes sir."
> He did a three-point kick on a folding chair lunging at me, and I ran out of the rehearsal hall and down to the bowels of CBS to all the places where the electronics stuff goes on and up another stairwell up into the executive suites and into Norman's office.[22]

Though it is unclear whether this confrontation was, in fact, what led to Rich ultimately leaving *AITF* at the end of the fourth season (a decision he later said "upset" Norman),[23] he would nevertheless remain very much a part of the Tandem stable, going on to direct *Family*'s one-hundredth show guest-starring Henry Fonda the following season, along with early episodes of *Good Times* and *The Jeffersons*, as well as scores of other sitcoms throughout the remainder of his life, including *Barney Miller*, *Benson*, *Newhart*, and *Murphy*

Brown. About the incident with Struthers, Rich wrote in his memoir: "In frustration, I kicked a folding chair standing near my podium. . . ."

> I exited the room, slamming the door behind me. Had a camera been in the hallway as I entered that space, it would have caught me grabbing my foot in agony and exhibiting a "pain take." . . . Then I limped to my office and called an orthopedist. . . .
>
> After lunch [and X-ray studies at the doctor's office that showed no break but a severe strain that required a short plaster cast], when I returned to rehearsal, Sally apologized and everyone had a good laugh, including me. We never did find out what was bothering her that day.[24]

As Tandem and Norman's statures continued to grow, his strife with O'Connor and Struthers and the consternation between the two actors and John Rich was only the tip of the iceberg. In January 1974, for example—six months before O'Connor did the same at *AITF*—Redd Foxx had walked off the set of *Sanford and Son* in a dustup that was a combination of money and Foxx's increasing dissatisfaction with how the show's still predominantly white writing staff were depicting African Americans, a frustration he increasingly took out on Yorkin, Norman, and Aaron Ruben.

Increasing also were Foxx's addictions to alcohol and cocaine. As *S&S* got more and more popular and the comedian became more famous, he indulged in both with greater frequency. Although he would return to the show for another three seasons with practically all his demands met, Foxx's nine-episode absence permanently soured his relationship with Yorkin and Ruben who were subsequently replaced by producers Saul Turtletaub and Bernie Orenstein for the remainder of the series.

Then there was another matter in December 1973, when Bill Macy made some off-color remarks that nearly resulted in *Maude* being permanently banned from the Emmys. The transgression occurred when Norman and Yorkin were being feted with the "Man of the Year Award" by the Hollywood chapter of the National Television Academy of Arts and Sciences during a black-tie gala in the grand ballroom of the Beverly Wilshire Hotel.

With many of Hollywood's highest-wattage A-listers in attendance and *The Tonight Show*'s first host Steve Allen serving as the emcee, virtually no expense was spared. And with Norman and Yorkin having graciously insisted that the people who worked on their shows also receive awards, everyone (except for Carroll O'Connor who refused to attend, and Rob Reiner who was said to be undergoing his own contractual disagreements with Tandem at the time and claimed to have another commitment) was there.

The logistics of the festivities had been arranged to have Norman and Yorkin standing on a stage where they would call out the names of the various actors and writers from each show, upon which a spotlight would shine on their table as an usher came over to present whoever it was with their award as they stood, took a bow, and sat back down.

Up first was Vincent Gardenia, the gregarious Italian stage actor who'd played the mayor of the fictional town in Norman's film satire about quitting smoking, *Cold Turkey*, which also costarred Jean Stapleton. But ever since being cast as the Bunkers' next-door neighbor Frank Lorenzo on *All in the Family*, Gardenia had increasingly grown frustrated over not having enough to do on the show. And at this exact moment he was to receive the award, he was slightly inebriated, so when the usher gave it to him, he stood up and yelled, "Norman, I don't know what I'm doing in the show, but I love you."[25]

Setting the tone for the rest of the night, up next was still-then *Sanford and Son* producer Aaron Ruben, who was at the height of being at crosshairs with Foxx who'd shown up at the event high and had reportedly been passing his stash around his table, where several members of the cast and crew from *Maude* were sitting. During the cocktail hour earlier in the evening, Foxx had already said something offensive to Bea Arthur who shot right back. Then, later, just as Yorkin was about to present Ruben with his award, Foxx announced audibly that he was going to the men's room.

At which point, the famed composer Henry Mancini, who was within earshot, became so enraged at Foxx that he reprimanded him verbally, and a brawl nearly broke out. According to Foxx's biographer, Michael Starr: "The famous composer grabbed Redd by his lapels and shook him, which pissed Redd off even more. The two men began shouting at each other and had to be separated before a fistfight broke out."[26]

But even this dustup couldn't trump what was about to happen as Bill Macy took to the stage with Norman—and then grabbed the microphone, turned toward the audience, and at the top of his lungs, shouted, "Cocksuckers of the world, unite!"

At the same time the room fell silent, there were nervous titters of laughter. "This was my first black-tie affair ever and as soon as he said it, my first reaction was, 'Oh God, Bill,'" said costar Adrienne Barbeau. "And then I looked around and people began leaving. I seem to remember that Henry Mancini got up and walked out."[27]

"Bill's friends and I will never understand what possessed him to behave in such a bizarre manner," recalled Betty Garrett. "Of course, he'd had a little too much to drink, but it may be that his long run in *Oh! Calcutta!*, the first Broadway show to feature full frontal nudity, made him equate success and admiration with scatological behavior. He obviously thought he'd get a laugh. Today, what he did would get a great giggle, but at the time it could have been devastating to his career."[28]

Explaining what may have led to Macy's lapse in judgment as she encapsulated both the general mood of the evening and how the untoward deed went down, the actor's widow Samantha Harper Macy, also remembered: "That's when Norman fell in love with me as an actress because there were all these tables with all his different shows, and they were supposed to be surrounded by other TV stars who'd come to honor him."

He was kind of being a bad boy on stage. He'd say, "Thank you so much, Mary, for coming to see my show," referring to Mary Tyler Moore, who wasn't there. "And thank you, Valerie Harper," who wasn't there either. None of the people he was talking about were there, and it was real embarrassing, which he did to embarrass the audience.

Bill and I were sitting at the *Maude* table, and there was every kind of booze in the world, bottles of it, and as it was, he was having trouble with the director Hal Cooper, who treated him as an underling and kicked him in the pants one time when he flubbed a line. Bill would come home and he would be just freaked, so he was in hell. We went to this party; he was drinking a lot of liquor, and he got this idea that he would take a chair, push it up against the apron of the stage and at some point, he'd jump up there with Norman, which he did.

In the meantime, Redd Foxx was sitting at our table, and he gave Bill something to snort, and he snorted it. And then, Redd got totally freaked because he could see that Bill was really out there, and so he left. He went and he hid in the bathroom. Meanwhile, super-stoned Bill was sitting at the table and when Norman started to talk and said, "The *Maude* table," Bill jumped up on stage with him and started fighting with him for the mic until Norman took it away from him and said, "Our father who art in heaven."

Well, that's when Bill grabbed it back from him and said, "Cocksuckers of the world unite!" He thought he was going to get great applause and that everybody in the building would understand that the people in this business were cocksuckers . . . and they'd all get the joke and he would get a great laugh. Of course, he did not get a laugh. And then Norman took the mic back and said, "Our father who art in heaven, hallowed be thy name . . ."

He started doing the Lord's Prayer again, and the joke was kind of blowing over and Bill didn't like it. Not only had he not gotten a huge laugh, but now Norman was covering it up making nice, so Bill said, "Well, if I can't talk, I'll . . ." And then he just did something. He didn't drop his pants, but he made a hand gesture as if he were jerking off and that was a big thing. It caused some serious damage for a while.[29]

So severe was the fallout that, despite multiple nominations, *Maude* never won an Emmy Award until its second-to-last season when Bea Arthur finally took home the statue for Outstanding Lead Actress in a Comedy Series in 1977. In the immediate aftermath, CBS also threatened to fire Macy until Norman intervened. "The network wrote us a letter that they could fire him for good reason and were thinking about firing him," said Samantha Macy. "And Norman said, 'Absolutely we're not doing this show without Bill.'"

A few weeks later, he called us and said, "I hear some bad things about you guys. I want you to come to my office right now." So we went to Norman's office, and I said, "What have you been hearing bad about us?" And he said, "That you're taking this seriously. I'm going to protect you. They're not going to take your job away and you do not have to worry. I'm going to take care of you." It was very loving and kind because Bill was innocent, and he thought people could take a joke that had a little sexuality to it. And they couldn't at that time. They just couldn't.[30]

At around this same time of the Television Academy debacle with Macy, there were also cracks starting to surface in Norman's marriage to Frances. They had been married for almost seventeen years by then, Kate and Maggie were now in their mid-teens, and Ellen, Norman's oldest daughter with his first wife Charlotte, was now twenty-six. Many of their marital problems had to do with the fact that Frances felt dwarfed by Norman's astronomical success and fame over the past couple of years on top of her general disdain for the Hollywood limelight.

Observed TV producer Barbara Gaines, who worked as a production assistant on *Maude*:

She was very complicated, and I think their marriage was already over by then. But Frances was interesting. She was a pioneer woman and probably maybe a little jealous of Norman's success. [But] I got along with her, and I always wanted to have a baby, so [anyway] one day I can't remember where we were, but Norman was standing there and she said to me right in front of him, "Norman wants another baby. Why don't you do it with him?" And she was serious. Really, she wasn't kidding, and I thought, "Well, no, I don't think that's a good idea," but in any event, she was stringent, she blurted it out. She just blurted out what she thought. She really did give Norman a lot of grief when I knew them even though I think he was always trying to please her, and it was not happening.[31]

On the other hand, on par things continued to look rosy for Norman. In many respects, he was just getting started.

CHAPTER 20

New Additions

With a keen eye toward future distribution and having full ownership of its shows, in 1972 Tandem began ramping up its leadership team. Among the most significant new recruits enlisted by Norman to become director of development that year was Al Burton, the diminutive veteran TV theme song composer and producer whose knack for recognizing talent would help to launch the careers of George Clooney, Leonardo DiCaprio, Jimmy Kimmel, Valerie Bertinelli, Michael J. Fox, Rick Schroeder, Sarah Jessica Parker, and many others. Along with Norman at Tandem (and later T.A.T. Communications and Embassy Television), Burton would be a major catalyst for such shows as *The Jeffersons, One Day at a Time, Mary Hartman, Mary Hartman, Fernwood 2 Night, America 2 Night, Diff'rent Strokes, The Facts of Life,* and *Silver Spoons.*

Then in 1973 after being introduced by Frances, Norman hired Virginia Carter, a Canadian-born former aerospace engineer and early spokesperson for the women's liberation movement, to become director and later vice president of creative affairs. In this capacity, she formed a film division specifically devoted to making made-for-television movies. After starting their careers there, many of the other executives who also joined Tandem back then often remained with the company and its later incarnations for decades. Among them were chief financial officer Daryl Egerstrom, business affairs executive Kelly Smith, director of syndication Gary Lieberthal, casting director and wardrobe coordinator Jane Murray and Rita Riggs, and longtime producers Patrica Fass Palmer, Rita Dillon, George Sunga, and Ken Stump.

But of those who came aboard during this time, none left more of an indelible mark than Jerry Perenchio, the swashbuckling billionaire media mogul, real estate magnate, art collector, and philanthropist who would turn Tandem on its ear.

Together with Perenchio—whom Norman once described as a "piece of finery who wore his Italian heritage like a glove"[1]—they were unstoppable. Yet in many ways, the two men were diametrical opposites, especially when it came to politics and their respective upbringings, which may have been part of their winning formula. While Norman was one of Hollywood's most outspoken liberals, Perenchio was a lifelong Republican and staunch supporter of GOP causes and candidates, including serving as co–finance director for John McCain's 2008 presidential bid. Whereas Norman's father was a huckster who served time in prison for selling fake securities, Perenchio's dad ran wineries in Napa Valley and later managed the Greek Theatre at Griffith Park in Los Angeles.

Perenchio was born in Fresno, California, in 1930. As a young boy, he often helped load baskets of grapes into a flatbed truck for his immigrant grandfather's produce import business before attending Black Foxx Military Institute in Los Angeles when he was fifteen. While studying at UCLA as an undergraduate business major, he started his first company, which booked bands and catered parties.

Following graduation in 1954 and a three-year Air Force enlistment as a flight trainer and jet fighter pilot, he began his entertainment career at MCA as a junior agent in the Band and Act department in 1958, where he was quickly anointed to become the youngest vice president in the history of the agency and then promoted to MCA's West Coast head of concerts. It was around this time also that he first met Norman and Yorkin after being dispatched by MCA's head honcho Lew Wasserman to procure a musical group they wanted singer Andy Williams to hear.

Perenchio flourished at MCA. A natural salesman with a gift for gab, he lived by instinct and a business philosophy later published in the *Wall Street Journal* called "20 Rules for the Road": "Supreme Self-Confidence, never arrogance"; "Teamwork"; "No Nepotism, no hiring of friends"; "When you suit up each day, it's to play Yankee Stadium or Dodger Stadium. Think big"; etcetera.[2] But shortly after his first encounter with Norman and Yorkin, Perenchio left MCA in 1962 after the Justice Department shuttered its talent management division following an anti-trust lawsuit.

Setting up his own shop soon afterward and merging it with another firm to form Chartwell Artists, his new venture rapidly grew into the fifth-largest talent agency in the world, handling the likes of Richard Burton and Elizabeth Taylor, Marlon Brando, Jane Fonda, Henry Mancini, Johnny Mathis, and Glen Campbell. Aside from repping talent and being an early cable television pioneer who cofounded National Subscription Television (ON-TV) in 1977, throughout his career, Perenchio would also be responsible for some of the most lucrative deals in the history of the entertainment industry, including the $60 million sale of Caesar's Palace in Las Vegas in 1969, and in 1989 and 1993, the sales of A&M and Motown Records to Polygram.

In 1986, he also paid $14 million for the Bel-Air estate known as the "Clampett Mansion" seen in the opening sequence of *The Beverly Hillbillies*, where he lived for the rest of his life. Another consequential early professional feat was booking a little-known British pop singer named Elton John, who had just recorded his first album, into the famed Troubadour club in Hollywood for a two-week engagement in the summer of 1970. Unofficially becoming the launch pad for John's spectacular career in the United States, word spread so quickly after the opening night performance that he became an overnight sensation.

Not long afterward, Perenchio sold Chartwell to another agency in 1971. No doubt spurred by his positive experience with John at the Troubadour, he decided to turn his attention to promotions full-time. Almost immediately, he found himself center ring as the promoter of what became known as the "Fight of the Century" between current heavyweight boxing world champion Joe Frazier and former undisputed world champ Muhammad Ali (who had lost his title because of his refusal to enter the draft for the Vietnam War) at New York's Madison Square Garden on March 8, 1971.

Perenchio landed the coveted assignment after raising the $5 million purse from then–Los Angeles Lakers owner Jack Kent Cooke. He then successfully negotiated the pay-per-view TV rights for over one hundred countries, and with the help of concert promoters, sold 1.5 million tickets to the historic celebrity-filled bout. Among the famous spectators were Dustin Hoffman, Woody Allen, Barbra Streisand, and Norman Mailer, while Burt Lancaster provided ringside commentary and Frank Sinatra took pictures for *Life* magazine.

After fifteen nail-biting rounds, Frazier defeated Ali, and Perenchio and Cook split the estimated $10 million profits. Perenchio's next event was perhaps an even bigger spectacle. In September 1973, he promoted the historic, $100,000 winner-take-all "Battle of the Sexes" showdown between then-twenty-nine-year-old, still-in-her-prime tennis champ Billie Jean King and her longtime adversary, the formerly great chauvinistic fifty-five-year-old braggart Bobby Riggs. Taking place at the Houston Astrodome and televised during prime-time on ABC—with King winning in three sets—it was the highest-rated broadcast of that year and the most attended live tennis match ever.

It was also during this same period that Perenchio, who had been toying with the idea of branching out into movies and television, fell in with Norman and Yorkin again. Though he hadn't kept in touch with Norman since their first meeting a decade earlier, he still socialized occasionally with Yorkin and his wife, Peg, who were close friends of his former client Henry Mancini.

And then when Atlantic Records was preparing to release the first *All in the Family* LP album in the fall of 1971, Yorkin, seeking advice about the contract, reached out to Perenchio, who reviewed it and made recommendations pro bono. But when Yorkin called again several months later about a similar request for a forthcoming *Sanford and Son* album that was being released by RCA, Perenchio insisted on being compensated. In turn, this is when Norman suggested putting him on Tandem's payroll as CEO to oversee the company's business operations.

Though Perenchio was indeed intrigued by the prospect, in keeping with his reputation as a tough-as-nails bottom-line negotiator, he insisted on the following terms: total anonymity when it came to Tandem's business side, having the final say in all budgets, and being the deciding factor in instances when the business and creative sides of the company overlapped. He also insisted on having the option to buy a third of the company at book value and putting everything in writing.

At this same time—and as Norman and Yorkin consulted with Tandem's attorneys and accountants about the feasibility of such an arrangement—Perenchio was actively on the lookout for a protégé he could groom to become his number-two man in whatever his next big endeavor might be, the same way MCA had trained him. He knew he wanted someone with a solid background in business, who was smart, savvy, and ambitious. Who they were or where they came from didn't matter as long as they had no prior connection to the entertainment industry.

After months of searching in vain and interviewing nearly sixty candidates, the young wunderkind he chose was Alan Horn, a recent Harvard MBA, who was referred to Perenchio by a friend. Born in New York and raised on Long Island in Riverhead, Horn at the time was living in Cincinnati working for consumer-packaged goods giant Proctor & Gamble as an assistant brand manager for Ivory Soap. Perenchio, meanwhile, had been in Greensburg, Pennsylvania, canvassing door to door trying to drum up subscribers for what would eventually become ON-TV.

After a series of phone calls, Horn agreed to fly to Pittsburgh in the winter of 1972 and meet with Perenchio in person at the airport. But when Horn, then twenty-nine, showed up at the information booth where they'd agreed to rendezvous, he looked nothing at all like the preppy Ivy League type Perenchio had been expecting. Though he was tall, slim, and attractive, he had a lofty, wiry afro and a thick bushy moustache. He also wore a gold diamond pinky ring and made his entrance clicking across the concrete floor in a pair of Cuban heel shoes.

Yet despite his appearance, which Perenchio initially found off-putting, he was equally impressed by Horn's charm and intellect, and they immediately hit it off. At Perenchio's insistence, they met again about a month later, this time at the New York Athletic Club. During the meeting, Perenchio instructed Horn to give him his best elevator pitch for why he should hire him—at which point Horn, who was a fifth-degree tae-kwon-do black belt, in his enthusiasm, accidentally dented a wall with his fist.

As much as anything, this undoubtedly made such an impression on Perenchio that he hired him on the spot. "I had no experience in the entertainment business, I had never been to Hollywood and I didn't know anyone there," Horn told the *Harvard Business School Alumni Magazine* in 2016. "He said, 'You're perfect,' and hired me. He wanted a blank slate."[3]

Perenchio also offered Horn a starting salary of $25,000 a year, the same as he'd been making at Proctor & Gamble, on top of moving expenses that included shipping his Austin-Healy sports car across the country from Cincinnati to California by train. At first, though, exactly what Horn would be doing when he got there appeared to be a blank slate too, because by this point Perenchio still didn't have a formal deal in place with Norman and Yorkin.

After months of back-and-forth—and initially with no contract—Perenchio officially joined Tandem as president and CEO in January 1973, with Horn working underneath him. In addition to helping to procure new studio space and production offices at Metromedia in Hollywood after CBS Television City became too cramped and negotiating the deal for *All in the Family's* first syndication package in 1975 with Viacom, in 1974 Norman and Perenchio formed a second production company called T.A.T. Communications, deriving the acronym from the Yiddish expression *tuches ahfen tisch*, which translated as "enough talk—put your ass on the table."

Still, all was not hunky-dory even as both Tandem and T.A.T grew exponentially throughout the remainder of the decade. Within months of Perenchio's and Horn's arrival, Norman was said to have privately told Perenchio that he no longer wanted to be partners with Yorkin after nearly fourteen years together.

Yorkin left Tandem in the fall of 1974, always maintaining that his split with Norman and Perenchio, with whom he later teamed up to produce the 1982 science-fiction thriller *Blade Runner* starring Harrison Ford, had been amicable. Formally making the announcement to the *New York Times*, he said, "There's nothing wrong with our relationship. I've decided doing both films and TV is too strenuous for me."[4]

In early 1975, Yorkin formed Bud Yorkin Productions, where his first project was the short-lived *Sanford and Son* spinoff *Grady* starring Whitman Mayo. Then in 1976, he joined forces with *S&S* producers Saul Turtletaub and Bernie Orenstein to form TOY Productions whose two sitcoms *What's Happening!* and *Carter Country* were modest hits for ABC before TOY was acquired by Columbia Pictures Television in 1979.

Meanwhile, with Perenchio eventually making Horn president of Tandem before later becoming chairman of Embassy Television at Norman's behest, the three would continue to work together for the next fifteen years. Following the sale of Embassy to the Coca-Cola Company in 1985 for $485 million in Coca-Cola stock, Perenchio went on to produce the 1989 film *Driving Miss Daisy* costarring Morgan Freeman and Jessica Tandy. In 1992, he partnered with Mexican billionaire Emilio Azcarraga to purchase Univision for $550 million, turning it into the largest US Hispanic TV network and selling it in 2007 for $13.7 billion.

Horn would also go on to enjoy a similarly spectacular career. Soon after leaving Embassy Television in 1986, he became president of 20th Century Fox shortly after it was acquired by Rupert Murdoch. Then in 1987, he cofounded Castle Rock Entertainment with Rob Reiner, overseeing such films as *The Green Mile*, *When Harry Met Sally*, and *A Few Good Men* along with TV's *Seinfeld*. He later became president and chief operating officer for Warner Brothers, where he ran the studio for more than a decade and executive-produced such films as the *Harry Potter* series, *The Dark Knight Trilogy*, and *The Hobbit Trilogy*, before becoming chairman of Walt Disney Studios in 2012.

CHAPTER 21

Spinning Off a Spin-Off

It might seem out of sync that the idea for a sitcom spun off from another show could exist first. However, that's precisely what happened in the case of Tandem's next big hit *Good Times*—TV's first spin-off of a spin-off, and the first to feature a two-parent African American family in the main roles—which was descended from *Maude* in 1974.

Here's how the roundabout gestation happened. Flush from his success playing the Bunkers' next-door neighbor Lionel Jefferson on *All in the Family* and looking to expand the role, in late 1971 actor Mike Evans enlisted the help of Eric Monte, a young African American writer whose rags-to-riches rise and subsequent epic fall was nothing if not astounding. Monte, whose real name was Kenneth Williams, was the middle of three children raised by a single mother in Chicago's infamous Cabrini Green housing project.

His mother, Anna, was a voracious reader, and it was her influence on top of escaping to the movies every Saturday with his older sister that fueled Monte's early passion to become a writer. With a particular affinity for Westerns, the fuse that lit his fire ignited when he was just five years old. While playing cowboys and Indians one afternoon on a street corner near his apartment building, the aha moment occurred when a white man told Monte he couldn't be the Lone Ranger because he was Black.

It was right then and there, after seeing the fictional character again on the big screen and realizing the white guy was right, that he decided he was going to create some Black heroes of his own someday, which is precisely what he set out to do. "The only things the Lone Ranger wore that were black were his mask, gun holster and boots," Monte recalled. "I soon came to realize the only blacks I saw in the movies and on television were servants, buffoons, and worse, clowns. For the first time in my life, I felt ashamed. So I made a vow that when I grew up I would become a writer and create black heroes."[1]

Still imbued with this dream as a teenager, and despite the discouragement of his mother who feared he was setting himself up for failure, Monte—a precocious but unmotivated high school student—dropped out during his junior year, and after a brief stint in the army, hitchhiked to California with one suitcase and five dollars. Though it was with such dogged determination that Monte set out to take Hollywood by storm, the cross-country trek took almost two years, with stopovers in Phoenix and Las Vegas, where he supported himself working in a car wash, selling drugs, and gambling.

After finally arriving in Los Angeles in 1967, he lived and panhandled in Pershing Square Park for another year until his life took a positive turn when he enrolled in a playwrighting class at L.A.'s City College. With tuition covered by the G.I. Bill, he showed great promise and soon wrote his first play called *If They Come Back* about a group of young activists after the civil rights movement that was produced on campus.

Around that time, he met Mike Evans, who had been a first-year acting student at City College, before being plucked by *All in the Family* director John Rich to play Lionel during an open casting call at CBS. Impressed by Monte's talent after seeing his play, the two became fast friends, and Evans at some point asked him to write an *AITF* spec script centered around his character, which he showed to Norman, who bought it.

What has never been clear, however, is what the script was about because it was never produced, nor did Monte ever formally receive a writer's credit for any *All in the Family* episode. Also unfounded were his later claims that it was he and not Norman who came up with the idea to spin the Jeffersons off into their own series in 1975, and that it was because of him that the characters of George and Louise, Lionel's parents, existed to begin with. As for the accuracy of the latter, Isabel Sanford made her first appearance during the eighth episode of season 1, "Lionel Moves into the Neighborhood," which would have made Monte's assertions impossible. And while Sherman Hemsley didn't appear until the third episode of season 4, "Henry's Farewell," he was mentioned numerous times before that.

Yet despite these inconsistencies, never in question—at least by all outward appearances—was the affinity for both Monte and Evans that Norman seemed to have early on, saying that, "I was charmed by Eric Monte and, having worked for years with Mike, liked him a lot too."[2]

Around this same time, Monte and Evans began collaborating on a pilot for a new sitcom loosely based on Monte's life. Setting it in the gritty, rough-and-tumble reality of the Cabrini Green Chicago housing projects, he envisioned the show to be about a poor but proud African American family struggling to make ends meet that realistically confronted topics plaguing low-income Black communities, including poverty, unemployment, racism, teenage pregnancy, drugs, gangs, and guns.

Though it would do so with a sense of humor and make audiences laugh, in keeping with Monte's early determination to create positive Black role models, he insisted that none of the characters would act buffoonish or reinforce racial stereotypes. Instead, they would be intelligent and aspirational and have depth. Also, they would be a complete nuclear family, including a husband and wife, three kids, and a boisterous next-door neighbor. The show's working title was *The Black Family*.

In the meantime, midway through *Maude*'s first season in 1973, Norman was already trying to figure out a way to give the Findlays' outspoken, feisty maid Florida played by actor Esther Rolle, her own starring vehicle. The maid first appeared in "Maude Meets Florida," the eponymous third-season episode in which the well-intentioned Maude makes a fool of herself trying to prove her liberal progressive mettle only to quickly discover she'd met her match. Here Rolle's impeccable comedic timing was in evidence from the get-go as Florida made it abundantly clear that she was anything but another subservient domestic sitcom servant.

In his book *Primetime Blues*, African American author and pop culture historian Donald Bogle summarized the essence of the character and the much-needed breath of fresh air she infused: "On *Maude*, Rolle's Florida was outspoken, clever, realistic, the embodiment of 1960s-style political correctness, yet at times a surprising symbol for preserving the status quo."

> Maude insisted that Florida could use the front door rather than the back one. Not only could she take her meals with the family, she could also have cocktails with them every day. . . .
>
> [Florida] informed Maude that she'd prefer using the back door because she could carry the groceries in more easily there. She wanted to eat by herself. And as for cocktails—well, she didn't drink during the middle of the day.
>
> Florida preferred to be a traditional maid *except* when it came to expressing her views. Weekly, she did so, and it was funny to see an African American woman so readily and knowingly matching wits with her employer. The scripts just congratulated themselves on their own liberalism. Quiet as it was kept, the scripts were also sometimes condescending in trumpeting the character's assertiveness.

What a surprise, the writers seemed to be saying, to find a middle-aged African American woman who could think for herself.[3]

When Rolle, then fifty-one, was cast in the part for which she would become best known, she had already had an estimable résumé as a stage actress. Born the tenth of eighteen children to Bahamian immigrants in Pompano Beach, Florida, after graduating from Spellman College in Atlanta, she decided to pursue her long-simmering passion for theater in New York, where her older sister was also an actress. After arriving in New York, she continued her education at Hunter College, then the New School and eventually the Yale School of Drama, although she held various jobs for many years in New York's garment district. Finally, at the age of forty-two, she made her stage debut as one of the founding members of the Negro Ensemble Company, whose later famous alumni included Lawrence Fishburne, Denzel Washington, Ruby Dee, Angela Bassett, and Phylicia Rashad.

Additionally, Rolle was an early member of Sierra Leonean musician and choreographer Asadata Defora's dance troupe Shogolo Oloba (later renamed the Federal Theater African Dance Troupe), where she became artistic director in 1960. A string of Broadway appearances followed, including such shows as *The Crucible*, *Purlie Victorious*, *Blues for Mr. Charlie*, and *The Amen Corner*, as well as television on the ABC daytime soap *One Life to Live*. Rolle then returned to Broadway in 1972 in her critically acclaimed performance as Miss Maybelle in Mario Van Peebles's hit musical *Don't Play Us Cheap*, which is where Norman first discovered her and asked her to audition for the role of Florida on *Maude*, although she resisted at first.

Later explaining her rationale to the *New York Times*, Rolle recalled: "I kept telling them, 'I won't leave New York to go out there and be a Hollywood maid.' Then Norman said, 'We don't want a Hollywood maid, Esther, we want a human being.' I said, 'You gonna let me have a say?' When he said yes, I accepted because people follow images."[4]

Once Norman decided he wanted to give Rolle her own series early into *Maude*'s run, the next question was what the premise would be. Then there was finding someone suitable who could play Florida's husband to make the transition as seamless as possible whenever the time came. The actor he selected was John Amos, who was seventeen years Rolle's junior, and had recently appeared in the *Sanford and Son* episode "A Visit from Lena Horn" as Luther, one of Fred's pool hall buddies.

New Jersey born and bred, Amos had originally hoped to become a professional athlete and had been a Golden Gloves boxing champion and a football player at Colorado State University. After graduating as a sociology major in 1964, he was signed as an NFL free agent with the Denver Broncos only to be eliminated during the second day of training because of a hamstring injury. While he recovered well enough to play on several minor league teams and was signed a second time as an NFL free agent in 1967, this time with the Kansas City Chiefs, he was dropped again almost immediately and returned to play for the minors, where he spent the next year with the Spokane Steelers in Washington State.

Amos then moved to New York, where he briefly worked as an advertising copywriter and a social worker for a nonprofit agency before deciding to try his luck in show business. At first performing as a stand-up comic on the Greenwich Village coffeehouse circuit, this eventually took him out west to Los Angeles. In 1969, he landed a coveted gig as a staff writer on singer Leslie Uggams's CBS variety show. It was here that one of the sketches he wrote prophetically turned out to be a popular recurring segment called "Sugar Hill" about a struggling blue-collar inner-city African American family on which one of the performers was also coincidentally Johnny Brown, the singer, actor, and comedian who would go on to appear on *Good Times* as rotund building super Nathan Bookman.

Though *The Leslie Uggams Show* was canceled after only two months because of low ratings, Amos's talents did not go unnoticed. Not long afterward in the fall of 1970, he was hired to play weatherman Gordy Howard on *The Mary Tyler Moore Show*, a recurring part as the comic foil to *MTM*'s smug anchorman Ted Baxter.

During this period also, he guested on such popular TV programs as *The Bill Cosby Show*, *The New Dick Van Dyke Show*, *The Tim Conway Comedy Hour*, and *Love, American Style*. He made his stage debut in 1971 in a play that was interestingly titled *Norman, Is That You?*, which won a nomination from the Los Angeles Drama Critics for "Best Actor" and prompted Amos to form his own theater company and mount a national tour of the show. He also made his debut on Broadway that following year in the play *Tough to Get Help*, which despite being directed by Carl Reiner, closed after just one performance and was savaged by critics. Harshest of all was the *New York Times*'s Clive Barnes, who called it "good for the occasional laugh" but "clumsy as well as slight."[5] However, in another interesting twist, one of the performers was Ralph Carter, who would go on to play Amos's youngest son Michael on *Good Times*.

In the meantime, after ten episodes and four seasons on *The Mary Tyler Moore Show*, Amos's hopes of becoming a regular cast member looked to be less and less likely even as he remained optimistic and appeared again on two more episodes at the end of the series. "I felt like in time it would come, and

I would be accepted the way the rest of the cast was," he said. "Mary's show was the launch of the sitcom careers for several actors. The main thing was that it put them right where they wanted to be, and I saw that opportunity coming for me down the road."[6]

But instead—and exactly one month after appearing on *Sanford and Son*—Amos was first introduced to viewers on *Maude* as Florida's husband Henry in "Florida's Problem," the eighteenth episode of the first season, originally airing on February 12, 1973. In it, Henry, who works as a firefighter, demands that Florida quit her job, because he no longer wants her working for white people. Once again showcasing Esther Rolle's pitch-perfect comedic timing, the episode featured some of her best lines ever, while also planting the seeds for Amos as the proud, no-nonsense character (later renamed James) he would portray on *Good Times*. According to Amos, Rolle was easy to work with, and despite their almost-two-decade age difference, they had instant chemistry:

> [As soon as] I read with Esther, it was like talking to someone or having dialogue with someone I had known all my life. It was a very natural union, and I think that was part of the success of our relationship as actors, that it looked so natural and felt so natural, because we were both in an environment that we knew candidly. We knew it by heart, and I was blessed when she gave her approval to Norman and said, "He'll do just fine" or words to that effect, letting him know she felt the same way I did that we had potentially great chemistry, and we did, as proven by the subsequent episodes.[7]

As he was beginning to assemble the pieces for what became *Good Times*, Norman also got a taste of some of the problems that would perpetually confound the series throughout its six-year run. Originally conceived as a daytime drama to be the first series about a family from the ghetto, his first roadblock was Rolle, a staunch supporter of the NAACP, who adamantly refused to play a single mother the way he'd envisioned it. "I told [the producers and Norman] I couldn't compound the lie that black fathers don't care about their children. I was proud of the family life I was able to introduce on television," said Rolle.[8]

Although he complied with her wishes, even more problems arose when he abandoned plans to do the show as a daytime drama in favor of another sitcom. Then after deciding to develop it around Eric Monte's and Mike Evans's concept for *The Black Family* and asking them to write a pilot and several episodes, Norman didn't think their material was up to snuff.

As for what may have happened, Jay Moriarity, who, along with his creative partner Mike Milligan, wrote the season-2 *Good Times* episode "The IQ Test" and worked closely with Evans on *The Jeffersons*, surmised:

> My understanding is that when Norman decided to do the *Good Times* spin-off, he went to Mike Evans and asked if he knew any writers, and the writer he happened to know was Eric Monte, who grew up in Cabrini Green in Chicago where the show took place. They met with Norman, he asked them to write something, they took Mike Evans's last name [as the last name for the Evans family on the show] and then they wrote something like *Good Times*. Mike Evans would have probably been the first guy to tell you he wasn't really a writer, Eric Monte had his idea of how he thought the show should go, but that's not how things work on a sitcom and Norman was a genius. He was the guy. He knew what he wanted to do, and it wasn't what Eric wanted. And they weren't going to take Eric's thing and shoot it. They were going to totally rewrite it even though Eric and Mike got the "created by" credit and made a lot of money. Eric didn't like that at all. He thought he should be running the thing.[9]

To punch up the pilot script, Norman recruited former *Rowan & Martin's Laugh-In* head writer Allan Mannings, who would go on to cocreate the original *One Day at a Time* with his wife, Whitney Blake, and whose other notable sitcom credits then included *Leave It to Beaver*, *McHale's Navy*, and *The Lucy Show*. And then in due course, after assuring her she'd have a husband on the show, Rolle finally agreed to *Good Times*. Yet, despite his clout at the time and the success of *All in the Family* and *Maude*, Norman still wasn't sure he could sell CBS programming chief Fred Silverman on the concept of doing a sitcom with an all–African American cast after he'd already rejected *Sanford and Son* two years earlier.

As it turned out, however, Silverman was looking for just such a property to replace *Roll Out*, a low-rated, mixed-race army comedy from *M*A*S*H* creators Larry Gelbart and Gene Reynolds, and immediately greenlit thirteen episodes of *Good Times*. Also, as it turned out, he did so on November 8, 1973, which was Esther Rolle's fifty-second birthday.

With *Good Times* set to air Friday nights at 8:30 beginning that February, Norman's next task was casting the show's supporting roles, which included the Evanses' three children and their neighbor. The first part he cast as their studious, politically minded eleven-year-old son, Michael "the Militant Midget," was actor and singer Ralph Carter. Then thirteen, Carter was appearing at the time on Broadway as Travis Younger in the musical *Raisin*, based on the Lorraine Hansberry drama *A Raisin in the Sun*, for which he scored a 1973 Drama Desk Award, a 1974 Theatre World Award, and a 1974 Tony nomination. However, he almost couldn't accept the role on *Good Times* because of his commitment in *Raisin*, and actor Lawrence Fishburne initially played Michael during the early rehearsals until Norman was eventually able to buy out Carter's contract.

The second person Norman cast was Michael's older brother James Jr. (J.J.), an aspiring artist who dreams of making it big someday. It would, of course, go to Jimmie Walker, the Brooklyn-born, Bronx-bred, beanpole comedian, who began his career in entertainment as a radio engineer for WVUR in New York and was just seven years younger than John Amos. In the early 1970s, Walker began honing his comic chops at Budd Friedman's iconic New York Improv (then known as the Improvisation) in Hell's Kitchen and Rick Newman's Catch a Rising Star on Manhattan's Upper East Side, alongside such other young stand-up start-ups as Jay Leno, Freddie Prinze, Richard Lewis, and Andy Kaufman.

In fact, it was at the Improv where Allan Mannings, who would go on to become one of *Good Times*'s head writers and producers, had first seen Walker perform and recommended him to CBS casting director Pat Kirkland. At the time, Walker, who had already appeared on the ABC talk show *Jack Paar Tonight* and was earning a decent living on the road, was the warm-up comic on another CBS sitcom that was filmed in New York. According to Walker's 2012 autobiography *Dynomite! Good Times, Bad Times, Our Times—A Memoir*, when Kirkland first approached him he was suspicious about her sincerity:

> Now she was casting a new series starring Esther Rolle who played the black housekeeper on *Maude*.
>
> I said, "Sure, let me know," and walked away. I didn't think any more about it. There are so many people in show business who say they are this or that—and aren't; who are going to do this and that for you and—and don't; who say, "give me your card" and "here's my card"—and never call that you end up not believing anybody. So many gigs and TV shows had fallen through for me that I was skeptical of everyone and everything. My line is "Everyone is a liar . . . until proven full of shit." If I had a dollar for every person who came into Improv with a business card that said "Producer," I would have already been a rich man.[10]

As Thelma, J.J. and Michael's sixteen-year-old sister, Norman hired Bernadette Stanis, a twenty-year-old dancer and former teen-beauty pageant contestant originally from Brooklyn. At the time, she was enrolled as a second-year drama student at New York's prestigious Juilliard School studying under the famed British actor John Houseman when her manager arranged for her to fly to Hollywood to try out for *Good Times*. During her audition, Stannis so dazzled Norman with her natural stage presence that she beat out two other actors, including Chip Fields, who later played Janet Jackson's abusive mother on *Good Times* and was the real-life mother of actor Kim Fields, best known for her role as Tootie on the 1980s, Norman-produced sitcom *The Facts of Life*.

The final role to be filled was Willona Woods, Florida's gossipy best friend and the Evanses' next-door neighbor. That went to veteran Broadway actor and singer, Ja'Net Dubois, who was then forty-two and had appeared with Louis Gossett Jr. in Lorraine Hansberry's *A Raisin in the Sun* and *Golden Boy* with Sammy Davis Jr. She also appeared in the play *The Hot l Baltimore* in 1973, which Norman later optioned into a sitcom and is where he first saw her, becoming so enamored of DuBois's performance in the play that he cast her for *Good Times* without an audition.

With the full main ensemble in place, the next task was phasing out the characters of Florida and Henry from *Maude*. To do so, Florida and Maude exchange tearful farewells and hugs in the episode "Florida's Goodbye," which aired on February 5, 1974, in which Florida quits her job after Henry gets a promotion. Although they promise to stay in touch, they of course never do, nor was Florida's name ever mentioned again.

And then magically, just three days later, *Good Times* premiered on February 8, 1974, with Florida and Henry (now James) having acquired the last name Evans and three kids now living in Chicago. Listed in the credits were Eric Monte and Mike Evans as cocreators followed by the words "Developed by Norman Lear."

In the gospel-tinged opening theme song—co-written by Dave Grusin and Alan and Marilyn Bergman, and containing such lyrics as "not getting hassled, not getting hustled," "temporary layoffs, "easy credit ripoffs," and "scratchin' and surviving"—viewers got a quick sense of the Evanses' hardscrabble lives as the camera panned above the Chicago skyline, then into the blighted neighborhood of their new home in the Cabrini Green public housing project, followed by an up-close exterior shot at the end of their dilapidated high-rise at 721 North Gilbert Avenue.

Adding to the authenticity was the Harlem dance hall motif of artist Earnie Barnes's "Sugar Shack" painting seen in the closing sequences of the show's earlier seasons. With the original premise about the travails of the Evans family, led by James—an honest, hardworking, but frequently unemployed laborer—trying to make the best out of life and always doing so with plenty of love despite their circumstances, the show was almost universally praised by critics from the start. In the *New York Times*, John J. O'Connor said: "On the one side, Black viewers are being afforded material that provides immediate personal and psychic identification. They no longer have to be content with *Father Knows Best*, which was unreal even for many white Americans. On the other side, whites are being given glimpses of Black life that, however simplified, can't help but weaken racial barriers."[11]

And in its review published the day before the *Good Times*'s premiere, the *Christian Science Monitor* said, "Producer Norman Lear breeds television shows like racehorses. His latest—*Good Times*—had great lineage: *All in the Family* and *Maude*. In this case, those bloodlines really tell and CBS's new show premiering tomorrow at eight-thirty p.m. Eastern Time looks like another champion for Bud Yorkin-Norman Lear Tandem Productions."[12]

With buzz about spin-offs already spreading before *Good Times* started, it was yet another monster hit for Norman right off the bat. Ending its first season as the seventeenth-highest-rated program of the year, tying with the ABC detective series *Barnaby Jones*, starring Buddy Ebsen, by the following year *Good Times* had climbed to number seven with an estimated 25 percent of all American households tuning in each week.

With most of the action taking place inside the Evanses' cramped seventeenth-floor apartment—authentically fashioned by set designers from the grimy walls and peeling paint to the beat-up furniture and graffiti that covered the outer hallway—in typical Norman fashion, the show also dove headfirst into tackling controversial issues from day one with scripts that were enhanced by topical political and social references and trenchant dialogue. In the debut episode "Too Old Blues," James gets squeezed out of a union apprenticeship because of his age. In episode two, "Black Jesus," the Evanses' values are challenged when one of J.J.'s paintings and an unexpected run of good luck creates a religious conflict. Then in "Getting Up the Rent," the third episode written by Eric Monte, the family, despite James's two jobs working as a dishwasher and in a car wash, isn't enough to spare them from an eviction notice as he is forced to take drastic action.

Week after week (and particularly during its first two seasons), it seemed that *Good Times* dared to take on subjects that even *All in the Family* and *Maude* didn't want to confront. For example, during episode eight, "Junior the Senior," the show addressed the issue of overcrowding in inner-city public schools when J.J. was promoted to the twelfth grade, despite failing grades. In the next episode, "The Visitor," a spotlight is shone on the squalid living conditions of many urban housing projects when an irate official from the Chicago Housing Authority shows up at the Evanses' apartment after Michael writes an angry letter to a local newspaper. Later in "The Check-Up," which was the twelfth and second-to-last episode of the first season, the family is concerned James might have hypertension after he comes home worn down and more irritable than usual from the frustration and stress of ghetto life and throws a chair. Fortunately, he's okay, although at the end of the show it is revealed that he does have high cholesterol necessitating a change of diet.

When season 2 started that September, the opener "Florida Flips" dealt with women's rights. As the episode began, Florida was in a foul mood and no one could figure out why as she stormed out of the house and attended a women's support group with next-door neighbor Willona, later informing James that she wanted more out of life than just taking care of the house and family and demanding to be treated as an equal. Next, in a two-parter about racial profiling, J.J. was falsely arrested for holding up a liquor store on his eighteenth birthday. This was followed by the episode "Crosstown Buses Run All Day, Doodah, Doodah" in which Michael refused to take part in a busing program for academically gifted students even though it meant forfeiting the chance to attend a better school in Chicago's affluent, predominantly white Rogers Park neighborhood.

Other notable episodes that season included "The I.Q. Test," which dealt with racial bias in standardized testing; "The Gang," another two-parter in which J.J. was forced to join a street gang against his will and gets shot; teenage alcoholism in "Sometimes There's No Bottom in the Bottle"; and "The Dinner Party," where the Evanses worried the meat loaf an elderly neighbor brought over for dinner might be made with dog food after they discovered that the old woman has been reduced to eating it herself because her Social Security benefits have been cut.

"I have great memories of some of the early shows," said Amos. "We discovered each other's abilities as actors to really almost improvise because at times we would come up with lines that we knew intuitively and ethnically were absolutely the correct lines to say. We accepted them and embellished them. Everybody had a contribution to make to the scripts it seemed, and those contributions were quite welcome."[13]

At the same time, however, discord among the cast—especially Esther Rolle and John Amos—was already beginning to brew with Norman and the show's other predominantly white writers and producers. The culprit initially was a word that Jimmie Walker said casually during early rehearsals that found its way into the third episode.

The word was *dynamite*, and it was literally explosive. Beginning in the early 1970s, catchphrases became a sitcom staple that soon spilled over to other genres. On Norman's other shows alone, there was *Meathead, dingbat,* and *stifle* on *All in the Family;* "You big dummy," "How 'bout five cross your lip," and "You hear that, Elizabeth? I'm coming to join you, Honey," on *Sanford and Son;* and *Maude's* "God'll get you for that" and "I'll rip your heart out." Then there was "Who loves, ya, Baby!" (*Kojak*), "Kiss my grits!" (*Alice*), "Up your nose with a rubber hose!" (*Welcome Back, Kotter*), and "Goodnight, John Boy!" (*The Waltons*).

But *dynamite*, which became *Dy-no-i ite!*, was the grandaddy of them all. According to Walker, here's how it got started:

> I was doing whatever . . . rehearsing . . . and I said to whomever it was, "Hey that's dynamite," and then we went on with the scene. John Rich was our director and he said, "I love that dynamite thing." I said, "What about it?" He says, "You've got to do that, man. That's what we need."
>
> I said, "Dynamite?" And he said, "Yeah," and he went out to the middle of the room and showed me how to do it—*"DY-NO-MITE!"* He said, "You've got to put your teeth out there, the whole thing." I go, "Really?" He says, "Yeah, we'll just do it, you'll take a random bite, something will happen—*DY-NO-MITE!* I don't want like dynamite, I want out there, teeth, smiling, gold, eyes, everything."[14]

As the first season led into season 2 and it became clearer and clearer that Walker was fast becoming the show's breakout star—with J.J.'s womanizing ways and flashier wardrobe that often included his trademark blue-denim bucket hat creeping more and more into each episode—Rolle and Amos grew increasingly resentful, though at first Amos tried to take things in stride.

> "I understood the writers had found with Jimmie a wonderful relief that they didn't have to write three or four pages of comedy material," Amos said. "All they had to do was bring him in with a funny hat at the appropriate or sometimes most inappropriate time and they could coast. As a writer myself, I knew this, so I looked at it objectively and said, 'I can see that he's comic relief. We do a lot of serious issues on this show and people don't want to get beat over the head when they turn on the boob tube.' So the bottom line was that I saw it for what it was initially but then too much emphasis was being put on him and the balance was lost on the rest of us."[15]

Noted author Donald Bogle: "When J.J.'s coonery was criticized, the writers sought to round him out. For some reason, they thought it would help if J.J. were turned into a ladies' man. But Walker always played the character in such a broad manner—with eye pops and facial contortions—that it was hard to believe any woman could ever take him seriously. . . . Plain and simple, he just seemed jive, juvenile and asinine. In time, viewers could anticipate Walker's every move and gesture. Built into the scripts was an element of self-mockery, but not for the character. Rather scripts mocked and parodied Jimmie Walker's performing style, his looks and his persona."[16]

As the goofiest aspects of J.J. increasingly became centerpieces of the show, Walker was suddenly a household name. Branded "the hottest skinny in comedy" by the *New York Daily News*, soon there were "Dy-no-mite!" T-shirts, belt buckles, pajamas, lunch boxes, and even a series of J.J. talking dolls. He became a fixture on the talk show circuit, appearing on *Mike Douglas*, *Dinah Shore*, and *Merv Griffin*, as well as on *Soul Train* and *The Love Boat*, and in concerts alongside Smokey Robinson, Gladys Knight and the Pipps, and Dionne Warwick.

Additionally, he appeared in such films as *Let's Do It Again*, *The Rabbit Test*, and *Airport '79*, and recorded a comedy album, *Dy-no-mite!*, which sold over one hundred thousand copies. And he became a top draw at The Comedy Store in Los Angeles and a headliner at Caesar's Palace in Las Vegas, at one point employing a staff of comedy writers that included Jay Leno, David Letterman, Elayne Boosler, and future Weather Channel owner Byron Allen.

But toward the end of the second season on *Good Times*, the roof was starting to cave in. In addition to Rolle's and Amos's dissatisfaction with how Walker's character had come to dominate the show, they were also progressively more frustrated with how the writers were portraying low-income African Americans in general. Said Amos, recalling one particularly contentious incident: "The writers would very often have James react in such a way that I knew was contrary to the Black culture, and let's face it, that's who we were, a Black family living in Chicago."

> In one episode, I can point this out as an example of where I laid down the law and I didn't do it in the most diplomatic way. We had a scene with two men who represented authority figures. I can't remember if they were law enforcement officers or whatever, but they represented authority figures and they were dressed as you might expect in raincoats, suits and ties, two white guys. They came into the house and on the pretext of whatever it was they were there to discuss, one of them chose to spit on the Evanses' living room floor, which was not in the script. This

was the actor's choice and I yelled, "Cut!" Now, you don't do this in a sitcom. No actor has the authority or the right to say cut. [But] I said, "Fuck that, I'm saying cut," so we stopped, and I drew it to the director's attention who was up in the booth invisible. I said, "Cut, you're not shooting another fucking foot of me until that shit is wiped off the floor. Nobody comes into the Evans house and spits on the floor." And I walked off.[17]

Cocreator Eric Monte, upon whose life *Good Times* had been based, was even more vocal about his unhappiness with what he felt was a lack of authenticity on the show. He had also been at constant odds with Norman ever since he'd turned over the pilot script to Allan Mannings to be rewritten before he sold it to CBS. Fed up with the fighting while trying to extend an olive branch, in late 1974 Norman told Monte about an opportunity with another film producer named Steven Krantz who had been looking for an African American writer for a new film he was directing about a group of inner-city high school students in 1960s Chicago.

Soon after meeting with Krantz, Monte left *Good Times* in mid-1974, though he would continue to be listed as one of the cocreators throughout the remainder of the series. The name of the film was *Cooley High* for which Monte wrote the screenplay based on and named after his alma mater Cooley Vocational High. Released in June 1975, it would eventually morph into the ABC sitcom *What's Happening!* produced by Bud Yorkin.

Meanwhile, three months later, as *Good Times*'s third season got underway, word of the friction behind the scenes had gotten out to the press. That September, *Ebony* magazine published a cover story with the headline "Bad Times on the *Good Times* Set" in which journalist Louie Robinson aptly summarized:

> The characters who people *Good Times*, the CBS Tuesday night presentation that is one of the top shows on television, offer the tube's best effort to date at showing a real slice of ghetto black life. Yet, there are some bad times at *Good Times*, and although the show has much to recommend in its comparison with TV's usual servings of silliness and violence, it has been thigh-deep in problems, which range from questionable scripting to salary disputes and include a tinge of personal antipathy.[18]

In a no-punches-pulled point-counterpoint in the same article, Rolle said of the J.J. character: "He's eighteen and he doesn't work. He can't read and write. He doesn't think. The show didn't start out to be that. Michael's role (finely etched by fourteen-year-old Ralph Carter) of a bright, thinking child has been slowly reduced. Little by little—with the help of the artist, I suppose, because they couldn't do that to me—they have made him (J.J.) more stupid and enlarged the role. . . . Negative stereotypes have been quietly slipped in on us through the character of the oldest child. I resent the imagery that says to black kids that you can make it by standing on the corner saying, 'Dy-no-mite.'"[19]

As for Walker's rebuttal, he said: "I play the way I see it for humor. I don't think anybody twenty years from now is going to remember what I said. I am not trying to have my lines etched into some archives or on a wall someplace. I don't think any TV show can put out an image to save people. My advice is do not follow me. I don't want to be a follower or a leader . . . just a doer."[20]

Also featuring comments from Allan Mannings and the other cast, absent from the article was Norman who declined to participate, and Amos, who was in the middle of a contract dispute over money that delayed production of the third season by three weeks. Reflecting on his state of mind at the time four decades later, he said: "Suffice it to say I had lost my balance, and the show became more important to me than anything."

> I was preoccupied with getting it right and it was just consuming me. I felt like I had the responsibility of playing every black father, every black man in the United States. Of course, in retrospect I know exactly why I put it on myself. I was there on TV, the most powerful, educational medium in the world on a regular basis, so I had to portray someone that would make other black men feel proud and say, "Yeah, that's the kind of dad I'd like to be or that's the kind of dad I wish I had." I wanted to be someone they would want to emulate and so I tried. In my efforts to do that—to be something above and beyond what was called for as opposed to just having a regular acting job, doing it and going home—I took it on as the ultimate responsibility.[21]

While Amos would return for season 3—one that saw the Evanses dealing with teenage marriage, drug abuse, venereal disease, and the expensive cost of hospital stays—his relationship with Norman and the other producers continued to go south. "It had become intolerable for me," he said. "I thought I'd much rather be unemployed, and much rather go back to what I was doing before this if at all possible because *Good Times* had become antithetical to everything I wanted to be doing on television."[22]

After appearing in the season finale, "The Rent Party," in which the Evanses throw a fundraiser for an elderly neighbor who is behind in her rent, airing on March 2, 1976, Amos got his wish. During that summer's hiatus, he received a call from Norman telling him he'd been fired. To eliminate his character, season four opened with the two-part episode "The Big Move," which saw the family preparing to leave Chicago and return to their native Mississippi, where James had been offered a lucrative partnership as a mechanic in a garage, only to have their lives shattered when they learn he'd been killed in a car accident. During the wake after the funeral in the second installment, a stoic Florida put on a happy face for the three kids and other mourners—until finally, at the end of the episode, she broke down—smashing a punch bowl, screaming, "Damn, Damn, Damn!" (in what became one of the most memorable lines of the entire show) and sobbed uncontrollably as she embraced Thelma, Michael, and J.J.

And then, poof, James was gone and almost never mentioned again.

With Amos now out of the picture, the Evanses' sassy next-door neighbor Willona and their hefty building janitor Bookman, whom Willona called "buffalo butt," took on more prominence. But more pronounced also was J.J.'s tomfoolery as he got involved with a series of get-rich-quick schemes, some skirting on lawlessness, including bookmaking, trying to manage a singer and a comedian, and even selling underwear so he and the kids could send Florida on a vacation.

This did not sit well with Rolle, who, in addition to her opposition to no longer having a husband, became even more disillusioned with the show. "Little by little, they've made J.J. more stupid. What kind of image is that for black children to follow?"[23] Rolle was also angered by the producers' decision to give Florida a new love interest—atheistic fix-it shop owner Carl Dixon, played by actor Moses Gunn—who appeared during six episodes toward the end of season 4.

In the two-part season finale, Carl planned to propose to Florida only to break up with her after learning he had lung cancer, although they reconciled by the end of the episode and decided to get married while he underwent treatment. As Rolle and the producers continued to butt heads during the summer hiatus, and still at odds as the fifth season got underway as she missed the first two episodes, they decided to go their separate ways.

Yet that still didn't stop her from expressing her wrath over how the show decided to explain the character's whereabouts by having Florida and Carl move to Arizona where they had gone on their honeymoon for his health. Protested Rolle: "What kind of mother would go traipsing across the country, leaving her three children to fend for themselves? It was bad enough James

Evans had been erased; now they had the mother marrying a man she barely knew and moving away."[24]

The show then took another unexpected twist after returning for season 5 as Willona became a surrogate mother figure to the Evans children and a mother herself. In the four-part season opener, "The Evanses Get Involved," the family befriended Penny Gordon, an abused child who lived in the building whom Willona legally adopted in the episode's final installment. To play the little girl, Norman drafted singer Janet Jackson after seeing her perform on her older brothers' variety show *The Jacksons*. During the audition in his office, he asked Jackson to improvise a scene with him in which he instructed her to cry after pretending to give him a present he didn't like—and then on cue, she turned on the waterworks, and he hired her on the spot.

Remembered Michael Baser, who wrote eleven episodes and served as story editor for twenty-four others with longtime creative partner Kim Weiskopf during season 5: "Janet was a very sweet, talented girl and her parents and brothers would come watch her do the show. It was right around the time that Michael released his first solo album and he'd be there too."[25]

But while the addition of Janet Jackson did inject some much-needed new life into *Good Times*, without Rolle the ratings tanked as Norman made numerous attempts to try and get her to return to no avail. Finally, in the spring of 1978, he managed to convince her to come back for one last season by giving her a raise, final script approval, and the promise to make J.J. a more serious character. Another enticement was Michael Moye, an aspiring young African American playwright at North Carolina State University. After winning a student playwrighting contest sponsored by Norman in which the first prize was a chance to write for any of his shows, Moye chose *Good Times* and was hired on the staff in the spring of 1978. From there, he would go on to write and produce for *The Jeffersons*, later going on to cocreate such sitcoms as *Silver Spoons*, *227*, and *Married . . . with Children* starring Norman's goddaughter Katey Sagal.

And so, sans her new husband Carl—and never mentioning him again—Rolle resurfaced that September in another multipart season opener called "Florida's Homecoming." As Thelma prepared to marry Keith (Ben Powers), a star college football player about to turn pro, at first it seemed as if the Evanses' fortunes were finally changing until Keith accidentally tripped over J.J. during the wedding ceremony and shattered his knee, sending the family right back to where they were.

Ultimately, though, it didn't matter, nor did Rolle's return, as the ratings continued to plummet. In December 1978, CBS pulled it from the schedule, although the show returned that spring before airing its final episode on

August 1, 1979. As *Good Times* ended its six-year run after 133 episodes, it did so on a positive note as each of its characters got a happy ending: J.J. sold a syndicated cartoon strip for a healthy advance; Keith's knee recovered, and he signed a contract with the Chicago Bears; Thelma got pregnant and asked Florida to move in with them; Michael planned to live on campus at the local college he was attending; and Willona was promoted to head buyer of the clothing boutique where she worked—with all of them getting out of the ghetto—and by happy coincidence remaining together, as it was revealed that Willona and Penny would be living downstairs from Keith, Thelma, and Florida in the same apartment building on Chicago's upscale North Side.

Despite its problems behind the scenes, the show's legacy as TV's first sitcom about a two-parent African American family lives on more than forty years later. Yet another often-overlooked part of that legacy, meanwhile, is that it also gave many future stars, including Debbie Allen, Philip Michael Thomas, Louis Gossett Jr., and even Jay Leno some of their first major TV exposure.

Consistently popular in reruns and spoofed on such shows as *The Wayans Bros.*, *Saturday Night Live*, and *The Bernie Mac Show*, in April 2024 there was even a short-lived animated version of *Good Times* that premiered on Netflix in conjunction with the show's fiftieth anniversary, produced by *Family Guy* creator Seth MacFarlane, that was universally panned by critics and original cast member Bern Nadette Stanis.

As for the other original cast members—and aside from Janet Jackson who, of course, went on to become an international pop superstar—the one whose career flourished the most was John Amos.

After getting fired from *Good Times* in 1976 and almost immediately landing the coveted role of the adult Kunta Kinte in the 1977 megahit miniseries *Roots*, he went on to a prolific career as a character actor, appearing in such TV shows as *Hunter*, *The West Wing*, *Two and a Half Men*, and *30 Rock*, as well the films *Coming to America*, *Diehard 3*, and *Lock Up*. Having long since mended fences with Norman, in 1994 Amos also starred in the short-lived sitcom *704 Hauser* about a Black family who moves into Archie Bunker's old house. In 2021, he also made a cameo appearance playing shady Chicago city councilman Fred C. Davis during a reenactment of *Good Times* on Norman's *Live in Front of a Studio Audience* with Jimmy Kimmel.

Of all those involved in the original series, the one who sadly fared the worst was cocreator Eric Monte. Claiming Norman had not only stolen his idea for *Good Times*, but that *The Jeffersons* was also his creation and that he had been the one who recommended Redd Foxx for *Sanford and Son*, Monte sued Norman, along with his agent, CBS, and ABC for $4 million in 1977.

He also sued Bud Yorkin, Bernie Orenstein, and Saul Turtletaub, similarly claiming they'd stolen his idea for *What's Happening* based on the film *Cooley High*, even though, as with *Good Times*, Monte's name was listed on the credits as one of the creators and he got paid.

While he was offered a $1 million joint settlement and a small percentage of *Good Times*'s residuals, Monte was blackballed by the industry, and his life hit the skids. Badly battered and addicted to crack cocaine, by the early 2000s Monte was living in a Los Angeles homeless shelter before finally getting clean and moving back to Chicago, and more recently Portland, Oregon, where he currently lives with his only daughter.

Although Norman never directly commented on the case, in 2006 he did tell the *Los Angeles Times*, "Whatever the credits reflect, I'm happy to go along with. Eric is a lovable, knowledgeable, sweet human being who just had no control of himself. He got in his own way emotionally. He was a dear lost soul. It wasn't a pleasant time dealing with Eric."[26]

CHAPTER 22

The Jeffersons Move on Up

One afternoon in 1974, early into the inaugural season of *Good Times*, three unannounced visitors managed to get past security guards at CBS Television City and upstairs to Norman's office. The men were members of the Black Panthers, the influential Black Power political organization. Heatedly calling *Good Times* "garbage" and Norman "the garbage man," they had come to vent their outrage over how James Evans was constantly underemployed.

Evidently, the message got through loud and clear because it was in such a manner after conferring with Tandem's director of development, Al Burton, that *The Jeffersons*—Norman's next sitcom and ratings bonanza—was born that same afternoon. The Jeffersons themselves had, of course, been on *All in the Family* from day one, starting with Lionel, who appeared in the first episode and quickly became a fan favorite as Archie's comic foil.

Lionel also appeared in "Archie Gives Blood," the fifth episode in which an ignorant Archie, thinking that only white people were eligible to donate blood, was caught off guard when he saw Lionel at the local blood bank. After getting Archie's goat once more by pretending to be the janitor, it was soon decided that Lionel would be the Bunkers' new next-door neighbor, beginning in the eighth episode "Lionel Moves into the Neighborhood," which aired on March 8, 1971. To play Lionel's mother Louise, Norman and director John Rich chose Isabel Sanford, the raspy-voiced actor who went on to become the first and still only African American woman to win an Emmy for Best Actress in 1985.

Although she had been acting for nearly three decades when she was cast in *All in the Family*, Sanford, then fifty-four, didn't get her first big break until four years earlier when she appeared as Tillie the housekeeper in director Stanley Kramer's classic 1967 film *Guess Who's Coming to Dinner*, costarring Spencer Tracy, Katharine Hepburn, and Sidney Poitier, which is where she caught the eye of Norman. Since then, she had been much in demand as a TV guest star on such shows as *Bewitched*, *The Mod Squad*, *Daniel Boone*, *The Mary Tyler Moore Show*, *The Interns*, *Love, American Style*, and *The Carol Burnett Show*, where she was a semi-regular.

She had also just seen *All in the Family* for the first time when her agent called to tell her Norman and Rich wanted her to audition for the part of Louise. But while she would, of course, go on to win the role, the part she initially read for wasn't Louise. It was for Louise's unnamed sister, which is who Sanford was supposedly playing during her debut on *AITF* when Archie mistook her for a maid.

Five episodes later, she then officially made her first appearance as Louise Jefferson in "The First and Last Supper," which was the thirteenth and final show of season 1, airing on April 6, 1971. In the story, Archie circulated a petition trying to prevent more Blacks from moving into the neighborhood as Edith accepted a dinner invitation with the Jeffersons at their house. Refusing to go, Archie ordered Edith to call Louise and tell her they couldn't come because she'd sprained her ankle. But when Louise offered to bring dinner over instead and Edith accepted, sparks flew between Archie and Louise's husband (introduced by name for the first time as George) until it was revealed at the end of the episode that he was really her brother-in-law Henry (played by Mel Stewart). George, as it turned out, was just as bigoted as Archie and refused to have dinner with white people, which is why he wasn't there.

It turned out also that the real reason George wasn't in the episode was because the only actor Norman had in mind to play him wasn't available. Instead, for the next two seasons, Mike Evans and Isabel Sanford continued to appear together and separately as Lionel and Louise in sixteen more episodes (including "Sammy's Visit" with Sammy Davis Jr.), only sporadically mentioning George and occasionally with Mel Stewart appearing as Henry.

Finally, on October 20, 1973, America got its first glimpse of George Jefferson, the swaggering, diminutive dry-cleaning store owner, who was also at first frequently described as a Black Archie Bunker. Appearing in the episode "Henry's Farewell," the actor who played him to perfection was Sherman Hemsley, who was twenty-one years younger than Sanford. A Korean War veteran and former postal worker originally from Philadelphia, Hemsley first moved to New York to pursue acting in 1967, where he joined the Negro Ensemble Company. A series of successful off-Broadway roles soon followed, including a double bill in 1969 in the plays *Old Judge Mose Is Dead* and *Moon on a Rainbow Shawl*. That following year, Hemsley got his big break in the Broadway musical *Purlie*, costarring alongside Cleavon Little, Melba Moore, and Robert Guillaume as plantation worker Gitlow Judson.

When Norman saw the show in 1971 around the time that he was conceiving the character of George Jefferson, Hemsley's appearance made such an impression that he decided to keep the role open until the actor became available. On *All in the Family*, Hemsley then appeared in fifteen episodes during seasons 4 and 5 before the Jeffersons were spun off into their own series, which Norman sold to CBS programming chief Fred Silverman sight unseen. "It just seemed like natural," Silverman said. "This is the [Bunkers'] next-door neighbors who we don't use that much but they've got the recognizability and they're funny."[1]

As a premise, Norman decided George's dry-cleaning business would expand into a small chain as he, Louise, and Lionel moved on up and into a luxury high-rise apartment building on Manhattan's Upper East Side—hence the symbolic motif for one of television's most unforgettable theme songs—written and sung by Ja'net DuBois who played Willona on *Good Times*. As showrunners and co-creators, Norman chose Don Nicholl, Mickey Ross, and Bernie West, who had served as head writers, producers, and story editors on *All in the Family* during its first five seasons.

With the core production team and story in place, Norman set out to flesh out the supporting characters. First, was Lionel's fiancée Jenny and her parents Louis and Helen Willis, an interracial couple who were to become George and Louise's upstairs neighbors. Interesting to note is that they were already semi in development nearly a year before the new series even aired, having been introduced clandestinely in the *All in the Family* episode "Lionel's Engagement" in which an unwelcome Archie attended Lionel's engagement party against George's explicit wishes. No sooner had he showed up than Archie insulted George's mother when he called her a mammy, an all-out war nearly broke out as Archie and George learned that Jenny's parents were a mixed-race couple, and then at the end, the two men clinked glasses in a "What's this world coming to?" toast.

Interesting to note also is that of all the actors who were in this episode, only one of them—Zara Cully—reprised the role on *The Jeffersons*. Then eighty-two, Cully had already amassed a half century of theater, film, and TV credits when Isabel Sanford recommended her to Norman to play George's tart-tongued mother Olivia. Recast as the Willises with Louis renamed Tom, meanwhile, were actors Roxie Roker and Franklin Cover who knew one another from working on Broadway, which is where Norman had first seen them, though they had never performed together before.

Roker, a distant cousin of *Today Show* weatherman Al Roker, had majored in drama at Howard University and studied Shakespeare in England before launching her professional acting career with the Negro Ensemble Company in New York in the early 1960s. Like her TV alter ego, Roker also had a white husband, named Sy Kravitz. They met in New York in 1961 at NBC, where Roker worked as a secretary to support herself while auditioning and performing, and Kravitz, who later became a high-ranking television producer, was a page. After marrying in 1962, they had a son, Lenny, who went on to become the internationally renowned rock guitarist and singer.

Roker was also a reporter for WNEW-TV in New York and hosted the public affairs program *Inside Bedford-Stuyvesant*. After returning to acting full-time, she appeared in several off-Broadway plays, including *The River Niger*—which made it to Broadway, where Roker won an Obie Award and was nominated for a Tony Award in 1974—resulting in her becoming Helen Willis on *The Jeffersons*.

Franklin Cover, Roker's heavyset onscreen husband whom Norman once described as a "great white polar bear," was a Shakespearean-trained actor who had appeared on Broadway in 1968 in *Forty Carats* and on such TV shows as *Naked City*, *The Defenders*, *The Jackie Gleason Show*, and the CBS soap opera *The Secret Storm*. For the part of the Willises' Black daughter Jenny, that went to the Charolotte, North Carolina, native Berlinda Tolbert, then twenty-six, who had recently appeared on *Sanford and Son*, *That's My Mama*, and *The Streets of San Francisco*.

For the Jeffersons' sassy, scene-stealing maid and George's comic foil Florence Johnston, Norman chose Marla Gibbs, a then-relatively-unknown actress originally from Chicago who was in her late thirties. Though she'd scored bit parts in little theater, in such films as *Sweet, Jesus Preacherman*, *Blackbelt Jones*, and *Yours, Mine and Ours*, costarring Henry Fonda and Lucille Ball, and on television's *Doc* and *Barney Miller*, Gibbs was still supporting herself at the time as a reservations agent for United Airlines and didn't join *The Jeffersons* as a series regular until the middle of season 2.

At the top of Norman's wish list for George and Louise's eccentric British next-door neighbor Harry Bentley, was American actor Paul Benedict. Norman had first seen him perform in 1968 in the off-Broadway play *Little Murders*. However, despite having already appeared as a Zen Buddhist in Norman's 1970 film *Cold Turkey*, Benedict—who then also had a recurring role as "The Mad Painter" on *Sesame Street*—repeatedly turned him down.

What finally tipped the scales was when he told Norman he couldn't do the show because the taping of *The Jeffersons*'s pilot conflicted with a movie he was appearing in that same day, whereupon Norman called the director and persuaded him to delay the shooting. In the end, Benedict was so flattered by his persistence that he immediately flew to Hollywood to take the part. Eventually introduced into the show also were Ned Wertimer, who played the Jeffersons' tip-hungry white doorman Ralph, and later Jay Hammer as Allan, the Willises' white son and "white sheep" of the family, who lived on a commune in New Mexico and didn't get along with Tom, and Ernest Harden Jr. as Marcus Garvey, a teenager from Harlem who worked as a delivery boy for George.

On *All in the Family*, George and Louise bid farewell to the Bunkers in the backdoor pilot "The Jeffersons Move Up," which aired on January 11, 1975. After a tearful goodbye with Edith, Louise and George leave Queens in style in a rented limousine as they head for Manhattan to their new home in the Colby East, a posh high-rise on the Upper East Side. Ecstatic about his sudden wealth and being away from Archie, George enthusiastically shows off the new digs to Lionel and Jenny. Then their neighbor Bentley, an interpreter for the United Nations, stops by—and after noticing George's small stature—asks him to walk on his bad back, which became a frequent site gag, as did George slamming the door in Bentley's face mid-conversation. Afterward, George and Louise are astonished when they discover he's British, just as Bentley had been about them when he first realized they were Black.

A little later, George's caustic mother who constantly criticizes Louise drops by. Finally, Jenny's parents Tom and Helen stop in, and George goes ballistic when he discovers they live right upstairs. Deriding them as "zebras," he vehemently tells Louise they are going to move but quickly changes his tune after Bentley tells him that his banker, H. L. Whittendale, also lives in the building.

That following week—on Saturday January 18, 1975, at 8:30 p.m. Eastern—*The Jeffersons* premiered as a stand-alone series that was Norman's first show produced by Tandem's sister company T.A.T. Communications. In the debut "A Friend in Need," George—who at the beginning of the show was even more of an unsympathetic character than Archie, plus loud, obnoxious, and ever eager to show off his newfound wealth—pressures Louise to hire a maid. However, she doesn't want to because she was once a maid herself and having one makes her uncomfortable. As the brouhaha builds, many of George's worst personality traits—from his frequent verbal abuse toward Louise whom he also loves deeply and calls "Weezy," to his overt hatred of white people whom he often refers to as "honkies"—are on full display.

At the forefront also was the first interracial married couple American television viewers had ever seen, who, despite George's scorn, were well-adjusted, happy, and seemingly never concerned about what others thought. Twenty minutes into the episode, Norman had Tom and Helen kiss. The setup of the scene was that George caused a ruckus after the Willises told him they seldom fought, to which he responded that they couldn't fight, because if they did and it really got bad, Tom would be calling her the N-word within five minutes. Both were outraged, and as Helen rebuffed George, telling him that she'd never thought about calling Tom a "honkey," he insisted she had thought about it because of how quickly she said it.

As the Willises stormed out into the hallway, Helen wondered out loud why she'd said it as Tom embraced her and they shared a long, passionate kiss. Right before the show aired, CBS predictably got nervous. "One day a vice president cornered me," remembered Jack Shea, who directed the episode. "He was shaking. He said, 'You can't let them do that. You can't show an interracial couple kissing.'"[2]

But not surprising either was that after standing his ground, Norman prevailed, and *The Jeffersons* became yet another instant smash, finishing its first season at number four. One major reason for the show's success undoubtedly was Marla Gibbs, who, after learning that the Jeffersons and the Willises both had an apartment in the building during her first appearance as Florence in the first episode, uttered the unforgettable line: "How come we overcame—and nobody told me?" and she brought the house down.

As to why that one line had such abundant resonance, *TV Guide* observed: "[It was] a laugh that acknowledged Florence, like the medieval Fool of old, spoke the deepest truth and the greatest wisdom of all. We all know full well that the majority of black people are not living in a high-rise dream world of mink, Ultrasuede and corporate investments. Florence reflects a long and dignified tradition of the servant who is often wiser than her employer. She has a crusty belligerence that 'don't take no stuff' off her employer even though they are materially better off than she is."[3]

Yet while *The Jeffersons* was an immediate hit, critics were less bullish. Atypical of his almost always glowing reviews of Norman's other shows, John J. O'Connor, writing in the *New York Times*, said: "Despite some fascinating touches, the comedy's situation is somewhat shaky. The character of Jefferson, snobbish and given to frequent temper tantrums, verges on the unattractive. Even Archie Bunker is an 'appealing bigot.' And much of [*The Jeffersons*'s] humor is based on insult, what used to be called 'playing the dozens' when content can become secondary to delivery. On *The Jeffersons*, too much of the content is."[4]

Lukewarm also was *TV Guide*'s Cleveland Amory, who had been one of *All in the Family*'s most ardent early supporters, describing *The Jeffersons* as "not good, pretty good or even fairly good" but "at best, it's not bad."[5] In the *Washington Post*, Joel Dreyfuss decried George as "simply irrational and unthinkable," adding, "while we know that television's version of reality usually has little to do with the real thing, there is a dangerous political message in a program that presents the fears of a black man in America as a simple aberration" and "if Lear gets some black input into the writing end of this program, it might move away from the brink of absurdity and develop into a pretty good television program."[6]

Ebony, meanwhile, opined that for "those who may still be looking for a deep and satisfying social significance in black shows on television, the wait goes on. Although *The Jeffersons* portrays blacks on television at a different socioeconomic level than other Black TV shows, it is nevertheless, like the others, broad comedy and has to be accepted as such."[7]

And as indeed it was, which is why Black and white viewers alike watched week after week. Unlike *All in the Family*, *Maude*, and *Good Times*, *The Jeffersons* never postured or overtly aimed to be anything other than pure entertainment, something that longtime writer and executive producer Jay Moriarity attributed to the show's first showrunners Don Nicholl, Mickey Ross, and Bernie West. "After *All in the Family*, these guys burned themselves out on serious comedy, which is basically what Norman wanted them to do," Moriarty said. "But on *The Jeffersons*, he left them alone because he trusted them, and they just wanted to make people laugh."[8]

Conversely, the show was never shy about tackling important issues either. Among other things, this included early episodes about adult adoptees looking for their birth parents, suicide, male chauvinism, racial quotas, organ donation, and even transgenderism. Yet even so, with Norman having delegated much of *The Jeffersons*'s day-to-day operations to Nicholl, Ross, and West, many of these topics might never have seen the light of day were it not for Jay Moriarty and his writing partner Mike Milligan, who joined the show's writing staff early during season 2 and went on to become story editors, then co-executive producers from 1978 until 1981. "Norman influenced me a lot. Mike and I tried to keep the Norman thing going by doing serious stories like *All in the Family* was doing," Moriarty said.[9]

However, unlike *All in the Family* and the strife-ridden sets of *Good Times* and *Sanford and Son*, the general atmosphere behind the scenes at *The Jeffersons* was mostly calm, especially among the writers and cast. Ascribing part of the conviviality to the fact that they never did a crossover episode with *All in the Family*, Moriarty noted that "Don [Nichol] was the alpha dog of the whole team with NRW, and he didn't want *The Jeffersons* cast to see how the *All in the Family* cast reacted when they did a table read. To show you how the attitude on *All in the Family* was different, they'd do a table read and the actors would say 'not funny' after a joke. Rob Reiner actually had rubber stamps made that said, 'NF' for not funny and the entire cast had one. Norman called it 'creative communism' and it worked great for *All in the Family* I guess, especially when he was there to control everything. But Don, Mickey and Bernie did not want our show to be a place where the inmates were running the asylum."[10]

Mike Evans, on the other hand, wasn't happy with the writing, nor with what he perceived to be the paltry amount of airtime that was given to his character Lionel, who at the beginning of the series was an engineering student at a local university and appeared in eleven of the thirteen episodes during season 1. Two of them, "Lionel the Playboy" and "Lionel Cries Uncle," even revolved around his character, though he still wasn't satisfied. Having been the first of the Jeffersons to appear on *All in the Family*, Evans felt he should not only be the star of the spin-off but the centerpiece of each show and bitterly complained to Nichol, Ross, and West. After his grievances fell on deaf ears, he then confronted Norman and was summarily fired. Although Norman never said anything directly about the incident in either his memoir or other interviews, in author Rick Mitz's *The Great TV Sitcom Book*, he was quoted as saying, "There was no question of money. He was unhappy, and speaking for myself, I was unhappy. It was by mutual agreement."[11]

And hence, Mike Evans's departure from *The Jeffersons* at the end of season 1 became effective immediately.

Replacing him was another young actor who coincidentally shared the same last name: Damon Evans. Then twenty-six, Evans was already a decorated singer and stage performer who was born in Baltimore and raised in New York. After attending high school at the prestigious Interlochen Arts Academy in Michigan on a *Reader's Digest* scholarship, he continued his education at the Boston Conservatory of Music, appearing in local productions of *Hair*, *Two If by Sea*, and *The Corner*.

In New York, Evans also appeared off and on Broadway in such shows as *A Day in the Life of Just about Everyone*, *Bury the Dead*, *The Me Nobody Knows*, and *Lost in the Stars*. He also performed in the national touring company of *Jesus*, the authorized concert version of Andrew Lloyd Webber's iconic musical *Jesus Christ Superstar*, before being plucked to play the second Lionel on *The Jeffersons*. "Chosen as the new Lionel was a young man Norman supposedly saw and liked in a TV commercial named Damon Evans—no relation to

Mike," recalled Jay Moriarity in his memoir *Honky in the House: Writing and Producing* The Jeffersons.

> Damon was a handsome and clean-cut young man with a preppy appearance and persona; where Mike had a slight street edge, which I thought made him more accessible and believable as someone who had grown up in Harlem and Queens. But no one could question Norman's proven expertise in casting. *All in the Family* had introduced Bea Arthur as Maude, *Maude* had introduced Esther Rolle as Florida, and Florida begat *Good Times*, the first black sitcom . . . and me and Mike Milligan's first writing credit.[12]

Though Evans—who is now openly gay but was then closeted—would appear for three seasons in seventy-two episodes before going on to star as the young Alex Haley in the 1979 miniseries sequel *Roots: The Next Generation*, his experience on the show wasn't a pleasant one. According to candid comments he made to author and classic TV historian Herbie J. Pilato in 2023, the main source of his problems was Isabel Sanford. "I worked together with Isabel in the mid-1960s, before *The Jeffersons*," Evans said. "We appeared together [on Broadway] in the James Baldwin play *The Amen Corner*. She was brilliant. But she didn't like me. Isabel was always trying to 'out' me. She was always criticizing me for something or would ask me to do these ridiculous errands that had nothing to do with *The Jeffersons*." Evans also told Pilato things once got so bad that Roxie Roker had to intervene. "Roxie just had to come over and bring me away from Isabel." [13]In addition to Evans's ongoing problems with Sanford was his overall discontent with the role, which was compounded by the producers' unwillingness to let him sing because it didn't fit in with the character. "Damon had to be continually reminded that that wasn't a musical variety series—the star is George Jefferson, not George Harrison," recalled Jay Moriarity.[14]

He did, however, get one opportunity to croon, but it wasn't a solo. It happened during the season-4 Christmas episode, "984 W. 124th Street, Apt. 5C," in which Louise got suspicious after she discovered George had been playing secret Santa to a family at a mysterious address, and Lionel, Jenny, Florence, Helen, and Tom sang "Silent Night" at the end.

Then, prophetically, two shows later, Evans was a no-show for the taping of the episode "Lionel Gets the Business." In the premise, George hired Lionel at the cleaners when he was laid off from his engineering job and then had to figure out a way to fire him after he messed things up. On this particular day, as the rest of the cast arrived at noon to begin rehearsals in the studio for that evening's show, Evans was MIA. "Everyone was on pins and needles, especially Don [Nicholl]," recalled Moriarity. "When Damon finally did appear, it was close to tape time and he was rushed into makeup and wardrobe. From what I could gather, Damon offered no real excuse for his absence. So in a case of life imitating art, George fired Lionel on stage and Don pink-slipped Damon off-stage, informing the singer's agent there was no longer any need for Damon to show up for work."[15]

With this and no explanation offered, Lionel was nowhere to be seen for the remainder of season 4 and all of season 5, even as Berlinda Tolbert continued to appear occasionally as Jenny. But then in early 1979, shortly after Moriarity and Milligan had been named executive producers, Sherman Hemsley ran into Mike Evans at a local beach in Los Angeles and persuaded him to return.

With Evans now set to reprise his role for the sixth season, it was then decided that Lionel and Jenny would become first-time parents, injecting a new thrust for the show, along with multiple storylines spread across eight episodes, culminating with the birth of the Jeffersons' and the Willises' first grandchild, Jessica. During the span of those shows, meanwhile, a new decade began.

As the 1970s transitioned into the start of the Reagan-era 1980s, *The Jeffersons* transferred well with the times. As the series evolved, it became less about race and more about ambition, achievement, and acceptance, even though there was still an episode in the seventh season in which George discovered there were members of the Ku Klux Klan living in the building, one of whom called him the N-word even after he had a heart attack and George administered CPR. The episode ended with his sad but true statement, "See that? They never change. You save their lives and they still don't change."[16]

Yet the character of George changed in ways that were both pronounced and profound. Though he was still a show-off prone to shooting from the hip and shooting off his mouth every week, he was also more tolerant. Most noticeably is that he stopped referring to white people as "honkies" and became friends with the Willises, no longer calling them "zebras" and "Mrs. Night and Mr. Night." As a matter of fact, Tom and George even eventually went into business together.

"What kept George human—and somewhat humane—" surmised author and screenwriter Rick Mitz, who later worked with Norman on the short-lived sitcom *a.k.a. Pablo*, "was the fact that underneath his obnoxiousness there was a great deal of sadness. He had struggled all his life, thinking that money was the key—and when he got it, he found out that the key didn't open all the doors. He was afraid to express his love for fear he'd be hurt, and later in the series when he did loosen up, it was truly touching. *The Jeffersons* was all about the bittersweet American dream and the silly side of success."[17]

Meanwhile, audiences of all races embraced and were emboldened by the fact that George was in absolute control of his own destiny even as they still laughed at his shortcomings. Observed *Essence* magazine:

> But nobody laughs at his ability to pay the note on the dee-luxxe apartment in the sky-y-y. The fact that the show has avoided turning Black success into the brunt of the humor, that the story lines have not evolved into George's buying Cadillacs and mismanaging his business to the point where Louise has to fire Florence and apply for welfare, is a fear all by itself—and an indication of how far we've come to dispelling certain stereotypes. If one of the goals of the Civil Rights Movement was to gain equal opportunity, then George Jefferson doesn't really contradict what black people have said we always wanted: he finally got a piece of the pie.[18]

What the show offered at its core, for all intents and purposes, was something for everyone, never siding with the rich or the poor, and always falling somewhere in between. It was also Norman's longest-running sitcom, lasting eleven seasons and 253 episodes until that was that. After multiple time-slot changes and no series finale, *The Jeffersons* was canceled unceremoniously without warning in the spring of 1985. Receiving the news while the show was on hiatus, the cast was predictably upset, and no one more so than Isabel Sanford. "The other sitcoms, they had a closing show—*Mary Tyler Moore*, *M*A*S*H*, and the others that were playing with us at the same time," she told the Television Academy Foundation in 2002. "They all had a closure and I thought we should at least have that respect. We had been running as long as they had but we didn't get it."[19]

Others, however, were more circumspect. Said Oz Scott, who directed the last two seasons and would go on to direct both Sherman Hemsley and Marla Gibbs in their next shows *Amen* and *227*: "I came in during the tenth season and it was very thin. I remember Glenn Padnick, the script supervisor, telling me, 'Your job is to inspire the actors who we feel are getting bored to see if we can get one last season.' They got the eleventh season, but everything was standing sets—the living room, the kitchen, the hallway and the bedroom—the entire eleventh season was nothing outside of those sets."[20]

Owing at least some of its inertia to the inevitable effects of aging, *The Jeffersons*, despite all its achievements, had also by then long since become more of a traditional slapstick sitcom even as it still occasionally wove in topics like prostitution, gun control, and illiteracy. But by then, there was also a surge of other highly popular sitcoms about upwardly mobile African American families where race was rarely mentioned and almost never the main emphasis.

Thanks in no small part to the innovations of Norman and *The Jeffersons*, who had already paved the way, race no longer had to be the emphasis. Instead, African American family sitcoms in the post-*Jeffersons* era could now simply focus on being families—and funny.

CHAPTER 23

Humps and Bumps

Just six days after George and Weezy moved on up to their new dee-luxe apartment in the sky-y-y on *The Jeffersons*, Norman had what turned out to be his first big-time flop with *Hot l Baltimore*, also produced by T.A.T. and codeveloped with Rod Parker from *Maude*. Premiering on ABC on January 24, 1975, it was something altogether different.

Unlike Norman's other shows about different slices of domestic life, *Hot l* took place at the seedy, soon-to-be demolished Hotel Baltimore in Baltimore, adopting its title from the burned-out *E* on the once-grand establishment's neon sign. It was also his first sitcom adapted from a play: Lanford Wilson's *The Hot l Baltimore*. Set in the fictional hotel's dingy lobby, the action centered around a series of conversations between the down-on-their-luck residents who lived there, who were facing eviction and an uncertain future after the building was condemned.

After seeing the play off Broadway not long after it opened in 1973, Norman was immediately interested in bringing it to the small screen. A big part of its appeal no doubt was the controversial main characters—including two prostitutes, one of whom was an illegal alien, and an openly gay couple—which was still unmined territory on television that seemed ripe for the picking. He had also, of course, had massive success turning the Broadway plays *Come Blow Your Horn*, *Never Too Late*, and *Divorce American Style* into box office gold. And with five hit shows currently on the air, including the number-one sitcom in America for the last five years in a row, Norman was now the most prolific producer in television. He had every reason to believe that *Hot l Baltimore* would be another winner.

It was therefore a complete surprise, if not a shock, when both CBS and ABC turned it down. No more enthusiastic were the brass over at ABC who had twice rejected *All in the Family*. But then, just when it seemed like he had exhausted every possible avenue and the project was dead, it got a reprieve.

Norman's white knight was future Disney chief Michael Eisner. In 1969, when ABC sacked the second *All in the Family* pilot, he was a young assistant to Barry Diller and had been running the projector during the ill-fated screening. And then as luck would have it, not long after rising to become the network's head of programming in 1974, he took such a liking to *Hot l*'s premise that he green-lit thirteen episodes.

As casting got underway, Norman's first hire was character actor Conchata Farrell—later best known as Charlie Sheen's gruff housekeeper on the early-2000s sitcom *Two and a Half Men*, who also guested on *Maude*, *Good Times*, and *One Day at a Time*—reprising her role from the original play as one of the two prostitutes, April Green. For the part of April's illegal alien counterpart, Suzie Marta Rocket, was Jean Linero, whose credits included film roles in *The Godfather*, *Heaven Can Wait*, and on television in numerous guest spots on Norman's other shows, including *All in the Family*, *Maude*, and *One Day at a Time*.

Though *Hot l* didn't have any stars, and the cast were all featured players, one interesting common denominator is that, like Farrell and Linero, several of the actors either already had or would appear on at least one or more of Norman's other shows. For example, sharing the billing in the opening credits with Farrell was James Cromwell who played desk clerk Bill Lewis. Cromwell had recently been on *All in the Family* in the recurring role of Archie's lug-headed loading dock coworker Stretch Cunningham and would go on to appear as a series regular on Norman's short-lived ABC sitcom *The Nancy Walker Show* and in one episode of *Mary Hartman, Mary Hartman* as Reverend Buryfield. As Clifford Ainsley, *Hot l*'s young hotel manager, was the Yale School of Drama–trained actor Richard Masur. Having first surfaced in the Norman-verse on *All in the Family* as a mentally impaired grocery delivery boy who had a crush on Gloria, Masur also then later became Ann Romano's young love interest during the first two seasons of the original *One Day at a Time*.

Charlotte Rae—most famous for her role as Edna Garrett, the nasally voiced housekeeper and later boarding school house mother on *Diff'rent Strokes* and *The Facts of Life*—had guested on *All in the Family* as a Tupperware saleslady, then as a department store personnel manager who turned James down for a job seven weeks later on *Good Times* in 1974. On *Hot l*, she played Ms. Bellotti, an eccentric woman with a psychotic never-seen son named Moose, who delighted in such off-stage pranks as staging *The Poseidon Adventure* in the bathroom, collecting a menagerie of unusual pets, and buttering the hallways. There was also actor Gloria LeRoy, who played an airheaded waitress named Millie, and had first worked with Norman in the 1968 film *The Night They Raided Minsky's* and subsequently appeared on *All in the Family* as the voluptuous Mildred "Boom Boom" Turner. The Norman newcomers of *Hot l* included actor Al Freeman Jr. as the wise middle-aged Charles Bingham; Lee Bergere and Henry Calvert as middle-aged gay couple George and Gordon; Stan Gottlieb as grumpy old man Mr. Morse; and Jackie, a young runaway and tomboy played by Robin Wilson.

Coincidentally, on the same day James Cromwell was approached about doing the new series, he learned that *All in the Family* wanted to make his character Stretch Cunningham a regular. "After I did my third *All in the Family*, I was riding down in the elevator at CBS one afternoon and Rod Parker from *Maude* said to me, 'Listen, we're developing a new series and we'd like you to star in it,'" Cromwell recalled.

> I said, "Holy mackerel, that's great. What is it?" He said, "It's called *Hot l Baltimore*. It's from a play in New York and you're the desk clerk. Sort of everything revolves around the lobby and your desk, and it's a hotel full of misfits and ne'er do wells and two homosexual guys." I said, "Wow, that's great," and then I walked into the rehearsal hall for *All in the Family* and they told me they were going to offer me a regular role and I told them I couldn't do it because I'd said yes to *Hot l Baltimore*. It was the same day, and I didn't know what I had missed because I chose *Hot l Baltimore*.[1]

Production for *Hot l* got underway in early 1975. However, despite the keen enthusiasm of Michael Eisner who attended every taping, and an all-out media blitz—including a full-page ad in *TV Guide* and on-air promos calling it "another comedy milestone"—it quickly became apparent to everyone involved that *Hot l Baltimore* was indeed going to be a hot potato that was doomed from the start.

Adding to the agita was that the first director Norman hired was from Broadway and had no previous television experience. So at the eleventh hour before the premiere episode was supposed to tape, he brought in Bob LaHendro, a seasoned pro who had already directed multiple episodes of *All in the Family*, *Sanford and Son*, and *Good Times*, and LaHendro saved the day, becoming *Hot l*'s full-time director.

But even with LaHendro's Midas touch, many of the actors still had difficulty. "First of all, it's a very well-written play and the transition to television was in my mind done very well, but it was not a simple situation," said James Cromwell. "This was an ensemble and people had to be on the same page in terms of the approach to their characters and balancing the reality of who they were. In other words, they had to create them as real people without commenting on them, or making fun of them, or diminishing them with judgments because they felt uncomfortable.

"I remember when we did the first run-through of the first script, Norman was pissed. He was very pissed at me, and he said, 'What are you doing? Play the character.' I thought I had to send it up. I didn't realize, 'Oh, there's ground, there's substance here, and it has to be invested.' Once he told me, I got it."[2]

Unfortunately, while the cast may have attempted to put its best foot forward, the characters were still decidedly campy and failed to ignite onscreen. Most pointedly were the hotel's resident homosexual couple Gordon and George, who frequently played up the "old queen" stereotype even as the show tried to make the audience laugh with them and not at them in awkward scripts that were chock-full of sexual inuendo and racy dialogue.

Out of an abundance of caution, ABC, as it never had before with any previous program, also aired each episode with a disclaimer warning. However, there were still stations—including WJC, then the network's Baltimore affiliate (now CBS)—that refused to run it at all. And then after a disappointing premiere at 9 p.m. eastern on January 24, 1975, *Hot l* never recovered. Four episodes into the run, Eisner informed Norman that it wouldn't be picked up for a second season even though ABC agreed to honor their original thirteen-week commitment, with the final show airing on June 6, 1975.

On top of his first dud—and ironically one month before the last episode of *Hot l Baltimore* aired—Norman received another difficult blow when Fred Silverman, who had been one of his biggest allies at CBS, jumped ship to become president of ABC's Entertainment Division in May of 1975. Like Norman at the time, Silverman was already legendary within the television industry and one of the first behind-the-scenes figures to become well known outside of it.

Under his three-year watch at ABC, the perennially third-ranked alphabet network catapulted to number one practically overnight, with Silverman almost single-handedly shepherding such hits as *Happy Days*, *Laverne and Shirley*, *The Bionic Woman*, *Three's Company*, *Fantasy Island*, *Mork and Mindy*, *The Love Boat*, *Charlie's Angels*, *Rich Man, Poor Man*, and the record-breaking miniseries *Roots*. For Norman, Silverman's departure meant not only the loss of one of his staunchest supporters at CBS, but also an important lieutenant in what turned out to be one of the biggest censorship battles of his career. In the fall of 1974, ceding to public outcry over what it perceived to be the increased amount of sex and violence on television, Federal Communications chairman Richard Wiley met with executives from all three networks in Washington to discuss possible solutions.

Leading the cause among the broadcasters was then–CBS president Arthur Taylor, who had been one of Fred Silverman's biggest nemeses, said to be a major catalyst for him leaving and a frequent thorn in Norman's side. Though Taylor was against the idea of government interference, he was in favor of taking some sort of action. Publicly vowing that CBS would no longer air programs that were not family-friendly before 9 p.m., NBC and ABC quickly followed suit.

With that, amid mounting pressure from Wiley, in January 1975, the National Association of Broadcasters officially ratified what became known as the Family Viewing Hour. As that following fall when it was scheduled to take effect approached, producers were understandably livid, and none more so than Norman, whose sitcoms would take an obvious direct hit. "It went down their throats like a chicken bone,"[3] said outgoing CBS programming chief Robert Wood at the time. Additionally, as author Sally Bedell Smith summarized in her book *Up the Tube*: "It was a canny ploy that many believe forced CBS to transfer *All in the Family* from its powerhouse position at the head of Saturday night to nine o'clock on Mondays. . . . The primary victims of the Family Viewing Hour were the adult comedies still scheduled before nine o'clock. The producers of both *Rhoda* and *M*A*S*H* on CBS endured countless battles over topics deemed unacceptable by the new standards. Pressure from CBS censors also dulled the topicality of the MTM spin-off *Phyllis*. The same sort of controversies swirled around Barney Miller at ABC, an offbeat comedy about life in a police station, and *Fay*, a show about a divorcee that NBC first sanitized, then killed after only three weeks on the air."[4]

When he received word from Bob Wood that CBS was planning to move *All in the Family* to another night following the ruling, Norman, who was vacationing in Paris at the time, vowed to take action. With the support of both the Writers Guild of America and the Screen Actors Guild, he and a group of other producers—including James L. Brooks, Danny Arnold, and Larry Gelbert—filed a $10 million lawsuit against the FCC in a Los Angeles federal court in October 1975.

Joining them in the fight were Carroll O'Connor, Mary Tyler Moore, Hal Linden, and Alan Alda. Among other things, the lawsuit charged that Wiley had violated their constitutional rights by forcing the network's hand into agreeing to the Family Viewing Hour. Though at first it wasn't enough to prevent *All in the Family* from getting moved to Monday nights where it went up against ABC's powerhouse *Monday Night Football*, it did engender widespread encouragement from the press.

In one such show of support, the *Boston Globe* wrote: "Norman Lear's *All in the Family*, *Maude*, *The Jeffersons*, and other shows are popular entertainment, topical and sometimes unsettling, but they are about the real world. And although they do little obeisance to the rituals of conventional morality, their underlying themes are honesty, decency, candor and brotherhood."[5]

All in the Family also got in a few jabs of its own at the network's expense that fall when the cast did a parody that ran as an advertisement for the new time slot called "These Are the Days, with the lampooning lyrics sung to the show's theme music by Carroll O'Connor, Jean Stapleton, Rob Reiner, and Sally Struthers around the Bunkers' piano.

But then finally, on November 4, 1976, U.S. district court judge Warren J. Ferguson declared the Family Viewing Hour unconstitutional exactly one month before CBS president Arthur Taylor was fired by CBS chairman Bill Paley citing personal differences, although Taylor would land on his feet, going on to start his own investment company before becoming dean of Fordham University's graduate school and later serving as president of Muhlenberg College in Pennsylvania.

In the meantime, Norman was already savoring the success of two new hit shows.

CHAPTER 24

Keep on Doing What You Do

.

Near the end of 1975—bookending the respective success and failure of *The Jeffersons* and *Hot l Baltimore*—Norman introduced TV's first divorced mother on what would become one of his most popular and favorite shows: *One Day at a Time*. With Norm himself a divorced father of three daughters, its premise was certainly a subject he could relate to, having also made it the theme of one of his earliest films.

By the mid-1970s, single-parent sitcoms were hardly a novelty either. From *The Andy Griffith Show*, *My Three Sons*, and *The Courtship of Eddie's Father* to *The Lucy Show*, *The Partridge Family*, *Gidget*, and *Julia*, unmarried mothers and fathers had been cropping up all over the dial for well over a decade. However, the circumstances surrounding the unmarried status of these shows' characters were ambiguous at best, leaving it largely up to the viewers' imaginations.

At the same time, while the subject of divorce cropped up occasionally, it was only in passing, so the notion of putting it front and center as the major focus of an entire series was indeed a watershed moment for television in 1975. But with divorce rates surging and the stigma gradually fading as more states adopted no-fault divorce laws, the timing was also perfect. From Norman's vantage point, the prospect seemed no less controversial than Maude Findlay getting an abortion and Edith Bunker going through menopause.

With this in mind, in December 1974, he began developing a pilot for a new show called *Three to Get Ready*. Collaborating with him were *Good Times* producer Allan Mannings and his wife, Whitney Blake—best known for her role as Dorothy "Missy" Baxter on the 1960s sitcom *Hazel* (and the real-life mother of actor Meredith Baxter, best known for playing Michael J. Fox's mom Elyse Keaton on the 1980s sitcom *Family Ties*)—who would be listed as cocreators. As *Three to Get Ready* was first conceived, the action centered around Ann Benton, a thirty-eight-year-old single mother living with her rebellious eighteen-year-old daughter Julie (whose last name was Cooper) in an Indianapolis apartment building.

Norman, however, had a slightly different vision. Though the setting would remain the same, he felt the emphasis should be on a slightly younger Ann as a newly minted divorcee trying to find her own identity. Aiming to do with Ann for divorced women what Archie Bunker had done for bigoted men by making them comically respectable characters, he said at the time, "Our divorcee isn't a chicly turned-out woman of the world. She was vulnerable and scared."[1]

What's more, as the father of two teenage daughters, Norman also thought that the daughter Julie should be a much bigger part of the story. Although Ann was also envisioned to be a feminist, she was the antithesis of her two-decades-older counterpart on *Maude*. She was "not a liberated loudmouth, but a reasonable feminist," noted TV historian Rick Mitz. "She didn't burn her bra and stop shaving her armpits, but Ann lived out the principles of feminism."[2] As originally conceived also, she was supposed to be a nurse with a love interest named Carl Silver, who was a doctor. Ann also had an upstairs neighbor named Gaye Morris. In the pilot, Ann and Carl's first date is disrupted when Ed, Ann's ex, comes to pick Julie up for the weekend.

Norman fortunately had no problem selling the concept to Fred Silverman, who as it happened, had been on the lookout for a new female-centric show with a modern theme—and in one of his last acts at CBS before moving over to ABC—gave him the nod immediately. Accordingly, Norman and Mannings wrote a script and began assembling the cast.

To play Ann, Mannings originally wanted to cast his wife Whitney Blake, but Norman had someone else in mind: thirty-two-year-old actor, singer, and dancer Bonnie Franklin, whose first television appearance had coincidentally been on *The Colgate Comedy Hour* when she was nine. However, Norman remembered her from her Tony-nominated turn in the Broadway musical *Applause*—which, in another interesting coincidence, was written by Lee Adams and Charles Strouse, who'd also written the theme song for *All in the Family* and the score for *The Night They Raided Minsky's*. "I loved the stride, the purposeful way she moves across a stage," he recalled.[3] Franklin's performance was so mesmerizing, in fact, that when she recorded *Applause*'s title track for the cast album, it became the most-listened-to Broadway song of the year, with Franklin's vocals upstaging the show's star Lauren Bacall. *Vogue* magazine also took notice, publishing a photo spread in

July 1970, predicting that Franklin, Sandy Duncan, and Melba Moore were all destined for major careers.

Allan Manings also remembered seeing Franklin in the 1974 NBC made-for-TV film *The Law*, in which she played a character like Ann named Bobbie Stone opposite Judd Hirsch and Gary Busey. After realizing that they both now wanted the same actor once it had been decided that Mannings's wife and series cocreator Whitney Blake wasn't going to star in the new series, Norman called Franklin and told her not to accept any more jobs until he'd heard from her as she soon did.

Cast as Franklin's daughter, Julie, was sixteen-year-old Mackenzie Phillips, the real-life daughter of the rock-folk group the Mamas and the Papas's frontman, John Phillips. Two years earlier, she had made a splash in mega-director George Lucas's coming-of-age comedy film *American Graffiti*, playing Carol Morrison, a young girl who gets picked up by a hot-rodding teenager, followed by small television parts on *Baretta* and *The Mary Tyler Moore Show*. More recently, Phillips had appeared in the film *Rafferty and the Gold Dust Twins*, starring Alan Arkin. Here she played a teen runaway named Rita Sykes, a role for which she got buzz in one of the first issues of *People* magazine, along with a profile in pop artist Andy Warhol's *Interview* magazine comparing her to a young Bette Davis.

She also caught the attention of Norman, who, as he'd been with Franklin, was so bowled over by Phillips's performance that he hired her on the spot. "I just met with Norman Lear, whom I knew was the brilliant creator of *All in the Family* and *Sanford and Son* and the deal was done," she recalled in her 2011 memoir *High on Arrival*.[4] For Ann and Julie's upstairs neighbor, Norman chose singer and actor Marcia Rodd, who had also originally played Maude Findlay's single daughter in the pilot of *Maude* before being replaced by Adrianne Barbeau.

Preparations for the pilot taping at CBS Television City began during the spring of 1975. At first everything seemed fine, but then as the taping day approached, trouble began. Initially at issue was the network's programming practices honcho Ray Cunneff, who took umbrage with the script. Though he was only thirty-two, Cunneff's views on what was and wasn't acceptable for prime-time television were more in line with his parents' generation. He was also deeply religious, bordering on being a born-again Christian. Cunneff demanded that Norman and Mannings delete twenty-six lines from the twenty-six-minute script.

They ran into still more problems after rehearsals began with the cast, who also disliked many of the lines and began having doubts about the legitimacy of their characters. And so as a gesture of goodwill in an effort to bolster morale, Norman and Mannings reluctantly agreed to meet with them to make revisions. That took up an entire day—by the end of which twenty-two of the twenty-six lines Cunneff had found objectionable were scrapped.

But then in a moment of déjà vu, just as he had during the premieres of *All in the Family* and *The Jeffersons*, Norman put his foot down. He insisted that the four remaining lines, two of which were Julie's graphic descriptions of teenage romance—including one in which she talks about how a boy at a party tried to put his hand up her sweater and another where she said "b.a." in substitute for "bare ass"—stay in the script.

However, CBS refused to budge, most likely attributable to the Family Viewing Hour, which would not be declared unconstitutional by US circuit court judge Warren Ferguson for another year. Then on the day the pilot was scheduled to tape, Norman and Mannings were informed that unless the lines were eliminated, the show wouldn't air even though they were still contractually obligated to make it. In an article published nine months later, the *New York Times Magazine* gave the following account of the ticking time bomb backstage:

> All of a sudden, the gloom was so thick in the dressing room, you could cut it with a clapboard. For the dozen or so actors frozen in various stages of temporary shock, the sudden turnabout meant an early end to a grueling production week and, if the pilot were sold, the chance to be gainfully employed possibly for years, at salaries hitherto only figments of their agents' fervid reveries. For Norman Lear and a handful of CBS executives, it meant a confrontation had been building slowly for months, one that was both inevitable and surprising, humorous in its unfolding and deadly serious in its implications—in short, the kind of confrontation that makes for the best of all first-act curtains.[5]

Still unwilling to acquiesce, Norman and Mannings went ahead with the taping as planned with the four lines still intact. And then, with the first episode in the can before the studio audience started filing out, Norman shouted up to the sound engineer in the control booth, instructing him to keep the audio on. According to this account in the same *New York Times Magazine* article: "He announced that the network considered the program they had just watched unfit for family viewing and asked if anyone agreed with CBS. Dead silence. 'Does anyone disagree?' Enthusiastic applause. It would be the last sound network officials who reviewed the tape in New York would hear."[6]

But despite winning the round, Norman still hadn't won the fight, at least not yet. Even after he and Mannings got rid of three of the four lines,

CBS still wasn't happy with the script. Complaining this time that it was too bland, they asked him to rewrite it again and reshoot it, which he did, this time changing the title and making some adjustments to the cast.

Now called *One Day at a Time*, out for the second time on two of his shows was Marcia Rodd. Norman also changed Ann's last name from Benton to Romano and gave her a second daughter named Barbara, played by fifteen-year-old Valerie Bertinelli, whom Norman had seen in the short-lived CBS drama *Apple's Way* and who reminded him of his daughter Maggie. "The first time I met him, I remember being in awe, even at that young age of fifteen, knowing that he was something special," she recalled. "I think it was my fourth callback for the show, and I sat right next to him at this big round table. I remember being very comfortable, which is not usual for those situations because I was really uncomfortable anytime I had to go and interview for any show. We read it once and he said, 'Well, try it again and do this, that and the other,' and I was so raw I didn't know what I was doing. Now granted, I look a lot like his daughter, Maggie, is what he said, and I think that probably inspired him to give me a chance, knowing how green I was. I guess he saw something in me, and I'm glad he did because he changed my life."[7]

Additionally, Ann got a meddlesome building superintendent—Dwayne Schneider, who in the beginning of the show had the hots for her—played by Pat Harrington Jr., who won both an Emmy and a Golden Globe for the role. The son of a vaudevillian who worked as an ad salesman for NBC after serving in the Air Force during the Korean War, Harrington had first risen to fame in the late 1950s, appearing on Jack Paar's *Tonight Show* as the linguistically challenged golfer Guido Panzini after being discovered by comedian Jonathan Winters, who was a frequent guest host. Harrington also played Panzini on *The Steve Allen Show*—where he was also a member of Allen's comedy troupe the "Men on the Street" alongside Don Knotts, Tom Poston, and Louis Nye—in addition to making scores of other TV appearances on such shows as *The Man from U.N.C.L.E.*, *The Munsters*, *McHale's Navy*, *Marcus Welby M.D.*, *The Beverly Hillbillies*, *F. Troop*, and *Alfred Hitchcock Presents*, as well as Elvis Presley's film *Easy Come, Easy Go*. After being cast on *One Day*, where he beat out nearly one hundred other actors and came to the audition wearing the same denim vest he wore in the series, Harrington (whom Norman once described as "the comic strength of the show")[8] had a recurring role on the ABC legal drama *Owen Marshall: Counselor at Law* as a district attorney.

Added last to the *One Day* ensemble was David Kane, Ann's lawyer-turned-boyfriend who was eight years younger, played by Richard Masur. At the time, Masur—then appearing in Norman's about-to-be-canceled *Hot l Baltimore*—also had a recurring role on the CBS sitcom *Rhoda* as Nick Lobo, the sleazy accordion-playing lounge lizard and boyfriend of Rhoda's younger sister Brenda. "It was not long after that that I did *Rhoda* or maybe I had done *Rhoda* already," Masur recalled. "Then Norman came to me. I got a call from his office. Could I come in and have a meeting? Let's have lunch."

> So we're sitting up there eating bad Chinese food and he says to me, while we were shooting *Hot l Baltimore*, he made a pilot [for a show called *Three to Get Ready*] that Lew Stadlen, a friend of mine, was playing a role in. . . .
>
> Norman said to me, "The show didn't sell but I'm making another pilot and I want you to play a combination of the part that Marsha [Rodd] played and the part that Lew played. So you're going to be this kind of funny, smart guy, who also has a big crush on her." I was married to a woman at the time who was older than I was, and Bonnie was older than I was. I said, "You know what's interesting to me, we'd be doing something about an older woman and a younger man because I haven't seen that." He said, "That's great. That's what we'll do."[9]

However, when it came time to shoot the second pilot during the midsummer of 1975, Norman encountered even more resistance from CBS. The major sticking point now was the network's opposition to a line in the new script by Julie in which she referred to mooning somebody in a car, even though it was just talk and no mooning actually occurred. But they still objected. In fact, on the day of the actual taping after the first one had already been shot with a second one planned for later that same evening, Perry Lafferty, CBS's West Coast vice president who was a close ally of Norman's, informed him that unless he eliminated the line, CBS not only wouldn't air the show, but they also wouldn't pay him either. For Norman, the prospect of going through this again was something he was simply unwilling to do. So even after Lafferty delivered the ultimatum, he decided to proceed with the second taping as planned at 8 p.m., with the line still in even though he was well aware of the financial risk. Aware also that there would likely be even more fallout while he was away on a long-planned vacation to Hawaii with Frances and his daughters the following week, as soon as the taping was over, the first thing Norman did was ask *One Day*'s associate producer Patricia Fass Palmer to put copies of both the original and backup tapes in his car, which he then took home and locked away in his garage for safekeeping before leaving for Hawaii the next morning.

It was the best possible option he could think of—a game of psychological sleight of hand that was old hat to him by now—to stall the network until he had a chance to convince them to come around to his way of thinking as he already had so many times before.

And once again, it worked. Several days later, Norman received a telegram from Fred Silverman, telling him that CBS wanted to see the tapes immediately and that they had every right to have them because they'd been the ones who'd financed the pilot. Norman, however, argued that because his company was producing it, it was still *his* show, and he had the right to keep the tapes—although after some coaxing from Silverman, he eventually consented to letting CBS have them under the condition that the line they wanted to take out would remain in. In the end, of course, CBS agreed, and the show went on the air, although because of the late date, it was put on ice until a time slot became available.

One Day at a Time finally debuted as a mid-season replacement on December 16, 1975, one week before Christmas. Airing Tuesday nights at 9:30, it was distributed under Norman's T.A.T. Communications production arm and initially filmed at CBS Television before moving to Metromedia Square in Hollywood, where it shared studio space with *The Jeffersons*. In the first episode, "Ann's Decision," the storyline sees a newly divorced Ann—who has taken back her maiden name and, at the beginning of the series, works as a cosmetics saleslady for Avon and later as an advertising executive—trying to adjust to life as a single mother raising her two teenage daughters, the headstrong, boy-crazy Julie and her bright-eyed, button-nosed younger sister Barbara.

Almost immediately, mother and daughter butt heads when Ann refuses to let Julie go on a camping trip with boys from her high school. A typically defiant Julie becomes argumentative, while the more levelheaded Barbara is simply content to have made the basketball team. In the meantime, two other characters enter the picture, momentarily distracting Ann: Schneider, the macho, pencil-mustachioed building super, who at first comes off as smarmy and always lets himself into the apartment with a passkey, and David, Ann's younger boyfriend, who proposes marriage even though the ink on her divorce papers is barely dry.

Soon, however, Ann's fight with Julie comes to a head when Julie gives her an ultimatum that she's going to live with her father if Ann doesn't let her go on the camping trip—whereupon Ann calls the recalcitrant teen's bluff and gives her bus fare as Julie storms out. With this, Ann feels guilty, wishing she'd had more patience with Julie, who then returns under the pretense that she's come back to retrieve her Elton John albums, until finally, they reach a compromise. The episode ends with Ann having a heartfelt conversation with her two daughters about the slippery slope of being a single mother.

Like most of Norm's other shows, *One Day at a Time* was another massive hit right off the bat, scoring high ratings and mostly positive reviews, as well as once again demonstrating Norman's Midas touch. It also trounced another short-lived NBC sitcom about divorce called *Fay*—starring actor Lee Grant and created by future *Soap* and *Golden Girls* creator Susan Silver, with Alan Arkin and James Burrows directing—that never caught on even though Grant was nominated for an Emmy that following year for Best Lead Actress in a Comedy Series. As for Norman's secret sauce, Franklin observed: "He's a good mixer. He makes people express themselves. He makes us create."[10]

As he had done with all his other shows also, *One Day at a Time* never shied away from tackling tough issues, including teen suicide, teen runaways, teen pregnancy, xenophobia, epilepsy, mental retardation, and sexual harassment, just to name a few. Particularly as they related to the perils of adolescence, Norman often referred to the show's story conferences as "group therapy for fathers." One of them even resulted in the season-1 episode "All the Way"—in which Julie is torn over whether or not to have sex with her boyfriend—that actually came from a real-life incident involving Norman's then-sixteen-year-old daughter Maggie, who'd gone through a similar dilemma and said no. However, despite her pleas to the young man to respect her wishes, Maggie's boyfriend refused. "The next night my daughter came home crying—he had all but stripped her," Norman recalled. "And that's how a show came about in which Julie faced the same problem."[11]

Likewise, through Franklin as Ann Romano, *One Day* realistically portrayed and promoted the lifestyle of the single, independent woman and working mother with depth and sensitivity as she tried, and in the beginning often struggled, to maintain a healthy balance between her career and raising two teenage daughters. In this sense, her character was often a study in contrasts, if not a journey through multiple dimensions. While her voyage didn't necessarily have a specific destination, for viewers and especially women in similar situations, Ann was someone they could easily relate to and draw inspiration from. Though she was scared and unsure of herself at times, she never let it show. She was always in control of her destiny, which made the character even more appealing to audiences, not only because she embraced it, but also because she had a lot of fun doing things on her own without anybody to answer to.

And so it went for nine seasons and 209 episodes. Thrown into the mix—besides Schnieder, the building super, who was always dropping in to the Romanos' apartment unexpectedly (usually wearing a tool belt and white T-shirt underneath his denim vest with a pack of cigarettes rolled in the sleeve) and who regarded himself as the Rudolph Valentino of Indianapolis, and Ann's boyfriend, David, who left after season 2—was the addition of several new recurring characters. They included Nanette Fabray as Ann's overbearing mother Katherine; the Romanos' man-hungry upstairs neighbor Ginny Wrobliki (Mary Louise Wilson), who worked as a cocktail waitress in a singles bar; William Kirby as Julie's boyfriend Chuck and Scott Colomby as Barbara's boyfriend Cliff; John Hillerman and Charles Siebert as Mr. Connors and Mr. Davenport, Ann's bosses at the advertising agency where she worked; and Bob Morton, Barbara's girl-shy high school friend, played by Jean Stapleton's son, John Putch. "I wouldn't have gotten *One Day at a Time* had I not been partying in my mom's dressing room after one of the *All in the Family* tapings when I was fifteen," Putch recalled. "[Norman's casting director] Jane Murray walked by, stuck her head in and invited me to come read for the part, and when I asked my mom if I could she said yes. That's how I got on that show."[12]

Unfortunately, as *One Day* progressed, all was not okay with Mackenzie Phillips behind the scenes. On the show, her character Julie had evolved from a rebellious teen into a more responsible young woman who fell in love with Max Horvath, an airline flight steward (played by actor Michael Lembeck) and married early during season 5 in a two-part episode called "Julie's Wedding." However, at that same time Phillips's own personal life was coming apart at the seams.

The problem was a crippling addiction to drugs, the seeds of which may well have started being sown when she was just ten and her father, John Phillips, who was also a heavy user, showed her how to roll her first joint, which she later described as a "rite of passage."[13] At age eleven, she had already experimented with cocaine. By the time she was fourteen, she was also a heavy wine drinker and cigarette smoker, which escalated from there.

Then in 1977, around the time of her eighteenth birthday, during *One Day*'s third season, Phillips's world collapsed when she was arrested and charged with disorderly conduct. According to an account from *People* magazine at the time, she was found "semiconscious on a West Hollywood Street under the influence of alcohol or drugs." Additionally, according to the article, "the DA said they also found a small trace of cocaine in a straw."[14]

Phillips, meanwhile, asserted that it was all a bum rap, claiming in the same article that "some guy [whom she later identified in her memoir thirty-two years later as a friend of her father's named Yipi] came up and said, 'Here, take this. It'll make you feel better.' Like a stupid, dumb shit, I took it. It was a Quaalude. I'd never taken it before. My knees were like jelly. I asked the guy to take me to a coffeeshop, but I fell over just when a deputy took me in."[15]

That following day, Phillip's arrest made front-page headlines in the *L.A. Times* with a report also on the *ABC Evening News* by gossip columnist Rona Barrett saying, according to Phillips's memoir, that "I'd been arrested with enough Quaaludes in me to kill a horse."[16] As a result, she was sentenced to six months' probation that required her to remain in treatment with the same psychotherapist whom she'd already been seeing for eight months, telling *People* at the time, "It's called diversion therapy. And I'm happily diverted."[17] She was also allowed to remain with the show, which managed to keep things tightly under wraps and essentially ignored the actor's drug problem at first (on which, at its peak, by the actor's own estimate, she spent nearly $400,000 a year for cocaine)[18] as things spiraled further and further out of control.

It wasn't surprising then that by the end of 1979 the wheels had come off completely. Having by now grown increasingly concerned about her physical appearance and erratic behavior, that November Norman and the producers ordered Phillips to take six weeks off and enter rehab. More troubling, however, was that she returned in early January 1980 in even worse shape. Two weeks later, she was given the option to either resign or be fired.

Phillips chose the latter, although the official statement given to the press was that her departure had been by mutual agreement as *People* magazine once again reported it. This time it was a cover story by journalist Sue Reilly, with an obviously airbrushed photograph of Phillips pouting and standing next to Franklin and Bertinelli who were both smiling. Describing the mood on the set at the time as "a situation [that is] bitter even by Hollywood's savage standards," even though "her colleagues agree that Mackenzie is a sweet person and perhaps the most talented actress on the show,"[19] the article featured candid quotes from multiple sources who spoke on and off the record, including one unnamed executive from Norman's T.A.T. Communications who said, "For two years, we've had nothing but trouble from that girl."[20] Barbara Brogliatti, who was Norman's chief publicist at the time, didn't try to spin the situation either, adding: "She has a drug-related medical problem. She just can't work. I consider this firing a step towards saving a child's life."[21]

The article also recounted two occasions when the cast became so concerned for Phillip's safety they sent paramedics to her house in the middle of the night. Said the coworker who wasn't identified: "When Mackenzie came out of it, there was no thanks. She wanted to know who was going to pay for 'all this.' She's impossible not to like, but everyone's disgusted. Everyone's gone out of their way to help, but you can only do so much."[22]

"*One Day at a Time* should have been my salvation," Phillips later said in her memoir. "It was exactly what I needed. Coming from a fragmented family, to have a place to go every day where everyone's talking, laughing, telling stories, bonding, and creating was heaven. But as time went on and my demons started taking over, holding onto the feeling of belonging was like trying to grab smoke."[23]

With Phillips off the show, many of the storylines focused on Barbara, who was now in college. Ann's mother Katherine also became a more frequent visitor after her husband died and she moved to Indianapolis. Ann, meanwhile, got laid off from Connors & Davenport and decided to start her own ad agency, also opening another storyline as she got a new love interest (her first serious one since David even though she'd dated and had a fling with a married man), named Nick Handris played by actor Ron Rifkin. Nick was a divorced commercial artist whom she met on the unemployment line. At first, they couldn't stand each other, but then after collaborating on a freelance assignment—with Nick doing the artwork and Ann writing the copy—they decided to go into business together and eventually fell in love.

Tragically, their relationship was cut short when Nick was suddenly killed by a drunk driver at the beginning of season 6 as two other characters who had already been appearing on the show were given expanded roles. One of them was Francine Webster, Ann's beautiful but conniving former nemesis from Connors & Davenport, played by Nanette Fabray's real-life niece Shelly Fabares, the actor and singer best known for her roles as Mary Stone on the 1950s sitcom *The Donna Reed Show*, as Elvis Presley's leading lady in the films *Spinout*, *Girl Happy*, and *Clambake*, along with her 1962 Top-40 hit "Johnny Angel."

The other character was then-fourteen-year-old Glenn Scarpelli as Nick's son Alex, who came to live with Ann and Barbara following Nick's death. Scarpelli's real father was the longtime Archie Comics illustrator Henry Scarpelli. Before asking Valerie Bertinelli to recommend him to Bonnie Franklin, the young thespian had already appeared on TV in the soap opera *Search for Tomorrow* and in ads for Celeste frozen pizza and Prego pasta sauce, as well as on Broadway in *Golda* with Anne Bancroft in 1977 followed by the revival of *Richard III* opposite Al Pacino in 1979. "I'd been watching *One Day at a Time* ever since it first went on the air and I never missed a single episode," Scarpelli recalled. "It was also around this same time when I was just starting out in the business and I was out in L.A. with my parents doing a bunch of TV pilots."

One of them was with Scott Colomby who played my older brother. He was also Valerie's boyfriend on *One Day at a Time*, and they were dating in real life. The producers of the pilot I did with Scott basically said, "You guys should hang out outside of rehearsing because chemistry is what this whole thing is about." So Scott asked my parents if he and his girlfriend could take me out to dinner. My parents were like, "A night in L.A. alone without my kid. Absolutely."

The next evening, Scott called me from the lobby of the hotel where we were staying in Westwood. He said, "Do you want us to come up and get you?" I gave him our room number and told him to come up and he walked in with Valerie Bertinelli. I was like, "Dude, you know, you should have mentioned that part." So anyway, we had a wonderful dinner and Val and I connected from the moment we met.

I was only ten or eleven years old at that point and then cut to around four years later in 1980. My mother had read an article in *TV Guide* where they talked about the fact that they were going to be adding a fourteen-year-old to the show. At first, I was like, "huh?" And then somehow, I managed to track Valerie down in San Francisco where she was doing a movie and she told me she had just spoken to Bonnie that day and they were looking for someone with theater credits.

I had just finished doing a Peter Bogdanovich film called *They All Laughed* with Audrey Hepburn and right after that wrapped there was an actor's strike, so they weren't really allowed to cast. Instead, we had an informal meeting at the Plaza Hotel where I met Al Burton and *One Day at a Time*'s casting director Eve Brandstein. They didn't put me on tape. It wasn't technically an audition but we certainly all got along great. At that point, they were also looking for the Nancy McKeon character Jo on *The Facts of Life*.

Nancy and I jumped on board the Tandem/T.A.T. bandwagon at the same time. And then literally, the day the strike ended I came home from school and my mom was packing because *One Day at a Time* had called to tell us that Bonnie Franklin and Norman wanted to meet with me the next day. We took the red eye and when we got to L.A., we checked into our hotel and I was whisked off to the studio to audition.[24]

Scarpelli appeared in sixty-six episodes during seasons 6 through 8 as the rest of *One Day*'s principal cast and many recurring characters remained intact. Phillips was also invited to return to the show at the beginning of season 7 in the two-part episode "Julie Shows Up." But things didn't go well.

After relapsing the following year and collapsing on the set, she was fired permanently when she refused to take a drug test, although she would continue to occasionally appear on a guest-starring basis. She also continued to struggle with various substance abuse issues before finally getting clean for good following a 2008 arrest for cocaine and heroin possession at the Los Angeles airport. Since that time, Phillips has been a drug and alcohol counselor at the Breathe Life Healing Center in West Hollywood. Additionally, she has continued her acting career, most notably costarring with Cara DeLizia in the Disney Channel series *So Weird* and appearing on such shows as *ER*, *7th Heaven*, *Cold Case*, *Beverly Hills 90210*, and *Without a Trace* as her relationship with Norman came full circle.

"Over the years, all through the years of my struggles, whenever I would see him at an event, he would grab me by my face, gently, and say, 'That punim, look at that punim! I've known you since you're a baby! I love you,'" Phillips told the entertainment website *Vulture* in 2022. "That friendship was a slow growth because I would see him in passing, and sometimes I would be in a stage of recovery and sometimes I wouldn't. Now, when I see Norman, I feel as though he has deep respect and trust for me, as I do for him. It's more of two grownups interacting. When I was forty, I still felt like a child around him. I don't feel like a child around Norman anymore. He saw something in me that I certainly didn't see in myself. He's just a good man."[25]

After Phillips left the show as a series regular in 1982, the show would continue for two more years as Barbara married a dental student named Mark Royer (Boyd Gaines), and in an interesting twist, Ann wound up marrying his father Sam (Howard Hessman) before the series wound down in the spring of 1984, with divorce having now long since become a non-issue on television largely thanks to *One Day at a Time*. To tie things up, in the next-to-last episode, Ann was offered a job in London. As she tearfully said goodbye to her family and her Indianapolis apartment (complete with a flashback clip from the first episode in which she tried to explain to Barbara and Julie that they all had to work together to navigate their new life), she gently closed the door as the series faded to black.

That following week, however, the show was back with another episode, this time as a backdoor pilot for another sitcom starring Schneider starting a new life in Florida, where he got a new job as the maintenance man for a boardwalk carnival and became a foster parent to his brother's two young children, although the new series never aired.

However, this wasn't the last of *One Day at a Time*. Following a perpetually successful run in reruns, on DVD, and a 2005 reunion with the original cast on CBS, twelve years later in 2017 the show was given a second life on Netflix with a reimagined reboot, this time focusing on a Cuban American family living in Los Angeles costarring Justina Machado and Rita Moreno. Developed by Gloria Calderón Kellett and Mike Royce, it was co-executive-produced by Norman and his business partner Brent Miller. Also involved in the series was Mackenzie Phillips, who interestingly appeared in two episodes playing a counselor named Pam Valentine.

CHAPTER 25

More Flops and Mary Hartman Mania

During the same time that the original *One Day at a Time* was becoming another humongous hit for Norman, he also had three other clunkers on all three networks. The first was *The Dumplings*, based on the syndicated Canadian newspaper comic strip of the same name, which aired on NBC from January 28 until March 31, 1976, and was canceled after only ten episodes. It costarred James Coco and Geraldine Brooks as an overweight married couple who ran a luncheonette on the ground floor of a Manhattan office building, with singer Steve Lawrence performing the show's theme song "Two by Two, Side by Side."

Next was *All's Fair*, premiering on CBS on September 20, 1976. It costarred actor Richard Crenna as Richard C. Barrington, a conservative Washington newspaper columnist romantically involved with a much younger and more liberal freelance photographer named Charlotte (Charley) Drake, played by Bernadette Peters. With many of the storylines revolving around their age difference and opposing political ideologies—on top of which Richard was a gourmet cook who already had a girlfriend when he first met Charley who was a vegetarian—*All's Fair* also featured actor Michael Keaton in one of his earliest television roles as Lanny Wolfe, who worked as an aide to President Jimmy Carter. However, despite a Golden Globe nomination for Peters and mostly positive reviews—including one from John J. O'Connor, writing in the *New York Times* that "The casting is first-rate and the finger-snapping pace of the show leaves just about everything looking easy and unintimidating"[1]—it never managed to gain a foothold and was canceled after only one season, airing its twenty-fourth and final episode on May 30, 1977.

This was followed by one of Norman's biggest flops ever, if not his biggest disappointment, with *The Nancy Walker Show*. Premiering on ABC on September 30, 1976, just one week after *All's Fair*, it was canceled after only thirteen episodes, one of which never aired. Norman had intended it to be a starring vehicle for Walker, the veteran comedienne and stage actor, who gained a newfound following in the mid-1970s both for her recurring roles as Rock Hudson and Susan Saint James's brassy housekeeper Mildred on the NBC detective series *McMillan & Wife* and as Rhoda Morganstern's meddlesome mother Ida on *Rhoda*, as well as her appearances as Rosie the waitress in a series of popular TV ads for Bounty paper towels.

On *The Nancy Walker Show*, she played Nancy Kittredge, a Los Angeles talent agent who operated her eponymous firm out of her swanky Hollywood apartment, which was frequented regularly by a steady stream of showbiz wannabes, has-beens, and a few who were semi-famous, all coming to her to either help them get their big break or jump-start their careers. In the ensemble also were Nancy's husband Kenneth (William Daniels), a lieutenant in the navy who was frequently away on assignment; their neurotic, hypochondriac grown daughter, Lorraine (Beverly Archer), and her newlywed husband, Glen (James Cromwell), who lived nearby; Terry Folsom (Ken Olifson), an unemployed gay actor represented by Nancy who also lived in her spare bedroom and worked as her secretary to pay room and board; network television executive Teddy Futterman (William Schallert); and Michael (Sparky Marcus) as his precocious young son.

While *Nancy Walker* was notable for being one of TV's first shows to feature an openly gay character, and there was one memorable episode in which Nancy and her husband smoked what they thought was marijuana only to learn that it was a regular cigarette, the show never got off the ground in part because her occupation as a talent agent who worked from home never lent itself to providing her with a real workplace like a restaurant, a newsroom, or a traditional office. As a result, the storylines lacked the necessary backdrop for the characters to play off one another in the same vein of other classic workplace comedies like *The Dick Van Dyke Show*, *The Mary Tyler Moore Show*, *The Bob Newhart Show*, *Taxi*, *Cheers*, and later *NewsRadio*, *Just Shoot Me*, and *30 Rock*. Norman was also less personally involved than he had been in his other shows, and it was less topical, something he lamented years later, saying, "I adored Nancy Walker's talent, and it added time to my life to work with her, but it was one we didn't get right at all."[2]

Even so, Walker still had the upper hand. Realizing that things might not work out even with Norman's stellar batting average, she had shrewdly negotiated to have it stipulated in her contract with ABC that she would be cast in another series if the show got canceled, which she quickly was, after the proverbial ax fell two days before Christmas on December 23, 1976. In early 1977, she was hired to star in producer Garry Marshall's *Happy Days* spin-off *Blansky's Beauties*, with Walker's character once again working in show business—this time in the title role of Nancy Blansky, who was first introduced on *Happy Days* as Howard Cunningham's cousin—now playing a den mother to a group of beautiful Las Vegas showgirls who live in the same apartment complex. However, *Blanksy's* went as fast as it came and was also canceled after just thirteen episodes, earning Walker the distinction of having starred in two failed series on the same network in one season, although she was immediately rehired as Ida Morganstern on *Rhoda* that following fall.

In the meantime, Norman wasted no time recruiting two of the actors from *The Nancy Walker Show*—James Cromwell and Sparky Marcus—for what would become his next and, as it turned out, last big hit of the decade, the already-in-progress late-night soap opera parody *Mary Hartman, Mary Hartman*. By the time it finally came to fruition and went on the air in early 1976, the idea for the project had been kicking around in Norman's mind for nearly a decade—even before he acquired the American rights for *Till Death Us Do Part* and began developing *All in the Family*.

In fact, not long after ABC had signed on to finance the first *AITF* pilot in 1968, he pitched them his idea of doing a five-day-a-week soap opera spoof airing late at night, and they immediately expressed interest. No doubt seeing dollar signs following the massive success of the prime-time soap opera *Peyton Place*, which was one of the network's few hits back then, to sweeten the pot the network even offered to pay Norman to write the first ten scripts. But then they twice reneged on the deal to do *All in the Family*, and the other project effectively died on the vine as Norman became busier and busier with his other shows.

One of the main catalysts for bringing the idea back to life was Al Burton, who had joined Tandem as Norman's creative affairs director in 1972. As soon as Norman told him about it, Burton was as enthralled with the idea as ABC had initially been and persistently encouraged him to pursue it, convinced it would be another winner for Tandem and T.A.T. The genre of daytime soap operas was also hotter than ever in the 1970s. Attracting more younger viewers and even men with edgier storylines, all three networks were brimming over with them, along with a proliferation of new fan magazines dedicated exclusively to the soaps and their actors. In addition to the older shows that had been around for decades like *Guiding Light*, *The Edge of Night*, *Another World*, and *As the World Turns*, there were also newcomers such as *All*

My Children, The Young and the Restless, and *Ryan's Hope,* with many of the top sudsers averaging ten million viewers an episode.

When it came to the premise of his latest project, Norman also knew precisely what he wanted: high-concept campy with the goal of satirically examining the impact of commercially driven consumerism on the American family, especially housewives, chock-full of bizarre characters, even weirder storylines, and no shortage of sexual innuendo and double entendre taped without a live studio audience or a laugh track. The title of the show featuring the titular character's name—neither of which he had figured out yet—would be mentioned twice, the notion of doing so having come from his observation that soap opera dialogue was often repeated more than once.

To add authenticity and give the illusion of a real soap opera with a long history, the dramatic instrumental opening theme—"Premiere Occasion," which had been written by British composer Charles Kingston under the pseudonym Barry White and copyrighted a decade earlier in 1965—would be selected from the Southern Library of Recorded Music's stock music catalog. There would also be incidental background music by Earle Hagen, the veteran composer who had also been behind the catchy opening tunes for *The Dick Van Dyke Show, I Spy, The Mod Squad, The Andy Griffith Show,* and *That Girl.*

But while Norman may have known exactly what he wanted the show to be about, when it came to finding writers who could execute the idea, he suddenly found himself at a stalemate. In addition to his usual stable of scribes, he also interviewed dozens of others, including Madelyn Pugh and Bob Carroll Jr., the longtime head writers of *I Love Lucy* and Lucille Ball's other sitcoms. Though not for a lack of trying, none of them cut the mustard. The one who could—and did—was Ann Marcus, a former journalist for the *New York Daily News* and *Life* magazine, who had been on the staff of *Peyton Place* and served as head writer for the soaps *Love Is a Many Splendored Thing, Love of Life,* and *Search for Tomorrow* (and later *Days of Our Lives* and *General Hospital*), along with having written scripts for *Lassie, Dennis the Menace, The Debbie Reynolds Show,* and *Gentle Ben.*

Marcus soon came up with the name of the main character Mary Hartman that became the title of the show, and she was named cocreator. She also brought in three other writers: Gail Parent, whose credits had already included *The Carol Burnett Show* and *Rhoda,* before later going on to write and produce *The Golden Girls* and Tracy Ullman's HBO sketch comedy series *Tracy Takes On . . . ,* in addition to writing the screenplays for Barbra Streisand's *The Main Event* and *Confessions of a Teenage Drama Queen*; Jerry Adelman, who was also originally from New Haven and had written for *My*

Little Margie, *The Bob Cummings Show*, *Bonanza*, and *Rawhide*; and Daniel Gregory Browne (then going by his birth name Ken Hartman), who, like Marcus, had written for *Peyton Place* and *Love Is a Many Splendored Thing*.

Norman lucked out also when it came to finding a director—Joan Darling who, as it turned out, happened to be a very distant cousin and was the first woman ever nominated for an Emmy for directing. Her credits at the time included the classic "Chuckles Bites the Dust" episode of *The Mary Tyler Moore Show* and its two spin-offs *Rhoda* and *Phyllis*, as well as *M*A*S*H* and acting appearances in *The Defenders*, *Marcus Welby M.D.*, *Owen Marshall, Counselor at Law*, *The Six Million Dollar Man*, and *Police Woman*.

With his core team in place and a pilot written, in the summer of 1974 Norman began selecting the cast starting with the whiny, wacky, pigtailed main character Mary Hartman. To help him narrow down a list of viable candidates, he first sent a copy of the script to his old friend Charlie Joffee, who, along with his rumpled, cigar-chomping partner Jack Rollins, made up the legendary New York comedy-management and -producing team Rollins and Joffee, which represented director Woody Allen. Joffee immediately recommended Allen's ex-wife, actor Louise Lasser, then thirty-five. She was already well known for her neurotic personality, which was exactly what Norman was looking for. Though her marriage to Allen only lasted two years, they remained close friends, and she had been in several of his most-famous films, including *What's Up, Tiger Lily?*, *Take the Money and Run*, *Bananas*, and *Everything You Always Wanted to Know About Sex* (*But Were Afraid to Ask)*. She had also appeared in director Otto Preminger's 1971 film *Such Good Friends*, on Broadway as Barbra Streisand's understudy in the musical *I Can Get It for You Wholesale*, and on television on the NBC soap opera *The Doctors*, along with *Love, American Style*, *The Bob Newhart Show*, and *The Mary Tyler Moore Show*.

But while Lasser had been intrigued by the script and flattered by Norman's interest, at first, she couldn't figure out what the character was all about (not unlike Bea Arthur's initial reaction to Maude Findlay), nor why he thought she was right for the part. Additionally, Lasser's recollection of how Norman first discovered her differed from his, on top of which she wasn't interested in doing any more television. "Norman had seen me in something," she recalled. "I can't think of the name of it, but he had seen me do a little part in something and he said, 'I want her.' This is what I was told, this is how he talked to me, and he said he wanted me to do it."

> I was thrilled when he called, that Norman Lear, big, shining Norman Lear, would come after a little orphan girl like me even though my

agent knew I didn't want to do a soap opera and I didn't want to do a series. I thought it stunted your growth and I didn't want to commit to anything, but Norman was relentless. I had five meetings with him in L.A., although we didn't audition or anything. He said I didn't have to audition. He just wanted to give me the part, so we talked about it on an intellectual basis. Each of the meetings was to try and get me to do it, but anytime I read Mary's lines, I saw a blank spot. I just didn't get it and I told him that. I kept saying, "There's a hole here" and he kept telling me I had to fill it in until gradually I came to realize that anything I did could fill it and all I had to do was what I was doing.[3]

During this period when Norman was still trying to get Lasser to make up her mind—and with the idea already in mind that *Mary Hartman, Mary Hartman* (also sometimes referred to under the acronym *MH2*) would be set in the fictional town of Fernwood, Ohio, where Mary's spouse would be an assembly line worker in an automobile plant—he next turned his attention toward finding someone to play her unfaithful husband, Tom. It was indeed then a delightful surprise when Greg Mullavey sauntered into an early casting session with the perfect look and the acting and improvisational skills to match.

All three attributes were in abundant evidence as soon as Mullavey—who had already appeared on television in everything from *Gomer Pyle U.S.M.C.*, *Ben Casey*, and *Gidget* to *The Fugitive*, *The Jackie Gleason Show*, *Daniel Boone*, *Adam-12*, and in the 1969 film *Bob & Carol & Ted & Alice*—took one look at the script and began performing a bedroom scene lying down on a conference table with Lasser following suit. "By nature, I like to take risks and make bold choices when I audition," explained Mullavey, who also made one appearance on *All in the Family* as Mike's stuck-up college friend Stewart Henderson.

"[During the *Mary Hartman* audition], we were in a conference room in Norman's offices, there was a big table and the scene Louise and I were reading for was supposed to take place in a bedroom, so I got up on the table as if it were the bed and Louise got on the table with me. That bold choice happened during my very first meeting with Norman, and he loved that choice."[4]

So, too, apparently did Lasser, who, after much hesitation, finally agreed to do the show and remembered about her audition with Mullavey that "we were very intimate and did it right on the table."[5] While their pairing was a defining moment in the casting, there were still numerous other principal roles to fill as Norman aimed to move quickly. The other major female character—Loretta Haggers, Mary and Tom's naive, bouffant blond, aspiring-country-singer next-door neighbor—went to twenty-seven-year-old actor Mary Kay Place.

Originally from Oklahoma, Place had started out as a secretary at Tandem several years earlier before becoming a writer's assistant on *Maude*, where she quickly learned the tricks of the trade, retyping scripts and occasionally even punching up dialogue. It was also around this time that Place became friends with an aspiring young comedy writer from Missouri named Linda Bloodworth-Thomason, whose budding friendship soon led to them becoming writing partners—and their first spec script—which they submitted to *Maude* producer Rod Parker's agent, who agreed to represent them. Consequently, they landed a series of plum TV writing assignments on *M*A*S*H*, *Paul Sand in Friends and Lovers*, *The Mary Tyler Moore Show*, *Phyllis*, and a Lily Tomlin special. They were also invited to take a whack at one of the early pilot scripts for the original *One Day at a Time*.

However, as much as she enjoyed her fruitful creative collaboration with Bloodworth-Thomason, who would go on to create the hit sitcoms *Designing Women* and *Evening Shade*, Place's even bigger passion was acting and singing, both of which she also got to do courtesy of Norman, beginning on an episode of *All in the Family* the year before teaming up with Bloodworth-Thomason. In the fall of 1972, shortly into the first season of *Maude*, Place was having lunch one afternoon with another friend of hers named Patty Weaver at the Farmer's Daughter restaurant across the street from CBS Television City. At some point during the meal after a couple of glasses of wine, she began telling Weaver—an aspiring actor and singer who would go on to appear on *Days of Our Lives* and *The Young and the Restless* and as an opening act for George Burns, Bob Newhart, Don Rickels, and Jerry Lewis—about a song parody she'd been working on. "I always used to like the Miss America pageants," Place recalled, "because they had the most insane talents. And so, I created this character who had an original oration on communism versus democracy for her talent . . . and then I wrote that song called 'If Communism Comes Knocking at Your Door, Don't Answer It.'"

> One day I met my friend Patty who was working in the news department at KTTV at the time for lunch. She was raised in Ohio in a very fundamentalist family, and she was a beautiful singer who sang harmony. After a glass of wine during lunch, I started telling her about the lyrics to my song. We were both a little tipsy, and as we were walking back to CBS afterward harmonizing and singing it, we ran into Mickey Ross and Bernie West who were two of the head writers and producers on *All in the Family*. They were also just returning from lunch and when

they heard us, they said, "What's that song you're singing?" I was like, "Oh, it's just a stupid song I wrote for a contest" and they said, "Oh, that's great."[6]

After exchanging a few more pleasantries, the four went their separate ways as the two women returned to the production offices of *Maude* and the men headed back to *All in the Family*. But then, about fifteen minutes later, as Place was seated at her desk and Weaver was preparing to leave, in walked Ross and West with Norman following behind them. "Sing that song for Norman," one of them said. "My throat just clutched . . . I got so nervous," Place recalled. "So did Patty, but we said, 'okay' and we sang the song and when we finished, Norman had this huge smile on his face."[7]

Norman liked the song so much that he invited them to perform it on an upcoming episode of *All in the Family* called "Archie Goes Too Far." In the storyline, Archie invades Mike and Gloria's privacy, snooping through their bedroom and infuriating everyone, including Edith, as they all storm out of the house. Later in the episode, they converged at the apartment of Gloria's best friend Trudy—including a disgusted Mike and a remorseful Archie, along with Place and Weaver playing two of Gloria's other friends who are sisters from Texas named Betty Sue and Joanie—who showed up also and proceeded to sing the song.

When the episode aired on January 27, 1973, Place's and Weaver's performance engendered such a huge response that the *Los Angeles Times*'s chief TV critic, Cecil Smith, wrote an entire feature article on it. As for Place—whose sizzle reel would later include everything from *ABC After-school Specials, Thirtysomething, Law & Order: Special Victims Unit, King of the Hill, Family Guy, The West Wing*, and the films *The Big Chill* and *Terms of Endearment*—she also soon went on to appear in both *M*A*S*H* and *The Mary Tyler Moore Show* in addition to writing for them before landing the coveted role of Loretta on *MH2*. "Once I'd started writing, Norman called me in one day and said, 'We're going to do this crazy show with Louise Lasser and I would like for you to read for the part of her sister' and I said, 'Great.' But then I came home and read the script. As soon as I saw Loretta, I thought, 'I've got to be Loretta!'"[8]

As Loretta's much-older husband, Charlie Haggers—whom she called "Baby Boy" and who was also Tom Hartman's best friend and coworker from the auto plant—Norman cast Canadian character actor Graham Jarvis, who had appeared on *All in the Family, Maude, Sanford and Son*, and in Norman's film *Cold Turkey*. Playing Mary's daffy mother, Martha Shumway, who talks to plants, was heard uttering the phrase "Mary Hartman, Mary

Hartman!" in the show's opening theme, and had a voice once described as "sounding like a Tweetie Pie cartoon bird strangling on peanut butter,"[9] was Dody Goodman. The actor's major claim to fame at that point had been an appearance on Jack Paar's second *Tonight Show* episode in 1957 after which she briefly became a regular, with Paar later writing in his memoir that her "whacky endearing quality" made her "his first big hit," although of his decision to drop her a year later, he also said that he felt "like the announcer on *The Dody Goodman Show*."[10]

Other *MH2* principals, meanwhile, included: Debralee Scott as Mary's seductive sister, Cathy; Phillip Burns as George Shumway, Mary and Cathy's father and Martha's exasperated husband; Victor Kilian as Grandpa Raymond Larkin, who is revealed to be a flasher in the premiere episode; and Claudia Lamb as Mary and Tom's troubled young daughter, Heather. Additionally, the show would have sundry supporting players, with each one as off-kilter, if not more so, than the regulars. Among them were actor Bill Macy's wife Samantha Harper Macy as Grandpa Larkin's nymphomaniac young social worker Roberta Wolashek, who fell in love with him; Bruce Solomon as Fernwood police sergeant Dennis Foley, who had the hots for Mary and eventually ran off with her; Shelley Fabares—also Ann Romano's conniving colleague and eventual business partner on *One Day at a Tim*e—whom Tom Hartman fell in love with after Mary left him for Sergeant Foley; Michael Lembeck (another *One Day at a Time* convert) as local TV news reporter Clete Meitzenheimer; Martin Mull as wife-beater Garth Gimble, who impaled himself on the aluminum star of a Christmas tree, died, and then returned as Garth's polyester-clad talk show host twin brother Barth on the *Mary Hartman* spin-offs *Fernwood2Nite* and *America2Nite*; Doris Roberts as faith healer Dorelda Doremus; Ed Begley Jr. as Cathy's deaf ex–love interest Steve; former MGM star Gloria DeHaven as Annie "Tippy-toes" Wylie, a bisexual CB radio afficionado who had an affair with Tom; Dabney Coleman, best-known for his role as the sexist boss in the 1980 Dolly Parton–Jane Fonda–Lily Tomlin film *9 to 5* as Fernwood's devious mayor Merle Jeeter; and Jimmy Joe Jeeter (Sparky Markus), Merle's child evangelist son who died by electrocution when a TV set fell into the bathtub while he was watching.

"When Norman saw the first script, he thought I would be perfect to play the social worker who sees Grandpa Larkin after he's convicted of being the Fernwood Flasher and then falls in love with him after giving him the Rorschach ink blot test," recalled actor Samantha Harper Macy of her role as Roberta.

He got me that part on the show and he was my hero in so many ways, but then he saw the first takes and didn't like them. He called me and said, "I wanted you to fall in love with grandpa." Grandpa's character was eighty-eight and I was thirty-two, but Norman said, "I want you to fall in love with him because he's wonderful not because you're so neurotic. I don't want you to play a neurotic person. I want you to be in love with him." We went back and shot it the next day and I came up with my character.[11]

With a $100,000 budget, Norman shot the *Mary Hartman, Mary Hartman* pilot consisting of two episodes under the Tandem umbrella in December 1974. However, as had been the case with *Hot l Baltimore* (and would be with several of his other later endeavors), he found no takers—including CBS, which foot the bill for the pilot—the general consensus being that *MH2* was simply too out there. Yet, as usual, Norman did not despair. "They all turned us down and Norman said to me, 'this is what they're like,' and then he said, 'We're still going to press. We're still pressing for it because we still think this is a great idea,'" Lasser recalled.[12]

With Jerry Perenchio prodding him, Norman also believed that, given how off the wall the show was, it might do even better on independent stations, which, by design, could afford to be more experimental and were less restrictive. What's more, a show like *Mary Hartman* had never been done before, nor had a sitcom ever been syndicated during its original run. "It was our greatest gift that the networks didn't want us because we needed that autonomy to make the kind of show we really wanted to make," said Mary Kay Place.[13]

As it turned out also, that following summer of 1975, the National Association of Television Programming Executives (NAPTE) would be in San Francisco for their annual convention attended by many of the industry's biggest movers and shakers. With a renewed enthusiasm, Norman's next order of business was to hire a salesman named Jim Packer and his company Mission Argyle Productions to whet their appetites. At Packer's recommendation that August, Norman invited a group of A-level TV executives who were responsible for buying content for nearly thirty station groups at over one hundred independent stations around the country to fly down to Los Angeles during the convention and attend a seated dinner party at his Brentwood home. It was held outside on the back lawn on a warm late-summer evening, and Norman's wife Frances along with their daughters Ellen, Kate, and Maggie served as cohosts, with violinists subtly strolling in between the white linen–covered and flower-adorned tables throughout the meal to help set the mood. Also on hand were Al Burton, Jerry Perenchio, and Alan Horn from Tandem.

Following dessert and coffee, the group repaired to Norman's movie theater–sized private screening room to watch the pilot. Before it began, he made his final sales pitch, also telling the executives how much his own family had liked it in the hopes of sealing the deal. With light applause after the screening was over, the reaction was generally positive, albeit not resoundingly enthusiastic, with some executives no doubt hesitant to respond either way in front of their biggest competitors.

But then, just as Norman was about to begin talking again, Al Flanagan, one of the most influential and conservative TV buyers in the country who was then-president of Combined Communications before going on to head up Gannet Broadcasting, raised his hand and asked how soon he could have the show, with several other executives quickly following his lead. Remembered Louise Lasser, who had been invited to come as an added attraction: "It was all very exciting and when I walked into the party, Norman said to me, 'We sold it.' It happened completely out of the blue and they sold it to like fifty stations."[14]

Filmed at KTLA in Los Angeles, the first station to syndicate the show was KING-TV in Seattle. With more than 128 other independent outlets soon carrying it, most of them airing it after eleven o'clock, the ones who did jokingly became referred to as "affiliates of the Mary Hartman Network." In the preposterous inaugural episode premiering on January 5, 1976, Mary worries about the mass murder of the Lombardi family down the block, all five of whom have been summarily rubbed out by Davey Jessup, a young sociopath who eventually kidnaps Mary. Witnessing the murders are Mary's daughter Heather and Raymond Larson—Mary's grandfather, who is revealed to be the "Fernwood Flasher" and gets arrested—though Mary is seemingly far more concerned about the yellow waxy buildup on her linoleum kitchen floor.

Also in the debut, viewers got their first peek into the private lives of the Hartmans' next-door neighbors, Charlie "Baby Boy" and Loretta Haggers—the May-December married couple who appear to be both physically and chronologically mismatched—complete with twenty-two-year-old Loretta dressed in a red peekaboo nightie and forty-six-year-old Charlie's ape-haired, bare-chested, middle-aged spread fully on display. In the episode as well was the first of many bedroom scenes between Mary and Tom, in which, while played splendidly by both actors, Tom nonetheless came off at first as having zero depth and being unbelievably sexist, though the character evolved as the series progressed.

And progress it did, quickly earning a cult following and becoming the most-talked-about show in America as *All in the Family* had been five years earlier—in some respects, even more so. Within its first six months on the air alone, *Mary Hartman* made the covers of *TV Guide*, the *New York Times Magazine*, *People*, *Rolling Stone*, and *Newsweek* and was parodied by everyone from Bob Hope and Carol Burnett to Donny and Marie Osmond. What's more, by the end of its first month, the cost of advertising during *MH2* had already increased twice on some stations as it also bolstered the ratings of shows that aired before or after it.

Around the country, fan clubs emerged as the *New York Post* published daily plot synopses, and several songs that Mary Kay Place wrote and sang on the show, including "Baby Boy" and "Vitamin L," were released as singles by Columbia Records in mid-1976. The producers even cleverly arranged to weave in Dinah Shore's eponymous talk show into an episode, with Loretta appearing on it and singing "Baby Boy," which spent thirteen weeks on *Billboard* magazine's Hot-100 chart, as Place then released a full LP of Loretta's music on Columbia Records entitled *Tonight at the Capri Lounge, Loretta Haggers!*

Rising even more alongside *Mary Hartman*'s popularity was Norman's public profile. In addition to now having seven of the top twenty shows on the air, in April 1976 he was interviewed by Mike Wallace for a segment on *60 Minutes*. This was followed by an invitation from Lorne Michaels to guest-host the second episode of the second season of *Saturday Night Live* that fall on which Norman's daughter Kate helped warm up the studio audience, featuring a series of prerecorded cameos with actors from several of his shows, including Jean Stapleton, Carroll O'Connor, Sherman Hemsley, Isabel Sanford, and Bea Arthur, all showering him with lavish praise, and even O'Connor calling him a "genius."

But amid Norman's public acclaim following *M2H*'s astronomical success, there were also mounting problems with its star, Louise Lasser. Toward the end of the first season—which would end with Mary landing in a psych ward after having a nervous breakdown on national television on *The David Suskind Show*—in May 1976, Lasser was arrested in Beverly Hills on charges of cocaine possession and causing a public nuisance.

The incident occurred at an upscale boutique after she didn't have enough money to pay for a dollhouse she wanted to purchase as a birthday gift for *MH2*'s costume designer and the actor's American Express card was also declined. After being told the store didn't accept traveler's checks and refusing to leave without the dollhouse, the manager then called the police, who originally arrested Lasser for jaywalking and two unpaid traffic tickets until, after searching though her purse, they found a vial of cocaine. "It was my friend Sandra's birthday that night, I was throwing a party for her at my house, and I had recently seen this dollhouse in this store window. I thought it would be great as a gift because of all the costumes she could have made for the little dolls," Lasser recalled.

> So I went back to get it and I wasn't feeling well at all that day. I had like a 103 temperature, but I figured I'd just pick up the dollhouse and pick up a birthday cake. I didn't have the right amount of cash; they wouldn't take my credit card and I was very childlike back then. When they wouldn't give me the dollhouse, I sat down in a chair and I wouldn't budge. I said, "I'm not leaving here without the dollhouse."
>
> I may have even started to cry and then the next thing I knew the cops were there. They were arresting me for two traffic tickets that were outstanding that I didn't even know about [and then they found the cocaine]. I wasn't a heavy user, but everyone smoked pot and did cocaine among the people I knew back then. It was part of being famous.[15]

Lasser was later released that same afternoon on a $1,631 bail, and her friend's birthday celebration went ahead as planned, with the actor spending most of the evening in her bedroom. Following her return to the *MH2* set two days later, Norman got her an attorney, and Lasser was ordered by the court to undergo psychiatric treatment, a requirement that was easy to fulfill, since she'd already been seeing a shrink anyway. In the meantime, the producers managed to work the incident into a storyline in which Mary refused to leave a local toy store in Fernwood without a dollhouse right before she was scheduled to appear on *The David Suskind Show* and then had a nervous breakdown during the first-season finale on July 2.

Two weeks later, Lasser flew to New York to host the second-to-last episode of *Saturday Night Live*'s first season where another series of bizarre incidents occurred.

Most memorable was her rambling opening monologue during which she walked out in the middle of it and barricaded herself in her dressing room until Chevy Chase, dressed in a shark's costume in preparation for a forthcoming sketch parody of the film *Jaws*, coaxed her out with the promise of appearing on the cover of *Time* magazine.

But first, earlier that evening twenty minutes before airtime, Lasser had announced she wasn't going to do the show at all unless another sketch she'd been at odds over with producer Lorne Michaels all week was eliminated. "They wanted Gilda Radner and me to do this sketch about the size of men's organs and I didn't want to do it," Lasser recalled. "I thought it was in poor taste, but Lorne kept leaving it on the list until finally my manager Jack Rollins had to tell him I wasn't going to do it, so they were mad. I don't know how many of them were mad, but they persisted and when we got to dress rehearsal, I put my foot down because I didn't want my father seeing me do the sketch."[16]

Though Lasser did go on after Jane Curtain agreed to take her place in the sketch, it still ranks as one of the worst shows in *SNL*'s history—and one that, along with Milton Berle's dreadful guest turn during season 4—Michaels never allowed to be shown in reruns. As for the rest of Lasser's performance, aside from the introduction, she only appeared in one other sketch with a regular cast member from the Not Ready for Primetime Players—again alongside Chase—this time staring silently into his eyes and pretending to be lovers in a lackluster parody of Ingmar Bergman's films. There was also another bit in which Lasser was seen by herself talking to a dog, as well as a short film that took place in a diner where she and her boyfriend (played by *SNL* writer Alan Zweibel) tried to break up and she kept forgetting her lines.

Worst, however, was Lasser's disjointed five-minute closing monologue at the end. It started off with her meandering onto the stage in bare, white-stocking feet struggling to put on her shoes and ruminating over the fact that she was doing so in front of twenty-two million people at one thirty in the morning. With piano music lightly playing in the background and her legs crossed Indian-style, she then proceeded to launch into another rambling, self-indulgent soliloquy about how she was initially reluctant about accepting the part of Mary Hartman, her meteoric rise to fame, and her recent drug bust. But the most surreal moment of the monologue was when she began incoherently recounting the moments leading up to her arrest. "They booked Mary," she said, staring off into space eerily in character and singing a few lines from composer George M. Cohan's classic "Mary's a Grand Old Name" off-key.

Norman, watching the show at home in Los Angeles, was not amused. "Each time during my monologue, I would switch between talking and singing and go 'And it was Mary!' and then the next morning I got a phone call from Norman," Lasser recalled. "He was furious. I can't tell you how angry he was with me because he thought I was blaming everything that happened to me on Mary, and I wasn't. I didn't even think about that."[17]

At the same time, back on the *MH2* set there were other issues aside from Lasser's erratic behavior. One of them was money, which, despite the show's success, T.A.T Communications was bleeding enormous amounts of week after week because of soaring production costs, on top of which were the expenses of selling, distributing and dubbing copies of each episode for every station around the country that was airing it. As a result, Norman was forced to cut expenses to the bone.

For the cast and crew, meanwhile, their experiences working on the show and with Norman were decidedly mixed. Comedian, actor, and political commentator Ben Stein, who served as one of the writers, for example, said in his 1978 memoir that "I enjoy it so much, I can hardly call it working,"[18] while Lasser told *TV Guide* in 1976: "I'm exhausted. It's not physical fatigue; I'm emotionally exhausted. The strain is unbelievable. Thank God for make-up."[19]

Lasser's onscreen husband, Greg Mullavey, who used transcendental meditation to help recharge his batteries in order to keep pace with the frenetic, five-day-a-week production schedule, said of his time on the show with Norman, "What I loved about him was that if you wanted to see him, he was almost always available no matter how busy he was."[20] On the other hand, screenwriter Dennis Klein—who also wrote the season-3 *All in the Family* episode "The Taxi Caper," as well as episodes of *The Partridge Family*, *The Odd Couple*, and *The New Dick Van Dyke Show* in addition to cocreating *The Larry Sanders Show* with Garry Shandling and serving as head writer during season 2 of *Mary Hartman, Mary Hartman*—described Norman as "controlling" and *MH2* in general as "schlocky."[21] He also added that "Norman hardly ever came to the set, and when he did it was to show directors how to direct. He wanted the show to be like his other shows, very rhythmic, very sitcom-y, and I think he was miserable in the end that *Mary Hartman* was more real."[22]

Notching 325 episodes in seventeen months—one of which famously featured author Gore Vidal who phoned Mary from his home in Rome and asked her to write a book with him and then visited her in the mental hospital where she voluntarily recommitted herself before they both appeared on *The Merv Griffin Show*—an exhausted Lasser left *MH2* in July 1977. With her character having run off with Sergeant Dennis Foley, the show was renamed *Forever Fernwood* and followed the lives of Mary's family and friends without her.

In the summer of 1977 also, *Forever Fernwood* spun off the satirical comedy talk show parody *Fernwood 2 Night*—created by Norman, produced by Alan Thicke, and costarring Martin Mull and Fred Willard—which ran for twenty-four episodes from July 4 until September 30, 1977.

That following spring, *Fernwood 2 Night* reemerged as *America 2 Night*—also created by Norman and produced by Thicke and again costarring Mull and Willard—and netting sixty-four more episodes. But by then, Norman was also ready to walk away from the grinding demands of weekly television, which is precisely what he soon did.

Part Four

The Later Years

CHAPTER 26

Changes at 704 Hauser Street and Shifting Priorities

The addition of Archie's grandson, Joey, in the middle of *All in the Family*'s sixth season at the end of 1975 marked the beginning of another evolving phase in the sitcom's trajectory. In addition to Mike and Gloria becoming parents, Mike graduated from college and became a sociology professor as the Stivics moved into George Jefferson's old house next door, clearing the way for a series of bold new storylines.

In the two-part "Birth of the Baby," for instance, TV cameras were allowed into the delivery room for the first time as Gloria was seen waist up in the stirrups, an event that was in stark contrast to television's first childbirth twenty years earlier on *I Love Lucy* when Lucy Ricardo couldn't even say the word *pregnant*. On *All in the Family*, meanwhile, Archie showed up at the hospital for his grandson's arrival in blackface after performing at a minstrel show at his lodge. Two weeks later, he was seen diapering the newborn with the infant's genitalia fully exposed in the episode "Archie the Babysitter," which aired January 12, 1976, on what was also the fifth anniversary of the series premiere.

Then in seasons 7 and 8, *AITF* tackled some of the most controversial topics of its entire run. They included gay bashing, draft dodging, Archie accidentally joining the Ku Klux Klan, and the attempted rape of Edith on her fiftieth birthday in a storyline that was originally intended for Ann Romano on *One Day at a Time*. In another provocative *Family* episode about sexual orientation, Edith's cousin Liz died, and her female roommate confessed to Edith that they were lovers. In the meantime, to spice things up and drive Archie crazy after Mike and Gloria moved out, Archie and Edith briefly had a Puerto Rican woman living under their roof—Teresa Betancourt (Liz

Torres)—a hospital worker who admitted Archie for a gallbladder operation and whom the Bunkers subsequently took in as a boarder to help them pay expenses while he was recuperating.

At the same time, Norman would continue to push the boundaries on all his shows, most notably *Maude*, in the season-5 two-parter "Walter's Crisis" in which Walter started drinking again and attempted suicide after his appliance business went belly-up. The year before, Norman had shot the flames even higher in the episode "The Analyst a.k.a. Maude Bares Her Soul" as Bea Arthur—in what was perhaps the finest performance of her career—delivered a tearful twenty-two-minute monologue from a psychiatrist's couch.

But as groundbreaking as *Maude*, *All in the Family*, and Norman's other signature sitcoms still were, by the mid- to late-1970s, the novelty had mostly worn off. All this while, too—on top of the abysmal failures of *Hot l Baltimore*, *The Dumplings*, *All's Fair*, and *The Nancy Walker Show*—were two more colossal flops. The first was *A Year at the Top*, a fantasy sitcom costarring then-*Saturday Night Live* musical director and future David Letterman bandleader Paul Shaffer and Greg Evigan as two struggling musicians who make a pact with the devil for a year's success, which was yanked after just five episodes on CBS from August 5 to September 2, 1977.

The second clunker was *The Baxters*, a quasi-reality series/sitcom that also began in 1977, originally as a local production of Boston's ABC affiliate WCVB. It was the brainchild of Hubert Jessup, a former Harvard Divinity School student–turned–talk show host, who launched it as an eleven-minute vignette segment on his Sunday morning public affairs program. According to New England–based journalist Tim Weisberg:

> It was part of the station's late-'70s initiative to produce its own programming rather than rely on first-run syndication and network reruns, overseen by General Manager Bob Bennett, whom Lear once told the *New York Times* was "the best local broadcaster in the nation." The show told the story of the Baxter family, an average American family facing the social issues of the day. The first fifteen minutes of the program would be the family tackling whatever the issue was that week; the second fifteen minutes would feature a live studio audience interacting with panelists to discuss that issue in depth.[1]

As *The Baxters* attracted a large, local following, Norman learned about the show shortly after its premier and immediately sensed the possibilities. Convinced he could make a go of it as a national show, which he did during the 1979–1980 TV season under T.A.T. Communications, he wasted no time offering to take over production and selling it in first-run syndication. Before any of that transpired, though, he gave the series an overhaul, relocating the family to suburban St. Louis, changing their first names, recasting them with nationally known actors, and coming up with a series of plots that seemed like they were straight from the playbook of *Mary Hartman, Mary Hartman*. One involved them having to decide whether to commit the elderly Mother Baxter to a nursing home. In another, they learned their son Jonah's teacher was gay and worried he might be harmed. In turn, each episode was presented as a mini-sitcom that confronted a different controversial issue every week, after which a live studio audience in each city where the show was being carried was invited to weigh in about how the cast should handle things.

Unfortunately, *The Baxters* never managed to take off. Norman was forced to throw in the towel after only one season amid soaring production costs, though the series was later picked up by a production company in Canada and ran for another year. In the meantime, the press began to take a more pessimistic view of America's sitcom king. Now with nearly as many flops as he had hits—and many of his most successful shows entering their twilight years—some started to speculate that his golden touch was tarnishing.

In fact, one journalist—John J. O'Connor of the *New York Times*, who had long been one of Norman's biggest cheerleaders—even said as much in an article titled "Is Norman Lear in a Rut?"—writing that "the Lear product has become noticeably strained."

A good deal of the humor has settled into a monotonous groove of hostility. The situations, particularly those dealing with sex, are getting predictable enough to trigger charges of easy exploitation.

One Day at a Time is getting healthy ratings on CBS, where it follows the vastly superior *M*A*S*H* on Wednesdays at nine-thirty. Despite a good cast and a promising premise—a divorced woman attempting to raise two teenage daughters—the series has been generally mediocre. The character of the older daughter, something of a hysterical brat, is positively repulsive. Mr. Lear counters that any strong reaction to a TV character may be worthwhile. Possibly, but not when the reaction is strong enough to get the TV set turned off.[2]

At the same time, by the late-1970s, both *All in the Family* and *Sanford and Son* were already reaping healthy profits in daytime reruns, as would *The Jeffersons*, *Good Times*, and *One Day at a Time* within a couple of years. While *Maude* initially proved to be a harder sell, it quickly got a major boost after Norman enlisted the aid of none other than former First Lady Betty Ford, who had recently left the White House and was one of the show's biggest fans. When Norman asked Ford to help him peddle it at a dinner party he was having at his home in the spring of 1977 for a group of broadcasting suits who were in L.A. for the National Association of Television Production Executives' annual convention, she couldn't say yes fast enough. Cohosted by Norman's wife, Frances, and their three daughters, the event's embossed invitation read: "Mrs. Betty Ford, Beatrice Arthur and Norman Lear."

In the positives column then, too, was his unexpected discovery of a precocious ten-year-old child actor from Chicago named Gary Coleman. At the time, Norman was in the middle of a nationwide casting search for an upcoming remake of *The Little Rascals* when a talent scout from Tandem visited the Windy City and spotted the diminutive young thespian in a TV ad. As author Joal Ryan recounted in her 2000 book *Former Child Stars*:

> In 1976, one of Lear's minions caught Coleman's act in a local Chicago bank commercial (a commercial in which Gary stressed to viewers "You can never save too much money"). While he was in Los Angeles on yet another commercial shoot (for Bisquick), Gary was summoned to a meeting at Tandem. Lear liked him, signed him to a contract, and cast him as Styme in the *Rascals* pilot. The show didn't go, but Lear had plenty of other up-and-running shows to let Gary play in, including *Good Times* and *The Jeffersons*.[3]

Though, of course, Coleman soon went on to mega-stardom in another one of Tandem's biggest hits—the late-1970s NBC sitcom *Diff'rent Strokes* about a white millionaire (played by and built around actor Conrad Bain from *Maude*) who adopts two Black orphans—such victories for Norman were becoming fewer and farther between. The mighty wheels on his sitcom bus kept turning, yes, but by the end of the decade, prime-time television was also undeniably on a different route.

What's more, Norman lost one of his staunchest supporters at CBS when Fred Silverman left the network in 1975 to take over as president of ABC, and then in 1978, at NBC. It was Silverman, in fact, who green-lit *Diff'rent Strokes* in what would prove to be one of his only successes during his tumultuous three-year reign at the Peacock network. By the same token, it had been Silverman—who, during his spectacular tenure at ABC, had almost single-handedly been responsible for the success of such nostalgia shows as *Happy Days* and *Laverne and Shirley* along with introducing what would become known as "jiggle TV," featuring buxom, often scantily clad young women in such programs as *Charlie's Angels*, *Battle of the Network Stars*, and

Three's Company—that, while legendary in the annals of television, were also the anthesis of the more socially conscious fare that had been Norman's stock and trade.

But the growing preference for such programs, and especially sitcoms, that in many ways were a throwback to their innocuous ancestors from the 1950s and 1960s wasn't Norman's only challenge. Even more pressing was his growing concern about the mounting political sway of the Christian Evangelical Right. Of particular alarm were religious zealots like the Reverend Pat Robertson and Moral Majority leader Jerry Falwell, who had labeled Norman the "number one enemy of the American family," a sobriquet he considered a badge of honor and wore as proudly as being on Richard Nixon's Enemies List.

Such radical extremism, Norman felt, was a grave threat not only to American democracy, but also the fabric of mankind. He had also increasingly come to believe that the only way to conquer it was to confront it head-on. And so, as the 1970s receded, he decided to step away from the control booth and heed the call. For Norman, it was a no-brainer. He had already changed television; he was now going to try and change the world.

CHAPTER 27

End of an Era

Still impressively ranked at number-four in the Nielsens, *All in the Family* opened its eighth season on Sunday, October 2, 1977, with the two-parter "Archie Gets the Business" in what originally aired as a one-hour special. In the story, Tommy Kelsey, the proprietor of Archie's local watering hole, has a heart attack and decides to sell his eponymous bar. After forging Edith's name on a home mortgage agreement to foot a bank loan, for which she eventually forgives him, Archie then becomes the new owner.

What none of the cast knew yet was that this was to be the sitcom's final year with Rob Reiner and Sally Struthers, although both actors already had one foot out the door. In fact, Struthers had to miss three episodes at the beginning of the season because she was filming the made-for-television movie *Intimate Strangers*, in which she played a battered housewife.

She had also recently inked a lucrative contract with CBS to star in a new series and do more TV movies, including 1979's *. . . and Your Name Jonah* and 1981's *A Gun in the House*. Though he was itching to direct films by this point, Reiner, too, was under contract with ABC to star in and produce what turned out to be the short-lived sitcom *Free Country*, cocreated with writing partner Phil Mishkin, in which he played a Lithuanian immigrant who had recently moved to New York. As for Norman, on top of wanting to pursue other interests, he was simply tired of the weekly grind.

While Carroll O'Connor and Jean Stapleton remained on the fence, and recently minted CBS programming chief Robert Daly wanted *AITF* to continue without Reiner and Struthers, by the mid-fall of 1977, rumors in the press about the show's presumptive fate had begun swirling around like a whirling dervish. Seeking to put an end to the speculation, in January

1978, Tandem officially released a statement in which Norman emphatically asserted that, indeed, this season would be *All in the Family*'s last. The following month, he told the *New York Times*: "I think it's time to move on. When Rob and Sally leave, the show is going to lose three of the important relationships that make the program what it is—between Archie and his son-in-law; between Archie and his daughter; and between the kids. We've had a good eight years. It's time to let others compete for that half-hour. The entity we call *All in the Family*, the song that leads into it, that particular location in Queens, will all be gone. But if Carroll and Jean want to do a show called *Archie and Edith*, I wish them well."[1]

Sometime either shortly before or thereafter, Norman assigned writers Mel Tolkin and Bob Schiller with the difficult task of trying to figure out how the Bunkers and the Stivics would go their separate ways. The premise they came up with was that Mike, Gloria, and Joey would move cross-country after Mike accepted a teaching position as an associate sociology professor at the University of California, Santa Barbara. Meanwhile, in yet another superb acting tour de force from O'Connor and Reiner, viewers finally learned what was at the root of Archie's prejudices after he and Mike got locked in the storeroom of Archie's saloon in the episode "Two's a Crowd," which aired in February 1978, one month before the season finale.

That March, the show would also be immortalized forever when the Smithsonian Institute announced plans to house Archie and Edith's chairs as part of its National Museum of American History's permanent collection alongside such other pop culture artifacts as Dorothy's ruby slippers from *The Wizard of Oz*, Muhammed Ali's boxing robe, the original Kermit the Frog puppet, J. R. Ewing's cowboy hat, *The Waltons*'s radio, Fonzie's leather jacket, and Mister Rogers's cardigan sweater. With a ceremony in Washington planned for that September, on hand alongside Norman, Reiner, Stapleton, and Struthers would be U.S. district judge John Sirica, Arizona senator Barry Goldwater, CBS programming chief Robert Daly, and Reiner's then wife, actor Penny Marshall. The festivities began on an even grander scale when Norman and the Bunkers were feted by Jimmy and Rosalynn Carter during a champagne reception in the Oval Office, also attended by Bette Davis, who was covering it as a special correspondent for *The Dinah Shore Show*.

∾

Taping for the hourlong episode "The Stivics Go West," was in mid-February 1978. Between Norman, the *AITF* cast and crew, and the studio audience, there was not a dry eye in the house. According to this account offered by Rick Mitz in *The Great TV Sitcom Book*:

> That last show with the entire family was a particularly hard one to shoot. Mike and Gloria were moving to California where he had a job waiting as an associate professor. Said one writer: "That last scene of the show required one hundred rehearsals because the stars weren't in any shape to do it. Carroll O'Connor finally broke down and Reiner had to leave." Lear got so upset, he had to wear dark glasses to cover his reddened eyes. The laugh-track on that show is not so much chuckles as sobs, sniffs and handkerchief-rustling.[2]

Airing on March 19, 1978, the most gut-wrenching scene of all was at the end as the Stivics were leaving for the airport and Mike—after assuring Archie that Gloria and Joey would be well taken care of—hugged him and Archie meekly returned the affection. Seconds later, as the sound of the Stivics' cab pulling off was heard in the distance, Archie finally sat in his chair and began to sob.

Then Edith, after fetching him beer, joined Archie in the living room in her chair and broke down also as the screen faded to black. That following week, *People* magazine ran a cover story in its March 27 issue featuring a photograph of the four actors accompanied by the headline: "Farewell to the Family: We'll Miss Them and They'll Miss Us." As Struthers confided to the magazine about the emotional aftermath, especially her close bond with O'Connor:

> I feel the way you do after you've been to a friend's funeral. The weeping has stopped, but you're not adjusted to the loss. I have to get used to not seeing these people who were my friends—my best friends—the last eight years. . . . [Carroll O'Connor] saw me through an engagement, dates, boyfriends. He always disapproved of them because he thought none of them was good enough for me. Just like my own father would have.[3]

Abundantly expressing their gratitude also was CBS, which took out a full-page ad in *Variety* thanking Norman for giving them "a dazzling variety of high comedy enriched with humanity."[4] But while Mike and Gloria were no longer on the show, their exit wasn't the last America would see of Archie and Edith—at least not yet. That June, newspapers around the country ran a story intimating that O'Connor was still game for doing another season if

All in the Family was renewed, with the actor quoted as saying, "I probably wouldn't play a better role as long as I live. There's no sense in walking out on that."[5]

Adding further grist to the rumor mill was the *New York Post*, which around this same time also reported that "the final show has already been planned for next year. It will have Archie and Edith retiring from the bar and going off to California to join Mike and Gloria."[6] Though Norman would continue to squelch any speculation about his own involvement—telling Les Brown of the *New York Times* that "I've been thinking of taking a deep breath, having a look around and trying out some new muscles"[7]—true to CBS's desires, that summer with nineteen Emmys and a Peabody Award under its belt, *All in the Family* was green-lit for a ninth season with Norman serving as a consultant.

To help fill the void left by Reiner and Struthers, a new member of the cast was added with the arrival of ten-year-old child actor Danielle Brisebois, who had recently played the youngest orphan Molly in the smash Broadway musical *Annie*, where both Norman and O'Connor had seen her. On *AITF*, she played Edith's orphaned Jewish niece Stephanie, who showed up on the Bunkers' doorstep in the season-9 opener and whom Archie grew to adore. "I remember watching *All in the Family* and Norman's other shows as a young girl and really loving them because they were so much fun, but I don't think I was aware yet of what a big deal he was," Brisebois recalled.

> Around the time Rob and Sally left *All in the Family*, I was getting too old for *Annie* and Charles Strouse, who was a good friend of Norman's, offered to make an introduction. My mom and I flew out to California to meet with him, and I brought a giant portfolio with me of articles and pictures and reviews. As we were about to leave, my mom said, "Sing for him," and I did. When I finished singing, Norman said, "You've just done so much for me, what can I do for you?" And then the next thing I knew, they were writing the role of Stephanie for me into the show.[8]

However, despite Brisebois's powerful pipes and nimble acting ability, the season itself was milquetoast, almost completely devoid of any of the sitcom's previous snap, crackle, pop. The only real highlights were a two-part Christmas episode in which Archie, Edith, and Stephanie visited the Stivics in California and it was revealed that Gloria had been cheating on Mike, and a celebration of *Family*'s two hundredth episode that spring. Hosted by Norman, the Oscar-style, black-tie gala was held at the Mark Taper Forum in Los Angeles in front of an audience of one hundred couples from forty-eight states who had been faithful viewers of the show and were flown out to California at Norman's expense.

In the meantime, within a week of the Christmas episode airing and ratings through the roof, Jean Stapleton announced she was ready to call it quits, saying, "Nobody's coming back as far as I know. It's our last year. No one has even discussed our tenth year. I'm quite certain I wouldn't do another year."[9]

While the press began floating the same question about the show's future around this same time, a spokesperson from Tandem confirmed Stapleton's desire to leave, also saying that Norman no longer wished to continue. Yet even so, America still hadn't seen the last of the Bunkers. With CBS founder and chairman Bill Paley cajoling him (and even calling him personally to request a meeting in person in New York, which was something he'd never done before in the nine years *All in the Family* had been on the air), Norman reluctantly agreed. As he recounted in his memoir, Paley told him: "Archie belongs to the American people, Norman, and so long as they want him, and I would add *need* him, it's our obligation to serve that need."[10]

And so, with O'Connor also aboard—and after what marked *All in the Family*'s 205th and final episode, another tear-jerker called "Two Good Edith," in which Edith nearly died from a blood clot that concluded with a passionate kiss between Archie and Edith in bed together—work began on what became *Archie Bunker's Place*, where the action now shifted to Archie's bar. Though Norman would not be involved in the production at all, before signing off, he made CBS agree to allow Stapleton to appear in the new series on a recurring basis during the first season to maintain continuity.

And so it went. Airing during *All in the Family*'s previous Sunday-night time slot following *60 Minutes* at 8 p.m.—with an instrumental version of the old theme song and an aerial view of the New York skyline panning into Queens and a tight exterior shot of Archie's bar—*Archie's Place* debuted on September 23, 1979. In addition to several of *AITF*'s directors and writers, making the transition also were Brisebois and Alan Melvin and Jason Wintergreen, respectively reprising their roles as Archie's friend Barney Hefner and Harry Snowden, who was Archie's bartender.

Added to the cast were veteran character actor Martin Balsam as Archie's new (and Jewish) business partner Murray Klein and comedienne Anne Meara as Archie's salty Irish cook Veronica Rooney. As per Norman's wishes, Stapleton also appeared in five episodes, including a two-part Thanksgiving show for which Rob Reiner and Sally Struthers also returned and that was another ratings blockbuster.

However, with Edith having been diminished to little more than an occasional prop and Stapleton unequivocally declaring by then that she no longer wanted to play the part, it was decided in early 1980 that the character would be permanently written out. The vexing question, of course, was *how* they would explain the disappearance of one of the most iconically beloved and unforgettable characters in the history of television. The writers and producers also knew that having Edith take off for an extended vacation to visit Mike, Gloria, and Joey in California or divorce Archie simply wasn't plausible.

The only viable solution, it seemed, was to kill Edith off, although Norman would have no talk of such a grisly demise. In the end, out of respect for his wishes and reverence for the character, it was mutually decided that spring that Edith would suffer a massive stroke in her sleep and die off-camera. In April, after Norman himself made the announcement of her impending death to the press, viewers were predictably outraged. As *Archie's Place* producers received hundreds of letters in protest, print media outlets from around the country published obituaries and memorials.

While flattered, Stapleton, on the other hand, politely urged Edith's grieving fans to get a grip. "It's like talking about something that doesn't really exist," she told one reporter. "Edith still exists in the imagination. . . . We must encourage people to realize that Edith doesn't die because she never really lived. You can't kill something that's an idea, can you?"[11] In the character's honor, Tandem established an Edith Bunker Memorial Fund, donating a half million dollars to the cause of the ERA and women's rights.

In the heartbreaking, hourlong season-2 opener "Archie Alone," which aired on September 23, 1979, the episode begins after Edith's funeral four weeks hence as Archie refuses to acknowledge the reality of her passing. With the house in complete disarray, food rotting in the refrigerator, and Archie refusing to sign the death claim on her life insurance, he sleeps on the sofa as pleas from his family and friends fall on deaf ears. He also ignores Stephanie's wishes to visit the cemetery—until finally—upstairs alone in their bedroom, Archie sees one of Edith's slippers and dissolves into tears.

Sans Stapleton and Norman, *Archie's Place* would continue for two more seasons. But despite decent ratings—and strong enough to displace comedian Robin Williams from his Sunday-night stronghold on *Mork and Mindy*—the show was essentially toothless save for a handful of memorable episodes. Aside from Edith's death, another notable show included Sammy Davis Jr. making a command performance in "The Return of Sammy" during which the entertainer stopped by the bar after Archie called into a talk show he was appearing on—and then after getting over the shock that Archie's partner and niece were both Jewish—the singer sat down to his meal and started to choke before Archie saved his life by performing the Heimlich maneuver.

Other noteworthy storylines included Stephanie's temple getting bombed, Veronica confronting her alcoholism, Archie coming to the defense of his Black housekeeper after one of his lodge buddies utters a racial slur, and baseball great Reggie Jackson showing up at the bar in a 1982 episode following the Super Bowl. However, after thirteen years, Archie Bunker's time had finally come, and CBS canceled the show in the spring of 1983. Though O'Connor was livid that the network didn't give them an official send-off, that following fall *TV Guide* paid tribute to both *Archie's Place* and *All in the Family* in a commemorative edition featuring a caricature of Archie, Edith, Mike, and Gloria on the cover with the headline "A Special Farewell." Also getting the ax was the short-lived *Archie's Place* spin-off *Gloria*, which had Struthers reprising her most famous role, now as a newly minted divorcee and single mother living in Upstate New York and working as an assistant to a crusty veterinarian played by actor Burgess Meredith.

Five years earlier, as Rob Reiner and Sally Struthers left *All in the Family* in the spring of 1978, *Maude* also voluntarily followed suit in what was attributed to a mix of declining ratings and Bea Arthur, who was in the middle of a contentious divorce from her husband, film director Gene Saks, having grown tired of the role. "Six years is a long time with anything," she told the *New York Times*. "That long in a part can be very rewarding; you can grow into it, but after a while it has to stop. I don't think Maude was a challenge to me anymore. Yes, the show would continue to be good but where would it go?"[12]

Together, Arthur and costar Rue McClanahan would, of course, go on to have a second sitcom resurgence in the mid-1980s playing housemates on the NBC hit *The Golden Girls* while Conrad Bain would immediately land another successful sitcom run on *Diff'rent Strokes*, also produced by Tandem and airing on NBC.

To wrap things up on *Maude*, it was decided that the Findlays would head for Washington after the governor of New York appointed Maude as a Democratic congresswoman, with Carol and Phillip moving to Denver and the Harmons leaving Tuckahoe for Idaho. Ever the creator, Norman attempted to replace the show with another sitcom that had originally been intended as a follow-up series for Arthur, who wasn't interested. It was called *Mr. Dugan*, and it cast actor Cleavon Little as a Black congressman. But it was canceled before it ever aired. Norman then reimagined the project a second time, this time casting Bill Macy as a former pro-football player–turned–university president, costarring John Amos, and calling it *Hanging In*. Additionally, he tapped Rue McClanahan to headline another show called *Apple*

Pie, where she played a lonely hairdresser living in Kansas City during the Great Depression opposite Dabney Coleman.

Both efforts tanked miserably, and while Norman had effectively decided to walk away from weekly television to devote more time to activism by this point, he would return to the small screen again and again for the rest of his life.

CHAPTER 28

1979–2023

As a symbolic mark of his A-list Hollywood status, shifting focus and the dawning of a new decade, in 1979 Norman purchased the rural Shaftsbury, Vermont, estate called the Gulley that had once belonged to poet laureate Robert Frost, and then later to the famed abstract painter Kenneth Noland, who was a major fan of *All in the Family*. Norman, too, had long been an admirer of Noland's work and owned several of his paintings. He and Noland serendipitously met that same year when Norman was in Pasadena on an art-buying spree with his old friend Richard Dorso, the former William Morris agent, Hollywood haberdasher, and TV producer best known for such hits as *The Fugitive*, *The Outer Limits*, and *The Doris Day Show*. Having acquired his first painting when he was just twenty-one, Dorso was also a well-respected art collector, whom Norman considered to be something of a mentor, once saying: "I learned what I know about modern art from Dick Dorso, and more importantly, I developed a taste for collecting myself directly from him."[1]

It was at some point during their excursion to Pasadena when Noland's name and the subject of his Vermont home, which had once been a working farm, came up. When Dorso told Norman it was for sale and that the original owner had been Robert Frost, his ears perked up. After procuring the painter's home phone number, Norman called him the following day and was thrilled to learn the house was still on the market.

Equally elated was Noland who lit up as soon as he heard Norman's voice on the other end of the line and told him how much he loved *All in the Family*. He also asked how soon he could come east to see the house and sweetened the pot by offering to charter a private plane to meet him at Kennedy

Airport and fly him up to Vermont. Noland assured him it would take no more than four hours round trip from New York, and as Norman recalled: "I stepped out of the prop plane in Bennington into the embrace of a man about my age who oozed something I came to think of as enthusiastic kindness."[2]

In 1963, Noland had purchased the estate directly from Robert Frost's family and converted the large barn behind the house into his art studio. That afternoon, while touring the lush grounds and the sunlit main house, Norman felt the most relaxed he'd been in years, describing the home in his autobiography as "warm and welcoming like a hug."[3]

He was also taken aback after seeing the bronzed National Historic Landmark plaque that hung from one side of the long, secluded driveway and the adjacent cottage where Frost had written some of his most famous poems. Not long afterward back inside the main residence, Norman spotted one of Noland's stripe paintings on the living room wall, and without hesitation, asked how much he wanted for the property.

With that, and the artist agreeing to throw in the painting as part of the package, the two men shook hands and struck a deal. Apart from its serene, bucolic setting and heritage, what truly made the place so special to Norman in the years to come was that it would serve as the home base for the entire Lear clan, or as he often called it, "my Hebrew Hyannis Port."

On the creative front, meanwhile, Norman increasingly began downsizing his duties at Tandem and T.A.T. Communications by delegating many of the daily responsibilities of his remaining sitcoms to Alan Horn. One exciting TV project he did devote his full attention to during this period was a new CBS drama he cocreated with Pulitzer Prize–winning *Roots* author Alex Haley called *Palmerstown, U.S.A.* Set in rural Tennessee during the Great Depression, it told the story of two nine-year-old boys (one white and one Black) who become best friends in the segregated South and featured talented young newcomer and recent Canadian transplant Michael J. Fox as Willie-Joe Hall, one of the two young boys.

"Alex Haley and I were good friends," Norman explained to author, historian, and National Public Radio television critic David Bianculli about the show's gestation in the 2016 book *The Platinum Age of Television*. "And we were having dinner one night, and he told me about his best friend, when they were nine or ten years old, who was this white kid. They were so close that their two families were closer than other families were comfortable with, in this small southern town. And then, when puberty set in, the culture called on them to separate. . . . It would just move them to see less of each other, and eventually none of each other. And I said, 'My God! That's such a great show! We follow these kids until puberty, and then we see how the culture ruptures their relationship.' And that's what we set out to do."[4]

But try as they did—and despite Fox's outstanding performance on the cusp of becoming one of the decade's biggest superstars as Alex P. Keaton on the hit NBC sitcom *Family Ties* and in such films as *Back to the Future* and *Doc Hollywood*—*Palmerstown* never managed to find enough of an audience and was canceled after just one season. In the meantime, as *Palmerstown* was struggling to get on its feet, Norman was also preparing to launch the other endeavor for which he would become nearly as renowned as his 1970s sitcoms, the nonprofit progressive advocacy group People for the American Way (PFAW).

Cofounded by Democratic Texas congresswoman Barbara Jordan and the then–Time Incorporated chairman and CEO Andrew Heiskell, PFAW was officially incorporated in September 1981. The organization's unofficial introduction to the public came in the form of a television ad/public service announcement that fall produced by Norman. The sixty-second spot was commandeered by a hardhat-clad Average American Joe, dressed in jeans, a denim work shirt, and blue jacket, as he stood in front of a forklift, and without uttering his name, took direct aim at Norman's nemesis, Moral Majority leader Reverend Jerry Falwell, and his propagandist view that being a good Christian meant voting a certain way.

In conjunction with PFAW that following year on March 21, 1982, in what was billed as a "salute to freedom" as part of George Washington's two-hundred-fiftieth birthday, Norman produced the celebrity-studded two-hour television special *I Love Liberty* for ABC. It was filmed the month before in front of some ten thousand spectators at the Los Angeles Sports Arena with millions more watching at home. With former president Gerald Ford and ex–First Lady Lady Bird Johnson serving as cochairs of the event, other famous guests from both sides of the political aisle included Barbra Streisand, Jane Fonda, Robin Williams, Burt Lancaster, Dionne Warwick, Patty Duke, Walter Matthau, Mary Tyler Moore, Martin Sheen, Christopher Reeve, and tap dancer Gregory Hines.

Backed by the US Air Force Band, Streisand sang "America the Beautiful" while Williams delivered a comedic monologue on patriotism dressed as the American Flag. With an introduction by Big Bird and then Miss Piggy dressed as both George Washington and Abraham Lincoln, the Muppets performed a comic reenactment of the Second Continental Congress. Burt Lancaster delivered an electrifying performance as Federal Justice Learned Hand giving a speech on the spirit of liberty as Christopher Reeve and Walter Matthau did a spot-on reenactment of a debate over religious freedom set in eighteenth-century New England. Seventeen years before his starring turn playing the commander in chief on *The West Wing*, Martin Sheen donned a powdered wig and strode onstage reading an open letter to George Washington from the American people. Introducing what was the evening's most elaborate production number performed by sixteen hundred people, including unicyclists, baton twirlers, and five marching bands, was Norman's longtime friend, Arizona Republican senator Barry Goldwater.

In his review for the *Washington Post*, Pulitzer Prize–winning television critic Tom Shales described the extravaganza as "America's first left-wing patriotic rally," also writing that: "As television, it's unimpeachably wholesome. One could watch it and have innumerable misgivings about it and yet not doubt that Norman Lear's heart is in the right place."[5] The *Christian Science Monitor* also hailed *Liberty* as "an unabashedly patriotic, flag-waving, freedom-loving, electronic paean to America's diversity of people and attitudes."[6]

Over the next four decades, People for the American Way would remain the chief cornerstone of Norman's activism life, engendering the support of such high-profile political figures, philanthropists, and actors as Julian Bond, Frances Berry, James Hormel, Seth MacFarlane, Jane Lynch, and Alec Baldwin, all of whom served on its board. Shortly after PFAW's founding, the organization also launched the People for the American Way Foundation dedicated to research and educational initiatives for progressive causes and later the political action committee the People for the American Way Voters Alliance. Three years later in 2004, Norman established the national nonpartisan, nonprofit campaign Declare Yourself to encourage eligible eighteen- to twenty-nine-year-olds to vote.

With many of his efforts also channeled directly through the Lear Family Foundation, other initiatives over the years included: the Norman Lear Center at the University of Southern California's Annenberg School of Communications, which studies the impact of media on society and was named in his honor following a $5 million donation made by Norman and his third wife, Lyn, in 2000; the national nonpartisan campaign nonprofit Declare Yourself created in 1994 to encourage eligible young people to vote; and the Business Enterprise Trust, cofounded in 1989 with Johnson & Johnson chairman and CEO James Burke to promote business ethics.

During the 1970s and 1980s, Norman was also actively involved in another progressive organization called the Malibu Mafia. They were a group of wealthy Jewish men in L.A. who met informally to discuss liberal political causes and find ways to fund them, including filling the defense coffers for Daniel Ellsberg and keeping the *Nation* magazine financially afloat.

On the heels of Norman's fabulous success with *I Love Liberty* in March of 1982 was the beginning of his seventh decade five months later. Despite the ever-mounting strains of their now-twenty-five-year-old marriage—marked by Frances's ongoing resentment of Norman's success, her general dislike of Hollywood, and manic-depressive mood swings—she went all out. Early on the evening of his sixtieth birthday on July 27, 1982, they drove to Van Nuys Airport in a chauffeured car, and with Norman blindfolded, boarded the awaiting private plane and circled Los Angeles for the next hour.

Deducing by the distance of the flight that they were either heading to Palm Springs or Las Vegas, upon landing and still blindfolded, Norman was ushered into another car and driven to the Beverly Hills Hotel about a half hour away. After being escorted by Frances through the palatial lobby and down a flight of stairs into the audibly hushed sounds of the hotel's overflowing main ballroom, moments later, after finally getting the blindfold removed, Norman was greeted by the enthusiastic sounds of family, close friends, colleagues, and the stars of some of his most famous sitcoms shouting, "Happy Birthday!"

Among the partygoers were his longtime business partner Jerry Perenchio singing the Mel Torme standard "I've Got a Crush on You" and Bea Arthur, who jumped out of a cake and belted out a baritone-heavy rendition of "My Man." On hand also were songsmith spouses Alan and Marilyn Bergman—who had written the theme songs for *Maude* and *Good Times* and were just fresh off penning the score for that year's biggest film *ET*—feting Norman with a song parody from the film *Guys and Dolls* complete with the lyrics "We've got the guy right here, his name is Norman Lear . . ."

Of the many other approbations that night, the most poignant came from Frances and Norman's daughter Kate, who, on behalf of all three Lear progeny, called Norman someone who "walks through life's peaks and valleys with equal wonder."[7] Conspicuously absent, however, were any remarks from Frances—who, as Norman surmised in his memoir, "didn't join the toasters, likely for the same reason I'd wanted to save our daughters from having to salute our steadily deteriorating marriage several months earlier."[8]

At the same time, despite their problems, Norman and Frances still loved and respected each other deeply. Aside from their shared intellectual and political interests, she had also long been one of his most trusted sounding boards, and, of course, there were Kate and Maggie, who were their greatest pride and joy. So in order to spare his family from having to put on a happy face, not to mention the dreaded task of having to hear—and worse, make—a series of obligatory toasts publicly proclaiming their marital bliss, Norman decided to surprise Frances with a cruise instead.

He got the idea when he was at home in Brentwood one night in the early spring of 1982 with author Gore Vidal and a group of other friends watching a James Bond film in his private screening room. One scene that caught Norman's attention was that of a yacht anchored at bay in the Greek Isles looking down from a panoramic mountaintop, the exact locale of which Vidal not only pinpointed, but also knew the owner of the yacht, which was called the *Paget*.

Norman's antenna no doubt rose as high as it had been when he'd first learned that Robert Frost's former home in Vermont was up for grabs, and he soon made plans to take a three-week cruise of the Mediterranean with Frances on a private yacht of their own early that summer, including stopovers in Samos, Rhodes, Corfu, Santorini, and Mykonos. With three spacious guest staterooms and a valet and chef at their disposal, Norman invited nine other couples to join them at sea for a week each. One of the pairs was Emmy-winning talk show host and author Bill Boggs and his former wife and close friend, bestselling author and veteran *Vanity Fair* senior editor Leslie Bennetts, then a reporter for the *New York Times*, who was a close friend of Frances's.

"Norman was going to surprise Frances and take her on a long vacation for their anniversary," Boggs remembered. "He somehow got her to Europe where the boat was docked and with two glasses of champagne in hand, he said, 'Happy anniversary! I chartered this yacht and we're not getting off for three weeks. Enjoy yourself.' Despite their difficulties, this came about in the most loving and romantic way on Norman's part. We all had an incredible time, and the memories are still vivid. I've always loved the story of how it happened."[9]

Added Bennetts, who first met Frances shortly after joining the *Times* in 1978 and remained a close family friend for the rest of her life: "My overriding takeaway from that whole experience was really admiring the fact that Norman, unlike a lot of other really powerful men, was taking time out to enjoy his success as much as possible and share it with the people he loved. His friends were important to him, and he and Frances were still very close in many ways at that point."[10]

But as momentous as Norman's birthday party and the cruise were, nothing could erase the painful memory of when Frances attempted to take her life for the third time and nearly succeeded as they were expecting dinner guests one evening several years earlier. Visting the Lears' home for a party in their honor on this night were theater producer Wynn Handman and his wife, Bobbie, the influential Democratic political activist and arts preservationist, who served as the executive director of People for the American Way's New York office for more than forty years.

Dinner had been scheduled for seven thirty, but when Norman arrived home from the office late that afternoon, Frances was nowhere to be found. Informed by the housekeeper that she'd been out all day, Norman, seeing no immediate cause for alarm, changed clothes and went back downstairs to greet their guests.

But with Frances still a no-show by seven o'clock, he became increasingly concerned and phoned her assistant, who, after some prodding, revealed that with the blessing of the psychiatrist she was seeing multiple times a week, Frances had rented a separate apartment, neither the address nor phone number of which the assistant had. Panic-stricken that Frances was trying to kill herself again, Norman immediately called the shrink on his emergency line and demanded the address and phone number of the apartment, which he didn't have either, though, providentially, as soon as they hung up, her assistant called again and told Norman that she remembered the apartment was located someplace on Beverly Glenn, south of Wilshire.

Seconds later, Norman was in his car, stopping at every apartment building within the vicinity and ringing the superintendent over the intercom in each one until finally—after hearing Frances's physical description and getting clearance from the owner with whom Norman threatened legal action if he didn't let him in—he was taken upstairs.

The modest studio apartment Frances had rented was nondescript and devoid of any personal effects except for a few photos of Kate and Maggie and a rug they'd purchased on a trip to Morocco several years earlier. As soon as they were inside, Norman spotted Frances lying on the rug semiconscious with a mostly depleted cup of pills in one hand and her mouth half-open with white liquid pooled around her lips.

Spotting a handwritten suicide note on the desk as he tried to feel her pulse, the super called 911, and Frances was rushed to Cedar-Sinai Hospital, where the attending emergency room physician told Norman she would have died within minutes if he hadn't found her when he did. Declared out of danger after pumping her stomach, she was admitted to a private room for observation as Kate and Maggie, who were now college students at Stanford and the University of Oregon, rushed to L.A. to be by Norman's side, with all three of them trying to comfort each other and struggling to make sense of what had just happened and *why again.*

Although he wasn't directly involved in any new shows at that time, the next major professional score for Norman—along with Jerry Perenchio and Bud Yorkin (who hadn't been actively working with Norman since the mid-1970s and would soon bow out altogether)—was the purchase of Avco Embassy Pictures for $25 million in January 1982. Following the acquisition and after folding Tandem and T.A.T.'s existing assets into the new entity, now called Embassy Communications, they would continue to be one of TV's biggest sitcom pipelines.

On top of older shows like *The Jeffersons*, *One Day at a Time*, *Diff'rent Strokes*, and *The Facts of Life*, among the new entries were *Silver Spoons*, *Who's the Boss?*, and *Square Pegs*, in addition to the big-screen version of the hit Broadway musical *A Chorus Line*, Ingmar Bergman's *Fanny and Alexander*, and the made-for-television movie *Eleanor, First Lady of the World*, starring Jean Stapleton. But for Norman, his biggest source of pride by far during this period was helping to launch Rob Reiner's film directing career, first with the cult rock mockumentary *This Is Spinal Tap* and *Stand by Me*, and later through a combination of his own funds and eventually his next company, Act III Communications, *The Princess Bride*.

In late 1983, nearly one year after launching Embassy Communications, Norman received word that he had been selected to be among the first inductees into the Television Academy of Arts and Sciences Hall of Fame alongside such other luminaries as Edward R. Murrow, Bill Paley, David Sarnoff, Paddy Chayefsky, Lucille Ball, and Milton Berle. He was, of course, thrilled, and one of the first people he called to share the news with was his mother back in Connecticut. Now eighty-four and confined to a wheelchair, Jeanette was unsurprisingly nonplussed. In a yarn he would spin repeatedly for the rest of his life, her response was, "Listen, if that's what they want to do, who am I to say?"[11]

Nevertheless, the old woman was overjoyed when he flew her out to California for the ceremony that following spring, and after telling the story during his acceptance speech, which was introduced by his old friend Bea Arthur, the camera caught a glimpse of Jeannette laughing in front of millions on national television. In the week leading up to the ceremony, she had also quickly become a major draw at several of the luncheons, dinners, and cocktail parties, holding court from her wheelchair and bedazzling the likes of Loretta Young, Burt Lancaster, Lucille Ball, Paul Newman, Groucho Marx, and Shirley MacLaine.

Itching to get back into the showrunner saddle in the interim, it was also around this same time that Norman mounted his first new sitcom in nearly five years as executive producer and cocreator of *a.k.a. Pablo*, which premiered on ABC on March 5, 1984. The premise centered around Paul Rivera, a struggling Hispanic stand-up comedian in Los Angeles—played by real-life comedian Paul Rodriguez—and his extended Mexican American family who still called him Pablo (hence the title) and which included a very young Mario Lopez playing his nephew.

However, despite the heavy hype, and even briefly beating out the hit NBC action-adventure series *The A-Team*, it was canceled after only one month, later earning the dubious distinction of ranking forty-fifth on *TV Guide*'s "50 Worst Shows of All Time" list. Another culprit was the timing, debuted during a time when the sitcom genre itself was severely on the wane and nearly thought to be extinct.

Long empty-nesters by the mid-eighties, Norman and Frances were still trying to make a go of their floundering marriage, which for all intents and purposes was over. They still fought almost constantly, plus Frances wanted to move to New York to be closer to Maggie and Kate, who were now both living there, while Norman—who could have been anywhere—wanted to remain in Los Angeles where the television industry was.

Since 1983, they'd both agreed to an open marriage/semi-trial separation in which they lived apart during the week and spent weekends together. That December, they also opted not to spend the holidays together, with Frances going to New York to be with the girls and Norman jetting off to St. Martin in the Caribbean, where he spent Christmas with his old pal Ben Bradlee, the legendary *Washington Post* editor, and his wife, Sally Quinn. After a relaxing time in the Caribbean, Norman flew back with the Bradlees to the nation's capital to attend the first of what turned out to be many annual New Year's Eve parties at their magnificent Georgetown townhouse, where he stayed in one of the guest rooms and rang in the new year with many of Washington's biggest movers and shakers.

Back in L.A after the holidays, Norman and Frances managed to forge a peaceful coexistence living apart and together as they both began dating other people, all the while keeping up appearances and continuing to host dinner parties, political fundraisers, and film screenings at their Brentwood home. At times, it seemed like the arrangement might work indefinitely.

Very quickly, however, all that changed one evening in 1984 when they invited their good friends Richard Dorso and his wife Betty, the longtime West Coast editor of *Glamour* magazine, over for dinner. There also was their mutual friend Dan Melnick—the then-president of Columbia Pictures responsible for such recent blockbusters as *Kramer vs. Kramer*, *The China Syndrome*, *Midnight Express*, and the just-released *Footloose*—on a blind date with an attractive young blond former teacher and psychology student named Lyn Davis, who, totally unbeknownst to either Norman or her, would become his next wife, the love of his life, and the mother of his three youngest kids.

Then thirty-seven and originally from Whittier, California, she had been raised by a father who, like Norman, had served in Italy during World War II, but returned emotionally scarred. She had also been unlucky in the marriage department. After marrying young, her first husband descended into schizophrenia, and following their divorce, she briefly dated actor Eddie Fisher. During the Lears' dinner party that evening—about which Davis later recalled of the palpable tension between Norman and Frances to *Town & Country* magazine that "you could feel the daggers going back and forth"[12]—one of the topics of conversation was People for the American Way and her PhD doctoral thesis. As it turned out, the subject she'd chosen was a comparison of two politically opposite church congregations, one liberal Unitarian, the other conservative fundamentalist.

Norman was instantly smitten, not only by Lyn's striking good looks, but also her intellect. Nevertheless, with Davis already there with another man and Frances also present, he didn't dare ask for her phone number, though he couldn't stop thinking about her. A few days afterward, Norman received a handwritten letter from Davis with her phone number asking for more information about People for the American Way, and he was over the moon.

This time it didn't take him any time at all to invite her to lunch a couple of days later. During the meal, their mutual attraction was abundantly obvious, especially for Norman, who could barely concentrate as he looked at Davis from across the table. According to his memoir: "What she took from our luncheon, as a result of my interest, was a new confidence in her thesis. What I took from it was a desire to 'be with her,' a more genteel way of expressing my desire to bed her."[13] According to Norman's memoir also, it was during their second lunch that he made his affections known while they were waiting for the appetizers. Within minutes of declaring his desire to kiss her, they were in the back seat of Davis's parked car around the corner from the restaurant making out like teenagers.

With Norman falling deeper and deeper in love with Davis and Frances continuing to see other people, their open marriage hung on by a thread until 1985 when they finally decided to call it quits for good. On a much happier note, in the early summer of that same year, their oldest daughter Kate married physician Dr. Jonathan LaPook in Los Angeles.

Among the guests were Carl Reiner and Mel Brooks who launched into an impromptu version of their classic comedy routine "The 2,000-Year-Old Man" during the reception, as well as Reiner's son Rob, Carroll O'Connor,

Jean Stapleton, Bea Arthur, Sherman Hemsley, and Isabel Sanford. As of this writing, the LaPooks have been happily married for thirty-eight years and reside in New York. Kate, who worked for Norman for many years, is currently a Broadway producer whose credits include *What the Constitution Means to Me*, *Of Mice and Men*, and *Catch Me If You Can*, and Jonathan is the longtime senior medical correspondent for CBS News. They have two sons, Noah and Daniel.

Norman and Frances's divorce became official in June of 1986, culminating in what was then one of the largest settlements ever recorded, estimated to be between $100 and $112 million. After relocating to New York, she invested $25 million of the settlement to launch the forty-plus women's magazine *Lear's* in 1988, which folded in 1994. In 1992, she also published her highly confessional memoir *The Second Seduction*, which barely mentioned Norman, though they remained friends, and he was devastated by her death when she succumbed to breast cancer in 1996 at the age of seventy-three.

Bookending Kate's wedding and Norman's divorce from Frances was also the sale of Embassy Communications to Columbia Pictures Television in June of 1985, then owned by the Coca-Cola Company, in exchange for $485 million in Coca-Cola stock. Minus Jerry Perenchio and Alan Horn, that following year, Norman would launch his next and last company Act III Communications, which he named such to signify his own third act, initially working alongside partner Tom McGrath and later Hal Gaba and Brent Miller. Act III's multiple entities over the next four decades included Village Roadshow Pictures, Concord Music Group, Village Roadshow Entertainment, Act III Broadcasting, Act III Theaters, Act Three Television, and Act III Publishing, among others. Some of the films and television shows were *Stand by Me*, *The Princess Bride*, and *Fried Green Tomatoes*, as well as *Channel Umptee-3*, *America Divided*, and *Tait Stages*.

~

With Norman's divorce from Frances finally on the books, he asked Lyn to marry him in May of 1986. The proposal took place on her thirty-ninth birthday while they were vacationing in Italy, where they were staying at the five-star Hotel San Pietro di Positano on the Amalfi coast. With the help of the hotel's pastry chef, he did so by asking her in Italian, with the words "Will You Marry Me?" written on a single slip of linen paper that was intricately folded inside her birthday cake, which the waiter translated for her.

With tear-filled eyes of joy, Lyn instantly said yes. Over that Fourth of July weekend two months later, in what was also a nationally televised four-day celebration of the two-hundredth birthday of the Statue of Liberty and its recent restoration, Norman threw a private engagement party for about forty guests in the middle of New York Harbor. The setting was the *Galaxy*, a two-mast, 160-foot boat he chartered. The morning after, he and Lyn flew to Africa for six weeks.

A little over a year later, Norman and Lyn were married on September 10, 1987. Though the idea of their father marrying a woman twenty-five years his junior would at first be difficult for his three adult children to accept—especially Norman's oldest daughter Ellen, who was the same age as Lyn—they would eventually all adjust. In fact, as the years wore on and the family expanded to include Norman and Lyn's three kids Ben, Madeline, and Brianna, as well as Maggie's husband Daniel Katz and their two children Griffin and Zoe, they all grew even closer.

Norman and Lyn's wedding was a small ceremony that took place at the suburban San Francisco home of Lyn's sister who served as her maid of honor. Norman asked longtime business partner Jerry Perenchio to be his best man and enlisted his friend Martin Marty, a Lutheran minister, to perform the service, which all three daughters and Kate's husband Jon LaPook attended, as did Lyn's other siblings and several close friends.

Their first home as husband and wife was a modest house that they rented in Brentwood on Manderville Canyon Road. And then within the first month of their nuptials, Lyn discovered she was pregnant. On top of this, they got another surprise they never anticipated when Lyn entered her fifth trimester and Norman discovered he was on the brink of financial ruin.

Unfathomable to him as it was, by the late 1980s Act III was leveraged to the hilt. In addition to several underperforming divisions in the company, another factor was the overall weakening economy at the time that had been exacerbated by the historic stock market crash of 1987, also known as Black Monday, resulting in the worst financial calamity on Wall Street up to that point since the Great Depression.

With some housecleaning and the help of Jerry Perenchio, Alan Horn, and Act III president and CEO Hal Gaba, Norman was eventually able to get things back on course. Auspicious was also the lifeline thrown by Gary Lieberthal, who had cut his teeth under Perenchio at Tandem/T.A.T. in the mid-1970s and had recently been appointed head of TV production at Columbia Pictures Television.

In early 1989, Lieberthal brokered a lucrative $3-million-a-year deal between Columbia and Act III for Norman to produce at least three new

TV pilots over the next three years. As he told the *New York Times* shortly after the arrangement was made: "My sense is that as quickly as Norman can come up with a program he loves, there won't be any problem finding a place for it on the networks."[14] Sharing these sentiments was journalist Richard Stevenson, who wrote the article and said: "Mr. Lear is certain to get a warm welcome from the three major networks. He is likely to be courted especially aggressively by CBS, which is mired in third place and desperately needs hit shows."[15]

On July 10, 1988, Norman's fourth child and only son, Ben, was born. For Norman, who had long felt remorseful about not being around enough for his three older daughters while they were growing up—a sentiment he often expressed in later interviews—Ben's birth represented a second chance to get it right. Mindful of this, he was a hands-on parent right from the start from accompanying Lyn in the delivery room to diaper duty.

However, not long after Ben's birth, as he was still trying to get out from underneath Act III's business problems, Norman was diagnosed with prostate cancer. Luckily for him again, though, was that it was detected early, and with his son-in-law Dr. Jon LaPook supervising, the surgery to have the benign tumor removed was successful.

With a new wife, young son, and restored physical and fiscal health, the 1980s ended on a high note for Norman as he also further expanded his activism footprint.

Befitting his planned return to weekly television as the 1990s got under-way was the twentieth anniversary of *All in the Family*. In recognition of the auspicious milestone, CBS aired a ninety-minute special on February 16, 1991, as it did just two days later for the also-turning-twenty *Mary Tyler Moore Show*.

For the *AITF* retrospective, all four cast members along with living viewers from around the country who had written into the show when it was originally on reminisced as Norman waxed nostalgic from the set of 704 Hauser Street accompanied by a series of vintage episode clips. A few days before the special, Norman and Rob Reiner appeared together on *The Arsenio Hall Show* to promote it.

At the time CBS aired the look-back, the network and Norman were gearing up for his much-anticipated return to weekly television that upcom-ing summer with *Sunday Dinner*, costarring actors Robert Loggia and Teri Hatcher. With the Lears' May–December marriage as the muse and Lyn coproducing, it was Norman's first sitcom produced under the Act III mar-quee and told the story of a Long Island businessman named Ben Benedict who falls in love with Thelma Todd (TT), a thirty-year-old lawyer with a deeply religious side.

In every episode, the typical high-decibel Norman-esque confrontations between the main principals and the other cast members unfolded amid controversial storylines, which, in this case, was the show's promotion of religion. With Norman back at the wheel, CBS was so certain *Sunday Dinner* would be a hit that they even pushed the always-reliable *Murder, She Wrote* back an hour to make room for it. To entice viewers to tune in, they also aired it with reruns of *All in the Family* following it.

In the end, however, such lofty expectations were sorely off the mark and *Sunday Dinner* quickly proved to be a fiasco, not only as evidenced by the low ratings that resulted in the axe falling after just six episodes, but also its sour critical reception. Ken Tucker, the influential *Entertainment Weekly* TV critic, called it "awful, fascinatingly awful."[16] And John J. O'Connor in the *New York Times* said: "Oddly enough for Mr. Lear, one of the shrewdest producers in the business, *Sunday Dinner* adds up to a series of staggering miscalculations. Apparently, it is meant to be a somewhat lyrical endorsement of May-September romances, sprinkled with new-age spirituality and environmental concepts of 'cosmic piety.' What emerges, however, is a decidedly silly and mean-spirited poke at young people."[17]

Nevertheless, as always, Norman persevered. Before the *Sunday Dinner* corpse was even cold, he was already in production for his next sitcom, the Washington political establishment satire *The Powers That Be*, cocreated by future *Friends* creators David Crane and Marta Kaufman, and helmed by John Forsythe and Holland Taylor on NBC. At the center of the action here was stodgy, liberal New England Democratic senator William Powers; his snobbish, status-hungry wife, Margaret; and their dysfunctional offspring, including the senator's illegitimate daughter Sophie from another relationship, as well as his current mistress and aide Jordan.

While this time reviews were considerably more favorable—including the 180-degree turnaround by *Entertainment Weekly*'s Ken Tucker, who said that *Powers* "could prove to be an upscale, uproarious *All in the Family* for the '90s"[18]—unfortunately, the show's vicious depiction of Washington's inside-the-beltway political scene of that time proved to be too much to handle. As a result, and despite surviving two discombobulated seasons, its shelf life, too, was short-lived.

The cancellation of *The Powers That Be* was Norman's second of two sitcom failures within as many years. While the press again had a field day speculating as to whether he had lost his Midas Touch as it did in the late-seventies, Norman, who was now in his early seventies, continued to come out swinging. And regardless of the disappointing outcomes of these more recent efforts, he could still rest on his laurels with his indelible place in the pantheon of pop culture having long been assured.

His next show, which was inspired by his accountant's admonishment that he was wasting money on storage fees for the old *All in the Family* set, was about an African American family now living in the Bunkers' former Queens home. The name of it was *704 Hauser*, starring former *Good Times* star John Amos.

Debuting in April 1994, the sitcom's seemingly perfectly timed arrival coincided with President Bill Clinton's first administration when conservative talk radio, particularly Rush Limbaugh, was at its peak. In an interesting twist, *704* represented a complete ideological reversal from the previous inhabitants on *All in the Family*. The parents, Ernie and Rose Cumberbatch, were working-class Democrats and Goodie, their son, was a conservative activist with a white, Jewish girlfriend.

Making a cameo in the first episode was a grown-up Joey Stivic dropping by to see his grandparents' old digs. And in another even more interesting twist, Rush Limbaugh was one of *704*'s biggest fans and even invited Norman to appear on his own show to promote it, which he did.

Still, none of this was enough to save the series from being yanked after only six episodes, including one that never aired. So as the 1990s hit mid-decade, Norman returned to the drawing board, still always in search of his next big hit and never looking back. By this time, too, he'd become a father again to identical twin daughters Madeline and Brianna who were also born in 1994.

~

By the beginning of the New Millenium, Norman was quickly cruising toward eighty. In 2001, he and Lyn purchased one of the few existing original copies of the Declaration of Independence for $8.1 million and over the next decade toured it across all fifty states in what was billed as the "Declaration of Independence Road Trip," which included stops at several presidential libraries, museums, Super Bowl XXXVI, the 2002 Olympics, and the Live 8 Concert in Philadelphia.

In addition to that victory under his belt, Norman and Rob Reiner teamed up to produce a dramatic filmed reading at Independence Hall on the Fourth of July in 2001. Although he didn't actively have any new shows of his own on the air then, Norman also continued to keep his fingers on the pulse of cutting-edge TV. In 2003, he made an appearance on the hit Comedy Central animated series *South Park* as the voice of Benjamin Franklin and served as a story consultant on two episodes. Then, in the second decade of the twenty-first century, as he was entering his nineties, his most famous sitcoms were back in vogue again thanks to an influx of new retro TV channels on cable, DVD releases, and the availability of 24/7 on-demand streaming services.

Bringing him another round of acclaim, too, was the publication of his memoir *Even This I Get to Experience* in 2014 followed two years later by the 2016 PBS American Master's documentary *Just Another Version of You*, with heartfelt tributes from family, friends, and other luminaries in the entertainment industry. Then ninety-four, Norman was still looking ahead and relishing every second of life with every bit of gusto he could grab. As he settled into the nonagenarian stage, whenever he was asked by interviewers how he got there, he would invariably say, "Two words. Over and Next," referring to his personal doctrine of living in the moment in order to remain focused and crediting laughter for adding years to his life.

But though he always emphasized the importance of looking ahead, Norman also relished the steady procession of awards and tributes he received during his later years. Adding to his already-formidable collection, just some of them included becoming the oldest person ever to win back-to-back Emmys in 2019 and 2020 for two of his *Live in Front of a Studio Audience* sitcom reenactment specials with Jimmy Kimmel; the Carol Burnett Award for Lifetime Achievement at the 2021 Golden Globes; and in 2019, a building named after him on the Culver City lot of Sony Pictures, which owns the distribution rights to his extensive catalog.

In 2018, Norman started a scholarship at his alma mater, Emerson College, in Boston for aspiring screenwriters who are the first-generation members of their family to attend college. In appreciation, his friend Emmy-winning producer and Emerson trustee Kevin Bright commissioned a bronzed statue of Norman's likeness that now stands prominently in the middle of the main Boston campus. Following the unveiling that October, there was a tribute to Norman on an exact replica of the *All in the Family* set with sketches, songs, and speeches, including one videotaped by Jay Leno. On hand for the festivities also was then-Boston mayor Marty Walsh, who officially proclaimed it "Norman Lear Day" for the City of Boston.

In 2017, Norman also made national headlines when he was selected to become one of that year's Kennedy Center honorees and announced he wouldn't participate in any activities involving Donald Trump. "I will not go to this man's house," he told the *Washington Post*. "I will not go to my White

House as long as this man is president."[19] When fellow inductees choreographer Carmen de Lavallade, LL Cool J, Lionel Richie, and Gloria Estefan heard this, they also bowed out, although after the president and first lady announced they weren't coming either, everything went ahead as planned.

In 2017 also, Norman struck sitcom paydirt again for the first time in nearly forty years when Netflix rebooted a Latino version of *One Day at a Time*, setting it in Los Angeles and starring screen legend Rita Moreno and Justina Machado. With Norman and partner Brent Miller co-executive-producing, the showrunners were Gloria Calderón and former *Everybody Loves Raymond* writer Mike Royce, who first met Norman shortly after the release of his memoir when he interviewed him about the book for a Screen Actors Guild Panel. "It was like a two-hour interview and I'm not an interviewer, but it went well, and then when Norman and Brent were looking for someone to help them run the show, I was available and we met," recalled Royce.[20] In a separate recollection about Norman in the *Hollywood Reporter*, he also said:

> Norman Lear never stopped loving the process. He'd warmed up the crowds for his shows during his heyday, and at ninety-five-years old, he did the same for us on *One Day at a Time*. It was important to him, because he believed so strongly in the power of the audience, and the importance of earning those indelible, classic moments that elevate a sitcom to greatness. He would always rhapsodize about "watching a couple of hundred people come together as one, when something makes them laugh. I don't think I've ever seen a more spiritual experience." He knew what made the work good.[21]

With Norman's sage input, strong characters, and storylines that, because of the streaming platform, could be far edgier than the original, the new *One Day* notched such robust ratings and so many critical nods during its first season that it was listed as one of the best new shows of 2017. Also earning multiple Emmy nominations and a couple of wins, it was renewed for two more seasons in 2018 and 2019 on Netflix and then again on Pop TV in 2020.

As a result, Norman—still sharp as a tack and showing little signs of his nine decades except for diminished hearing and walking with the aid of a cane—was suddenly a hot property in Hollywood again. When he turned ninety-six in 2018, he even signed a new contract with Sony to have him continue to make new shows up until his one hundredth birthday. Disappointingly, most of these projects never materialized, including a sitcom about aging Norman had been peddling for years called *Guess Who Died?* that died quickly after NBC dumped the pilot in 2018.

What did transpire, however, was Norman teaming up with Jimmy Kimmel in May 2019 for the first of three ABC TV specials called *Live in Front of a Studio Audience* on which original episodes of *All in the Family* and *The Jeffersons* were re-created with all-star casts, including Woody Harrelson and Marisa Tomei as the Bunkers and Jamie Foxx and Wanda Sykes as *The Jeffersons* with a cameo by Marla Gibbs. A second special with another episode of *All in the Family* and *Good Times* (and another cameo by John Amos) aired that December followed by a third in 2021 redoing *Diff'rent Strokes* and *The Facts of Life.*

The other thing that happened was that among American comedy's true greats of the past seventy years, Norman was now one of the last reigning elder statesmen, a rarified club also including fellow nonagenarian funnymen Carl Reiner, Mel Brooks, Dick Van Dyke, and Bob Newhart, who were all in great demand on the talk show and podcasting circuit. In fact, Norman, Reiner, Brooks, and Van Dyke would appear together in 2017 on the HBO documentary about aging *If You're Not in the Obits, Eat Breakfast*, produced by Reiner's nephew, the legendary comedy manager and *Seinfeld* creator George Shapiro.

And in between all his other projects, by 2015 Norman was also podcasting on Spotify with a new show of his own called *All of the Above with Norman Lear.* Then there was social media. Starting in 2020 until almost the end of his life, he began releasing a series of short videos on Facebook called "Breakfast Thoughts." With topics typically about politics, pop culture, or whatever else came to mind, usually these tongue-in-cheek chats took place from his Los Angeles home in the morning, with Norman holding court from his kitchen table noshing, sipping coffee, and dressed casually in a jogging suit and his trademark white hat.

With the world beginning to return to some sense of normalcy following the COVID-19 lockdown, 2021 started out on an up note for Norman. Clad in a blue jogging suit and his white hat with a wispy ponytail jutting out from underneath, in early January he was profiled on *CBS Sunday Morning* in a ten-minute segment entitled "What Makes Norman Lear, at 98, Still Tick?" Interviewing him was his son-in-law and longtime CBS News chief medical correspondent Dr. Jonathan LaPook.

The discussion was for the most part filled with affectionate, lighthearted banter, including one portion with Norman and LaPook singing "There's No Business Like Show Business," peppered by sound bites from Lyn and Norman's daughter Kate interspersed alongside various video clips from his long career. Two of the most prominent topics were how Norman managed to stay young and his most famous sitcom *All in the Family*, which was turning fifty that same month. But then, on a more somber note, the segment ended with Norman talking about death and insisting he didn't fear it.

In a *Town & Country* magazine profile that following fall, Norman offered a similar sentiment via Lyn who said: "We talk about it all the time. Norman admits no fear. 'The leaving is difficult,' he says, 'but the going I'm fine with it.'"[22] Yet, with Norman approaching his ninety-ninth birthday and the future swathed in uncertainty, the inevitable was a still a topic that few in his inner circle were willing to broach with him. In the same article, Sony Pictures chairman and CEO Tony Vinciquerra said: "We haven't talked about that yet. I'm enjoying him too much as it is."[23] Act III president Brent Miller also said there hadn't yet been any discussions about what might happen upon Norman's passing, adding: "There's no formal plan. We'll keep moving until he can't move anymore."[24]

And as such they did. In mid-February, Norman was feted with the Carol Burnett Award during the seventy-eighth annual Golden Globes ceremony in Los Angeles. While he didn't attend in person due to COVID, after being introduced by Tina Fey and Amy Poehler, Norman delivered the following remarks on video live from his home:

> Hello and good evening, everyone, thank you for this wonderful night. It knocks me out to be introduced by Amy Poehler and Tina Fey. At close to ninety-nine, I can tell you that I've never lived alone, I've never laughed alone and that has as much to do with my being here today as anything else I know. And once more, thank you and bless you, Carol Burnett, for everything you have meant to me by way of joy, surprise, delight, and laughter. So glad we had this time together.[25]

Remaining mostly at home that winter, Norman attended meetings over Zoom and stayed socially distanced from visitors who came to see him at his 8.29-acre Westridge Road estate in Brentwood, which he sold that year for $27 million. Additionally, he spoke to a handful of reporters who were writing retrospectives about *All in the Family*'s fiftieth anniversary, including a special issue of *Life* magazine, alongside a series of other interviews to promote a coffee table book he did about the show with entertainment journalist Jim Collucci with a foreword by Jimmy Kimmel called *All in the Family: The Show That Changed Television*.

That spring, his routine remained essentially the same, venturing out only occasionally to restaurants or small gatherings with Lyn and his kids, and sometimes pictured with a walker or in a wheelchair. In the early summer of 2021, Norman and Lyn moved from their longtime Westridge Road home where Ben, Madeline, and Brianna grew up into a smaller house they leased in Beverly Hills, also shedding their penthouse New York condo at 15 Central Park West the following year for $17.5 million. In July, meanwhile, they flew east to their Vermont summer home for Norman's ninety-ninth birthday where his entire family would join them.

For Norman's one-hundredth one year later, they did the same. Not surprisingly, the momentous milestone generated a groundswell of media coverage. That same day, Norman penned an op-ed in the *New York Times* reflecting on his life and what he deemed the "alarming" condition of the United States. "Reaching my own personal centennial is cause for a bit of reflection on my first century—and on what the next century will bring for the people and the country I love," he wrote. "To be honest, I'm a bit worried that I may be in better shape than our Democracy."[26]

Also on his birthday, Norman received word that Amazon Freevee had just green-lit his latest sitcom *Clean Slate*, costarring actor Laverne Cox and comedian George Wallace. Additionally, he spoke to National Public Radio's *Morning Edition* and recorded a "Breakfast Thoughts" segment, where he sang the Dean Martin classic "That's Amore" and posted it on Instagram. Plans were also announced by Act III that day for a forthcoming one-hundredth-birthday TV special in the fall, although curiously, it would not air on CBS, which had been Norman's main television turf for decades, but instead on ABC.

On its website the same day, *People* magazine reported that Norman and Brent Miller currently had at least twenty-three new projects in the works, including a *Who's the Boss?* reboot starring Tony Danza and Alyssa Milano, a reboot of *Mary Hartman, Mary Hartman* for TBS, an animated revival of *Good Times* on Netflix, and more *Live in Front of a Studio Audience* specials on ABC.

The aptly titled pretaped *Norman Lear: 100 Years of Music and Laughter* aired on ABC on September 22 at 9 p.m. and began streaming on Hulu the following day. Later nominated for an Emmy Award, among the stars who showed up were Rob Reiner, George Clooney, Isabella Gomez, Tom Hanks, Rita Moreno, Jennifer Aniston, Marla Gibbs, John Amos, Valerie Bertinelli, Jimmy Kimmel, and Amy Poehler. Two of the highlights were the musical tributes playing homage to the theme songs of Norman's classic shows and Rob Reiner describing Norman as his second father.

In October, Norman was profiled on *CBS Sunday Morning* again, this time by Ted Koppel. Though at first his usual vigor seemed slightly diminished, he was animated as ever, discussing politics and his future plans, including a possible reimagination of the abortion episode of *Maude*.

But as it happened, the *Maude* reboot never did happen, and Norman's interview with Ted Koppel also turned out to be his last major television appearance. During the final year of his life, he stayed mostly at home in Los Angeles. Over the next nine months, pictures of Norman, often in a wheelchair and sometimes aided by oxygen, occasionally surfaced on social media, including one with actor and comedian Tyler Perry.

In June of 2023, Norman posted on X, formally Twitter, expressing his support for the writer's strike, although he never showed up at the picket line. He also for the first time in over forty years didn't spend the summer in Vermont. For his one-hundred-first birthday, picketing writers and actors threw a party in his honor on the CBS Television City lot, which he attended on Zoom. That day also, Norman posted a new "Breakfast Thoughts" video on Instagram, saying:

> It's Norman Lear here, dribbling a bit because he's entering his second childhood. I've just turned 101, and that is, they tell me, my second childhood. It feels like that, in terms of the care I'm getting. I get the kind of care at this age that I see children getting, toddlers getting. And so I am now a 101-year-old toddler, and I'm thinking about two little words that we don't think about often enough, we don't pay enough attention to: over and next. When something is over, it is *over*, and we have the joy and privilege of getting on to the next [thing]. And if there were a hammock in the middle between those two words, it would be the best way I know of identifying living in the moment.[27]

In the early evening of December 5, 2023, Norman Lear died peacefully in his sleep with Lyn and other immediate family members gathered at his bedside singing showtunes and the theme songs of his classic sitcoms. The official news came early the following morning from his longtime spokeswoman Lara Bergthold and was also confirmed on Norman's Instagram account, accompanied by a black-and-white photo of him smiling. The statement read:

> Norman lived a life in awe of the world around him. He marveled at his cup of coffee every morning, the shape of the tree outside his window, and the sounds of beautiful music. But it was people—those

he just met and those he knew for decades—who kept his mind and heart forever young. As we celebrate his legacy and reflect on the next chapter of life without him, we would like to thank everyone for all the love and support.[28]

Not surprisingly, Norman's passing triggered far more than the usual round of tributes that typically follow the death of a major showbiz celebrity of similar stature, including a three-page obit on the front page of the *New York Times*. They were more becoming of a national hero, which for much of the nation Norman was. "Norman Lear was a transformational force in American culture, whose trailblazing shows redefined television with courage, conscience, and humor, opening our nation's eyes and often our hearts," said President Joe Biden in a statement.[29]

As soon as the news went viral, all the major morning programs interrupted their broadcasts, and there were also long segments on that evening's news as CBS, NBC, ABC, UPN, and FOX all posted an in-memoriam card to Norman before the start of their prime-time hour. The following night, CBS aired an hourlong special called *Norman Lear: A Life on Television*, which was produced by *Entertainment Tonight*. As for some the other approbations:

- Jimmy Kimmel said: "His bravery, integrity, and unmatched moral compass were equaled by his kindness, empathy, and wit. Even at 101, Norman cared as much about the future, our children, and [our] planet . . . as anyone I have ever known. He was a great American, a hero in every way and so funny, smart, and lovely [a] man you almost couldn't believe it. The privilege of working alongside Norman and the opportunity he gave me and my wife to get to know him and his beautiful family has been among the great honors and pleasures of my life. We were all very lucky to have him."[30]

- George Clooney said: "It's hard to reconcile that at 101 years old, Norman Lear is gone too soon. The entire world of reason just lost its greatest advocate and our family lost a dear friend. A giant walked in his shoes."[31]

- Tyler Perry called Norman's sitcoms "the only thing that brought laughter and joy to me as a child, who was living a daily nightmare."[32]

- Bob Iger, CEO of Disney, remembered Norman as an "icon and the brilliant mind behind countless timely and meaningful shows that were full of heart and humor."[33]

Additionally, Rob Reiner told the *Hollywood Reporter*: "I saw him a lot over these last years. Right before he died, I was on the phone with him. He was awake but wasn't responding. He wasn't talking. But I was told he might be able to hear. So, I got on the phone, went upstairs and just talked into his ear. I told him I loved him. I told him I loved him every time I saw him, so it wasn't anything new, but I told it to him again. I don't know if he heard me, but I really hope he did."[34]

Both individually and in full totality, all were tributes befitting a king, who, through his artistic achievements and activism, lived to leave this world a better place than when he entered it. And, indeed, Norman Lear was and did.

His funeral was private. President Biden and his wife Jill attended the shiva while they were in California on a fundraising swing. Two weeks later, Norman's official cause of death was listed as cardiac arrest.

Afterword and Acknowledgments

As I mentioned earlier, I was just a small boy when Norman Lear became a personal hero of mine after discovering his classic sitcoms in the early 1970s. In a very real sense, writing this biography was not only a dream come true decades in the making, but it has also brought me full circle. The first of Norman's shows I ever saw was his most famous *All in the Family*, although I can't recall the exact episode. This was followed by *Sanford and Son*, which I vividly remember watching when I was around four or five, often munching on a box of raisins on Friday nights from the perch of a big red cushy chair in my parents' bedroom in our New York apartment.

And then there was *Maude*, *Good Times*, *The Jeffersons*, *One Day at a Time*, and *Mary Hartman, Mary Hartman*, which I often watched either with my grandparents Bill and Elizabeth Whetsell or my great-aunt Helen. Despite their very adult themes, the adults in my life always let me watch, although all I really knew back then was that Norman's shows were special and made me laugh. Along with more age-appropriate 1970s kids fare like *Sesame Street*, *Mister Rogers' Neighborhood*, *Captain Kangaroo*, and a handful of sitcoms that were already in reruns (*I Love Lucy*, *The Andy Griffith Show*, *The Dick Van Dyke Show*, *The Honeymooners*, etc.), these programs were the seminal TV treasures that helped shape my formative years. It was also television—and Norman's sitcoms in particular—as well as my love for film, theater, and stand-up comedy that fueled my ambitions to become a writer from a very young age.

Norman's sitcoms were also an escape from a childhood marred by learning issues and a formidable battle with attention deficit disorder that I began waging in kindergarten at a time when few people knew how to address either one. Though I also acted in a few plays, my first love was always writing, thanks largely to my mother, who wrote several articles for *New York* magazine, and my grandmother, who had an arts and entertainment column and reviewed books for her local newspaper in South Carolina for many years. With the influence of these two amazing women, I soon began channeling more and more of my energies in that direction also.

And I continued to watch Norman's sitcoms as much as I could. As a teenager in the 1980s, at a time when there was a bumper crop of new books about television shows, I even tried my hand at writing one on *All in the Family*, often at the expense of my schoolwork. Although I had the attention span of a gnat when it came to subjects like math and science, I always had laser focus when it came to the book, which became my saving grace.

This was especially true when I was seventeen and decided to take my first stab at trying to get it published. It coincided with a very unhappy stretch at a boarding school I attended in suburban Atlanta. On weekends, they used to take us to the mall for hours on end—where, invariably, I always made a beeline to the bookstore, poring over books about publishing and the latest issue of *Writer's Digest*, which listed the names and addresses of literary agents, several of whom I reached out to.

Almost everyone who knew what I was doing back then told me I was being "unrealistic," which made me even more determined to prove them wrong. But then, by some miracle, one agent I contacted in New York was interested. I remember receiving the letter in the mail from him like it was yesterday and calling him from a pay phone in the boarding school rec room, trying to sound like an adult as our conversation was drowned out by the sound of video games and other teenaged boys in the background. Of course, I was over the moon, and I'm not sure if the agent knew how young I was at the time, although several weeks later, after it quickly became apparent that I was in way over my head, he dropped me like a hot potato.

Still, my resolve to become a writer and publish my book never wavered, nor did my desire to attend college, where I also aimed high, despite barely passing grades and abysmal SAT scores. In fact, one particularly unsympathetic teacher at my boarding school even told me I should go to trade school instead. But then—luckily again—and because of a letter I wrote to the dean of admissions against the advice of my guidance counselor, I was conditionally accepted through a special program to the freshman class at Emerson College in Boston in the fall of 1990, where I majored in journalism, made lifelong friends, and thrived as I never had before. It is also important to note here that one of the reasons why I wanted to attend Emerson in the first place—aside from its reputation as one of the best communications and performing arts schools in the country—was my discovery that Norman had gone there.

It was during my four years at Emerson that I saw my name in print for the first time writing for the school newspaper and doing internships at *Boston* magazine and the *Boston Globe*. I also had the opportunity to take another incredible journalism class at Harvard during the summer between my junior and senior years with Pulitzer Prize–winning author Ron Suskind, where one of the highlights was a mock press conference with former 1988 Democratic presidential candidate and Massachusetts governor Michael Dukakis.

Immediately after graduating from college in the spring of 1994, I moved back to New York to make my mark as a writer. While there were several lean years and many hurdles along the way, I eventually managed to make a very good living working in public relations during the height of the dot.com bubble before slowly but surely succeeding at what I had set out to do. The turning point was another class I took at the New School in Manhattan that was so life-changing I wound up enrolling four times.

The instructor was an amazing woman originally from Michigan named Susan Shapiro. In a way, it felt like we were kindred spirits because, like me, she came from a family of doctors and had always wanted to be a writer. She also struggled during her early years in New York before finally learning the tricks of the trade, which is why she'd created this class: to teach others how to do the same. It was as if a light switch had suddenly been flipped on. If Ron Suskind and my professors at Emerson—especially Marsha Della Giustina—helped me pour the concrete for my career, it was because of Susan that I was able to build the house that now stands, including several plum assignments from the *New York Times*, the *Wall Street Journal*, the *New York Post*, and the the *New York Daily News* that I landed as a direct result of her class.

With my professional credentials building and my confidence renewed, it was around this same time that I dusted off what was clearly a very amateurish first draft of my *All in the Family* book from high school, and after a series of rewrites, began reaching out to literary agents again. Fortunately, it was at a time when you could still do so without a recommendation (something almost unheard of now), and I got several nibbles. One was from a very famous agent who handled many bestselling authors and represented me for nearly a year, although after spending months working on a proposal and shopping it around to all the major New York publishers, he couldn't sell it, and we amicably parted ways.

However, it was thanks to him—and because of him—that I won the jackpot in the spring of 2000 when he introduced me to Peter Rubie, my phenomenal agent and good friend for the past twenty-five years. Though he couldn't sell the *All in the Family* project for various reasons either, Peter has stuck by me through thick and thin, three previous books, and at least a dozen other ideas that have yet to come to fruition.

It has truly been one of the greatest fortunes of my life to have Peter in it, always having my back, never losing faith, and giving me a swift kick in the pants when I've needed it. It was also thanks to Peter that this book happened at all, literally bringing us full circle too, because he told Applause Books executive editor John Cerullo about the class I teach on Norman at Emerson College, and John suggested I write a biography. My deepest gratitude to John for greenlighting this project immediately without a proposal, for being there for me every step of the way, and for having the patience of Job. Thanks also to the incredible editorial team at Applause, particularly Barbara Claire for her enormous help in making photo selections, Emily Burr, Chris Chappell, Meaghan Menzel, and Emily Jeffers. On a separate but equally important note, thanks also to Susan Schulman, another literary agent extraordinaire, for her deft negotiating skills.

To my family for their continued love and support—my incredible parents Anne and Bill Whetsell; my sister and brother-in-law Holly and Gabe Coltea; my three precious nieces Libby, Cacie, and Annie, who are more like daughters; Porter and Carol Rodgers, my aunt and uncle who are more like parents; cousins Melissa Padgett (Brent), Melinda Couzens (John), and Susan Drumm, who are more like sisters and brothers; and their respective families. My thanks also to Heyward and Sherrill Whetsell, Jim Bratton, and Drew Tate.

I also want to acknowledge my other extended academic family at Emerson College. A major shout-out first and foremost to Martie Cook for helping me realize my other dream of becoming a professor, taking a chance on me, and along with Brooke Knight, saying "yes" to my Norman Lear class without which this book may never have seen the light of day. My many thanks to Barry Marshall for not only helping me navigate the sometimes-tricky ropes of academia, but also for being a great friend and one of my favorite people to talk about pop culture with; Tom Cooper, a true mensch and mentor without peer who continues to selflessly fulfill that role even though he's happily retired and living in Hawaii; and Jonathan Satriale—a.k.a. "Satch"—my now-colleague and good friend whom I've known since our undergrad days at Emerson more than thirty years ago; his wife, Liz; and their amazing son, Henry.

Because she deserves it and always stood in a class by herself, I want to acknowledge separately—and again—my beloved friend, mentor, and journalism professor Marsha Della Giustina, who sadly passed away in June

2023 as this book was being written and whom I think of every day. If we are lucky enough, we all have that one teacher whose influence is so powerful it remains with us for the rest of our lives, and for me, Marsha was *that* teacher. How I wish she could have been there with her red pen to help me put the finishing touches on this project as she did with so many others. I only hope I can make her proud.

I also owe enormous gratitude to many other Emerson greats present and past: Shaun Clarke, Lu Ann Reeb, Janet Kolodzy, Jan Roberts-Breslin, Kevin Bright, Greg Payne, Mike Brown, Anne Doyle, Matt McMahan, Manny Basanese, Mike Bent, Ed Lee, Maria Corrigan, John-Albert Moseley, Jim Delaney, Mako Yoshikawa, Jabari Asim, Cristina Kotz Cornejo, Bob Fleming, Pete Chvany, Tom Kingdon, Anthony Bashir, Bill Gilligan, and Vito Sylvestri. Abundant thanks also to Jennifer Williams in the American Comedy Archives and Erin Clossey in the Office of Communications for helping me gain access to photos of Norman's years at Emerson for the book that would not have been available otherwise. Additionally, I would like to thank Jay Bernhardt, who recently became Emerson's thirteenth president, and Jackie Liebergott, who was president when I was a student and took a leap of faith by allowing me to attend.

My deepest thanks as well to the many people who agreed to talk to me and share their memories about Norman—many of whom also helped open other doors—in particular, Adrienne Barbeau, John Amos, Mary Kay Place, Greg Mullavey, Louise Lasser, Samantha Macy, Jay Moriarity, John Putch, Glenn Scarpelli, James Cromwell, Candice Azzara, Bob LaHendro, Oz Scott, Elliot Schoenman, Michael Baser, Denis Klein, and Mike Royce. For her help in procuring vintage pictures of New Haven, Connecticut, where Norman was born, I thank Emma Norden of the New Haven Museum. I also thank Peter Malia for his keen historical perspective.

Further, I am grateful to two of my pals and biggest writing idols Marc Eliot and Richard Zoglin, whose respective biographies on Cary Grant, Jimmy Stewart, Clint Eastwood, Elvis, and Bob Hope were master classes in how to do one right. A very special thanks to my good friend Jesse Nash for always sensing the possibilities and encouraging me to shoot the flames even higher, as well as his colleagues Joe D'Imperio, Chris Munger, and Brian Hyland.

On another personal note, I am infinitely thankful to my many extraordinary friends whose support and encouragement provided much-needed emotional nourishment during this endeavor. A very special thanks to Susan Hersh whose sense of humor and joie de vivre perpetually puts a smile on my face and a spring in my step.

Another heartfelt thank-you goes to my dear friend Liz Temkin, an exceptional human being who enriches my life immeasurably every day and never ceases to amaze me. My heartfelt thanks as well—in alphabetical order, and with each one occupying a very important place in my life also—to Jeff Abraham, Linda Alexander, André Archimbaud, Tammi Armitage, Rob Bates, Tar Beaty, Steve and Sondra Beninati, Melinda Bickers, Bill Boggs, Pat Buckles, Megan Cogswell, Ronny Cohen, Tom D'Angelo, Joe Davis, Jamie DeRoy, Ted Faraone, Wayne Federman, Candyce Francis, Eddy Friedfeld, Alix Friedman, Beth and Zoe Friedman, Larry Haber, Damian Hall, Wayne Jacques, David Kogut, Mike Kornfeld, Rikki Kane Larimer, Steve Mittleman, Judy Orbach, Marie Raperto, Mike Reilly, Ellen and Steve Resnick, Richard Rubenstein, Frank Santopadre, Ernie Savage, Andrew Schmertz, Carol Scibelli, Roberta Sickles, Howard and Patrica Storm, Alix Strauss, Gary and Rene Susman, Neil Vineberg, and Alan Zweibel.

With great fondness, I also want to remember the late great George James, the late great Budd Friedman, the late great Rick Newman, and the late great George Shapiro.

I also must thank Norman's daughter Kate for her early support. And finally, I want to give a huge heartfelt hat tip to you, Norman. So many wonderful things have happened to me because of you. The impact you have had on my life is immeasurable. Thank you!

Norman Lear Complete Filmography

Listed below are Norman's television and film credits during a career spanning over seven decades as a writer, director, executive producer, developer, and creator from 1950 until 2023, including several projects that were still in progress at the time of his death presented chronologically and compiled from Internet Movie Database (IMDB). Also included are a list of Norman's notable television appearances, major awards, and other honors.

TELEVISION

As Writer Only

All Star Revue NBC, 1 episode, cowriter with Ed Simmons. December 6, 1950 (first official television screen credit).

Ford Star Revue NBC, 2 episodes, cowriter with Ed Simmons. Season 2, episode 1, January 4, 1951. Season 2, episode 6, February 15, 1951.

The Colgate Comedy Hour NBC, writer 12 episodes, 1950–1953. Season 1, episode 2, September 17, 1950: Cowriter with Harry Crane and Ed Simmons. Season 1, episode 6, October 15, 1950: Cowriter with Ed Simmons. Season 1, episode 10, November 12, 1950: Cowriter with Ed Simmons. Season 1, episode 37, May 20, 1951: Cowriter with Ed Simmons. Season 1, episode 42, June 24, 1951: Cowriter with Ed Simmons. Season 2, episode 8, October 21, 1951: Cowriter with Ed Simmons. Season 2, episode 10, November 4, 1951: Cowriter with Ed Simmons. Season 2, episode 35, April 27, 1952. Season 3, episode 1, September 21, 1952: Cowriter with Ed Simmons. Season

3, episode 11, November 30, 1952: Cowriter with Ed Simmons. Season 3, episode 33, May 3, 1953: Cowritten with Ed Simmons with special material by Danny Arnold. Season 4, episode 1, October 4, 1953: Cowritten with Ed Simmons, Danny Arnold, Arthur Phillips, and Rocky Kalish.

The Tennessee Ernie Ford Show NBC, writer 4 episodes, 1957–1958. Season 2, episode 13, December 26, 1957: Cowriter with Roland Kibbee and William Yagemann. Season 2, episode 21, February 20, 1958: Cowriter with Roland Kibbee and Bill Waterman. Season 2, episode 29, April 17, 1958: Cowriter with Roland Kibbee and William Yagemann. Season 3, episode 10, December 11, 1958, Cowriter with Danny Arnold, Howard Leeds, and Norman Paul.

As Writer, Director, Producer, Executive Producer, Series Creator, Co-creator, and/or Developer

The Martha Raye Show NBC, 1954–1956, writer 4 episodes, director 8 episodes, producer 18 episodes. Season 1, episode 1, January 23, 1954: Produced by Norman. Season 1, episode 2, February 20, 1954: Produced by Norman. Season 1, episode 3, March 20, 1954: Produced by Norman. Season 1, episode 5, May 15, 1954: Produced by Norman. Season 2, episode 1, September 28, 1954: Coproduced with Karl Koffenberg, cowritten with Ed Simmons, codirected with Grey Lockwood. Season 2, episode 2, October 26, 1954: Produced and directed by Norman, cowritten with Ed Simmons. Season 2, episode 3, November 23, 1954: Coproduced with Karl Koffenberg, cowritten with Ed Simmons. Season 2, episode 7, March 15, 1955: Produced and directed by Norman. Season 2, episode 8, April 12, 1955: Coproduced by Norman and Ed Simmons. Season 2, episode 9, May 10, 1955: Coproduced by Norman and Ed Simmons. Season 2, episode 10, June 7, 1955: Coproduced by Norman and Ed Simmons. Season 3, episode 1, September 20, 1955: Coproduced by Norman and Ed Simmons, directed by Norman. Season 3, episode 2, October 11, 1955: Coproduced by Norman and Ed Simmons. Season 3, episode 3, November 1, 1955: Coproduced by Norman and Ed Simmons. Season 3, episode 7, December 13, 1955: Coproduced by Norman, Karl Hoffenberg, and Ed Simmons. Season 3, episode 7, January 24, 1956: Produced and directed by Norman. Season 3, episode 8, February 14, 1956, directed by Norman. Season 3, episode 9, March 6, 1956: Codirected with Frank Brunetta and Ed Simmons; cowritten with Billy Friedberg and Mike Miller. Season 3, episode 11, April 17, 1956: Produced and directed by Norman.

The George Gobel Show NBC, 1958–1959, writer 7 episodes, director 5 episodes. Season and episode # unknown, September 23, 1958: Cowritten with Dan Beaumont, Phil Green, Tom Koch, and Leo Solomon. Season 5, episode 1, October 21, 1958: Cowritten with Dan Beaumont, Phil Green, Tom Koch, and Leo Solomon. Season 5, episode 3: Cowritten with Dan Beaumont, Phil Green, Tom Koch, and Leo Solomon, November 4, 1958. Season 5, episode 5, December 2, 1958: Codirected with Grey Lockwood, cowritten with Dan Beaumont, Phil Green, Tom Koch, Joseph Quillan, and Leo Solomon. Season 5, episode 6, December 16, 1958: Codirected with Grey Lockwood, written by Norman. Season 5, episode 7, December 30, 1958: Codirected with Grey Lockwood, cowritten with Dan Beaumont, Tom Koch, Joseph Quillan, Leo Solomon, and Paul Sully. Season 5, episode 8, January 13, 1959: Codirected with Grey Lockwood, cowritten with Dan Beaumont, Tom Koch, Joseph Quillan, Leo Solomon, and Paul Sully.

The Deputy NBC, 1959–1961. Half-hour Western starring Henry Fonda and the first episodic TV series created by Norman in collaboration with Roland Kibbee that aired for two seasons and 76 episodes from September 12, 1959, until July 1, 1961. Norman and Kibbee also cowrote many of the episodes, including the premiere, "Back to Glory."

Bobby Darin and Friends NBC, January 31, 1961. Coproduced with Bud Yorkin and cowritten by Norman with special material by Shirley Henry.

General Electric Theatre CBS, Season 9, episode 25, "Love Is a Lion's Roar," March 1961. Coproduced with Bud Yorkin.

The Danny Kaye Special CBS, November 6, 1961. Coproduced with Bud Yorkin and cowritten with Hal Kanter.

Henry Fonda and the Family CBS, February 6, 1962. Coproduced with Bud Yorkin and cowritten with Tom Koch.

The Andy Williams Special NBC, May 4, 1962. Cowriter and coproducer with Bud Yorkin.

The Andy Williams Show NBC, 1962–1963, 5 episodes. Executive producer with Bud Yorkin.

Barnaby unsold TV pilot, 1965. Executive producer with Bud Yorkin. Starring Sorrell Booke, who appeared in five episodes of *All in the Family*, including "Archie and the Editorial," Allan Melvin who had a recurring role on

All in the Family and *Archie Bunker's Place* as Archie's friend Barney Heffner, Frank Kabott, and Jane Shutan.

ABC Stage 67 ABC, Season 1, episode 3, "Where It's At," September 28, 1966, Co-executive produced with Bud Yorkin and cowritten with Dick Cavett, Ron Friedman, Larry Hovis, Tom Koch, and Pat McCormick.

Justice for All ABC, 1968. First unaired pilot for what would become *All in the Family*. Written by Norman with *Till Death Us Do Part* creator Johnny Speight also given a writer's credit. Starring Carroll O'Connor, Jean Stapleton, Tim McIntire, and Kelly Jean Peters.

Those Were the Days ABC, 1968. The second unaired *All in the Family* pilot with same script that was not seen by the public until 1998. Created and executive produced by Norman. Directed by Norman with Bud Yorkin. Starring Carroll O'Connor, Jean Stapleton, Chip Oliver, and Candace Azzara.

All in the Family CBS, 9 seasons, January 12, 1971–April 8, 1979, 205 episodes. Created by and executive-produced by Norman who also wrote seven episodes, including the premier "Meet the Bunkers" used for the two ABC pilots. **Directors:** John Rich, 81 episodes, seasons 1–5; Bob LaHendro, 34 episodes, seasons 3–4; Wes Kenney, 24 episodes, season 5; Paul Bogart, 97 episodes, seasons 6–9. **Starring**: Carroll O'Connor (Archie Bunker, 202 episodes, 1971–1979), Jean Stapleton (Edith Bunker, 205 episodes, 1971–1979), Rob Reiner (Mike Stivic, 184 episodes, 1971–1978), Sally Struthers (Gloria Stivic, 184 episodes, 1971–1978), Danielle Brisebois (Stephanie Mills, 1978–1979, 24 episodes). **Supporting Cast and Recurring Characters:** Mike Evans (Lionel Jefferson, 33 episodes, 1971–1975), Isabel Sanford (Louise Jefferson, 26 episodes, 1971–1979), Mel Stewart (Henry Jefferson, 1971–1973), Sherman Hemsley (George Jefferson, 15 episodes, 1973–1978), Betty Garrett (Irene Lorenzo, 24 episodes, 1973–1975), Vincent Gardenia (Frank Lorenzo, 10 episodes, 1973 and two other appearances in different characters), Allan Melvin (Barney Heffner, 25 episodes, 1971–1979), James Cromwell (Stretch Cunningham, 3 episodes, 1974), Danny Dayton (Hank Pivnik, 15 episodes, 1976–1979), Bob Hastings (Kelsey, 12 episodes, 1971–1976), Jason Wingreen (Harry Snowdon, 25 episodes, 1976–1979), Billy Halop (Munson, 10 episodes, 1971–1976), Liz Torres (Teressa Betancourt, 7 episodes, 1976–1977). **Primary Writers:** Michael Ross (written by 18 episodes, script supervisor 24 episodes, story editor 58 episodes, teleplay by 13 episodes, story by 2 episodes, 1971–1975), Bernie West (written by 18 episodes, story editor 58 episodes, teleplay by 13 episodes, story by 2 episodes, produced by 1 episode, 1971–1975), Don Nicholl (written by 20 episodes, story editor 10 episodes, teleplay by 10 episodes, story by 2 episodes, produced by 1 episode, 1971–1975), Larry Rhine (story editor 70 episodes, executive story editor 24 episodes, written by 31 episodes, teleplay by 4 episodes, 1975–1979), Lou Derman (script supervisor 24 episodes, story editor 23 episodes, written by 12 episodes, teleplay 4 episodes, 1974–1976), Mel Tolkin (written by 30 episodes, teleplay by 4 episodes, 1975–1977), Bill Davenport (story editor 23 episodes, written by 10 episodes, teleplay by 3 episodes, story by 2 episodes, 1974–1976), Milt Josefsberg (written by 17 episodes, teleplay by 3 episodes, story by 2 episodes, 1975–1979), Bob Schiller (written by 13 episodes, 1977–1979, teleplay by 5 episodes, 1977–1979, story by 1 episode, 1977–1979), Bob Weiskopf (written by 13 episodes, teleplay by 5 episodes, story by 1 episode, 1977–1979). **Notable Awards and Nominations:** 52 Emmy nominations and 22 wins, 8 Golden Globe wins and 22 nominations, 1 Writers Guild of America Award and 10 nominations. **Broadcast History:** Jan–July 1971, CBS Tue 9:30–10:00, Sep 1971–Sep 1975, CBS Sat 8:00–8:30, Sep 1975–Sep 1976, CBS Mon 9:00–9:30, Sep 1976–Oct 1976, CBS Wed 9:00–9:30, Nov 1976–Sep 1977, CBS Sat 9:00–9:30, Oct 1977–Oct 1978, CBS Sun 9:00–9:30, Oct 1978–April 1979, CBS Sun 8:00–8:30. **Theme:** Opening, "Those Were the Days" by Charles Strouse and Lee Adams sung by Archie and Edith at the piano, Closing, "Remembering You" by Roger Kellaway and Carroll O'Connor. **Production Company and Filming Locations:** Tandem Productions, CBS Television City 1971–1975 (Hollywood) and Metromedia Square 1975–1979 (Hollywood).

Robert Young and the Family CBS, March 6, 1971. Co-producer with Bud Yorkin.

Sanford and Son NBC, 6 seasons, January 14, 1972–March 25, 1977, 136 episodes. Codeveloped for American television by Norman with Bud Yorkin. Uncredited as executive producer with Yorkin whose name is listed onscreen.

Maude CBS, 6 seasons, 141 episodes, September 12, 1972–April 22, 1978. Created by, developed, and executive-produced by Norman. **Producers:** Rod Parker, Bob Weiskopf, Bob Schiller, Charlie Hauk, Gene Marcione. **Directors:** Hal Cooper (127 episodes, 1972–1978), Bill Hobin (9 episodes, 1972), Tony Csiki (2 episodes, 1976–1977, Bud Yorkin (1 episode, 1972). **Starring:** Bea Arthur (Maude Findlay, 141 episodes, 1972–1978), Bill Macy (Walter Findlay, 141 episodes, 1972–1978), Adrienne Barbeau (Carol Traynor, 126 episodes, 1972–1978), Conrad Bain (141 episodes, 1972–1978), Rue McClannahan (Vivian Cavender Harmon, 115 episodes, 1972–1978). **Supporting Cast and Recurring Characters:** Brian Morrison (Phillip Traynor

#1, 28 episodes, 1972–1976), Kraig Metzinger (Phillip Traynor #2, 11 episodes, 1977–1978), Esther Rolle (Florida Evans, 45 episodes, 1972–1974), Hermione Baddeley (Mrs. Nell Naugatuck, 68 episodes, 1974–1977), J. Pat O'Malley (Bert Beasley, 22 episodes, 1975–1977), Fred Grandy (Chris, 7 episodes, 1973–1974), Marlene Warfield (Victoria Butterfield, 8 episodes, 1977–1978). **Primary Writers:** Bob Schiller (story editor 39 episodes, written by 9 episodes, teleplay by 2 episodes, 1972–1974), Bob Weiskopf (story editor 39 episodes, written by 9 episodes, teleplay by 2 episodes, 1972–1974), Alan J. Levitt (story editor 39 episodes, written by 4 episodes, teleplay by 3 episodes, 1972–1974), Elliot Shoenman (story editor 22 episodes, written by 6 episodes, teleplay by 4 episodes, 1974–1977), Charlie Hauck (written by 14 episodes, teleplay by 4 episodes, story by (1 episode, 1975–1978), Arthur Julian (written by 13 episodes, teleplay by 4 episodes, 1976–1978, Budd Grossman (written by 8 episodes, teleplay by 7 episodes, 1972–1975, story by 1 episode), Bill Davenport (written by 12 episodes, 1, teleplay by 3 episodes, 1976–1978. **Notable Awards and Nominations:** 4 Emmy nominations and 1 win, 4 Golden Globe nominations, 4 Directors Guild of America nominations, 1 Writers Guild of America Award and 1 nomination. **Broadcast History:** Sep 1972–Sep 1974, CBS Tue 8:00–8:30, Sep 1974–Sep 1975, CBS, Mon 9:00–9:30, Sep 1975–Sep 1976, CBS Mon 9:30–10:00, Sep 1976–Sep 1977, CBS Mon 9:00–9:30, Sep 1977–Nov 1977, CBS Mon 9:30–10:00, Dec. 1977–Jan 1978, CBS Mon 9:00–9:30, Jan 1978–Apr 1978, CBS Sat 9:30–10:00. **Theme:** "And Then There's Maude" composed by Alan and Marilyn Bergman and Dave Grusin and performed by Donny Hathaway. **Production Company and Filming Locations:** Tandem Productions, CBS Television City 1972–1975 (Hollywood) and Metromedia Square 1975–1978 (Hollywood).

Good Times CBS, 6 seasons, 133 episodes, February 8, 1974–August 1, 1979. Created by Eric Monte and Mike Evans, developed by Norman. **Executive Producers:** Norman (1974–1975), Allan Mannings (1975–1977), Austin and Irma Kalish (1977–1978, Norman Paul (1978–1979). **Directors:** Gerren Keith (72 episodes, 1976–1979), Herbert Kenwith (57 episodes, 1974–1976), Bob LaHendro (3 episodes, 1974), Donald McKayle (3 episodes, 1974), John Rich (1 episode, 1974), Perry Rosemond (1 episode, 1974). **Starring:** Esther Rolle (Florida Evans, 109 episodes, 1974–1979), John Amos (James Evans, 61 episodes 1974–1976), Jimmie Walker (James "J.J." Evans Jr, 133 episodes, 1974–1979), BernNadette Stanis (Thelma Evans, 133 episodes, 1974–1979), Ralph Carter (Michael Evans, 133 episodes, 1974–1979), Ja'net DuBois (Willona Woods, 133 episodes, 1974–1979), Penny Woods (Janet Jackson,

48 episodes, 1977–1979), Ben Powers (Keith Anderson, 24 episodes, 1978–1978). **Supporting Cast and Recurring Characters:** Johnny Brown (Nathan Bookman, 58 episodes, 1975–1979), Albert Reed (Alderman Fred Davis, 7 episodes, 1974–1979), Teddy Wilson (Sweet Dady Williams, 7 episodes, 1976–1979), Helen Martin (Wanda, 7 episodes, 1974–1979), Moses Gunn (Carl Dixon, 6 episodes, 1977). **Primary Writers:** Norman Paul (executive story editor 24 episodes, story editor 13 episodes1974 teleplay by 12 episodes, written by 9 episodes, story by 7 episodes, 1974–1978). Jack Elinson (executive story editor, 24 episodes, story editor, 13 episodes, 1974, teleplay by 11 episodes written by 8 episodes story by 2 episodes, 1974–1976). John Baskin (story editor 17 episodes, written by 12 episodes, teleplay by 7 episodes, story by 1 episode, 1974–1977). Roger Shulman (story editor 18 episodes, written by 12 episodes, teleplay by 7 episodes, story by 1 episode, 1974–1976). Michael S. Baser (story editor 23 episodes, teleplay by 3 episodes, written by 3 episodes story by 1 episode, 1976–1978). Kim Weiskopf (story editor 23 episodes, teleplay by 3 episodes, written by 3 episodes, story by 1 episode, 1976–1978). Joeseph Bonaduce (story editor 24 episodes, teleplay by 3 episodes, story by 2 episodes 1978, written by 1 episode, 1977–1979). Bruce Howard (story editor 12 episodes, story by 3 episodes 1976–1978, teleplay by 3 episodes, written by 2 episodes, 1975–1979). Bob Peete (written by 12 episodes, 1974–1977). Sid Dorfman (teleplay by 5 episodes, written by 3 episodes, story by 1 episode, 1976–1978). Gene Farmer (story editor 7 episodes teleplay by 1 episode, written by 1 episode, 1977–1978). Michael G. Moye (written by 7 episodes, teleplay by 2 episodes, 1978–1979. Allan Mannings (teleplay by 6 episodes, 1974–1977. **Notable Awards and Nominations:** 4 Golden Globe nominations. **Broadcast History:** Feb 1974–Sep 1974, CBS Fri 8:30–9:00, Sep 1974–Mar 1976, CBS 8:00–8:30, Mar 1976–Aug 1976, CBS Tue 8:30–9:00, Sep 1976–Jan 1978, CBS Wed 8:00–8:30, Jan 1978–May 1978, CBS Mon 8:00–8:30, June 1978—Sept 1978, CBS Mon 8:30–9:00, Sep 1978–Dec 1978, CBS Sat 8:30–9:00, May 1979–Aug 1979, CBS Wed 8:30–9:00. **Theme Song:** "Good Times" composed by Dave Grusin and Alan and Marilyn Bergman and performed by Jim Gilstrap and Blinky Williams. **Production Company and Filming Locations:** Tandem Productions, CBS Television City 1974–1975 (Hollywood) Metromedia Square 1975–1979 (Hollywood).

The Jeffersons CBS, 11 seasons, 253 episodes, January 18, 1975–July 2, 1985. Created and developed by Norman with Don Nicholl and Michael Ross. **Executive Producers:** David Duclon, Ron Leavitt, Jay Moriarity, Mike Milligan, Michael Ross, George Sunga, Bernie West. **Producers:** David Duclon,

Ron Leavitt, Michael G. Moye, Jerry Perzigian, Donald Seigell, Jack Shea. **Directors:** Jack Shea (110 episodes, 1975–1979), Bob Lally (97 episodes, 1978–1983), Oz Scott (40 episodes, 1983–1985). **Starring:** Sherman Hemsley (George Jefferson, 253 episodes, 1975–1985), Isabel Sanford (Louise Jefferson, 253 episodes, 1975–1985), Roxie Roker (Helen Willis, 251 episodes, 1975–1985), Franklin Cover (Tom Willis, 252 episodes, 1975–1985), Marla Gibbs (Florence Johnston, 217 episodes, 1975–1985). **Supporting Cast and Recurring Characters:** Mike Evans (Lionel Jefferson #1, 62 episodes, 1975 and 1979–1985), Damon Evans (Lionel Jefferson #2, 74 episodes, 1975–1978), Paul Benedict (Harry Bentley, 203 episodes, 1975–1985), Berlinda Tolbert (Jenny Willis Jefferson, 166 episodes, 1975–1985), Zara Cully (Mother Jefferson, 75 episodes, 1975–1978), Ned Wertimer (Ralph the doorman, 77 episodes, 1977–1985), Jay Hammer (Allan Willis, 24 episodes, 1978–1979), Danny Wells (Charlie the bartender, 23 episodes, 1975–1985), Ernest Harden Jr. (Marcus Henderson, 8 episodes, 1975–1979), Jack Fletcher (Mr. Whittendale, 6 episodes, 1978–1984). **Primary Writers:** Mike Milligan (written by 20 episodes, teleplay by 7 episodes, story by 5 episodes, 1975–1981, Jay Moriarity (written by 20 episodes, teleplay by 7 episodes, story by 5 episodes, 1975–1981). Bryan Joseph (executive story consultant 26 episodes, teleplay by 3 episodes, written by 2 episodes, 1978–1980). Jerry Perzigian (written by 19 episodes, teleplay by 9 episodes, story by 2 episodes, 1979–1985. Don Seigel (written by 19 episodes, teleplay by 9 episodes, story by 2 episodes, 1979–1985. Peter Casey (written by 20 episodes 1985, teleplay by 8 episodes, story by 1 episode, 1979–1985). David Lee (written by 20 episodes, teleplay by 8 episodes story by 1 episode, 1979–1985). Michael G. Moye (written by 22 episodes, story by 1 episode, teleplay by 1 episode, 1979–1984). Gordon Mitchell (written by 15 episodes, teleplay by 5 episodes, story editor 2 episodes, 1975–1977). Lloyd Tuner (written by 15 episodes, teleplay by 5 episodes, story editor 2 episodes, 1975–1977. **Notable Awards and Nominations:** 2 Emmy Awards and 14 nominations, 8 Golden Globe nominations, Humanitas Prize nomination, 2 NAACP Image Awards, 1 Writers Guild of America Nomination. **Broadcast History:** Jan 1975–Aug 1975, CBS Sat, 8:30–9:00; Sep 1975–Oct 1976, CBS Sat, 8:00–8:30; Nov 1976–Jan 1977, CBS Wed 8:00–8:30; Jan 1977–Aug 1977, CBS Mon 8:00–8:30; Sep 1977–May 1978, CBS Sat 8:00–8:30; June 1978–Sep 1978, CBS Mon 8:00–8:30; Sep 1978–Jan 1979, CBS Wed 8:00–8:30; Jan 1979–Mar 1979, CBS Wed 9:30–10:00; Mar 1979–June 1979, CBS Wed 8:00–8:30; June 1979–Sep 1982, CBS Sun 9:30–10:00; Sep 1982–Dec 1984, CBS Sun 9:00–9:30; Jan 1985–March 1985, CBS Tue 8:00–8:30; Apr 1985, CBS Tue 8:30–9:00; June 1985, CBS Tue, 8:30–9:00; Jun 1985–Jul 1985, CBS

Tue 8:00–8:30. **Theme Song:** "Moving on Up" composed by Jeff Barry and Ja'net DuBois and performed by Ja'net DuBois **Production Companies:** T.A.T. Communications (1975–1982, seasons 1–8), NRW Productions (1975–1979, seasons 1–5), Ragamuffin Productions (season 7, 1980–1981), Embassy Television, seasons 9–11, 1982–1985. **Filming Locations:** CBS Television City (Hollywood, 1975), Metromedia Square (Hollywood, 1975–1982), Universal City Studios (Universal City, California, 1982–1985).

Hot l Baltimore ABC, 1 season, 13 episodes, January 24–April 25–1975. Created by Norman and developed with Rod Parker. Executive-produced by Norman with Parker also executive-producing 1 episode. **Producers:** Ron Clark and Gene Marcione (13 episodes). **Director:** Bob LaHendro (4 episodes). **Starring and Appearing in All 21 Episodes:** James Cromwell (Bill Lewis), Conchata Ferrell (April Green), Jeannie Linero (Suzie Marta Rocket), Richard Masur (Clifford Ainsley), Al Freeman Jr. (Charles Bingham), Gloria LeRoy (Millie), Robin Wilson (Jackie), Stan Gottlieb (Mr. Morse), Lee Bergere (George), Henry Calvert (Gordon), Charlotte Rae (Mrs. Bellotti). **Theme:** Composed by Marvin Hamlisch. **Production Company:** T.A.T. Communications.

The Dumplings NBC, 1 season, 11 episodes (1 unaired), October 4, 1975–March 31, 1976. Created and produced by Don Nicholl, Michael Ross, Bernie West and George Sunga, and developed by Norman. **Starring:** James Coco and Geraldene Brooks. **Broadcast History:** Jan 1976–Mar 1976, NBC Wed 9:30–10:00. **Opening Theme:** "Two by Two, Side by Side" performed by Steve Lawrence. **Production Company:** T.A.T. Communications.

Three to Get Ready 1975. Cocreated by Allan Mannings and Whitney Blake, developed by Norman. Unaired pilot for what became the original *One Day at a Time*. Cowritten by Norman and Allan Mannings. Directed by Joan Darling and Jim Drake. Starring: Bonnie Franklin, Mackenzie Phillips and Marcia Rodd.

One Day at a Time CBS, 9 seasons, 209 episodes, December 16, 1975–May 29, 1984. Cocreated by Whitney Blake and Allan Mannings, and developed by Norman. **Executive Producers:** Norman, Dick Bensfield, Jack Elinson, Perry Grant, Mort Lachman, Alan Rafkin. **Producers:** Dick Bensfield, Patricia Fass Palmer, Perry Grant, Katherine Green, Allan Mannigs, Bud Wiser. **Directors:** Alan Rafkin (123 episodes, 1978–1983), Herbert Kenwith (47 episodes, 1976–1978), Noam Pitnik (18 episodes, 1975–1984). **Starring:** Bonnie Franklin (Ann Romano, 209 episodes, 1975–1984), Pat Harrington Jr. (Dwayne F. Schneider, 209 episodes, 1975–1984), Valerie Bertinelli

(Barbara Cooper, 209 episodes, 1975–1984), Julie Cooper (Mackenzie Phillips, 131 episodes, 1975–1981, 1981–1983). **Supporting Cast and Recurring Characters:** Richard Masur (David Kane, 22 episodes, 1975–1976), Mary Louise Wilson (Ginny Wrobliki, 18 episodes, 1976–1977), Scott Colomby (Cliff Randall, 6 episodes, 1977–1978), Ed Cooper (Joseph Campanella, 8 episodes, 1976–1982), John Putch (Bob Morton, 14 episodes,1976–1983), Shelly Fabares (Francene Webster, 38 episodes, 1978–1984), Nanette Fabray (Grandma Katherine Romano, 46 episodes, 1979–1984), Michael Lembeck (Max Horvath, 61 episodes, 1979–1980; 1981–1984), Ron Rifkin (Nick Handris, 19 episodes, 1980–1981), Glenn Scarpelli (Alex Handris, 19 episodes, 1980–1983), Boyd Gaines (Mark Royer, 57 episodes, 1981–1984), Howard Hessman (Sam Royer, 16 episodes, 1992–1984). **Primary Writers:** Dick Bensfield (written by 44 episodes, story by 5 episodes, teleplay by 5 episodes 1975–1984). Perry Grant (written by 44 episodes, story by 5 episodes teleplay by 5 episodes 1975–1984. Bud Wiser (written by 20 episodes, teleplay by 4 episodes, 1976–1984. **Notable Awards and Nominations:** 2 Emmy Awards and 1 nomination, 3 Golden Globe Awards and 6 nominations,1 Humanitas Prize nomination, 1 Photoplay Awards nomination, 6 Young Artist Awards nominations. **Broadcast History:** Dec 1975–July 1976, CBS Tue, 9:30–10:00; Sep 1976–Jan 1978, CBS Tue 9:30–10:00; Jan 1978–Jan 1979, CBS Mon 9:30–10:00; Jan 1979–Mar 1979, CBS Wed 9:00–9:30; Mar 1979–Sep 1982, CBS Sunday 8:30–9:00; Sep 1982–Mar 1983, CBS Sun 9:30–10:00; Mar 1983–May 1983, CBS Mon 9:30–10:00; Jun 1983– May 1984, CBS Wed 8:00–8:30, May 1984–August 1984, CBS Mon 9:00–9:30; Aug 1984–Sep 1984, CBS Sun 8:00–8:30. **Theme Song:** "This Is It," composed by Nancy Barry and Jeff Barry sung in the opening by Polly Cutter. Closing theme "This Is It" (instrumental) composed by Ray Barry. **Production Companies and Filming Locations:** T.A.T. Communications, seasons 1–7, Embassy Communications, seasons 8–9; filmed at Metromedia Square, 1975–1984, Hollywood.

All's Fair CBS, 1 season, 24 episodes, September 20, 1976–April 30, 1977. Created by Bob Schiller, Bob Weiskopf, Rod Parker and developed by Norman. **Starring:** Richard Crenna, Bernadette Peters, and Michael Keaton in one of his first major TV roles. **Broadcast History:** Sep 1976–Aug 1977, CBS Mon 9:30–10:00. **Production Company:** T.AT. Communications.

The Nancy Walker Show ABC, 1 season, 13 episodes (one unaired), September 30, 1976–December 23, 1976. Created by Norman and Rod Parker, executive-produced by Norman (11 episodes) and produced by Parker (2 episodes). **Directors:** Alan Rafkin, 8 episodes, 1976; Hal Cooper, 1 episode,

1976. **Starring and Appearing in All 13 Episodes:** Nancy Walker (Nancy Kittridge), William Daniels (Lt. Cmdr. Kenneth Kitteridge), James Cromwell (Glen), Beverly Archer (Lorraine), Ken Olfson (Terry Folson), William Schallert (Teddy Futterman), Sparky Marcus (Michael Futterman). **Broadcast History:** Sep 1976–Dec 1976, ABC Thu 9:30–10:00. **Theme:** "Nancy's Blues" by Marilyn and Alan Bergman and Marvin Hamlisch. **Production Company:** T.A.T. Communications.

Mary Hartman, Mary Hartman Syndicated, 2 seasons, 325 episodes, January 5, 1976–July 1, 1977. Created by Gail Parent, Ann Marcus, Jerry Adelman, and Daniel Gregory Brown. Developed by Norman. **Producer:** Jerry Addler. **Directors:** Jim Drake (157 episodes, 1976–1977), Nessa Hyams (105 episodes, 1976–1977), Kim Friedman (23 episodes, 1976), Joan Darling (21 episodes, 1976), Hal Alexander (12 episodes, 1977), Jack Heller (7 episodes, 1976), Bob Lally (5 episodes, 1976), Giovanna Nigro (5 episodes, 1976), Dennis Klein (5 episodes, 1977). **Starring and Appearing in All 325 Episodes:** Louise Lasser (Mary Hartman), Greg Mullavey (Tom Hartman), Mary Kay Place (Loretta Haggers), Graham Jarvis (Charlie Haggers), Dody Goodman (Martha Shumway), Debralee Scott (Cathy Shumway), Victor Kilian (Grandpa Larkin). **Supporting Cast and Recurring Characters:** Claudia Lamb (Heather Hartman, 323 episodes), Phillip Bruns (George Shumway, 250 episodes), Dabney Coleman (Merle Jeeter, 148 episodes), Marian Mercer (Wanda Jeter, 118 episodes), Bruce Solomon (Sgt. Dennis Foley, 104 episodes), Dennis Burkley (Mac Slattery, 85 episodes), Susan Browning (Nurse Pat Gimble, 72 episodes), Sid Haig (Texas, 85 episodes), David Byrd (Vernon Bayles 53 episodes 1977), Martin Mull (Garth Gimble, 49 episodes). **Broadcast History:** 1976–1977, syndicated and network late night 30 minutes five nights a week. **Theme:** Opening, "Premiere Occasion" by Barry White with incidental music by Earle Hagen. **Production Company:** T.A.T. Communications.

Forever Fernwood Syndicated, 1 season, 130 episodes, 1977–1978. Follow-up series to *Mary Hartman Mary Hartman* following Louise Lasser's departure with Norman as executive producer and same primary cast and crew with several new additions, most notably Shelly Fabares as Eleanor Major, Tom Hartman's new love interest.

All That Glitters Syndicated, 1 Season, 65 episodes, April 18–July 15, 1977. Created by Norman and Ann Marcus, developed by Norman. **Producers:** Viva Knight, Stephanie Sills, Nicky Weaver, Virginia Carter. **Directors:** Herbert Kenwith, James Frawley. **Starring and Appearing in All 25**

Episodes: Lois Nettleton (Christina Stockwood), Barbara Baxley (L.W. Carruthers), Anita Gillette (Nancy Langston), Chuck McCann (Bert Stockwood), Vanessa Brown (Peggy Horner), Louise Shaffer (Andrea Martin), Davis Haskell (Michael McFarland), Linda Gray (Linda Murkland), Gary Sandy (Dan Kincaid), Marte Boyle Slout (Grace "Smitty" Smith). **Broadcast History:** 1977, syndicated, five nights a week. **Theme:** "Genesis Revisited," composed by Alan and Marilyn Bergman, performed by Kenny Rankin. **Production Company:** Tandem Productions.

Fernwood 2 Night Syndicated, 1 season, 65 episodes, July 4–September 30, 1977. Satirical comedy talk show spun off from *Mary Hartman, Mary Hartman* created by Norman and produced by Alan Thicke. **Directors:** Tony Csiki (11 episodes, 1977), Jim Drake (8 episodes, 1977), Louis J. Horvitz (8 episodes, 1977) and Howard Storm (3 episodes, 1977). **Starring:** Martin Mull (Barth Gimble), Fred Williard (Jerry Hubbard), Frank De Vol (Happy Kyne), and Tommy Tedesco (Tommy Marinucci). **Production Company:** T.A.T. Communications. ***Rebranded as *America 2–Night* with same cast and also airing for 65 more episodes in first-run syndication from April 10–July 7, 1978.

A Year at the Top CBS, 6 episodes, August 5, 1977–September 2, 1977. Created by Heywood Kling, developed and executive-produced by Norman with Don Kirshner also serving as co-executive prouder. **Producers:** Patrica Fass Palmer and Darryl Hickman. **Directors:** Marlene Laird and Alan Rafkin. **Starring and Appearing in All 6 Episodes:** Paul Shaffer (Paul), Greg Evigan (Greg), Gabriel Dell (Frederick J. Hanover). **Writers:** Heywood Kling, Sandy Veith. **Broadcast History:** Aug 1977, CBS Fri 8:00–8:30; Aug 1977–Sep 1977, CBS Sun 8:30–9:00. **Theme Music:** Composed by Greg Evigan, Paul Shaffer, Harry Greenfield. **Production Companies:** Don Kirschner Productions, T.A.T. Communications, Tandem Productions.

Norman Lear's New Little Rascals 1977. Unaired ABC pilot for proposed reboot of director Hal Roach's classic 1930s *Our Gang* series. Created and executive-produced by Norman, two pilots were filmed. The then-unknown child actor Gary Coleman, who would go on to star in the hit Tandem/Embassy Communications–produced NBC sitcom *Diff'rent Strokes* was cast as Stymie.

Mr. Dugan Unaired sitcom originally intended as a revamped continuation of *Maude* with three never-shown episodes created and executive-produced by Norman. After *Maude* star Bea Arthur decided not to do it, it was retooled to be about an African American former football player–turned–congressman in Washington (played by Cleavon Little) that was canceled by CBS before its scheduled premiere in March 1979. **Production Company:** T.A.T. Communications.

Hanging In CBS, 4 episodes, August 8–August 24, 1979. Norman's attempt to relaunch *Mr. Dugan*, this time as a starring vehicle for Bill Macy (Walter Findlay from *Maude*) as a former pro football player who becomes president of a fictional university. One episode also featured former *Good Times* star John Amos.

The Baxters Syndicated, 2 seasons, 50 episodes, September 1979–August 1981. An interactive sitcom originally begun as a local production on Boston's ABC affiliate WCVB in 1977. Norman revamped the series for one season in national syndication with a new set of actors, including Anita Gillette and Larry Keith, playing Nancy and Fred Baxter. After Norman ended his association due to low ratings it was subsequently picked up by a Canadian production company for season 2.

Palmerstown, U.S.A. (a.k.a. *Palmerstown*) CBS, 2 seasons, 17 episodes, March 20, 1980–June 9, 1981. Hourlong drama set in the rural South during the Great Depression and focusing on the lives of two young boys—one white and one African American—who become best friends. Based on the real-life childhood of *Roots* author Alex Haley who cocreated *Palmerstown* with Norman and served as executive producer with him, it was actor Michael J. Fox's first major role as a continuing character in an American TV series, where he played one of the two boys, Willie-Joe Hall.

I Love Liberty ABC, March 21, 1982. Two-hour all-star variety special billed as a "salute to freedom" and "America's first left-wing patriotic rally" coinciding with President George Washington's 250th birthday. Coproduced by Norman and Bud Yorkin in conjunction with Norman's free speech advocacy group People for the American Way, the event was originally filmed on February 22, 1982, at the Los Angeles Sports Arena. Guests in alphabetical order included: Christopher Atkins, Valerie Bertinelli, Jimmy Buffett, Ellen Burstyn, LeVar Burton, Nikki D'Amico, Patty Duke, Erik Estrada, Peter Falk, Jane Fonda, Bonnie Franklin, Anthony Geary, Arizona senator Bary Goldwater, Louis Gossett Jr., Valerie Harper, Jim Henson (as the Muppets), Gregory Hines, Judd Hirsch, Michael Horse, Waylon Jennings, Geri Jewell, Burt Lancaster, Michele Lee, Hal Linden, Shirley MacLaine, Melissa Manchester, Walter Matthau, Kristy McNichol, Mary Tyler Moore, Frank Oz, Helen Reddy, Christopher Reeve, Kenny Rogers, Martin Sheen, Frank

Sinatra, Madge Sinclair, Rod Steiger, Barbra Streisand, Dick Van Patten, Dionne Warwick, Robin Williams, Henry Winkler.

a.k.a. Pablo ABC, 6 episodes, March 6–April 10, 1984. Norman's first sitcom comeback attempt cocreated and coproduced with Rick Mitz about a struggling Hispanic stand-up comic in Los Angeles named Paul Rivera (played by real-life stand-up comic Paul Rodriguez) and his large Mexican American family who still call him Pablo. **Broadcast History:** Mar–April 1984, ABC Tue, 8:30–9:00. **Production Company:** Embassy Television.

Good Evening, He Lied 1984. Unaired pilot executive-produced by Norman about a TV newsroom based on treatment written by former Los Angles anchorwoman Marcia Brandwynne.

P.O.P. 1984 NBC telefilm cowritten by Norman and Steve Kunes and directed by Bud Yorkin about a con artist who moves back in with his wife and estranged son following a twenty-year absence starring Jane Anderson, Bea Arthur, and Beeson Carroll.

Heartsounds ABC, September 30, 1984. Telefilm executive-produced by Norman about a New York doctor who becomes a patient after suffering a heart attack starring Mary Tyler Moore, James Garner, and Sam Wannamaker. **Production Companies:** ABC Television and Embassy Television.

All in the Family 20th Anniversary Special CBS, February 16, 1991. Hosted by and executive-produced by Norman with appearances by Carroll O'Connor, Jean Stapleton, Rob Reiner, and Sally Struthers. Cast members and viewers reminisce about their favorite *All in the Family* moments supplemented by video clips from classic episodes.

Sunday Dinner CBS, 6 episodes, June 2–July 7, 1984. Created and executive-produced by Norman who also wrote the first episode, *Sunday Dinner* was loosely based on his third marriage to Lyn Lear, who was twenty-five years old younger, and chronicled the family conflicts caused by the May-December marriage between fifty-six-year-old widower Ben Benedict (Robert Loggia) and TT Fagori (Teri Hatcher) who was twenty-six years his junior. To try and entice viewers, CBS re-aired classic episodes of *All in the Family* alongside *Sunday Dinner*. **Production Companies:** Act III Television and Columbia Pictures Television.

The Powers That Be NBC, 21 episodes (5 unaired), 2 seasons, March 7, 1992–January 2, 1993. Political satire about a US senator and his dysfunctional family in Washington. Executive-produced by Norman and cocreated by David Krane and Marta Kauffman, it starred John Forsythe, Holland Taylor, and Eve Gordon with theme music composed by Marvin Hamlisch. **Production Companies:** Act III Television, Columbia Pictures Television, Castle Rock Entertainment.

704 Hauser CBS, 6 episodes (1 unaired), April 11–May 9, 1994. Final spin-off from *All in the Family* created and executive-produced by Norman about an African American family moving into Archie Bunker's old home. Spurred by Norman's accountant telling him how much money he was spending for storage of the original *All in the Family* set, *704* debuted at a time when conservative talk radio was in its infancy and experiencing its first surge in popularity, particularly Rush Limbaugh. John Amos (James Evans from *Good Times*) starred as family patriarch Ernie Cumberbatch, a liberal Democrat who is the political opposite of his conservative Republican son Thurgood "Goodie" who was named after Supreme Court Justice Thurgood Marshall. **Production Companies:** ELP Communications, Act III Television, Castle Rock Entertainment, Columbia Pictures Television.

Channel Umptee–3 (a.k.a. Umptee–3) WB, 1 season, 13, episodes, October 20, 1997–February 25, 1998. Saturday morning children's cartoon TV series co-created by veteran animator Jim George and Norman, co-executive produced by Norman and John Baskin, and produced by George. **Directors:** Chris Headrick, Don Jurwich, Mike Peraza, David Schwartz, Bob Seeley. **Featuring Voices of:** David Paymer (Sheldon S. Cargo), Rob Paulsen (Ogden Ostrich), Jonathan Harris (Stickley Rickets), Alice Ghostley (Pandora Rickets). **Opening Theme:** composed by Walter Murphy and performed by David Paymer, Rob Paulsen and Jonathan Harris. **Production Companies:** Adelaide Productions, Act III Productions, Enchanté George, Columbia TriStar Television.

Maggie Bloom 2000 TV movie produced by Norman starring singer Debbie Gibson. Network and original airdate unknown.

America Divided EPIX-TV, 2016. Released in conjunction with the 2016 presidential elections, *America Divided* was a multipart docuseries co executive produced by Norman, Shonda Rhimes and the rap artist and actor and rap artist Common among others featuring segments on inequalities in housing, healthcare, labor, education, the criminal justice system, and politics. Norman appears in the first two episodes originally airing on September 30 and October 7 and exploring gentrification in New York City and racial discrimination in housing.

One Day at a Time 4 seasons, 46, episodes, January 6, 2017–June 16, 2020, Netflix (seasons 1–3), Pop TV (season 4). Reboot of Norman's 1970s sitcom of the same title, this time revolving around a Cuban American family living in Los Angeles's Echo Park neighborhood. Tackling issues ranging from immigration, homophobia, racism, and gender identity, it starred Justina Machado, Todd Grinnell, Isabella Gomez, Marcel Ruiz, Stephen Tobolowsky, and Rita Moreno. Developed by Gloria Calderón Kellett and Mike Royce, it was executive-produced by Norman and producing partner Brent Miller with the original theme sung by Gloria Estefan during seasons 1 through 3.

Guess Who Died? 2018. Unaired comedy pilot for NBC about a group of residents living in a senior community in Palm Springs, California starring Hector Elizondo, Holland Taylor, Beth Lacke, Adrian Martinez, and Christoper Lloyd. Cocreated by Norman and screenwriter Peter Tolan who cowrote the pilot and served as executive producers along with Brent Miller. Had the series been picked up, it would have been Norman's first original sitcom in nearly twenty years.

Live in Front of a Studio Audience: Norman Lear's "All in the Family" and "The Jeffersons" ABC, May 22, 2019. The first in a series of specials reimagining Norman's classic 1970s sitcoms conceptualized and hosted by Jimmy Kimmell. The first special recreated "Henry's Farewell" from *All in the Family*, with Woody Harrelson and Marisa Tomei as Archie and Edith, Ellie Kemper and Ike Barinholtz as Mike and Gloria, and Jamie Foxx and Wanda Sykes as George and Louise Jefferson. In *The Jeffersons* re-creation, "A Friend in Need" (the first episode of the original series), Foxx and Sykes also appear as George and Louise with a cameo appearance by Marla Gibbs who played Florence in the original series. The first special was seen by 10.4 million viewers and Norman became the oldest Emmy winner in history for Outstanding Variety Special, sharing the honor with Jimmy Kimmel, Adma McKay, Justin Theroux, Will Farrell, producing partner Brent Miller, and Eric Cook.

Live in Front of a Studio Audience: Norman Lear's "All in the Family" and "Good Times" ABC. Airing on December 18, 2019, this was the second special re-creating another episode of *All in the Family* and *Good Times*, with John Amos who played James Evans in the original series making a cameo and winning a second Emmy for Outstanding Variety Special, making Norman the oldest Emmy winner in history two years in a row.

Rita Moreno: Just a Girl Who Decided to Go for It 2021. American Master's documentary on the life and career of legendary dancer, actor and singer Rita

Moreno co-executive produced by Norman and his third wife Lyn Davis Lear and Michael Kantor. Narrated by Moreno, Norman also appears in several scenes.

Live in Front of a Studio Audience: Norman Lear's "Diff'rent Strokes" and "The Facts of Life" ABC. Norman's third live special with Jimmy Kimmel airing on December 7, 2021, with cameo appearances by series originals Todd Bridges, Kim Fields, Mindy Cohn, and Lisa Whelchel (Blair from *The Facts of Life*) performing the theme song.

Additional TV Series Produced by Tandem Productions, T.A.T. Communications and/or Embassy Television/ Embassy Communications/ELP Communications

Diff'rent Strokes, 8 seasons, 189 episodes, November 3, 1979–March 7, 1986 (NBC, seasons 1–7); (ABC, season 8), Tandem Productions (1978–1986), Embassy Television (1985–1986).

Hello, Larry NBC, 2 seasons, 38 episodes, January 26, 1979–April 30, 1980, T.A.T. Communications.

McGurk: A Dog's Life Created by Charlie Hauck for NBC and the last television project developed by Norman to become a pilot, it aired for one episode on June 15, 1979, at 8:00 p.m. EST.

The Facts of Life NBC, 9 seasons, 201 episodes, August 24, 1979–May 7, 1988, T.A.T. Communications (seasons 1–3), Embassy Television (seasons 4–7), Embassy Communications (seasons 8–9), ELP Communications (season 9), Columbia Pictures Television (season 9).

Archie Bunker's Place CBS, 4 seasons, 97 episodes, September 23, 1979–April 4, 1983, Tandem Productions with The O'Connor-Becker Company (season 1) and UGO Productions, Inc. (seasons 2–4).

Checking In CBS, 4 episodes, April 9–April 30, 1981, T.A.T. Communications with Ragamuffin Productions.

Silver Spoons NBC, 5 seasons, 116 episodes, September 25, 1982–May 11, 1986, Embassy Television (1982–1986), Embassy Communications (1986–1987).

Gloria CBS, 1 season, 21 episodes and 1 pilot aired as *Archie Bunker's Place*, September 26, 1982–April 10, 1983, Tandem Productions.

Square Pegs CBS, 1 season, 20 episodes, September 27, 1982–March 7, 1983, Embassy Television.

Who's the Boss? ABC, 8 seasons, 186 episodes, September 20, 1984–April 25, 1992, Embassy Television (seasons 1–2), Embassy Communications (seasons 3–4), ELP Communications in association with Hunter/Cohan Productions and Columbia Pictures Television (seasons 4–8).

Double Trouble NBC, 2 seasons, 23 episodes, April 4, 1984–March 30, 1985, Embassy Television.

E/R CBS, 1 season, 22 episodes, September 16, 1984–February 27, 1985, Embassy Television.

227 NBC, 5 seasons, 116 episodes, September 14, 1985–May 6, 1990, Embassy Television (1985–1986, season 1), Embassy Communications (1986–1987, seasons 2–3), ELP Communications (1988–1990, seasons 3–5), Columbia Pictures Television (1988–1990, seasons 3–5).

The Charmings ABC, 2 seasons, 21 episodes (1 unaired), March 20, 1987–February 11, 1988, Embassy Communications in association with Columbia Pictures Television (1988, episodes 17–21).

Married . . . with Children FOX, 11 seasons, 259 episodes, April 5, 1987–June 9, 1997, Embassy Communications, ELP Communications and Columbia Pictures Television.

Everything's Relative CBS, 1 season, 10 episodes, October 3–November 7, 1987, Embassy Communications.

Free Spirit ABC, 1 season, 14 episodes (1 unaired), September 22, 1989–January 14, 1990, ELP Communications and Columbia Pictures Television.

Phenom ABC, 1 season, 22 episodes, September 14, 1993–May 10, 1994, ELP Communications with Gracie Films and Columbia Pictures Television.

TV Projects in Development at the Time of Norman's Death

The Corps, 10 episodes.

Mary Harman, Mary Hartman remake, 1 episode.

Fried Green Tomatoes, starring Reba McEntire.

Clean Slate, costarring George Wallace and Laverne Cox, 1 episode.

Good Times remake, 12 episodes on Netflix in April 2024.

Duino

Dads of Dewitt

K-Sun

Loteria

Who's the Boss

Gamergate

FILMS

As Producer and Writer

Cold Turkey 1971, United Artists. Produced and directed by Norman with screenplay by Norman, William Price Fox, and Margaret Rau. **Starring:** Dick Van Dyke, Pippa Scott, Tom Poston, Edward Everett Horton, Bob and Ray, and Bob Newhart. **Production Company:** Tandem Productions.

The Night They Raided Minsky's 1968, United Artists. Produced by Norman, directed by William Friedkin with screenplay written by Norman, Sidney Michaels, and Arnold Schulman based on the 1960 novel *The Night They Raided Minsky's* by Rowland Barber. **Starring:** Jason Robards, Britt Ekland, Norman Wisdom, and Bert Lahr. **Production Company:** Tandem Productions.

Divorce American Style 1967, Columbia Pictures. Produced by Norman and directed by Bud Yorkin with screenplay by Norman and Robert Kaufman. **Starring:** Dick Van Dyke, Debbie Reynolds, Jason Robards, Jean Simmons, Van Johnson. **Production Companies:** National General Production Inc., Tandem Productions, Columbia Pictures.

Never Too Late 1965, Warner Brothers. Produced by Norman and directed by Bud Yorkin with screenplay by Sumner Arthur Long who wrote the 1962 Broadway play of the same name. **Starring:** Paul Ford, Connie Stevens, Maureen O'Sullivan and Jim Hutton. **Production Company:** Tandem Productions.

Come Blow Your Horn 1963, Paramount. Producers: Norman and Bud Yorkin, directed by Yorkin with screenplay written by Norman from the Broadway play by Neil Simon. Starring: Frank Sinatra, Lee J. Cobb, Molly Picon, Barbara Rush, and Jill St. John. **Production Company:** Tandem Productions.

As Executive Producer Only

(***Studio and exact release date provided where available.)

Start the Revolution without Me, 1970, Warner Brothers.

This Is Spinal Tap, 1984, Embassy Pictures.

The Princess Bride, 1987, 20th Century Fox with Act III Communications and Buttercup Films.

Fried Green Tomatoes, 1991, Universal Pictures with Act III Communications, Electric Shadow Productions, and Avnet/Kerner Productions.

Things in Bob's Garage. Unproduced film written by C. Jay Cox optioned by Norman and Act III Productions in 1998.

Way Past Cool, 2000.

Declaration of Independence, 2003.

PBS American Masters, *Pete Seeger: The Power of Song*, 2007.

El Superstar: The Unlikely Rise of Juan Francis, 2008.

I Carry You with Me, Sony Pictures Classics 2020.

I Got a Monster, 2023

NOTABLE TV INTERVIEWS AND APPEARANCES

(****Network and exact air dates given where available.)

The Colgate Comedy Hour, 1952.

The Merv Griffin Show, 1971.

The David Frost Show, 1971.

The Dick Cavett Show, 2 episodes, 1972.

Tomorrow Coast to Coast with Tom Snyder, 2 episodes, 1974.

The Best of All in the Family CBS, December 24, 1974.

Dinah!, 4 episodes, 1975–1977.

Bob Hope's World of Comedy, 1976.

Saturday Night Live, guest host with musical guest Boz Scaggs, September 25, 1976.

Mary Hartman, Mary Hartman, 1 episode appearing as himself, 1976.

60 Minutes, profiled by Mike Wallace, 1976.

The 29th Annual Primetime Emmy Awards, presenter, 1977.

The Mike Douglas Show, 4 episodes, 1977–1979.

The 30th Annual Primetime Emmy Awards, presenter, 1978.

AFI Lifetime Achievement Award, 2 episodes, 1979–1980.

The 200th episode of All in the Family, host, CBS, March 4, 1979.

Over Easy, 1 episode, 1979.

Quiz Kids, host, 1981.

The Alan Thicke Show, 1981.

Television: The Ultimate Drug, 1981.

Late Night with David Letterman, 1982.

The 35th Annual Primetime Emmy Awards, presenter, 1983.

1st Annual American Comedy Awards, 1987.

All in the Family: 20th Anniversary Special, host, CBS, February 16, 1991.

The Arsenio Hall Show, 1991.

Alan King: Inside the Comedy Mind, Comedy Central, 1991.

The Tonight Show Starring Johnny Carson, 1 episode, 1992.

Late Night with Conan O'Brian, 1 episode, 1994.

The Roseanne Show, 1998.

CBS: The First Fifty Years, 1998.

Television: The First Fifty Years, 1999.

E! True Hollywood Story: All in the Family, 2000.

The '70s: The Decade That Changed Television, 2000.

TV's Most Censored Moments, 2002.

Everybody Loves Raymond, 1 episode, 2002.

She Turned the World on with Her Smile: The Making of The Mary Tyler Moore Show, 2002.

Inside TV Land, 3 episodes, 2000–2002.

Now on PBS, 2 episodes, 2002–2006.

South Park as the voice of Benjamin Franklin in the 4th episode of season 7 and the 100th episode of the series originally airing on April 9, 2003.

Intimate Portrait, Lifetime TV, 5 episodes, 2000–2003.

The Oprah Winfrey Show, 2004.

The Funniest Families of Television Comedy: A Museum of Television and Radio Special, 2004.

Real Time with Bill Maher, 2006.

The American Flag: Two Centuries of Concord and Conflict, 2007.

The Florence Henderson Show, 1 episode, 2009.

Make 'Em Laugh: The Funny Business of America, 2009.

TV Land Moguls, 1 episode, 2009.

TV's 50 Funniest Catchphrases, 2009.

America in Primetime, 2011.

TV Land Icon Awards, 2016.

The Today Show, 4 episodes, 1979–2016

PoliticKING with Larry King, 2016.

Tavis Smiley, PBS, 3 episodes, 2009–2016.

American Master's: Norman Lear: Just Another Version of You, 2016.

The History of Comedy, CNN, 2017.

Full Frontal with Samantha Bee, 2017.

The 69th Primetime Emmy Awards, presenter, 2017.

The Newspaperman: The Life and Times of Ben Bradlee, HBO, 2017.

If You're Not in the Obit, Eat Breakfast, HBO, 2017.

Sammy Davis Jr.: I've Gotta Be Me, 2017.

CBS: This Morning, 3 episodes, 2014–2017.

The Last Act, 2018.

Norman Lear: A Mini Documentary, 2018.

The History of Concord Jazz, 2019.

The Paley Honors: A Special Tribute to Television's Comedy Legends, 2019.

The Kelly Clarkson Show, 2020.

Jimmy Kimmel Live!, ABC, 2020.

2021 Golden Globe Awards, 2021.

The 2021 Just for Laughs Awards Show, 2021.

3rd Annual AAFCA TV Honors, 2021.

Late Night with Seth Myers, NBC, 2021.

History of the Sitcom CNN, 4 episodes, 2021.

Right to Offend: A&E Comedy Network A&E Network, 2022.

Entertainment Tonight, 4 episodes, 1983–2022.

Good Morning America ABC, 4 episodes: November 20, 1979, October 15, 2014, December 18, 2019, November 22, 2022.

CBS Sunday Morning with Jane Pauley, 4 episodes: January 10, 2016, July 5, 2020, January 10, 2021, October 16, 2022.

Norman Lear: 100 Years of Music and Laughter, self, ABC, September 28, 2022.

Dem Tinseltown Homiez, the Hollywood Guys, 2 episodes, 2023.

Being Mary Tyler Moore, HBO, 2023.

Norman Lear: A Life on Television, 2023.

Somebody Feed Phil, 2024.

EMMY AWARDS AND NOMINATIONS

(Boldface indicates wins)

1971—Outstanding Writing Achievement in Comedy—*All in the Family* for "Meet the Bunkers"

1971—Outstanding New Series—*All in the Family*

1971—Outstanding Series Comedy—*All in the Family*

1972—Outstanding Writing Achievement in Comedy—*All in the Family* for "The Saga of Cousin Oscar"

1972—Outstanding Writing Achievement in Comedy—*All in the Family* for "Sammy's Visit"

1972—Outstanding Series—*All in the Family*

1973—Outstanding New Series—*Maude*

1973—Outstanding Comedy Series—*Maude*

1973—Outstanding Comedy Series—*All in the Family*

1974—Outstanding Comedy Series—*All in the Family* shared with John Rich

1976—Special Classification of Outstanding Program and Individual Achievement—*Mary Hartman, Mary Hartman* shared with Viva Knight

1976—Outstanding Comedy Series—*All in the Family*

1982—Outstanding Writing in a Variety or Music Program—*I Love Liberty*

1985—Outstanding Drama/Comedy Special—*Heartsounds*

1991—Outstanding Informational Special—*All in the Family: 20th Anniversary Special*

2019—Outstanding Variety Special (Live)—*Live in Front of a Studio Audience: Norman Lear's "All in the Family" and "The Jeffersons"*

2020—Outstanding Variety Special (Live)—*Live in Front of a Studio Audience: "All in the Family" and "Good Times"*

2022—Outstanding Variety Special (Live)—*Live in Front of a Studio Audience: "The Facts of Life and Diff'rent Strokes"*

ADDITIONAL AWARDS AND HONORS

Nomination for Golden Laurel Producer's Award 9th Place, 1967.

Nomination for an Academy Award, Best Writing, Story and Screenplay for *Divorce American Style*, 1968.

Nomination for Writer's Guild of America Award, Best Written American Comedy for *Divorce American Style*, 1968.

Honorary Degree from Emerson College, 1968.

Winner of International Cinematographer Guild Publicists Showmanship Award for Television, 1973.

Golden Globe Award, Best Television Series for *All in the Family*, 1974.

Star on the Hollywood Walk of Fame, 1975.

Winner of Humanist Arts Award, American Humanist Association, 1977.

Winner of Peabody Award for *All in the Family*, 1978.

Winner of Valentine Davies Award, Writers Guild of America, 1978.

Winner of International Cinematographer Guild Publicists Showmanship Award for Television, 1978.

Winner of Golden Plate Award, Academy of Achievement, 1980.

Winner of Variety, Musical or Comedy for *I Love Liberty*, Writers Guild of America, 1983.

Television Academy Hall of Fame, Inaugural Inductee with Lucille Ball, Milton Berle, Paddy Chayefsky, Edward R. Murrow, William S. Paley, David Sarnoff, 1984.

Winner of Michael Landon Award, Young Artist Awards, 1984.

American Comedy Awards, Creative Achievement Award, 1987.

Casting Society of America, Lifetime Achievement Award, 1991.

Winner of Wise Owl Award for Television and Theatrical Film Fiction for *Fried Green Tomatoes*, Retirement Research Foundation, USA, 1992.

Winner of Writer's Guild of America Award, Laurel Award for TV Writing Achievement, 1993.

National Medal of Arts presented by President Bill Clinton, 1999.

Winner of Women in Film Lucy Award, 1999.

Online Film and Television Association Hall of Fame Inductee, 1999.

Winner of Television Critics Association Lifetime Achievement Award, 1999.

Winner of Inaugural Norman Lear Achievement Award in Television, 2006.

Winner of Producer's Guild of America Award for Lifetime Achievement in Television, 2006.

Winner of Brittania Award for Excellence in Television, 2007.

Nomination for the Gold Derby TV Award for Lifetime Achievement, 2007.

Winner of the Gold Derby TV Award for Lifetime Achievement, 2008.

Nomination for the International Documentary Association IDA Award for the PBS American Masters Documentary *Pete Seeger: The Power of Song*, 2008.

Winner of GLADD Media Award, Pioneer Award, 2014.

Winner of Evelyn F. Burkey Award, Writers Guild of America, 2015.

Winner of TV Land Impact Icon Award, 2016.

Winner with wife Lyn Davis Lear of International Documentary Association Americus Award, 2016.

Winner of All Def Movie Awards' Vanguard Award, 2016.

Kennedy Center Honors, 2017.

Winner of Peabody Award for Lifetime Achievement, 2017.

Winner of National Hispanic Media Coalition Media Icon Award, 2017.

Statue Dedication at Emerson College's Main Campus in Boston, 2018.

Building Dedication at Sony Pictures in Culver City, CA, 2019.

Humanitas Prize, Norman Lear Award, 2020.

Winner of Carol Burnett Award, Golden Globes, 2021.

Winner of African American Film Critics Association Legend Award, 2021.

Nomination for Online Film and Television Association Award for *Norman Lear: 100 Years of Music and Laughter*, 2023.

Notes

Chapter 1: Early Childhood and Youth

1. "All in Her Family," *Hartford Courant*, April 21, 1996.
2. Norman Lear, *Even This I Get to Experience* (New York: Penguin Press, 2014), 4.
3. Frazier Moore, "TV Pioneer and Sitcom King Norman Lear Pens a Book," Associated Press, October 16, 2014.
4. Lear, quoted in Cindy Sher, "Sitcom King Norman Lear on Finding Humor in Everything," *Times of Israel*, November 13, 2005.
5. Lear quoted in Michael Schneider, "How Norman Lear Devoted Himself to a Lifetime of Advocacy," *Variety*, September 17, 2019.
6. Schneider.
7. Lear, *Even This*, 18.
8. Lear, 43.

Chapter 2: College (Briefly) and Off to War

1. Lear, *Even This*, 44
2. Charles B. Hyman and Monika K. Piascik, "Retrospection: President Lowell's Quotas—A History of Discrimination Quotas and Policies," *Harvard Crimson*, March 15, 2015.
3. Norman Lear, interview with the American Comedy Archives at Emerson College with Bill Dana, May 26, 2005.
4. Pam Lambert, "The War That Was," *People*, August 7, 1995.

5. Norman Lear, interview with Morrie Gellman for the Academy of Television Arts and Sciences Foundation, February 26, 1998

Chapter 5: Major Break #1

1. Norman Lear, interview for "Norman Lear Seminars at the Museum of Broadcasting—the Marc Goodson Seminar Series, June 1986.
2. Lear.
3. Stephen Battaglio, *David Susskind: A Televised Life* (New York: St. Martin's Press, 2010), 35.

Chapter 6: Live from New York

1. William S. Paley, *As It Happened: A Memoir* (New York: Doubleday, 1979).
2. Sally Bedell Smith, *In All His Glory: The Life of William S. Paley, the Legendary Tycoon and His Brilliant Circle* (New York: Simon & Schuster, 1979), 270.
3. Jack Gould, "Milton Berle Appears on *Star Theatre*—CBS Offers *Toast of the Town*," *New York Times*, July 4, 1948.
4. Thomas J. Lueck, "Sylvester Weaver, 93, Dies; Created *Today* and *Tonight*, *New York Times*, March 18, 2002.
5. David Everitt, *King of the Half Hour: Nat Hiken and the Golden Age of TV Comedy* (Syracuse, NY: Syracuse University Press, 2001), 61.
6. Neil Simon, *Rewrites: A Memoir* (New York: Simon & Schuster, 1996), 50.
7. Simon quoted in Adam Bernstein, "TV Comedy Writer Danny Simon Dies," *The Washington Post*, July 28, 2005.
8. Lear quoted in Tim Gray, "Norman Looks Back on Early Days as TV Comedy Writer," *Variety*, October 30, 2015.
9. Jerry Lewis, interview with Sam Denoff for the Academy of Television Arts and Sciences Foundation, October 22, 2000.
10. Tim Brooks and Earl Marsh, *The Complete Directory to Prime-Time Network and Cable TV Shows, 1946–Present*, ninth edition (New York: Ballentine Books, 2007), 553.
11. Shawn Levy, *King of Comedy: The Life and Art of Jerry Lewis* (New York: St. Martin's Press, 1996), 91–92.
12. Lewis, Academy interview.

13. Jack Gould, "Martin and Lewis Score on TV Show: Madcap Comedians Perform in Hour-Long NBC Program of Slapstick and Bedlam," *New York Times*, September 18, 1950.

14. Gould, "Martin and Lewis Score."

15. Gould, "Martin and Lewis Score."

16. Levy, *King of Comedy*, 94.

17. Lear, Academy interview, Emerson College.

18. Lear.

19. Levy, *King of Comedy*, 97–98.

Chapter 7: Up and Down the Martin and Lewis Merry-Go-Round

1. Levy, *King of Comedy*, 115.

2. Levy, 115.

3. Levy, 115.

4. Levy, 120–21.

5. Levy, 120–21.

Chapter 8: Putting Words into the Big Mouth and Other Adventures

1. Jean Maddern Pitrone, *Take It from the Big Mouth: The Life of Martha Raye* (Louisville: University of Kentucky Press, 1998), 2.

2. David Everitt, *King of the Half Hour: Nat Hiken and the Golden Age of TV Comedy* (Syracuse, NY: Syracuse University Press), 68.

3. Everitt, 78–79.

4. Everitt, 68.

5. Lear, *Even This*, 149.

6. Jack Gould, "TV: *Martha Raye Show*," *New York Times*, October 12, 1955.

7. Enid Nemy, "Francis Lear, a Mercurial Figure of the Media and a Magazine Founder, Dead at 73," *New York Times*, October 1, 1996.

8. "Train Shatters Truck, Injures One in Windsor," *Hartford Courant*, April 27, 1955.

9. "Gloria Lockerman: TV's Million-Dollar Baby," *Jet*, November 10, 1955.

Chapter 9: Marriage #2 and Other Ups and Downs

1. Bud Yorkin Interview with Morrie Gellman for the Academy of Television Arts and Sciences Foundation, August 9, 2000.
2. Lear, Academy interview.
3. Jack Gould, "Forbidden Area; *Playhouse 90* Gets Under Way with Story about Red Spies, Sneak Attack Tennessee Ernie Ford Three-Ring Program," *New York Times*, October 5, 1956.
4. Lear, *Even This*, 171.
5. Herman Lear Obituary, *Hartford Courant*, December 24, 1957.
6. Lear, *Even This*, 173–74.

Chapter 10: In Tandem

1. Bud Yorkin Interview for the Academy of Television Arts and Sciences Foundation, August 9, 2000.
2. Yorkin.
3. Yorkin.
4. Yorkin.
5. Jack Gould, "*Fonda and Family*; Special Program Made Up of Sketches by Norman Lear and Tom Koch, *New York Times*, February 7, 1962.
6. "Dethroned King of Air: James Thomas Aubrey Jr.," *New York Times*, March 1, 1965.
7. Bosley Crowther, "*Come Blow Your Horn*': Sinatra Film Arrives at the Music Hall," *New York Times*, June 7, 1963.
8. Bosley Crowther, "Adaption of Broadway Play at Music Hall: Paul Ford Keeps Lead in Comedy by Long," *New York Times*, November 5, 1965.
9. Nadine M. Edwards, "Film Proves It's *Never Too Late*," *Los Angeles Evening Citizen's News*, November 12, 1965.
10. Roger Ebert, "I Attend the All-American Picnic at the Premiere of *Divorce American Style*," *Chicago Sun-Times*, June 25, 1967.
11. *Variety* review, 1967.
12. Bosley Crowther, "*Divorce American Style*: Solemn Topic Treated Too Much as a Joke," *New York Times*, July 20, 1967.

Chapter 11: Family Ties

1. Alex Simon and Terry Keefe, "William Friedkin: The Hollywood Flashback Interviews," *Hollywood Interview*, April 29, 2010.

2. John Lahr, *Notes on a Cowardly Lion: The Biography of Burt Lahr* (New York: Open Road Media, 2013).

3. "Bert Lahr's Part in Film to Remain, Says Producer," *New York Times*, December 6, 1967.

4. Ralph Rosenbloom and Robert Karen, *When the Shooting Stops, the Cutting Begins: A Film Editor's Story*, revised edition (New York: De Capo Press, 1996).

5. Roger Ebert, "*The Night They Raided Minsky's*," *Chicago Sun-Times* review, December 23, 1968.

6. Judith Crist, *New York* magazine review, December 23, 1968.

7. *Time* magazine review, January 3, 1969.

Chapter 12: On a Mission

1. Mike Barnes, Bud Yorkin, Overlooked *All in the Family* Legend, Dies at 89," *The Hollywood Reporter*, August 18, 2015.

2. Greg Braxton, "Norman Lear's Latest Emmy Nomination Writes His Partner Out of History—Again," *Los Angeles Times*, July 26, 2019.

3. Bud Yorkin, Academy interview.

4. Sam Roberts, "Bud Yorkin, Writer and Producer of *All in the Family*, Dies at 89," *New York Times*, August 18, 2015.

5. Ronald Brownstein, *Rock Me On the Water: 1974—The Year Los Angeles Transformed Movies, Music, Television* (New York: HarperCollins, 2021), 93–94.

6. Kory Grow, "Norman Lear Talks TV Today, Trump, *All in the Family* Feuds," *Rolling Stone*, July 7, 2016.

7. Alison Beard, "Life's Work: An Interview with Norman Lear," *Harvard Business Review*, November 2014.

8. Press Release: "That's TV to Show Missing Episodes of *Till Death Us Do Part* Not Seen on TV for Over 50 Years," September 1, 2022.

9. Allan Neuwirth, *They'll Never Put That on the Air: The New Age of TV Comedy* (New York: Allworth Press, 2006), 217–18.

10. Neuwirth, *They'll Never Put That on the Air*, 217–18.

11. Lear, *Even This*, 221.

12. Carroll O'Connor interview with Charles Davis for the Academy of Television Arts and Sciences Foundation, August 13, 1999.

13. Carroll O'Connor, *I Think I'm Outta Here: A Memoir of All My Families* (New York: Simon & Schuster, 1998), 150–51.

14. O'Connor, Academy interview.

15. O'Connor.

16. Lear, *Even This*, 223–24.

17. Neuwirth, *They'll Never Put That on the Air*, 220.

18. Candice Azzara, interview with the author, July 22, 2022.

19. Brooks and Marsh, *The Complete Directory to Prime-Time Network and Cable TV Shows*, 1056.

Chapter 13: Rube Tube Awakening

1. Smith, *In All His Glory*, 424.

2. Smith, 424–25.

3. William Grimes, "Michael Dann, TV Programmer Dies at 94, Scheduled *Horowitz* and *Hillbillies*," *New York Times*, May 30, 2016.

4. Cecil Smith, "Scene '70: The New TV Season," *Los Angeles Times*, September 13, 1970.

5. Brownstein, *Rock Me on the Water*, 93.

6. Sally Bedell Smith, *Up the Tube: Prime-Time TV in the Silverman Years* (New York: Viking Press, 1981), 43–44.

7. Yorkin Academy interview.

Chapter 14: On the Air

1. Lear, quoted in Brownstein, *Rock Me On the Water*, 96–97.

2. Jean Stapleton, interview with Karen Herman for the Academy of Television Arts and Sciences, November 28, 2000.

3. John Rich, *Warm Up the Snake: A Hollywood Memoir* (Ann Arbor: University of Michigan Press, 2006), 2.

4. Lear, *Even This*, 232.

5. Smith, *Up the Tube*, 45.

6. Robert Metz, *CBS: Reflections of a Bloodshot Eye* (Chicago: Playboy Press, 1973), 333.

7. TV Guide text and graphic reproduced in Donna McCrohan, *Archie & Edith, Mike & Gloria: The Tumultuous History of* All in the Family (New York: Workman Publishing, 1987), 32.

8. Rich, *Warm Up the Snake*, 3–5.

Chapter 15: The Makings of a Hit

1. Phil Carey, interview with Karen Herman for the Academy of Television Arts and Sciences Foundation, July 25, 2002.

2. John Leonard, "Bigotry as a Dirty Joke," *Life*, March 18, 1971.

3. Whitney M. Young Jr., "Irresponsible Television Production Aids Racism," *Los Angeles Sentinel*, February 4, 1971.

4. Cecil Smith quoted on *E! True Hollywood Story: All in the Family*, August 27, 2000.

5. McCrohan, *Archie & Edith, Mike & Gloria*, 194.

6. Cecil Smith, "Bigotry Used as a Laughing Matter," *Los Angeles Times*, January 12, 1971.

7. Telepic Review: *All in the Family*, *Variety*, January 13, 1971.

8. Cleveland Amory, "*All in the Family*: Review," *TV Guide*, February 27, 1971.

9. Amory.

10. Jack Gould, "Can Bigotry Be Laughed Away? It's Worth a Try," *New York Times*, January 21, 1971.

11. Merv Griffin, *Merv* (New York: Simon and Schuster, 2003), 83.

12. George Gent, "Scott and Lee Grant Get Best-Acting Emmys," *New York Times*, May 10, 1971.

13. Jason Hellerman, "50 Year Later, White House Tapes Reveal Richard Nixon Hated *All in the Family*," No Film School, February 17, 202, https://nofilmschool.com/nixon-all-in-the-family.

Chapter 16: Lightning in a Bottle

1. Fred Silverman, interview with Dan Pasternack for the Academy of Television Arts and Sciences Foundation, May 29, 2001.

2. McCrohan, *Archie & Edith, Mike & Gloria*, 118–19.

3. Laura Z. Hobson, "As I Listened to Archie Say Hebe," *New York Times*, September 12, 1971.

4. Hobson.

5. Norman Lear, "As I Read How Laura Saw Archie . . . ," *New York Times*, October 10, 1971.

6. Lear, *Even This*, 247–48.

7. Lear, 247–48.

8. Rich, *Warm Up the Snake*, 132–33.

9. Rich, 133–34.

10. Bill Dana, interview with Jeff Abraham for the Academy of Television Arts and Sciences Foundation, February 10, 2007.

11. Script excerpt from *All in the Family*'s "Sammy's Visit," written by Bill Dana. Original airdate, February 19, 1972.

12. Script excerpt from "Sammy's Visit."

13. Rich, *Warm Up the Snake*, 133.

Chapter 17: The Tandem Sitcom Machine Swings into High Gear

1. Aaron Ruben, interview with Morrie Gellman for the Academy of Television Arts and Sciences Foundation, February 25, 1999.

2. Michael Starr, *Black and Blue: The Redd Foxx Story* (Montclair, NJ: Applause Theatre & Cinema Books, 2011), 115.

3. Illunga Adell, interview with the author, July 3, 2022.

4. Lear, Academy interview.

5. Nick Ravo, "Redd Foxx, Cantankerous Master of Bawdy Humor, Is Dead at 68," *New York Times*, October 13, 1991.

6. Kendall Rivers: "'You Big Dummy!' An Essay on *Sanford and Son*, the Iconic Black Sitcom That Influenced Television Forever," Medium, July 23, 2012.

7. Donalde Bogle: *Primetime Blues: African Americans on Network Television*, (New York: Farrar, Straus and Giroux, 2001), 188.

8. Starr, *Black and Blue*, 118–19.

9. Herb Schlosser, interview with Karen Herman for the Academy of Television Arts and Sciences Foundation, May 10, 2007.

10. Tom Shales, "TV: A Massive Spring Facelift?" *The Washington Post*, January 9, 1972.

11. "They'll Be Saying Things," *Baltimore Afro-American*, December 28, 1971.

12. "Crossed Swords," *Sanford and Son:* Season 1, Episode 1, Written by Aaron Ruben, Ray Galton, and Alan Simpson, originally broadcast January 14, 1972, NBC.

13. Judith Kessler, "*Sanford and Son:* Change in Comedy?" *The Washington Post*, August 29, 1973.

14. Eugenia Collier, "*Sanford and Son* Is White to the Core," *The New York Times*, June 17, 1973.

15. Bogle, *Primetime Blues*, 190–91.

Chapter 18: . . . And Then There's Maude

1. Lear, Academy interview.

2. Lear.

3. "Gene, For Heaven Sake, Help Me!!" *TV Guide*, November 18, 1972.

4. Bea Arthur, interview with Karen Herman for the Academy of Television Arts and Sciences Foundation, March 15, 2001.

5. Arthur.

6. Lear, Academy Interview.

7. Samantha Harper Macy, interview with the author, June 20, 2022.

8. Adrienne Barbeau, interview with the author, June 29, 2022.

9. Rue McLanahan, *My First Five Husbands . . . and the Ones Who Got Away: A Memoir* (New York: Broadway Books, 2007), 147.

10. Bob LaHendro, interview with the author, May 31, 2022.

11. Elliot Schoenman, interview with the author, August 15, 2022.

12. Judy Stone, "She Gave Archie His First Comeuppance, *New York Times*, November 19, 1972.

13. "Fall Preview," *TV Guide*, September 9, 1972.

14. John J. O'Connor, "*Maude*, a Comedy Will Make Debut Tonight," *New York Times*, September 12, 1972.

15. Susan Silver, interview with the author, August 30, 2023.

16. Lewis Beale, "Maude's Abortion Fades into History, *Chicago Tribune*, November 13, 1982.

17. Kristen Baldwin, "How *The Golden Girls* Creator Susan Harris Changed TV Comedy Forever—and Why She Doesn't Watch It Now," *Entertainment Weekly*, October 15, 2018.

18. Rod Parker quoted in Beale, "Maude's Abortion Fades into History."

19. Kate Kilkenny, "Why Norman Lear Considers Himself a 'Bleeding-Heart Conservative,'" *Pacific Standard* magazine, April 27, 2017.

20. Barbeau, author interview.

21. Hal Cooper, interview with Karen Herman for the Academy of Television Arts and Sciences Foundation, December 11, 2003.

22. Lear, Academy interview.

23. Aljean Harmetz, "Maude Didn't Leave 'em All Laughing," *The New York Times*, December 10, 1972.

24. Sara Kettler, "How Bea Arthur and *Maude* Changed the Way Women Were Portrayed on Television," Biography.com, March 14, 2020.

Chapter 19: Tandemonium

1. Jay Moriarity, interview with the author, January 19, 2022.

2. Moriarity.

3. Betty Garrett, *Betty Garrett and Other Songs* (New York: Madison Books, 2000), 236.

4. John Putch, interview with the author, August 16, 2023.

5. Christopher Porterfield, "The New TV Season: Topping Old Taboos," *Time*, September 25, 1972, 50.

6. Yorkin quoted in Martin Kasindorf, "Archie & Maude & Fred & Norman & Alan: Inside a TV Empire," *New York Times Magazine*, June 24, 1973, 226.

7. Bill Macy quoted on *Beverly Hills View*, hosted by Joan Agajanian Quinn, originally broadcast October 26, 2018, Beverly Hills Television.

8. Rob Reiner quoted in Joseph Morgenstern, "TV: Speaking about the Unspeakable," *Newsweek*, November 29, 1971, 52–60.

9. Mike Evans quoted in Morgenstern, "TV: Speaking about the Unspeakable."

10. Sally Struthers quoted in Morgenstern, "TV: Speaking about the Unspeakable."

11. Schoenman, interview with the author.

12. O'Connor quoted in McCrohan, *Archie & Edith, Mike & Gloria*, 129.

13. O'Connor, *I Think I'm Outta Here*, 167.

14. O'Connor, Academy interview.

15. Lear quoted on *Larry King Now*, hosted by Larry King, originally broadcast October 29, 2014, Hulu.

16. Carrol O'Connor quoted in Bill Davidson, "The Uprising in Lear's TV Kingdom," *TV Guide*, April 13, 1974, 12–17.

17. O'Connor, Academy interview.

18. James Cromwell, interview with the author, July 7, 2022.

19. Carrol O'Connor quoted in Dwight Whitney, "An American Institution Rolls On," *TV Guide*, January 2, 1979, 14–18.

20. McCrohan, *Archie & Edith, Mike & Gloria*, 131–32.

21. Sally Struthers quoted in *Gilbert Gottfried's Colossal Amazing Podcast*, cohosted by Gilbert Gottfried and Frank Santopadre, originally broadcast January 10, 2022.

22. Struthers.

23. Rich, Academy interview.

24. Rich, Warm Up the Snake, 180–81.

25. Garrett, *Betty Garrett and Other Songs*, 192.

26. Starr, *Black and Blue*, 84.

27. Barbeau, author interview.

28. Garret, *Betty Garrett and Other Songs*, 192.

29. Macy, author interview.

30. Macy.

31. Barbara Gallagher, interview with the author, September 1, 2022.

Chapter 20: New Additions

1. Lear, *Even This*, 260.
2. "Jerry Perenchio's 20 'Rules of the Road,'" *Wall Street Journal*, August 13, 1999.
3. Alan Horn quoted in *Harvard Business School Alumni Magazine* profile, May 26, 2016.
4. Bud Yorkin quoted in A. H. Wieler "News of the Screen," *New York Times*, September 22, 1974, 55.

Chapter 21: Spinning Off a Spin-Off

1. Eric Monte quoted in Clarence Walker, "Black History: Screenwriter Eric Monte Fought to Change Black Stereotypes," *NewsBlaze*, February 28, 2018.
2. Lear, *Even This*, 269.
3. Bogle, *Primetime Blues*, 198.
4. Esther Rolle quoted in Judy Stone, "Florida Finds Good Times in Chicago," *New York Times*, May 5, 1974.
5. Clive Barnes, "*Tough to Get Help* at Royale," *New York Times*, May 5, 1972.
6. John Amos, interview with the author, July 12, 2002.
7. Amos.
8. Sean Campbell, *The Sitcoms of Norman Lear* (Jefferson, NC: McFarland & Company, Inc., 2007), 97.
9. Moriarity, author interview.
10. Jimmie Walker: *Dyn-o-Mite! Good Times, Bad Times, Our Times—A Memoir* (New York: Da Capo Press, 2012), 35.
11. John J. O'Connor, "Good Times for the Black Image," *New York Times*, February 2, 1975.
12. Arthur Unger, "Black Family Portrait," *Christian Science Monitor*, February 7, 1974, 18.
13. Amos, author interview.
14. Jimmie Walker, interview with John Dalton for the Academy of Television Arts and Sciences Foundation, February 7, 2017.
15. Amos, author interview.
16. Bogle, *Primetime Blues*, 203.
17. Amos, author interview.
18. Louie Robinson, "Bad Times on the *Good Times* Set," *Ebony*, September 1975.

19. Rolle quoted in Robinson.

20. Walker quoted in Robinson.

21. Amos, author interview.

22. Amos.

23. Rolle quoted in Christopher Paul Denis and Michael Denis, *Favorite Families of TV* (New York: Citadel Press, 1992), 138.

24. Rolle quoted in Denis and Denis.

25. Michael Baser, interview with the author, September 6, 2023.

26. Lear quoted in John L. Mitchell, "Plotting His Next Big Break," *Los Angeles Times*, April 14, 2006.

Chapter 22: The Jeffersons Move on Up

1. Silverman, Academy interview.

2. Jack Shea quoted in Bill O'Hallaren, "It Could Have Been the Kiss of Death," *TV Guide*, May 17, 1980, 23–23.

3. Mary Helen Washington, "As Their Blackness Disappears, So Does Their Character," *TV Guide*, July 30, 1983, 4–9.

4. John J. O'Connor, "TV's Lear's *The Jeffersons*, *New York Times*, January 17, 1975, 67.

5. Cleveland Amory, "Review: *The Jeffersons*," *TV Guide*, February 22, 1975.

6. Joel Dreyfuss, "All in the (Black) Family," *Washington Post*, January 19, 1975.

7. Louie Robinson: "The Jeffersons: A Look at Life on America's New Striver's Row," *Ebony*, January 1976.

8. Moriarity, author interview.

9. Moriarity.

10. Moriarity.

11. Rick Mitz: *The Great TV Sitcom Book* (New York: Perigee, 1983), 346.

12. Jay Moriarity, *Honkey in the House: Writing & Producing The Jeffersons* (Los Angeles: Antler Publishing, 220), 84.

13. Herbie J. Pilato: "*Jeffersons* Star Damon Evans and His Eclectic Career," Newsbreak.com, January 24, 2023.

14. Moriarity, *Honkey in the House*, 241–42.

15. Moriarity, 241–42.

16. "Sorry Wrong Meeting," *The Jeffersons*, originally broadcast February 15, 1981, CBS.

17. Mitz, *The Great TV Sitcom Book*, 344.

18. Bonnie Allen, "Movin' on Up: *The Jeffersons*," *Essence*, October 1981.

19. Isabel Sanford, interview with Brad Lemack for the Academy of Television Arts and Sciences, April 3, 2002.

20. Oz Scott, interview with the author, August 24, 2023.

Chapter 23: Humps and Bumps

1. Cromwell, author interview.

2. Cromwell.

3. Sally Bedell Smith: *Up the Tube: Prime-Time TV in the Silverman Years* (New York: Viking Press, 1981), 102.

4. Bedell Smith, *Up the Tube*, 101–2.

5. Gary Grossman, "Questioning Hollywood about Violence," *Boston Globe*, October 15, 1976.

Chapter 24: Keep on Doing What You Do

1. Mitz, *The Great TV Sitcom Book*, 365.

2. Mitz, 365.

3. Lear quoted in Dwight Whitney, "Portrait of an Overachiever," *TV Guide*, July 24-30, 1976, 33–35.

4. Mackenzie Phillips, *A Memoir: High on Arrival* (New York: Gallery Books, 2011), 29.

5. Richard M. Levine, "As the TV World Turns," *New York Times Magazine*, December 14, 1975.

6. Levine.

7. Valerie Bertinelli quoted in Josef Adalian, Stewart Miller, and Dan Reilly, "A Lifetime of Norman Lear: Rita Moreno, John Amos, Valerie Bertinelli, and Other Collaborators Reflect on Working with the TV Legend," *Vulture*, December 6, 2023.

8. Lear quoted in Mike Barnes, "Pat Harrington Jr., the Super on *One Day at a Time*, Dies at 86," *Hollywood Reporter*, January 7, 2016.

9. Joel Keller, "Richard Masur on *Transparent*, Norman Lear and Surviving *Heaven's Gate*," AVClub.com, February 3, 2016.

10. Bonnie Franklin quoted in Denis and Denis, *Favorite Families of TV*, 162.

11. Lear quoted in Denis and Denis, *Favorite Families of TV*, 163.

12. Putch, author interview.

13. Brent Furdyk, "The Tragic Real-Life Story of Mackenzie Phillips," NickiSwift.com, October 16, 2023.

14. Robert Windler, "*One Day at a Time* Seems Kids Stuff to Mackenzie Phillips—She's 18 and Wants It All Now," *People*, May 1, 1979.

15. Phillips quoted in Windler.

16. Phillips, *High on Arrival*, 43.

17. Phillips quoted in Windler.

18. Denis and Denis, *Favorite Families of TV*, 164.

19. Sue Reilly, "Why McKenzie Got Fired: The Sad Story of *One Day's* Troubled Star, March 18, 1980.

20. Reilly.

21. Reilly.

22. Reilly.

23. Phillips, *High on Arrival*, 44–45.

24. Glenn Scarpelli, interview with the author, April 5, 2022.

25. Phillips quoted in Adalian, Miller, and Reilly, "A Lifetime of Norman Lear.

Chapter 25: More Flops and Mary Hartman Mania

1. John J. O'Connor, "An Odd, Late Season That Is Full of Gaps: Few New Shows Promising, but Most Follow Formula Old Sitcom Return in Slightly Altered Guise," *New York Times*, September 20, 1976.

2. Lear quoted during appearance in author's class "Topics in Comedic Studies: "Norman Lear" at Emerson College, March 17, 2021.

3. Louise Lasser, interview with the author, June 23, 2022.

4. Greg Mullavey, interview with the author, May 26, 2022.

5. Lasser, author interview.

6. Mary Kay Place, interview with the author, August 9, 2022.

7. Place.

8. Place.

9. Douglas Martin, "Dody Goodman, 93, Television Actress, Dies," *New York Times*, June 24, 2008.

10. Martin.

11. Samantha Harper Macy, interview with the author, June 20, 2022.

12. Lasser, author interview.

13. Place, author interview.

14. Lasser, author interview.

15. Lasser.

16. Lasser.

17. Lasser.

18. Ben Stein, *Dreamz* (New York: Harper & Row, 1978), 75.

19. Lasser quoted in Bill O'Hallaren, "A Cute Tomato, a Couple of Slices of Baloney, Some Sour Grapes, a Few Nuts," *TV Guide*, June 19, 1976.

20. Mullavey, author interview.

21. Dennis Klein, interview with the author, February 23, 2023.

22. Klein.

Chapter 26: Changes at 704 Hauser Street and Shifting Priorities

1. Tim Weisberg, "When Norman Lear Took a Boston-Made TV Show National," Radio Transcript from 1420 WBSM (New Bedford, CT), December 6, 2023.

2. John J. O'Connor, "Is Norman Lear in a Rut?" *New York Times*, March 12, 1976.

3. Joal Ryan, *Former Child Stars: The Story of America's Least Wanted* (Toronto: ECW Press, 2000), 125–26.

Chapter 27: End of an Era

1. 1978 *New York Times* article quoted in McCrohan, *Archie & Edith, Mike & Gloria*, 161.

2. Mitz, *The Great TV Sitcom Book*, 258.

3. "Farewell to the Family," *People*, March 27, 1978.

4. Lear, *Even This*, 317.

5. O'Connor quoted in McCrohan *Archie & Edith, Mike & Gloria*, 163.

6. 1978 *New York Post* article quoted in McCrohan, *Archie & Edith, Mike & Gloria*, 163.

7. Les Brown, "Norman Lear Dreams Up a Twist in the Plot for Himself," *New York Times*, April 9, 1978.

8. Danielle Brisebois, interview with the author, June 3, 2022.

9. Stapleton quoted in *Archie & Edith, Mike & Gloria*, 165.

10. Lear, *Even This*, 317.

11. Stapleton quoted in *Archie & Edith, Mike & Gloria*, 167.

12. Kirk Honeycutt, "We Ran Out of Controversy: Bea Arthur Says Farewell to *Maude*," *New York Times*, April 16, 1978.

Chapter 28: 1979–2023

1. Lear quoted in catalog for *The Collection of Richard Dorso* (Los Angeles: Los Angeles Modern Auctions [LAMA], 2011).

2. Lear, *Even This*, 313.

3. Lear, 313.

4. Lear quoted in David Bianculli, *The Platinum Age of Television: From "I Love Lucy" to "The Walking Dead," How TV Became Terrific* (New York: Anchor Books, 2016), 289–90.

5. Tom Shales, "Miss Liberty's Left Hand," *Washington Post*, March 20, 1982.

6. Arthur Unger, "Norman Lear's *I Love Liberty*: Patriotism and Family Fun," *Christian Science Monitor*, March 19, 1982.

7. Quoted in Lear, *Even This*, 324.

8. Lear, 324.

9. Bill Boggs, interview with the author, December 4, 2023.

10. Leslie Bennetts, interview with the author, December 4, 2023.

11. Quoted in Lear, *Even This*, 345.

12. Lyn Lear quoted in Andrew Goldman, "Norman and Lyn Lear on How to Stay Married in Hollywood," *Town & Country*, December 2021.

13. Lear, *Even This*, 349.

14. Lieberthal quoted in Richard W. Stephenson, "Lear Joins with Columbia TV to Produce, Not Manage," *New York Times*, February 2, 1989.

15. Stephenson.

16. Ken Tucker *Entertainment Weekly* review of *Sunday Dinner*, quoted in Lear, *Even This*, 384.

17. John J. O'Connor, "Norman Lear's Sitcoms, Past and Present on CBS," *New York Times*, June 6, 1991.

18. Ken Tucker *Entertainment Weekly* review of *The Powers That Be*, quoted in Lear, *Even This*, 385.

19. Hank Stuever, "Norman Lear Put His Foot Down—and The White House Flinched," *Washington Post*, November 27, 2017.

20. Mike Royce, interview with the author, December 9, 2023.

21. Mike Royce, "Remembering Andre Braugher and Norman Lear: Together They Could Have Created a Hell of a Sitcom," *Hollywood Reporter*, December 14, 2023.

22. Lyn Lear quoted in Goldman, "Norman and Lyn Lear on How to Stay Married."

23. Tony Vinciquerra quoted in Goldman.

24. Brent Miller quoted in Goldman.

25. Norman Lear 2021 Golden Globe Acceptance Speech, quoted in Chrstina Dugan Ramirez, "Norman Lear Says, 'Nobody Has Made Me Laugh Harder Than Carol Burnett as He Receives Her Eponymous Award," *People*, February 28, 2021.

26. Norman Lear, "On My 100th Birthday: Reflections on Archie Bunker and Donald Trump," *New York Times*, July 27, 2022.

27. Lear quoted in Savanah Walsh, "Norman Lear Is Living in the Moment on His 101st Birthday," July 27, 2023

28. Lara Bergthold quoted in Joelle Goldstein, "Norman Lear's Cause of Death Determined Nearly 2 Weeks after Television Legend Died at 101," *People*, December 18, 2023.

29. Official Statement from President Joe Biden on the Passing of Norman Lear, December 6, 2023.

30. Jimmy Kimmell quoted in Jason P. Frank, "The Industry Pays Tribute to Norman Lear," *Vulture*, December 7, 2023.

31. George Clooney quoted in Frank.

32. Tyler Perry quoted in Frank.

33. Robert Igor quoted in Frank.

34. Rob Reiner, "My Second Father, Rob Reiner Rembers Norman Lear," *Hollywood Reporter*, December 11, 2023.

Index

"The Saga of Cousin Oscar," *All in the Family*, 123
Saks, Gene, 258
"Sammy's Visit," *All in the Family*, 127–29
Samuel Tilden High School, 13
Sanford, 140
Sanford, Isabel, 197–98; Evans, D., relation to, 205; Television Academy Foundation and, 207
Sanford, John Elroy. *See* Foxx, Redd
Sanford and Son, 132, 134, 137, 139–40, 167, 293; Silverman relation to, 135–36. *See also specific episodes*
Sanford Arms, 140
Sanicola, Hank, 78
Santopadre, Frank, 166
Saturday Night Live, 107, 136, 240, 241–42
Scarpelli, Glenn, 225–27
Schiller, Bob, 146, 253
Schlatter, George, 102
Schlosser, Herb, 136
Schoenman, Elliot, 146–47, 160
Schulman, Arnold, 88
Schulz, Charles M., 66
Schwartz, Edwin, 13
Schwartz, Elliot, 13
Scollay, William, 19
Scollay Square, 18–19
Scotch 'n Soda, 70
Scott, Debralee, 237
Scott, Oz, 207
Scott Field, Illinois, 21
Screen Actors Guild (SAG), 159, 213
Search for Tomorrow, 225
The Second Seduction (Loeb, F.), 270
Segelstein, Irwin, 110
Selznick, David O., 69, 71
Sesame Street, 200
The Session, 112
Sevareid, Michael, 164
704 Hauser, 195, 274, 303
Shaffer, Paul, 248
Shaftsbury, Vermont, 260–61
Shales, Tom, 263
Shapiro, George, 277

Sharri Zedek synagogue, 14
Shaver, Buster, 26
Shaw, George Bernard, 29–30, 95
Shawn, Dick, 88
Shea, Jack, 202
Sheen, Charlie, 210
Sheen, Martin, 263
The Sheik, 31
"The Sheik of Araby," 31
Shogolo Oloba, 181
Shore, Dinah, 240, 253
Shulman, Max, 71
Siebert, Charles, 223
Silver, Susan, 148–49, 222
Silverman, Fred, 109, 250–51; ABC and, 212–13; *All in the Family* relation to, 122–23; *Good Times* relation to, 184; *The Jeffersons* relation to, 199; *One Day at a Time* and, 221; *Sanford and Son* relation to, 135–36; Wood and, 110, 121
Silver Spoons, 305
Simmons, Ed, 9, 30–33, 51, 62, 64; *The Colgate Comedy Hour* and, 44, 45, 47, 51; *Ford Star Revue* and, 40, 42; Lewis, Jerry relation to, 50; Raye, M., relation to, 55
Simon, Alex, 88–89
Simon, Danny, 40–42
Simon, Irving, 41
Simon, Mamie, 41
Simon, Neil, 41–42; *Come Blow Your Horn* and, 14, 41, 76–77, 308
Simpson, Alan, 130–31
Sinatra, Frank, 24, 41, 63, 77–78
Sir Your Cur, or the Villain Gets It in the End (Lear, N.), 13
"Sixteen Tons," 65
60 Minutes, 240
The $64,000 Question, 59–60, 76
Skelton, Red, 60
Smith, Cecil, 109, 119, 236
Smith, Harry B., 31
Smith, Kelly, 172
Smith, Sally Bedell, 38, 105–6, 110, 115, 213